Additional Praise

In this provocative and highly original book, Matt Sekerke and Steve H. Hanke provide a fascinating account of the origins, development and workings of the modern monetary economy. The authors debunk some of the leading assumptions underlying modern monetary economics and explain some leading paradoxes in recent experience. The writing is clear and concise, and the style is stimulating. The book is a major achievement in monetary economics.
 —**George S. Tavlas**, *Alternate to the Governor of the Bank of Greece on the ECB Governing Council and Distinguished Visiting Fellow, Hoover Institution, Stanford University*

Making Money Work offers a daring and provocative solution to a perennial problem: how best to rewrite the rules of our financial system. Monetary and financial economists of all traditions will find much to take away from this highly original contribution to modern financial and monetary theory, which offers a novel policy conclusion – that the aim of monetary policy should be to make money as neutral as possible. This book deserves to be widely read.
 —**Kevin Dowd**, *Professor of Finance and Economics, Durham University Business School*

This book offers a refreshing, illuminating, and sorely-needed rethink of monetary economics. Sekerke and Hanke lucidly explain who creates money, how this creates imbalances, and the role of a "neutral" monetary policy in taming those imbalances. I highly recommend studying this book carefully.
 —**Harald Uhlig**, *Bruce Allen and Barbara Ritzenthaler Professor in Economics, University of Chicago*

An exciting and provocative book that goes far beyond traditional monetarism. Sekerke and Hanke mount a head on challenge to the mainstream macroeconomics which has been the only game in town for two decades, not to mention the source of multiple policy errors. Sekerke and Hanke's novel and comprehensive analysis, which from start to finish has money and finance at its center, is a strong contender for a replacement.
 —**David Laidler**, *FRSC, Professor Emeritus, University of Western Ontario and author of Taking Money Seriously*

Even the world's most influential economists are puzzled about how the quantity of money affects output, employment and inflation. *Making Money Work* is a vital contribution to the public debate, not just in the USA, but around the world. The book is both necessary and ambitious, trying to clarify key issues in debates which go back centuries. It is of the utmost importance to understand what Sekerke and Hanke are saying.
 —**Tim Congdon**, *CBE, Founder of Lombard Street Research (now TS Lombard), Professor, University of Buckingham, and Chair of the Institute of International Monetary Research*

This thought-provoking book strongly challenges received wisdom in the monetary field, not only on much current theory, but also on practice, both for regulation and policy setting. The authors make a strong case for their criticisms, and if they are right, then monetary theory and management have been badly misdirected in recent decades. Whatever your own preconceptions may be, the challenges laid down here are well considered, argued and presented. Their critiques in this book should be read, assessed and addressed.
—**Charles Goodhart**, *CBE, FBA, Emeritus Professor of Banking and Finance, London School of Economics*

The authors advocate a radical new approach to both monetary policy and regulation of the commercial banking sector. Highly recommended.
—**Christopher Wood**, *Global Equity Strategist, Jefferies*

Money and banks have been ignored for too long by both economic theory and monetary policy. It is a pleasure for a practitioner to discover this stimulating presentation, which puts them back in their proper place. It clearly explains how monetary policy and regulation should be designed—not to assist fiscal excesses, but to support investment and economic prosperity. A must!
—**Philippe d'Arvisenet**, *former Head of Economic Research, BNP Paribas*

Sekerke and Hanke's book is perfectly timed for both economics and policy. It shows how to modernize monetary policy for faster growth and defense of the dollar, unlocking banking as a vital engine of growth. Sekerke and Hanke rewrite the theory of monetary policy to include the impact of bank regulation and fiscal policy alongside the actions of the central bank.
—**David Malpass**, *former President of the World Bank Group and Under Secretary of the Treasury for International Affairs*

Sekerke and Hanke have made an important and timely contribution to the debate over our monetary and financial system. Bringing together fiscal, monetary and regulatory aspects, the authors offer readers a unified and integrated approach unique to the literature. Highly recommended for both scholars and practitioners.
—**Mark Calabria**, *former Director, the Federal Housing Finance Agency, and former Chief Economist to the Vice President*

This writer dubbed Steve Hanke the "Money Doctor" for designing inflation-slaying monetary regimes in nations from Montenegro to Argentina. Hanke also won *Fortune*'s praise as virtually the first expert to predict that a post-Covid explosion in M2 had unleashed a sustained rash of runaway prices. Here, Sekerke and Hanke champion a new architecture that would recharge our commercial banks to fund the high-risk, big-potential projects essential to ensuring America's future prosperity and wean our nation from a dangerous over-reliance on government funding.
—**Shawn Tully**, *Senior Editor-at-Large, Fortune Magazine*

In recent years, money supply has been disappearing from much macroeconomic research. Monetary policy without money is an oxymoron. The Sekerke and Hanke book is the antithesis of that paradoxical methodological direction.
—**William A. Barnett**, *Oswald Distinguished Professor of Macroeconomics, University of Kansas; Director, Center of Financial Stability; and Editor, CUP journal, Macroeconomic Dynamics.*

Sekerke and Hanke offer a uniquely comprehensive view of the US monetary system, showing how the Federal Reserve, the Treasury, and other regulatory agencies combine with banks and non-bank financial institutions to drive economy-wide trends and cycles in production, investment, and employment. They describe how this system broke during the financial crisis of 2008 and identify promising solutions to make it work again for the benefit of all Americans.
—**Peter Ireland**, *Murray and Monti Professor of Economics, Boston College*

The authors take us clearly through the institutional complexities of the modern financial system. They show why it is hard to be over-impressed with the basic fact of money creation by individual banks. They explore the consequences for monetary economics, for business cycles, and for our understanding of financial crises. More than most economic explorations, they leave us with new insights as to why and how money itself matters so fundamentally.
—**Roger Sandilands**, *Emeritus Professor of Economics, University of Strathclyde*

Making Money Work offers an insightful and compelling analysis of the modern financial landscape, challenging conventional views on banking, money creation, and monetary policy. Its unique approach—combining rigorous theory with practical reform proposals—makes it an essential read for anyone in finance and economics.
—**Abderrahim Taamouti**, *Professor and Chair in Applied Econometrics, University of Liverpool, and Fellow of the Econometric Society*

A must-read that combines the authors' knowledge of financial markets with an in-depth analysis of monetary theory.
—**Didier Cahen**, *Secretary-General of Eurofi*

Economic theory too often abstracts from the details of money and finance. This book offers a brilliant new approach to economics, firmly grounded in the institutional realities of the financial system.
—**Manuel Hinds**, *former Minister of Finance of El Salvador (1995–1999) and co-recipient of the Manhattan Institute's Hayek Prize (2010)*

Making Money Work

Making Money Work

How to Rewrite the Rules of Our Financial System

Matt Sekerke
Steve H. Hanke

WILEY

Copyright © 2025 by Matt Sekerke and Steve H. Hanke. All rights reserved.

Published by John Wiley & Sons, Inc., Hoboken, New Jersey.
Published simultaneously in Canada.

No part of this publication may be reproduced, stored in a retrieval system, or transmitted in any form or by any means, electronic, mechanical, photocopying, recording, scanning, or otherwise, except as permitted under Section 107 or 108 of the 1976 United States Copyright Act, without either the prior written permission of the Publisher, or authorization through payment of the appropriate per-copy fee to the Copyright Clearance Center, Inc., 222 Rosewood Drive, Danvers, MA 01923, (978) 750-8400, fax (978) 750-4470, or on the web at www.copyright.com. Requests to the Publisher for permission should be addressed to the Permissions Department, John Wiley & Sons, Inc., 111 River Street, Hoboken, NJ 07030, (201) 748-6011, fax (201) 748-6008, or online at http://www.wiley.com/go/permission.

The manufacturer's authorized representative according to the EU General Product Safety Regulation is Wiley-VCH GmbH, Boschstr. 12, 69469 Weinheim, Germany, e-mail: Product_Safety@wiley.com.

Trademarks: Wiley and the Wiley logo are trademarks or registered trademarks of John Wiley & Sons, Inc. and/or its affiliates in the United States and other countries and may not be used without written permission. All other trademarks are the property of their respective owners. John Wiley & Sons, Inc. is not associated with any product or vendor mentioned in this book.

Limit of Liability/Disclaimer of Warranty: While the publisher and author have used their best efforts in preparing this book, they make no representations or warranties with respect to the accuracy or completeness of the contents of this book and specifically disclaim any implied warranties of merchantability or fitness for a particular purpose. No warranty may be created or extended by sales representatives or written sales materials. The advice and strategies contained herein may not be suitable for your situation. You should consult with a professional where appropriate. Further, readers should be aware that websites listed in this work may have changed or disappeared between when this work was written and when it is read. Neither the publisher nor authors shall be liable for any loss of profit or any other commercial damages, including but not limited to special, incidental, consequential, or other damages.

For general information on our other products and services or for technical support, please contact our Customer Care Department within the United States at (800) 762-2974, outside the United States at (317) 572-3993 or fax (317) 572-4002.

Wiley also publishes its books in a variety of electronic formats. Some content that appears in print may not be available in electronic formats. For more information about Wiley products, visit our web site at www.wiley.com.

Library of Congress Control Number applied for:

Cloth ISBN: 9781394257263
ePDF ISBN: 9781394257287
ePub ISBN: 9781394257270

Cover Design: Wiley
Cover Image: © tomertu/stock.adobe.com

SKY10100554_032025

Cien pasos equivocados en el camino correcto
es mejor que
mil pasos correctos en el camino equivocado

Contents

Foreword		xvii
Introduction		xix

Part One: How Money Works: Institutions of the Monetary Economy — 1

Chapter 1:	Rethinking Monetary Economics	3
	Macroeconomics Without Money	4
	Broad Money and the Banking System	5
	From Interest-rate Policy to Quantity-based Policy	7
	Neutral Monetary Policy	9
	Productive Capital Markets	9
Chapter 2:	Fiat Money Systems	13
	Specifying Money So That Money Matters	14
	Money Is Essentially an Abstract Measure of Value	14
	Money Consists in a Claim or Credit	16
	The State, or an Authority, Is an Essential Basis for Money	18
	Money Is Not Neutral in the Economic Process	19
	Fiat Monetary Standards	21
	Metallic Standards	21
	Standards After Metallic Standards	23

	Foreign Exchange and the Quest for an International Monetary Standard	25
	Revisiting the Foundations of Monetary Economics	27
Chapter 3:	The Institutional Structure of the Monetary Economy	35
	The Government Sector	36
	The Fiscal Authority	36
	The Monetary Authority	38
	The Consolidated Government	39
	The Commercial Banking System	41
	Deposit Creation by Individual Banks	43
	Fallacious Accounts of Bank Funding and Deposit Creation	45
	Financial Intermediaries	48
	Asset Managers	49
	Money Market Funds	50
	Asset-backed Securities	51
	Consolidated Financial Intermediation Sector	53
	The Nonbank Public: Nonfinancial Firms and Households	54
	Nonfinancial Business	54
	Households	56
	The Rest of the World	57
	The Money Supply and Its Connections to the Nonbank Public	58
	The System of Claims as a Foundation for Monetary Theory	60
Chapter 4:	Financial Intermediation in the Capital Markets	67
	Savings and Investment: The Standard Macroeconomic Story	68
	Savings and Investment: The Microeconomic Foundations	70
	The NPV Criterion	71
	Information Asymmetry	72
	Equity Rationing	74
	Revising the Growth Model	75
	Financial Intermediation and Project Stratification	75
Chapter 5:	Credit Creation by the Commercial Banking System	81
	Savings and Investment: Expanding the Standard Story	82
	The Set of Bankable Projects	85
	Maturity Transformation and Bank Risk Management	88
	Credit Risk Management	89
	Interest Rate Risk Management	91
	Liquidity Risk Management	93
	Economic Growth with Credit and Capital Markets	96

Chapter 6:	Universal Banks and the Banking–Capital Markets Boundary	103
	Complementarities and Competition in Banking and Capital Markets Business	106
	Risk Transformation in Securitization Markets	108
	Risk Transfer Contracts	111
	Bank Lending to Nonbank Financial Institutions	114
	Risk Management in Universal Banks	116
	Part Two: A Broader View of Monetary Policy	**121**
Chapter 7:	Analytical Frameworks and Basic Monetary Facts	129
	The Equation of Exchange and the Demand for Money	130
	The Cambridge Equation	132
	The Equation of Exchange in Economic Theory	132
	Divisia Broad Money	135
	Constructing Divisia Indices	136
	Comparing Divisia and Simple Sum Aggregates	138
	Sources of Divisia Money	141
	Divisia Money by Sectors and Strata	144
	Evolution of Bank Balance Sheets from 1945 to 2023	149
	Broad Trends	150
	Finer Details	153
	Bank Lending Versus Capital Market Finance	156
	Three Big Questions	163
Chapter 8:	The Regulation of Universal Banks	173
	Bank Capital Regulation	176
	Defining Bank Capital	177
	Capital Adequacy Before the Basel Era	179
	Capital Adequacy After the First Basel Accord	180
	The 1996 Market Risk Amendment	182
	The Monetary Policy Impact of the Basel I Era	183
	The Problem of the Trading Book	184
	Regulatory Capital Under Basel III	187
	Bank Liquidity Regulation	189
	The Liquidity Coverage Ratio	190
	The Net Stable Funding Ratio	194
	Summing Up	195

Chapter 9:	Monetary Aspects of the Government Budget	203
	Stable Government Debt Dynamics and the Monetary Standard	205
	Stability Conditions	205
	Deposit Insurance	208
	Fiscal Influences on Aggregate Conditions	209
	Central Bank Transactions in Government Obligations	210
	Government-sponsored Enterprises and Financial Agencies	211
	Monetary Consequences of GSE Guarantees	213
	The Federal Home Loan Bank System	214
	Crowding-out in Capital Markets	216
	The Disaggregated Budget Arithmetic	217
	Some Examples of Sector-level Fiscal Influence	219
	Sectoral Impact of the Fiscal Impulse from Quantitative Easing	220
	Appendix 9.A Propagation of a Fiscal Impulse	223
Chapter 10:	Central Bank Policy	231
	Central Bank Policy Implementation Before and After the GFC	233
	Quantitative Easing and Its Consequences	234
	Reestablishing Control Over Short-term Interest Rates	237
	The Path to Normalization and the COVID Interventions	238
	Structural Changes in the Reserve Market	242
	Interest Rate Policy Transmission and Asset Prices	245
	An Unintended Period of Steady Broad Money Growth	247
	Prospects for Future Interest Rate Policy	251

Part Three: Rewriting the Rules of Our Financial System   259

Chapter 11:	Defining Neutral Monetary Policy	261
	Neutral Monetary Policy	262
	Defining Neutrality	264
	Why Neutrality?	266
	Efficient Use of Global Savings	267
	Formation of Investable Projects	268
	Formation of Bankable Projects	269
Chapter 12:	Universal Banks in the Monetary System	271
	Competition in Commercial Banking	273
	Competition in Capital Markets	276
	Competition Within Universal Banks	277
	Competition Versus Financial Stability	278

	Governance	279
	Regulation	281
Chapter 13:	**The Base of Investable and Bankable Projects**	**285**
	Of Savings Gluts and Safe Assets	286
	Shifts in the Balance of Domestic Saving	287
	Safe Assets as a Sink for the Saving Glut	288
	Après le deluge	289
	The Pathological Character of Land and Real Estate	290
	Investable Projects Involving Land	290
	The Bankability of Investable Projects Involving Land	292
	Exposure of the Banking System to Land Values	294
	Is Technology Making Fewer Projects Bankable?	296
	How to Expand the Base	297
Chapter 14:	**Rewriting the Rules**	**303**
	Toward a New Central Bank Operating Model	304
	Errors of the Old Monetarism	305
	Targeting Divisia Money	306
	Reserve Management	309
	Standing Facilities	309
	Monitoring the Distributional Impact of Broad Money Growth	311
	Fixing Bank Regulation	311
	Splitting the Banking Book and the Trading Book	312
	Neutral Credit Risk Weights	314
	Liquidity Risk Management	318
	Underwriting, Pricing, and Innovation	318
	Using Savings More Efficiently	320
	Reducing Government's Footprint in the Capital Markets	320
	Unwinding the Federal Reserve Balance Sheet	322
	Unfinished Business	324
	Appendix 14.A Neutral Credit Risk Weights	326
About the Authors		331
Index		333

Foreword

This book must be read for the following reasons:

1. It offers a theoretical view on money and monetary policy that is often overlooked; indeed, the authors explain why economic thinking fails to grasp the nature of fiat money.
2. It stresses that monetary policy is heavily influenced by fiscal conditions. The monetary impact of the government budget is an essential factor behind monetary policy. If you combine a "fiscal constraint factor" (money must finance the deficit) and regulatory banking measures (banks have to buy the issued obligations), you completely condition monetary policy. We should see to it that bank regulation is more neutral.
3. What is worth praising in this properly *extraordinary* book is the combination of monetary theory and the business-related imperative of *making money*. I have never seen (except perhaps in reading Keynes) such a skillful association.
4. The authors look at central bank policy from the viewpoint of the quantity of money. Far from being an old-fashioned method, my experience has showed me that this relationship is essential to determine the adequate mix of fiscal and monetary policy.

5. The proposals for reform contained in the book are geared to achieve neutrality in the monetary system. I have been working and battling during all my career to promote the benefits of neutrality. This is the crux of the book.
6. The pathological character of real estate as the essential bankable project and absorber of savings is well analyzed.

If monetary policy creates distortions—which is abundantly the case—the allocation of savings to investments is, by definition, skewed. Is this the right way of using monetary policy for productive investment purposes?

Obviously, no.

We need, therefore, to improve the performance of the monetary system and make a better use of aggregate savings.

In order to achieve these aims, it is absolutely essential to enforce neutrality as the main objective of monetary policy. We have to stop believing that we (and central banks) know better than the markets. Markets, not public officials, fix the long-term interest rates.

★ ★ ★

To sum it up, the authors have illuminated a compelling path toward a basic objective which I share: a quantitatively based monetary framework.

—Jacques de Larosière

Jacques de Larosière is a member of the French Académie des Sciences Morales et Politiques. In the past, he served as the Managing Director of the International Monetary Fund (1978–1987), the Governor of the Banque de France (1987–1993), and the President of the European Bank for Reconstruction and Development (1993–1998).

Introduction

The Global Financial Crisis of 2007–2009 (GFC) precipitated a deep recession and a comprehensive reckoning with the risks taken by the world's largest universal banks. Less obviously, the GFC introduced major disruptions to the conditions by which money is supplied to the wider economy. Commercial banks' ability to create credit was restrained by new lending guidelines and increases in their capital and liquidity buffers, and the production of money-like instruments by financial intermediaries in the "shadow banking" sector was sharply curtailed. Governments stepped in with "quantitative easing" (QE), filling the gap with varying degrees of success. As the banking system of the developed world slowly recovered, the center of global credit creation shifted to China, a situation which has proven unsustainable.

Fifteen years later, we can evaluate the post-GFC policy measures which continue to define the landscape for banking, the capital markets, and monetary policy. With banks straining under the burden of their capital markets business and their accumulated exposures to real estate, credit growth is grinding to a halt. As a result, the global economy is leaning heavily on global savings to finance investment, just as capital investment needs are reaching a generational inflection point. Investments in electricity generation and electrification, decarbonization, the reconfiguration of global supply chains, and the renewal of public infrastructure and common pool resource assets will require investments in the hundreds of trillions over the coming decades. That we are leaning increasingly on government finance for this purpose is a worrying sign.

Our task in this book is to explain why the commercial banking system is central to the monetary economy. Motivating our analysis and results requires an ambitious itinerary. We must explain not only why banks are so essential for investment and the monetary system, but also why the received wisdom on money, banking, and monetary policy is wrong. We must explain how a fiat money system works and why the economic thinking underlying contemporary policy is inadequate to the task of fostering and regulating it.

We focus on the United States throughout, though we believe our analysis is valid for most of the developed world. To present data for all the major economies would quickly become overwhelming, which is not to mention the endless differences in the design of central banking institutions, bank regulation, and capital markets prevailing in different jurisdictions. We hope that others who are more knowledgeable about specific territories will approach their systems with the same orientation. We have also decided to cut off our reviews of empirical data at the end of 2023. Sacrificing some up-to-the-minute timeliness was necessary to avoid continuous revisions to our data analyses as we drafted the manuscript.

We have been following developments in money and banking for decades, as a consultant to universal banks, in post-GFC litigation, and in designing reforms to monetary systems. Tracing each insight back to its source sometimes eludes us. We hope that those whose work is under-represented in the bibliography will forgive us.

The best way to follow the complete argument is to proceed straight through, but in a book of this size the reader may want to skip around or at least skim certain sections. Chapter 2 will be most interesting for those who want to understand why cryptocurrencies and decentralized finance are not viable alternatives to the system of fiat money. Chapters 4 and 5 describe the micro-foundations of bank lending and financial intermediation, and how the presence of banks and financial markets complicates standard models of economic growth. Chapter 6 and Part Two are heavy on institutional details.

We would like to thank William A. (Bill) Barnett, Dean Buckner, Mark Calabria, Warren Coats, Peter Colwell, Tim Congdon, Kevin Dowd, Charles Goodhart, Manuel Hinds, Peter Ireland, Clark Johnson, David Laidler, Marco Macchiavelli, Ross McLeod, Roger Sandilands, Kurt Schuler, Abderrahim Taamouti, George Tavlas, Andrew Willans, and Zachary Zolnierz for helpful comments on an earlier draft of the book. Caleb Hofmann provided valuable help in preparing the final manuscript. We alone are responsible for any errors that may remain. We appreciate the efforts of Bill Falloon, Stacey Rivera, Purvi Patel, Katherine Cording, Delainey Henson, and the rest of the team at Wiley.

Correspondence about the book can be addressed to the authors at sekerke@jhu.edu and hanke@jhu.edu.

Matt Sekerke and Steve H. Hanke
March 2025

Part One

HOW MONEY WORKS: INSTITUTIONS OF THE MONETARY ECONOMY

Chapter 1

Rethinking Monetary Economics

Money has disappeared from economic thinking, absorbed into Interest and Prices.[1] Its essential role in the economy is as invisible to economic theory as water is to fish. This is not just a problem for theory. When the monetary system breaks, it is the job of economists to fix it, and theory is the economist's sharpest tool.

The last great proponents of the view that money matters in the economy—monetarists like Milton Friedman, Karl Brunner, and Allan Meltzer—were humbled by the failure of Paul Volcker's "monetarist" experiment at the Federal Reserve from 1979 to 1982.[2] For the next 40 years, the Federal Reserve's monetary policy drove interest rates downward until they could go no lower.[3] We are now surrounded by the legacy of this policy: mountains of debt, insane real estate prices, eye-watering equity valuations, and Gilded Age levels of inequality. Perhaps the pathologies of an era that ignored the quantity of money as a factor in economic growth are a good reason to pay attention to the quantity of money once again.

Our goal is not to rehabilitate the old monetarism. Instead, we want to reexamine the role of money in the economy, taking the classic quantity theory of Irving Fisher and the Cambridge economists as a point of departure. We want to build a monetary economics that coheres with the current state of our financial architecture. The economic impact of money has not vanished from real life, even if we now carry less cash and the role of money has been abstracted away from economic theory. The quantity of money continues to affect growth, inflation, and asset prices. This book explains how.

Macroeconomics Without Money

The preferred tool of the vanguard in moneyless macroeconomic theory is dynamic stochastic general equilibrium (DSGE) modeling.[4] The paradigmatic DSGE model is the "real business cycle" (RBC) model in which large-scale macroeconomic fluctuations are traceable to changes in productivity or household preferences.[5] Random fluctuations or "shocks" affecting technology and tastes take center stage in contemporary macroeconomic analysis.

The RBC model supports a distinctive narrative about the macroeconomy. Developments in the economy are the result of technology-driven fluctuations in output and the efforts of households to optimize after observing them. Wages, interest rates, consumption, and investment adjust to the new state of technology through optimizing activity and quickly converge to their equilibrium values. All analysis can be carried out in terms of "real" variables, measured independently of their monetary values.

To achieve even a modicum of influence for money, some kind of external device is needed to extend the RBC model. "Neo-Keynesian" economists shoehorn an assumption about "sticky" wages or prices into a model that is otherwise largely identical to an RBC model.[6] These stopgap theoretical devices, reverse-engineered to generate the short-term effect on inflation they are meant to explain, are defended with elaborate handwaving about why sticky prices are obvious to economists but imperceptible to economic actors.

Sticky-price models of the economy include a "price level" whose changes can be interpreted as inflation. The price level establishes a one-size-fits-all exchange rate between monetary values and "real" quantities like aggregate consumption, aggregate output, and the opportunity cost of leisure. As the inverse of the price level, in effect, money is a redundant variable and may be excluded from the model. The price level is influenced in the short term by changes in an interest rate, which is set by a central bank and taken to capture the stance of "monetary policy." Everything one needs to know about money, it seems, is encapsulated in the interest rate (a price for consumption today versus consumption tomorrow) and the price level.[7]

Such grudging admission of an economic role for money via interest rates and the price level comes with the enormous caveat that changes in monetary conditions affect the economy only in the "short run," as "transitory" responses experienced on the way to a new, "long-run" equilibrium in which money once again takes a back seat to shocks in tastes and technology.

Given this state of consensus in macroeconomic theory, current thinking on monetary economics consists of situating the rate of interest controlled by the central bank relative to an unobservable rate of interest called "r-star," or the rate of interest that would prevail in capital market equilibrium. Monetary policy is tight or loose depending on whether the central bank's policy rate is above or below r-star.

Unsurprisingly, RBC and Neo-Keynesian models have little useful to say about phenomena like proliferating debt, asset price inflation, growing inequality, the Global Financial Crisis (GFC) of 2007–2009, or the post-COVID episode of inflation. We can hardly look to current monetary economics to understand our current situation.

Broad Money and the Banking System

The old monetarism defined money too narrowly, focusing on the liabilities of the central bank as the decisive instruments of control for monetary policy. Much of contemporary economics repeats the same error, limiting money to cash and reserves supplied by the central bank. The relevant quantity of money for economic activity is much broader. Most of it is deposit money supplied by banks. Accordingly, much of this book is devoted to centering banks in a conception of the monetary economy.

Contrary to what is taught in basic economics courses, banks do not lend pre-existing funds. They do not intermediate funds between depositors and borrowers or multiply the reserve money supplied by the central bank. Banks create deposit funding out of nothing.[8] Over the course of this book, we will justify this claim and refute the standard textbook stories.[9]

Banks create money when they make new loans. Deposit money is credited to a borrower on the books of the bank against the recognition of a loan asset. The deposit money created by the loan remains in circulation until the principal of the loan is repaid. Excess money balances can be exchanged for goods, services, or assets, but these transactions only transfer the ownership of the money balance. Society cannot collectively "get rid of" deposit money except by repaying loans.

The ability of banks to create their own funding in the form of deposit money has enormous consequences for economic analysis. It means that any investment that can be funded with bank credit need not draw on aggregate savings. Aggregate savings are costly because they can only be formed when someone in the economy reduces their consumption. Bank credit economizes aggregate savings. This was once well-known to economists like Walras, Fisher, Marshall, Wicksell, and the Keynes of the *Treatise on Money*. As the great Joseph Schumpeter wrote in his monumental *History of Economic Analysis*,

Banks do not, of course, "create" legal-tender money and still less do they "create" machines. They do, however, something ... which, in its economic effects, comes pretty near to creating legal-tender money and which may lead to the creation of "real capital" that could not have been created without this practice. But *this alters the analytic situation profoundly* and makes it highly inadvisable to construe bank credit on the model of existing funds' being withdrawn from previous uses by an entirely imaginary act of saving and then lent out by their owners. It is much more realistic to say that *the banks "create credit," that is, that they create deposits in their act of lending*, than to say that they lend the deposits that have been entrusted to them. And the reason for insisting on this is that depositors should not be invested with the insignia of a role which they do not play. The theory to which economists clung so tenaciously makes them out to be savers when they neither save nor intend to do so; it attributes to them an influence on the "supply of credit" which they do not have. The theory of "credit creation" not only recognizes patent facts without obscuring them by artificial constructions; it also *brings out the peculiar mechanism of saving and investment that is characteristic of full-fledged capitalist society and the true role of banks in capitalist evolution.*[10]

The meaning of those "patent facts" for that "peculiar mechanism of saving and investment" is the axis on which this book turns.

The centrality of banks in the monetary system points to the credit- and claim-based nature of fiat money. Bank money is not *backed* by reserves, fractionally or otherwise. Instead, it is *underwritten* by credible claims to future economic surpluses. The same is true for money issued by the government: the government's ability to redeem its debt and preserve the unit of account in terms of its monetary standard depends on the credibility of its claims to future tax revenues. We explore this and other aspects of fiat money systems at length in Chapters 2, 5, and 9.

Bringing out the role of banks in the contemporary economy is complicated by two main obstacles. First, academics tend to view banks through the same corporate finance lens as other firms, despite the special nature of banks' funding and their distinct legal organization. Second, the corporations that first come to mind when we think of "banks" are in fact large financial holding companies in which the true banking business is just one subsidiary. The credit-creating banking business is attached to multiple capital markets businesses which are concerned with financial intermediation. Two very different economic functions with very different risk profiles live under the roof of a "universal bank," competing with one another for business opportunities, capital, liquidity, and the attention of senior management. To make progress in monetary economics we must grapple with the peculiarities of the universal banking firm.

We separate the economic functions of universal banks into commercial banking and financial intermediation in Chapter 3 and trace the networks of claims that are characteristic of each. In Chapters 4 and 5, we distinguish the functions of financial intermediation and credit creation, digging into their microeconomic foundations and tracing their respective roles in financing investment and economic growth. We take particular care to explain why interest rates are not sufficient to determine equilibrium in either market. In Chapter 6, we consider the hybrid universal bank institution and its contribution to "shadow bank" activities.

If banks are central to the monetary system and live inside universal banks, then the regulation of universal banks is a matter of significant economic concern. Because universal bank regulation affects the volume of credit created by the banks and its allocation among different sectors of the economy, it is a powerful structural instrument of monetary policy. In Chapter 8, we explain how bank regulation affects monetary conditions.

A combination of competition, corporate governance, and regulation ensures that private firms perform their economic functions and maximize social welfare. In Chapter 12 we consider how well these forces have operated in the domain of universal banking. We ask whether any mix of competition, governance, and regulation can ensure that universal banks simultaneously and successfully perform their roles in the monetary system and the capital markets.

From Interest-rate Policy to Quantity-based Policy

In Part Two, we define monetary policy as the official mechanisms that govern the creation and destruction of the money supply. We think of monetary policy being much bigger than what the central bank does. Monetary policy is a complicated mix of bank regulation, fiscal policy, and central bank policy that conditions the production and distribution of money in the economy. It cannot be reduced to interest rates.

One's first lessons in economics involve drawing supply and demand schedules and finding the equilibrium where they cross. Competitive equilibrium yields an equilibrium price and an equilibrium quantity. If we conjure an idea of a "money market," applying the same tools will yield an equilibrium quantity of money at an equilibrium price: the interest rate. As a result, many economists see the interest rate and the quantity of money as two sides of the same coin: take care of the interest rate, and the quantity of money will take care of itself.

In Chapters 4 and 5, we explain why equilibrium in capital and credit markets is more complicated than these blackboard models would imply. Excess demands for equity and credit are a glaring, fundamental fact of economic life for all but the richest members of society. For example, economists like to think that people consume not based on their current income, but based on the "permanent income" they would earn over their lifetime. But to actually consume at this level, one would need to borrow against the entirety of one's future earnings, pulling late-career income forward by some decades to the beginning of one's working life. While consumer credit allows people to borrow against *some* of their future income, the volume of permitted borrowing is nowhere near the present value of one's late-career excess earnings. Offering to pay a higher interest rate does nothing to change the situation; instead, we have an equilibrium with an excess demand for money. The interest rate does not clear the market, and credit is rationed by other mechanisms. Commercial credit demand is also pervasively rationed, with firms able to borrow far less than what their expected future earnings would support.[11]

Credit rationing ensures that interest rates alone do not determine the quantity of money. The same phenomenon in capital markets—equity rationing—ensures that interest rates do not determine equilibrium between savings and investment, either. To describe the set of investments that can be funded by savings or credit at a particular interest rate, we propose the notions of *investable* and *bankable projects*. Many potential investments may have a positive net present value at current interest rates, but additional qualifications are needed to make the project investable and match savings to the project. For an investable project to become bankable requires further qualifications. The set of investments that obtain financing in rationed equilibrium is, therefore, determined not only by interest rates but also by a complicated mix of institutional and contractual features and the informational endowments of banks and investors.

Savings can flow to investable projects, and money can be created by underwriting bankable projects. Bank regulation tilts the set of bankable projects by making certain types of lending more costly. Fiscal policy can put funds into projects regardless of whether they are investable or bankable. It can also make projects investable or bankable by letting investors and banks transfer their risks to the government. When banks, bank regulation, and fiscal policy have so much power to shape the quantity of money, the central bank's field of action is relatively small by comparison. We consider their respective roles in monetary policy in Chapters 8, 9, and 10.

Neutral Monetary Policy

The money supply must be created and continually renewed by the banking system, the government, and nonbank financial institutions. The conditions of bankability that support the creation of deposit money are not evenly distributed in society. And while government money creation is zero in the aggregate, its net impact may be positive or negative for any given economic sector or stratum of the income distribution. As a result of credit rationing and fiscal policy, the money supply is not homogeneously distributed in society, and we do not expect money's impact on growth, inflation, or asset prices to be uniform within the economy. The supply of money will privilege incomes and prices in certain sectors at the expense of others. *Contrary to the received economic wisdom, money is not neutral in the short run or the long run.*

The non-neutrality of money is not detectable using economic aggregates. Its effect is distributional, privileging certain economic actors and activities at the expense of others. Special instrumentation is needed to see it. In Chapter 7, we marshal available data to show the heterogeneity of monetary conditions across segments of the economy. In Chapter 8, we show how regulatory credit risk weights reinforce heterogeneity in private money supply, and in Chapter 9, we present evidence that imbalances in money supply are not completely rebalanced by the intermediation of funds between segments.

We believe that an important goal for the monetary system is to create conditions in which the money supply is more neutral, a notion we define more precisely in Chapter 11. The availability of credit should not determine whether economic actors participate in certain markets or change the intensity of their effort devoted to economic activities. We must also be concerned about the *quality* of money.[12] When the money supply distorts the level and allocation of economic activity, productivity is lost, inferior investments are made, and concentrations of wealth accumulate. These are outcomes we should try to avoid.

Productive Capital Markets

If the obverse of credit rationing in credit markets is the non-neutrality of money, the obverse of equity rationing in capital markets is the proliferation of safe assets. Safe assets are the "default option" for aggregate savings whenever the supply of investable projects falls short. In lieu of risky projects with potential to produce excess economic returns, financial intermediaries must find or create safe assets to absorb surplus savings. Safe opportunities are found in the form of government debt. But they are also overwhelmingly made by plundering the supply of bankable projects, as we show in Chapters 7 and 13.

For the financial system at large, our overarching goal is to use the global supply of savings more efficiently by channeling more of it to risky investable projects. It is likely that global savings will be scarcer in the coming decades than they have been for the past 40 years. If so, it would be foolish to fund projects with scarce savings when they could be funded from bank credit instead. We argue that capital markets have extended their footprint deeply into bank business, cannibalizing bankable projects and channeling savings needlessly into funding low-risk projects and money substitutes. Global savings and the efforts of financial intermediaries would be better directed toward funding risky projects with greater growth potential.

In Chapter 14, we sketch our vision for a new monetary policy framework. This entails a novel central bank operating model, reforms to banking and bank regulation, and improvements to capital markets. We can only suggest a direction for reform. If we wanted to settle the details once and for all, we would fail to meet the moment. Hence our motto for the book: "One hundred flawed steps in the right direction are better than one thousand correct steps in the wrong direction." Or as Keynes said: "It is better to be approximately right than precisely wrong."

Notes

1. Woodford, M. (2003). *Interest and Prices.* Princeton University Press.
2. For a magisterial treatment of the development of monetarism in the United States, which involves much more than just the contribution of the three leaders mentioned, see Tavlas, G. (2023). *The Monetarists: The Making of the Chicago Monetary Tradition, 1927–1960.* University of Chicago Press.
3. Bianchi, F., Lettau, M., and Ludvigson, S.C. (2022). Monetary policy and asset valuation. *Journal of Finance* 77 (2): 967–1017.
4. See Laidler, D. (2024). Lucas (1972) a personal view from the wrong side of the subsequent fifty years. *European Journal of the History of Economic Thought*, doi: 10.1080/09672567.2024.2329045 for a discussion. The new approach rapidly conquered the field, to the point where a paper in macroeconomics without a DSGE model is almost unpublishable; see Colander, D. and Freedman, C. (2019). *Where Economics Went Wrong: Chicago's Abandonment of Classical Liberalism.* Princeton University Press: 149–152. For critiques of the DSGE approach, see Romer, P. (2016). *The Trouble with Macroeconomics.* Manuscript and Stiglitz, J.E. (2018). Where modern macroeconomics went wrong. *Oxford Review of Economic Policy* 34 (1–2): 70–106.

5. The touchstones in this area are Kydland, F.E. and Prescott, E.C. (1982). Time to build and aggregate fluctuations. *Econometrica* 50 (6): 1345–1370, Long, J.B., Jr. and Plosser, C.I. (1983). Real business cycles. *Journal of Political Economy* 91 (1): 39–69, King, R.G., Plosser, C.I., and Rebelo, S.T. (1988a). Production, growth and business cycles: I. The basic neoclassical model. *Journal of Monetary Economics* 21: 195–232, and King, R.G., Plosser, C.I., and Rebelo, S.T. (1988b). Production, growth and business cycles: II. New directions. *Journal of Monetary Economics* 21: 309–341. Black, F. (2011). *Exploring General Equilibrium*. MIT Press memorably boils DSGE down to 'technology and tastes.'
6. Gali, J. (2015). *Monetary Policy, Inflation, and the Business Cycle: An Introduction to the New Keynesian Framework and its Applications*, 2e. Princeton University Press, Schmidt, S. and Wieland, V. (2013). The new Keynesian approach to dynamic general equilibrium modeling: Models, methods, and macroeconomic policy extensions. In: *Handbook of Computable General Equilibrium Modeling* (eds. P.B. Dixon and D.W. Jorgenson), 1439–1512. Elsevier.
7. It is common among some monetary theorists to speculate unironically about a "moneyless limit" in which money disappears from the economy completely. See Woodford, M. (1998). Doing without Money: Controlling inflation in a post-monetary world. *Review of Economic Dynamics* 1: 173–219 and Woodford, M. (2000). Monetary policy in a world without money. *International Finance* 3 (2): 229–260 for some early steps in this direction.
8. McLeay, M., Radia, A., and Thomas, R. (2014a). Money in the modern economy: An introduction. *Bank of England Quarterly Bulletin* 2014 Q1: 4–13 and McLeay, M., Radia, A., and Thomas, R. (2014b). Money creation in the modern economy. *Bank of England Quarterly Bulletin* 2014 Q1: 14–27.
9. See Chapters 3 and 5.
10. Schumpeter, J.A. (2006 [1954]). *History of Economic Analysis.* Routledge: 1080 (emphasis added).
11. Holmström, B. and Tirole, J. (2011). *Inside and Outside Liquidity.* MIT Press. Credit rationing is (almost) obvious when contrasted with the Arrow-Debreu complete markets benchmark in which claims to consumption in any future state of the world can be traded among agents, for a price.
12. Put differently, we are concerned with the credit counterparts of money. See Congdon, T. (2024). *The Quantity Theory of Money: A New Restatement.* Institute of Economic Affairs.

Chapter 2

Fiat Money Systems

Monetary economics concerns itself with the connections between money, banking, and economic activity. The failure of economists to respond coherently to the Global Financial Crisis (GFC) is a failure of monetary economics. In this chapter, we confront several fundamental reasons behind the poor track record of monetary economists. Several foundational precepts of economic theory obscure and diminish the importance of money and banking in market exchange. The deepest misunderstandings stem from a misunderstanding of the nature of money itself, which is incorrectly defined as anything acceptable in exchange and deemed neutral with respect to the underlying "real" economy.[1]

In contrast to this view, we argue that money is primarily a unit of account that is made determinate by collective action through the state. Money is constituted as a nexus of credit relations, which are unevenly distributed in society and possible only under limited circumstances. As a result, the domains susceptible to monetization are limited, and the appearance of robust monetary systems is an exceptional occurrence. Monetary systems cannot merely be "stood up" anywhere by following a technocratic recipe. Changes in the quantity of money follow changes in patterns of credit relations and are decidedly *non*-neutral. Whereas economists have been content to *assume* the neutrality of money, neutrality must be made a *goal* of monetary policy.

The central role of the state in monetary systems focuses attention on the monetary standards they have devised and the tools for their enforcement. We present the metallic standards of early capitalist society as a fiat money standard. No historically important monetary system has spontaneously emerged from uncoordinated market action, and no system of exchange based on barter ever preceded the existence of money. Neither markets nor monetary systems are self-organizing.[2] The presence of an authoritative standard has always been essential for the existence of reliable money and market exchange.

We also explain how our analysis of the nature of money extends to foreign exchange markets, where an ongoing tension exists between market-driven efforts to consolidate trading around a limited set of "vehicle" currencies and transnational efforts to maintain convertibility through external devices and authorities.

Specifying Money So That Money Matters

Economics fails to capture the full scope and stakes of monetary economics because mainstream economic theory largely fails to specify money correctly. Economists struggle to understand and explain what money *does* because they misunderstand what money *is*.

Heterodox theorizing about money has coalesced around four themes adeptly summarized by Geoffrey Ingham: "that money is essentially an abstract measure of value; that money consists in a claim or credit; that the state, or an authority, is an essential basis for money; [and] that money is not neutral in the economic process."[3] While we will be concerned with the *macro*economic resonance of these propositions, each of them departs in an important way from foundational axioms of *micro*economic analysis—that is, claims about the behavior of individuals and firms that form the hard core of what economists most strongly believe to be true. In many ways, admitting the importance of money and banking to the economy brings mainstream economists into conflict with their basic worldview.

Money Is Essentially an Abstract Measure of Value

In economic theory, the preferred abstract measure of value is *utility*. So fundamental is utility to economic analysis that the description of individual choices in terms of their marginal contribution to an individual's utility is widely hailed as the "marginalist revolution" that set modern economics on its way beginning in the 1870s. Similarly, the analysis of *expected* utility across many possible states of an uncertain world is arguably the decisive innovation of postwar economics. Thus, it is absolutely standard for economists to assume that individual economic behavior may be analyzed as if individuals are equipped with a *utility function* that completely describes the desirability of alternative outcomes for consumption, wealth, and leisure without reference to monetary values, and that all decisions in the economy about production, consumption, investment, and labor supply are ultimately the consequence of individual actors maximizing utility. It is not such a huge leap from the planning of a solitary Robinson Crusoe figure to that of the economy at large, as both are coordinated by the utility calculations of a representative individual rather than monetary exchange.[4]

Given an index of utility and assumptions about the state of competition, prices for any good or service in terms of any other good can be expressed as ratios of marginal utilities in equilibrium. To get prices in terms of money, one simply chooses an available good to be the "numeraire" good which will henceforth be called "money." It does not matter which one, so long as everyone agrees on it.[5] However, economic theory is silent on the process that determines what form money will take, and *we have no historical examples* of a society spontaneously agreeing to use a certain thing as money. Even in prison, power is needed to establish cigarettes or packages of mackerel as the unit of account and medium of exchange.[6]

The availability of a *unit of account* supporting an abstract system of value eliminates the "double contingency" between buyers and sellers, who are unable to communicate about reservation prices and willingness to pay in terms of utility.[7] It also makes exchange fault-tolerant in the presence of different media of exchange, which do a better or worse job of *answering* to that unit of account. Without widespread social consensus on a *numeraire*, exchange remains chaotic because any potential trading partner may choose their own reference good. As Ingham puts it: "The very *idea* of money, which is to say, of abstract accounting for value, is *logically anterior and historically prior to market exchange*."[8] The cost of re-discovering values in every market situation, without the aid of money as a calculating device, would be prohibitive to efficient trading. By assuming the priority and anteriority of market exchange, economics assumes a system of value, while hiding it outside the scope of analysis.

Once an idea of money exists, it can be made concrete in terms of a particular *monetary standard* that establishes a scale of value and a unit of account. The unit of account is the unit in which socioeconomic obligations are denominated, such as fines and damages paid for violations of civil and criminal law and the tax owed to authorities—obligations that can arise quite apart from any exchange economy. They also include the amounts owed in debt contracts, the rates at which wages and salaries are paid, the interest and dividends earned on financial assets, and the prices of goods and services. It is significant that the unit of account is connected to the idea of accounting and double-entry bookkeeping. Money comes into being because of double-entry bookkeeping on the balance sheets of suitably empowered entities called banks, and good money allows its users to make plans in terms of its units.[9] Implementing the monetary standard involves the ongoing maintenance and defense of the unit of account in terms of the chosen scale of value.

To the extent that economics deals with money, it tends to prioritize money's function as a medium of exchange based on the supposed anteriority of exchange.[10] The historical existence of anything resembling a primitive barter economy has been thoroughly disproven.[11] It is only in the context of an abstract measure of value, made concrete by a monetary standard, that various objects or "money-things" can answer to the unit of account as a medium of exchange. The unit of account function of money is central and precedes any medium of exchange.[12]

Money Consists in a Claim or Credit

When economic theory defines the numeraire as a chosen good, money takes on the character of a good for any sort of economic analysis. Analyzing goods in economics is about as interesting as analyzing sets in mathematics or points in geometry. However, we point out that goods already exist when they are used and are the result of a process of production.

Money is *not* a good. Money is not a pre-existing resource, and the production that will redeem its value has not yet taken place. Money is a claim. The production of resources follows the production of money, which is only partly constrained by current resource endowments. The production of money therefore relies on credit—that is, the belief (*credere*) that the investments financed by money can redeem money's value without a debasement of the monetary standard.

The creation of money always involves a credible promise to pay. The fulfillment of that promise and the retirement of a corresponding claim *redeems* the value of money. At the end of the process, money does not become a fully embodied resource; *something else* does, creating a real economic surplus, and the monetization of that surplus allows the return of money to the authority that created it, after which it is destroyed. Among these promises to pay is the claim a government holds on firms and households within its jurisdiction to pay taxes, and the claim a bank holds on a firm or household to repay loan principal.[13]

The creation of money that accompanies the recognition of these claims is bounded by the ability of the state, the banking system, and other financial actors to identify and underwrite promises to pay about which there can be little doubt.[14] While the value of money is ultimately redeemed in terms of resources that have yet to come into existence, already-existing savings and property may be marshaled as collateral to liquidate the claims underlying created money, should future surpluses fail to materialize. The sale of the collateral allows the creditor (or debtor) to find money from another source which can redeem the obligation.

Money is destroyed when claims are repaid. Taxes, government debt issuance, and loan amortization retire money from circulation. One can say that the supply of money remains outstanding in the aggregate except for taxation and the repayment of loan principal. In lieu of massive prepayments of taxes, the only way the public can rid itself of money in the aggregate is to pay down loan debt ahead of schedule.

Thus, even though the money supply persists and generally increases over time, it must constantly be renewed as money underwritten by older claims is retired and replaced with money underwritten by new claims. The government and the banking system must produce money constantly, and its value must remain consistent with expectations for future surpluses if the monetary standard is to be protected.

Notions of money being created and destroyed are largely foreign to standard monetary economics. From that perspective, money is stuff that already exists: a medium of exchange, forged from value saved as the product of non-consumption, intermediated through the government and the banking system, and grudgingly held as a kind of tax on transactional convenience. Money does not get created and destroyed so much as change form into other financial liabilities as economic actors reorganize their portfolios. The choice to hold money is but one allocation made in the course of choosing an optimal portfolio, albeit an important one that controls one's overall risk exposure.[15]

Underwriting involves judgments about creditworthiness, and creditworthiness inevitably involves beliefs that cannot be fully substantiated with data or historical experience. Though shrouded in highly technical language and partly constrained by data, creditworthiness is a social construct *par excellence*, with far-reaching consequences for economic activity. Beliefs about creditworthiness emerge and grow within society from thousands of sources, coordinating economic activity for a time before being refuted. The impregnability of AAA credit ratings, residential property prices, and various sectors of the economy have all been spectacularly falsified in recent history. Yet prior to their falsification, these beliefs made large scale credit creation possible and resulted in a distribution of credit that did not correspond to *ex post* differences in productivity or earning capacity.

The credit enjoyed on the other side of a claim is the purchasing power of money. Out of nothing, the government and the banking system create the power to command goods and services, now. This purchasing power is exchanged by issuers of money for a claim on future savings, which are expected to become available as productivity is expanded. *The value of money consists in the successful and timely defense of such claims, rather than any correspondence between money and currently existing resources.* Money, as a claim or credit, is intrinsically forward-looking.[16]

At the same time, there is a stratum of the money supply that is fully funded by already-existing savings. Its existence likewise depends on the capacity of financial institutions to issue claims against credible promises to pay. However, this *store-of-value money* is distinct from the forms of money created by banks and the government that may be used to settle transactions and relies on its convertibility into these more certain forms for its monetary status, which can be threatened in times of distress. Store-of-value money is not always *medium-of-exchange money*, while medium-of-exchange money is always store-of-value money. This leads to our third claim.

The State, or an Authority, Is an Essential Basis for Money

It is the priority of society acting collectively through the state to say what money is.[17] Thus, all money is fiat money, and always has been. As the collector of taxes and civil penalties with legal recourse to punishment for non-payment, the state is free to specify the form in which its citizens or residents discharge their official liabilities. The value the state attributes to a unit of account in terms of tax compliance is sufficient to establish the value of things answering to that unit among everyone subject to taxation.[18] Similarly, the state's ability to demand and collect money-things as an ongoing enterprise establishes the value of government debt. The unlimited lifetime of a bank organized as a joint stock corporation is another historically important parallel. Whatever the state demands for payment of tax or issues in anticipation of tax collections has the primary claim to the status of money.

Money is one of the great inventions of mankind.[19] The existence of well-functioning fiat money is intrinsically connected to the rule of law and other fundamental constructs of capitalism and modernity. A unit of account is essential for contracting, and enforceable contracts are essential for the pursuit of unpaid claims.

Government's exercise of its fiat to establish a unit of account and ensure the convertibility of exchange media is historically prior to market activity on any material scale. Similarly, the state's role in establishing a monetary system entails the state's ability to delimit the bounds of "legitimate commerce" that may be transacted with its money. Today's strictures against money laundering and transactions with sanctioned entities have deep historical roots, such as limitations on the export of cash and the inspection of imports and exports at customs houses. The state and its agents expend significant effort to ensure the domains of money and legitimate commerce coincide.

Banks' power to create money is granted by the state and tightly controlled thereafter.[20] The state grants bank charters and undertakes measures to ensure the convertibility of bank-issued claims to state-issued claims at par.[21] Licenses to enter the banking business are more difficult to obtain than those for any other business, and banks are subject to immense bodies of distinct corporate and securities laws, as well as regulations concerning their governance, liquidity, and capitalization.[22] Likewise, the banking firm is *not a firm like any other* precisely because it is *not a corporation financed like any other*. Banks' ability to issue money in the form of deposits allows each individual bank to produce its own funding, which affords every bank significant leverage.[23]

The limits of measures ensuring convertibility to state-issued claims at par define the boundary between *medium-of-exchange money* and *store-of-value money*. Actors must be paid at least the rate of short-term government bonds to hold store-of-value money, while medium-of-exchange money is held at interest rates below the government rate, or even for no interest at all. The difference in user cost is an indication of the difference in "moneyness" enjoyed by each variety.[24] When adding up components of the money supply, it is essential to account for these differences.

It should be unsurprising that the state is directly implicated in any kind of monetary or financial crisis both as a cause of the crisis and as a means of its resolution. Crisis is essential to renewing the monetary order, just as it is to the political order.[25] Events that call the state's credibility into question inevitably undermine the value of the state's money. But it is impossible to end a financial crisis without the state re-establishing the basis for money. Such decisions nowadays take the form of decisions about the amount of inflation that is tolerable in re-establishing the monetary standard, the eligibility of assets as collateral at the central bank, the bounds of deposit insurance, and the institutional scope of government bailouts—but the essentially political nature of a financial crisis remains plain.

Money Is Not Neutral in the Economic Process

If money is just a numeraire good, as it is in the standard economic view, changing the value of money will change all of the exchange ratios between money and goods, but the relative prices of goods in terms of money will remain unchanged.[26] The value of money establishes a *price level*, but because *relative prices* do not change, economic actors make the same decisions as before, and money is taken to be *neutral* in the economic process.[27]

In fact, nothing could be more unlikely than the neutrality of money. The creation and destruction of purchasing power is unevenly distributed in society and the consequences of the diffusion of purchasing power have uneven effects on the prices of goods and services.

Most purchasing power is created by the lending activity of the banking system, which is not indifferent to the character of borrowers or the purposes for which loans are underwritten. The ability of economic actors to monetize their future surpluses via the banking system varies with their net worth, their possession of suitable collateral, and the alignment of their pursuits with what is currently deemed creditworthy. Firms and households with greater net worth have a greater ability to increase their purchasing power because they already possess the resources needed to retire credit claims against themselves. Their wealth reduces or eliminates the risk for a lending bank. When wealth is concentrated, lending opportunities are concentrated (and limited) as well. Similarly, firms that operate with more standardized physical assets have more borrowing capacity than firms that rely on human capital, which cannot be pledged as collateral. Economic actors who resist the *zeitgeist* will face more difficulties in funding their ventures than those who annex their ambitions to the latest hype cycle.

The uneven creation of credit affects the terms of trade between economic actors and sectors of the economy. It would be absurd to argue that, for example, the residential real estate mania of the past two decades had nothing to do with the willingness of banks (backstopped by capital markets) to create money against residential property collateral, that such willingness did not divert attention and resources from other kinds of economic activity, or that those who already had more wealth and more equity in real estate capital failed to reap more benefits from this newly created purchasing power than those without.

Economics fails to see these distortions because money and finance are defined out of the economic problem, which treats all investments as equally worthy destinations for society's accumulated savings based on their net present value (NPV). By defining bank lending as a subset of the intermediation of aggregate savings, mainstream economics reduces access to credit to the clearing of the market for loanable funds. Those seeking funds, like all borrowers, are rationed from the market only if they are unwilling or unable to pay the prevailing interest rate for loanable funds. Money is neutral because all sufficiently-productive investment projects are funded as the market for loanable funds clears.

Yet it is emphatically not the case that all borrowers who seek loans at the prevailing interest rate obtain them. Net worth is unevenly distributed because of differences in accumulated savings and rationing in capital markets. And because net worth and collateral are unevenly distributed and investment projects are not always aligned with prevailing ideas of creditworthiness, credit capacity varies widely, and money cannot be neutral. We discuss why the market for loanable funds fails to clear in Chapter 4 and distinguish banking from financial intermediation in Chapter 5.

We argue in Part Three that the neutrality of money needs to be made a *goal* of monetary policy, rather than a feature of monetary economics that is taken for granted. The activities undertaken in the economy and the efficiency with which they are pursued should not depend on the availability of credit. Rather, credit should be deployed to a wide spectrum of activities based on their ability to generate surpluses. Pursuit of this goal requires the notion of creditworthiness to operate over more domains than it has traditionally.

Similarly, monetary policy ought to recognize the impact of credit creation on the distribution of purchasing power, investment, and entrepreneurial activity to avoid distortions of economic activity and enable economic growth. It will be constrained in this pursuit by the monetary impact of tax policy, which may not be optimal from an economic perspective. In Part Three of the book, we will suggest reforms to monetary policy oriented toward monetary neutrality.[28]

Fiat Monetary Standards

Our approach to monetary economics places the power of the state's fiat at the center of a system that creates and destroys purchasing power in ways that potentially affect the size and character of the economy. We have accordingly expanded the potential scope and ambition of monetary policy in a fiat monetary system. Underpinning the system is the state's ability to maintain and defend a unit of account through the successful implementation of a monetary standard.

For money to carry out its unit of account function and establish an abstract system of value, another, more fundamental stipulation is needed as to the value of money in terms of some other thing. That other thing is the *monetary standard*.

The choice of the monetary standard is reserved to society acting collectively through the state. We take a standard to mean *the set of rules according to which the value of money is defined and authenticated*. Monetary standards have technical and process elements, focused on the mechanics of valuation and the performative visibility and protection of the valuation process, respectively.[29]

Metallic Standards

Metallic standards were important to the development of capitalist commerce and are frequently idealized. When properly understood, the early history of metallic standards well illustrates the differences between the unit of account, the value of coins used as media of exchange, and the standard according to which coinage is created and destroyed. In a system with many coinages and standards of varying quality, the early modern invention of banking reconciled the motley landscape of money to a standard unit of account, and transfers between banks became the preferred secure, low-noise channel for making payments.

Gold standards operated within an abstract system of value created by the Holy Roman Emperor Charlemagne. The unit of account was a *libra*, divided into 20 *solidi* (singular: *solidus*) and 12 *denarii* (singular: *denarius*) per *solidus*. The system was preserved from the ninth century through the decimalization of the British pound, previously divided into schillings and pence, and whose £ symbol recalls the initial letter of *libra*. These denominations were used continuously for quoting prices and specifying obligations in contracts, while multiple systems of coinage passed in and out of currency.[30]

The minting of coins was left to the authority of local rulers, who would specify the quantity of metal to be contained in each coin. It was typical to use gold for coins intended for large payments, copper for the smallest denominations, and silver in between. However the amount of metal used initially would vary, and in use, coins would lose metal upon being clipped or simply passed from hand to hand. Thus, payments were settled by weighing coins rather than counting them, and there was little sense in which the coins of the time had a "face value."[31]

Specifying gold and silver contents created implicit exchange rates between gold and silver which did not necessarily align with the relative scarcity of the metals. Abundant metal could be minted into coin, increasing its supply and driving coins made of scarce metal out of circulation. Merchants transacting business in multiple locales and coins could take advantage of differences in exchange rates to dispose of certain coins at a higher price and acquire them cheaply elsewhere.

Banking emerged in what is now Italy when moneychangers began accepting deposits of coins from their clients. Coins were weighed, and the client received a bank balance, denominated in the prevailing unit of account. Thereafter, a bank client could direct payment to other firms from their bank. The bankers would offset debits and credits among their clients and settle the net balances in metal. City governments established public banks to ensure the wide availability of such services, and government supervision and guild control were common features of early modern banking systems.[32]

The bank money which permitted payments to be settled in terms of the unit of account, rather than any metallic medium of exchange, was where the metallic standards reached their full expression. Bank money was assured convertibility into coin at the legal rate, whereas the convertibility of coin into the unit of account remained subject to multiple uncertainties. At the same time, the ability of banks to create credit relieved the system from the hard constraint of metal supply, while leaving the metallic standard intact. The state's fiat defining the metal content corresponding to the unit of account was defended with the highest fidelity in bank money.

Metallic standards remained subject to the whims of sovereigns and the winds of politics. Throughout the era of metallic standards, rulers changed mint prices, standards of metal content, and exchange rates between gold and silver; they debased coins and called old coins in for reminting. Standards were mutable, yet stable between interventions.

There is no reason to fetishize gold as the basis of a monetary standard. Gold has many qualities as a metal and as a token money-thing, but it is not any more intrinsically valuable than any other thing that commands a positive price in the market. It was the *standard*, rather than the *gold*, that made gold standards successful.

Metallic standards are distinguished from contemporary fiat standards by their connection to real resources, as well as by their relation to government finances. Few contemporary fiat systems offer two-way convertibility, or the opportunity to exchange the local currency for some other thing at a fixed exchange rate.[33] Many people spuriously seize on this fact as "proof" that non-metallic fiat money is simply made up and intrinsically worthless. Such observers would deny the possibility of linking a unit of account to anything other than a commodity, despite important successes of monetary standards implemented after the period of metallic standards.[34] Few monetary standards now involve periods of sharp deflation, for example.[35]

More importantly, metallic standards constrained government spending by more obviously connecting excessive government expenditures to devaluations of the currency, and by keeping the range of possible devaluations within reason. Shameless debasing of the coinage or enormous forced loans from the banking system would quickly undermine a government's pursuit of increased spending. Contemporary fiat systems place fewer obstacles in the way of government spending, making hyperinflations possible but ultimately changing none of the underlying math about a government's solvency.

Standards After Metallic Standards

The "real bills doctrine" employed by the early Federal Reserve System was also a monetary standard, a tentative step away from a pure metallic standard which aligned the quantity of currency and bank reserves with the supply of "real bills."[36] In addition to exchanges against gold and foreign currencies backed by gold, expansion in the supply of currency and bank reserves was permitted by trading "real bills" with the central bank. Real bills are short-term advances by banks used to finance trade and production. Short-term debt instruments issued against other collateral, including government debt, were not deemed acceptable for monetization by the Federal Reserve System. Embracing the real bills doctrine involved the use of government fiat, as written into the Federal Reserve Act, as well as a program of implementation by the newly established Federal Reserve System.

The Bretton Woods system linked the world's currencies to gold following World War II via the gold parity of the U.S. dollar. Gold parities for other world currencies were derivable from their fixed exchange rates with the U.S. dollar. Inevitably, gold would flow out of debtor countries and into creditor countries under the Bretton Woods system, while the newly established International Monetary Fund would serve as a foreign exchange dealer of last resort, making Special Drawing Rights available on a standby basis to bridge deficits. The balance of payments deficits rarely proved temporary, however. In response, the United States suspended the convertibility of the U.S. dollar into gold, and the international system of fixed exchange rates fragmented into a mix of fixed, pegged, and floating exchange rates linking a profusion of national monetary standards.[37]

Today, most developed economies embrace a consumer price standard implemented by a central bank. The value of money is established with reference to a basket of goods and services purchased by a representative household. Under a consumer price standard, central banks commit to a slow rate of decline in the ability of a representative household to purchase the reference consumption basket with the same expenditure of money. Wide consensus suggests that "a slow rate" means a low, single-percentage-point rate of inflation for the reference basket.[38] Again, there is nothing magical about the consumption basket of a representative consumer (whoever that might be) as the basis for the value of the monetary unit.

The consumer price standard is useful because it collapses the distinction between the unit of account and the value of money. The value of money is specified with reference to prices in general, and not the price of any one thing. While metallic standards risked non-market exchange rates between coins and the unit of account, the exchange rate between paper cash and the unit of account is defined by the face value of cash. Under the consumer price standard, all money is bank money, issued by a central bank or a commercial bank.

The consumer price standard is enforced by the actions that central banks take to achieve their targeted rate of consumer price inflation. The totality of these actions are largely what we mean by the implementation of monetary policy. The importance of the standard and its enforcement are underscored by official proceedings that hold central banks to account. Underneath the jargon, such proceedings are in large part a ritual in which society collectively acknowledges the sanctity of the monetary standard.[39]

Foreign Exchange and the Quest for an International Monetary Standard

Perhaps another reason metallic standards are so celebrated is their wide geographic acceptance in the early development of global capitalism. This was no accident, nor an embrace of an inevitable natural law. The same European powers who emerged from the commercial leagues of the Middle Ages preserved metallic standards within their home territories while imposing them on colonies and other possessions abroad. The near-universal establishment of metallic standards ensured the convertibility of the world's currencies into each other.

Since the end of the Bretton Woods system, the global economy has operated on a system of currency convertibility intermediated by a global network of dealer banks. Its growth and sustainability rest on a set of standardized agreements enforceable under New York and English law, the willingness of dealer banks to create credit to absorb payment imbalances, and the ability to settle payments through a network of correspondent banks connected by the SWIFT messaging system. It also depends closely on the willingness of central banks to function as foreign exchange dealers of last resort. All aspects of the nature of money—the primacy of units of account, credit relations, state underwriting, and non-neutrality—are also inherent in the market for foreign exchange.

The nature of post-Bretton Woods currency convertibility implies that foreign exchange rates—the price of one money in terms of another—are not overdetermined by barter terms between baskets of goods in two jurisdictions or by relative asset prices. They are also a function of the terms on which dealer banks are prepared to create credit over various horizons in each traded currency.[40] We can say that exchange rates are the price at which claims on receipts in different currencies trade in the foreign exchange market. Macroeconomics is again essentially blind to the nature of international money, eager as it is to reduce exchange rates to purchasing power parities (ratios of price levels) or interest parities (ratios of interest rates). Asset pricing studies, on the other hand, recognize the existence of risk premiums associated with the term of forward exchange rate agreements, which in turn recognize the uncertainty of rolling over multicurrency credit indefinitely.[41]

Settling payments in different currencies requires market participants to accumulate balances in each subject currency. When such balances cannot be obtained through sales of goods and services, they can be obtained through credit creation. Credit is created against the market participant's credible claim to a future surplus in the currency—perhaps as precise as a purchase order, or more generally based on their ongoing commercial operations. Once an actor is in possession of foreign currency balances, payments can be settled in that currency on the books of the dealer bank, or via the settlement system of the state issuing the currency, and ultimately in terms of reserve money.[42]

Dealer banks are willing to settle large volumes of payments with each other in multiple currencies due to the existence of master netting agreements that allow for the aggregation and offset of claims.[43] The ability to net payment flows in a trillion-dollar-a-day market significantly reduces dealer banks' risk that a failure to receive payment will endanger their financial position. And as with domestic settlement systems, the ability to settle international claims via cancellation or netting underpins the status of international money as money.

The pattern of credit created by and between dealer banks leads to significant exposures to future movements in foreign exchange rates and interest rates. Such exposures are traded among dealer banks and other market participants in deep international markets for derivatives. Though derivatives may ultimately settle at a date, months, or years in the future, collateral is exchanged daily to zero out banks' exposure to their counterparties. The suitability of various financial instruments as collateral for such purposes is likewise established by international master agreements between dealer banks. Suitable collateral thus functions as a kind of quasi-money for the interim settlement of risk exposures underlying foreign exchange dealing activity between international banks.[44]

The U.S. dollar sits at the center of the post-Bretton Woods currency convertibility regime and dealer bank risk management. The U.S. dollar serves as a standard of value for international transactions far beyond the borders of the United States, with trade being invoiced and settled in U.S. dollars in many non-U.S. jurisdictions. Virtually every participant in international trade and finance is thus obliged to hold U.S. dollar balances to maintain their own liquidity and solvency. Exchange rates between two non-U.S. currencies (for example, EUR/CLP) are frequently obtained as "cross rates" via the U.S. dollar (EUR/USD and USD/CLP) rather than directly. And U.S. Treasuries and government-sponsored enterprise (GSE) obligations have pride of place in collateralizing derivative transactions and other financial exposures between international banks.

The U.S. dollar's place at the center of international money and finance is well-reinforced, despite frequent reports of its impending displacement. Dealer banks are most comfortable creating U.S. dollar credit because it is the currency most likely to be received in trade, and if not, the currency most easily obtained by selling another. And in recent years, the Federal Reserve has expanded its role in the provision of international U.S. dollar liquidity, providing further confidence that the ability to transact in U.S. dollars will not be compromised in times of market distress.[45] Central banks hold ample U.S. dollar reserves following decades of accumulation in the 1990s and 2000s, and often seek to stabilize the price of their currencies in U.S. dollar terms.[46] For all its imperfections, the U.S. dollar has emerged as an international standard of value *par excellence* and the preferred mechanism through which transactions in goods and money alike are settled.

Though the U.S. dollar has enjoyed *de facto* dominance, efforts have been growing over the postwar period to synchronize the rules by which money is created across jurisdictions. The International Monetary Fund has emerged as a kind of global consultancy for central banks, offering technical assistance on everything from price index construction to monetary policy implementation, premised on a consensus around inflation-targeting central banks.

Somewhat less obviously, the rules for the creation and destruction of bank money are being progressively synchronized by a consensus on bank regulation emanating from the Basel Committee on Banking Supervision (BCBS). Though technically a working group between the banking supervisors of the G10 countries, the "Basel Accords" authored by the BCBS have set the agenda for bank regulation in most of the developed world since the 1980s.[47] The Basel Accords impose constraints on money creation that are binding on all internationally active banks, at least in principle, so that expansion of bank money must be bounded by growth in the equity held by the banking system.

However, we should not overstate the extent to which these international efforts define an international monetary standard. In addition to structural disagreement between debtor and creditor countries, which makes the right to contract debt in one's own currency a preferred sovereign right, the heterogeneity of conditions that permit the creation of money-supporting claims in each jurisdiction frustrates attempts at international alignment. Though banks may play by the same capital rules, the supply of bankable projects varies. And though central banks may coordinate policy, international agreements can be at cross-purposes with domestic commitments.

Revisiting the Foundations of Monetary Economics

This chapter has begun to unwind much of the mythology about money perpetuated by academic economics and corporate finance and recently amplified by proponents of cryptocurrencies and decentralized finance. We have seen that money is not a veil for the barter-like exchange of utilities or productive factors but primarily a unit of account which is constitutive of exchange. Money consists of credit created and destroyed continuously on the basis of credible claims to future surpluses. The state is an essential actor in establishing the unit of account, the terms on which claims are redeemed, and the fungibility of money issued according to valid rules of formation. Accordingly, we must be concerned with the legal constitution of money and its regulation. Finally, we argued that money is not neutral in the process of exchange. Structural imbalances exist about whose claims to future surpluses are deemed most credible, with consequences for the distribution of purchasing power. We have reviewed various ways in which states have established monetary standards and examined the domestic and international consequences of money's nature.

We hope this chapter buries, once and for all, the idea that fiat money is an arbitrary token that everyone agrees will exchange for goods and services. Behind every fiat money used in exchange lies a unit of account defined by a monetary standard. The standard may be flawed or have undesirable consequences, but it is not arbitrary, and the monetary standard makes fiat money's role in exchange possible. In subsequent chapters we will develop the idea that modern fiat monetary standards are underwritten by credible claims to future surpluses monetized by the government and/or the commercial banking system. The value of fiat money is only as good as the credibility of these promises. But without even the pretense of something that *redeems* the value of money—gold, a "real bill," or a future surplus—any token masquerading as money lacks value. Claims of a "Bitcoin standard" or anything like it are completely indefensible.[48]

In the next chapter, we will be concerned with the institutions of the monetary economy which are generally left out of economic analysis. We consider the government's roles as fiscal and monetary authority and the credit creation (commercial banking) and financial intermediation functions of the financial system. We show the connections between each of these sectors and the household and nonfinancial business sectors where consumption and production take place. We consider the contributions made by various financial sectors to money production. Finally, we examine how the symmetry of our sectoral accounting framework has led monetary economics into the error of treating money-producing sectors symmetrically with intermediary sectors and erasing the active role of credit creation in financial expansion.

Chapters 4–6 go deeper into the microeconomic conditions supporting the reallocation of savings in capital markets and the creation of credit in the banking system. While we will assume the legal existence of banks and financial intermediaries, we will not use financial regulation to explain equilibrium outcomes. We are concerned to demonstrate that equilibrium can be described without recourse to external rules and to recognize the relevant constraints that give each sector of the financial system its special character. The markets served by financial intermediaries, commercial banks, and shadow banking institutions are each bounded by different resources. But Chapter 6 acknowledges an uncomfortable truth: all of these unique financial system functions coexist in large, complex institutions that enjoy a great deal of discretion in how they direct resources to each subsector of the financial system.

Notes

1. Though we criticize economic theory throughout the book, we continue to draw intuition and arguments from what we believe to be a settled "core" of economic thinking. Hence our criticism of, say, DSGE models does not result in us discarding a general equilibrium orientation to the economy or the basic story of economic agents making choices involving tradeoffs between current and future output.
2. Mundell, R. (2000). The Euro and the stability of the international monetary system. In: *The Euro as a Stabilizer in the International Economic System* (eds. R. Mundell and A. Clesse), 57–84. Springer.
3. Ingham, G. (2004). *The Nature of Money.* Polity Press: 56.
4. At the same time, a literature has been developed analyzing rigorously the conditions under which the aggregation of preferences in a synthetic, representative individual (or household or firm) is possible. See for example, Gorman, W.M. (1959). Separable utility and aggregation. *Econometrica* 27 (3): 469–481. The conditions where it is possible are incredibly restrictive, but economists have largely chosen to embrace these unreal assumptions rather than think through the radical consequences of non-aggregability for economic analysis.
5. Arrow, K.J. and Debreu, G. (1954). Existence of equilibrium for a competitive economy. *Econometrica* 22 (3): 265–290; Kiyotaki, N. and Wright, R. (1989). On money as a medium of exchange. *Journal of Political Economy* 97 (4): 927–954. This error in analysis may be more responsible for the rise of cryptocurrency than any other.
6. To be sure, many economists have erroneously attributed the exchange of certain common items to the development of money. All this proves is that they are unimaginative anthropologists and historians. They are only "discoverers" of "universal" patterns of behavior because they cannot conceive of other reasons why the items would be exchanged. For example, Graeber, D. and Wengrow, D. (2021). *The Dawn of Everything: A New History of Humanity.* Penguin Books: 22–24 cite vision quests, traveling healers and entertainers,

gambling, and the exchange of heirloom treasures to spread one's name as reasons why objects erroneously identified as "primitive currencies" were exchanged, without any sort of "primitive trade" occurring.

7. We deliberately allude to the terminology of Parsons, T. (1951). *The Social System*. Free Press.
8. Ingham, G. (2004). *The Nature of Money*. Polity Press at 25.
9. Ingham, G. (2004). *The Nature of Money*. Polity Press emphasizes the explanation of banks and banking in Luca Pacioli's treatise on accounting. See also Soll, J. (2016). *The Reckoning: Financial Accountability and the Making and Breaking of Nations*. Penguin Books.
10. See, e.g., Kiyotaki, N. and Wright, R. (1993). A search-theoretic approach to monetary economics. *American Economic Review* 83 (1): 63–77.
11. Graeber, D. (2014). *Debt: The First 5,000 Years*, new and expanded edition. Melville House: 21–41 and cites therein.
12. In early modern commerce, the unit of account was defined with reference to a certain weight of gold, as we explain further. Multiple gold coins circulated with different gold content. There was no pretense that any of these coins—the media of exchange—were identical to the unit of account. Early banks performed the important function of reconciling the many coins of commerce to the established unit of account.
13. The connection between vocabulary of belief and redemption and the Gospel of St. Matthew, the patron saint of bankers is noted by Soll, J. (2016). *The Reckoning: Financial Accountability and the Making and Breaking of Nations*. Penguin Books: 23–24.
14. One could say that underwriting *deems* the returns of an investment to be "money-good," whereas the realization of the return *re-deems* the underwritten promise.
15. The classic articulation of this viewpoint is Tobin, J. (1963). Commercial banks as creators of "money." *Cowles Commission Discussion Papers No. 159*, which underpins the more expansive theory of Tobin, J. (1969). A general equilibrium approach to monetary theory. *Journal of Money, Credit and Banking* 1 (1): 15–29.
16. This line of reasoning also suggests that money creation is not indifferent to how the funds are used.
17. We are consciously paraphrasing the classic chartalist statement of Knapp, G.F. (1924). *The State Theory of Money*. Macmillan. See also Wray, L.R. (2015). *Modern Monetary Theory: A Primer on Macroeconomics for Sovereign Monetary Systems*, 2e. Palgrave-Macmillan and Mosler, W. (2010). *The Seven Deadly Innocent Frauds of Economic Policy*. Valence Co. Nobel Laureate Robert Mundell

would often claim among colleagues that Knapp was the greatest monetary theorist of all, and would quip, "Private money isn't worth a Hayek." We thank Clark Johnson for sharing the quip with us. When we speak of "the state" in this section, we have in mind the best kind of democratic institution, not an authoritarian regime.
18. Knapp, G.F. (1924). *The State Theory of Money*. Macmillan.
19. We thank Lars Jonung for emphasizing this point.
20. Omarova, S.T. and Steele, G.S. (2024). Banking and antitrust. *Cornell Law School Research Paper No. 24-03*.
21. Episodes of so-called "free banking" feature the issue of notes by commercial banks which circulate as currency in the hands of the public, in place of or in competition with notes issued by a central authority. This is not so much a market solution to the problem of money as it is a low-tech means for bank deposit money to exchange outside of the banking system. The value of these bank notes, like the value of deposits, depends on their convertibility into other banks' notes and deposits at par, which assumes a common denominator for exchange and a system of clearings. That common denominator has always been established by a state-determined monetary standard. The interest in free banking, thus, lies not in the evidence it provides for market-based money solutions but rather in the ability such systems enjoy in avoiding runs by liquidating deposits into notes that banks issue themselves. See Dowd, K. (2023). *The Experience of Free Banking*, 2e. Institute of Economic Affairs for the state of the art on free banking.
22. See, for example, Malloy, M.P. (2011). *Principles of Bank Regulation*, 3e. West.
23. The failure of Admati, A. and Hellwig, M. (2024). *The Bankers' New Clothes*, new and expanded edition. Princeton University Press to recognize the distinction between self-created bank funding and funds sourced from capital markets seriously impairs their analysis of the banking business and the leverage and capitalization of banks.
24. See the discussion in Chapter 7.
25. Cumming, R.D. (1969). *Human Nature and History: A Study of the Development of Liberal Political Thought*. University of Chicago Press.
26. This is the consequence of a mathematical property called homogeneity. See, for example, Tintner, G. (1948). Homogeneous systems in mathematical economics. *Econometrica* 16: 273–294 and Arrow, K.J. (1950). Homogeneous systems in mathematical economics: A comment. *Econometrica* 18: 60–62. Homogeneity is not an intrinsic part of a utility function. Rather, it is a property that economists want from in a utility function because neutrality is part

of the view they are seeking to axiomatize. Rather than being an ideological conspiracy, the point is usually to focus attention on some aspect of the economic situation that is unrelated to money.
27. Consider Hume's famous thought experiments of the quantity of money suddenly halving or doubling.
28. For a discussion of the notion of neutrality through history, see Lucas, R.E., Jr. (2013). *Collected Papers on Monetary Theory*. Harvard University Press: Chapter 16.
29. The work of Georg Simmel bridges the sociological aspects of money and its economic analysis. See Laidler, D. and Rowe, N. (1980). Georg Simmel's philosophy of money: A review article for economists. *Journal of Economic Literature* 18 (1): 97–105 for a discussion.
30. Lane, F.C. and R.C. Mueller. (1985). *Money and Banking in Medieval and Renaissance Venice. Volume One: Coins and Moneys of Account*. Johns Hopkins University Press: 7.
31. Lane, F.C. and R.C. Mueller. (1985). *Money and Banking in Medieval and Renaissance Venice. Volume One: Coins and Moneys of Account*. Johns Hopkins University Press: 11, 45.
32. Ibid, 65–89.
33. Countries with currency board systems enjoy two-way convertibility between their local currency and a foreign anchor currency. We are unaware of a modern system offering two-way convertibility between a local currency and a commodity.
34. To avoid confusion, our view is that most fiat monetary standards have been failures. However, this is a result of proliferating too many such standards in conditions that are not hospitable to money creation, rather than an intrinsic failure of systems not based on gold. The U.S. dollar, the Deutsche Mark, the euro, the Japanese yen, and the Swiss franc are a few successful postwar monetary standards not based on gold.
35. Bordo, M.D., Dittmar, R.T., and Gavin, W.T. (2003). Gold, fiat money, and price stability. *NBER Working Paper 10171* compare price stability under the gold standard, inflation targeting, and other monetary standards and find that inflation targeting actually provides more short-run stability than the gold standard.
36. Meltzer, A. (2003). *A History of the Federal Reserve, Volume 1: 1913–1951*. University of Chicago Press: 263–270.
37. Daunton, Ma. (2023). *The Economic Government of the World, 1933–2023*. Allen Lane: 143–168.

38. Bernanke, B.S., Laubach, T., Mishkin, F.S., et al. (2001). *Inflation Targeting: Lessons from the International Experience*, rev. ed. Princeton University Press.
39. Consider the Humphrey-Hawkins testimony of the Federal Reserve Chairman to Congress.
40. Mehrling, P. (2013). Essential hybridity: A money view of FX. *Journal of Comparative Economics* 41: 355–363.
41. Backus, D.K., Foresi, S., and Telmer, C.I. (2001). Affine term structure models and the forward premium anomaly. *Journal of Finance* 56 (1): 279–304.
42. Bank for International Settlements. (1993). *Central Bank Payment and Settlement Services with Respect to Cross-Border and Multi-Currency Transactions* (BIS), Bank for International Settlements. (1997). *Real Time Gross Settlement Systems* (BIS), Horii and Summers, B.J. (1994). Large-value transfer systems. In: *The Payment System: Design, Management, Supervision* (ed. B.J. Summers). International Monetary Fund, Van den Berg, P. (1994). Operational and financial structure of the payment system. In: *The Payment System: Design, Management, Supervision* (ed. B.J. Summers). International Monetary Fund.
43. Harvey, R. (2013). The legal construction of the global foreign exchange market. *Journal of Comparative Economics* 41: 343–354.
44. Singh, M. (2020). *Collateral Markets and Financial Plumbing*, 3e. Risk Books.
45. See the discussion in Chapter 10.
46. Mohanty, M.S. and Turner, P. (2006). Foreign exchange reserve accumulation in emerging markets: What are the domestic implications? *BIS Quarterly Review*, September, 39–52.
47. Goodhart, C. (2011). *The Basel Committee on Banking Supervision: A History of the Early Years*, 1974–1997. Cambridge University Press.
48. Bitcoin maintains a positive price largely due to holdup. It is not possible for bitcoin-denominated claims to be created on demand. If someone wants to obtain some bitcoin—for instance, to evade sanctions (Russia) or capital controls (China)—they must ransom a large enough quantity in U.S. dollar terms (usually) from existing holders. The holdup problem comes from bitcoin's limited supply and scheduled production in combination with its current holders' awareness of these conditions. Rises in the bitcoin price do not prove the intrinsic value (or network value, or whatever) of Bitcoin any more than a lack of homes for sale in a neighborhood makes those homes infinitely valuable. Holdup (or HODLup, if you like) is not viable as a standard of value.

Chapter 3

The Institutional Structure of the Monetary Economy

The previous chapter argued that money is intrinsically a claim or a credit, and that the value of fiat money is not *backed* but *underwritten* based on the quality of the underlying claims. A claim on an entity is an asset, whereas credit extended is a liability. A balance sheet collects assets and liabilities for an economic actor at a point in time. A system of balance sheets therefore provides a useful schema for the network of claims underlying the money supply.[1] We present such a schema in this chapter, which is a simplified version of flow-of-funds accounting. The balance sheets divide the economy into sectors: the government (divided into fiscal and monetary authorities), the banking institutions that create money, the financial institutions that intermediate savings, and the households and nonfinancial firms comprising the so-called "real" economy. Together, these sector balance sheets connect the monetary liabilities of the government, the banking system, and the financial sector to real assets and surpluses in the process of formation.

After laying out the balance sheet schema, we do two things. First, we show how to add up the economy's monetary liabilities to produce aggregates known as *broad money*. When economists speak of the money supply, they are usually talking about some more or less inclusive notion of broad money. Second, we connect changes in the money supply to *investment*. We consider investment at the microeconomic level of the individual firm and household, as well as in the aggregate. As we will explain in subsequent chapters, the growth of the money supply is intimately connected with the ability of the economy to generate certain kinds of investment opportunities that support monetary claims.

During our tour, we will toggle between balance sheets of individual institutions and the balance sheet of the consolidated sector. For example, we switch between discussing one bank's balance sheet and the balance sheet of the banking sector. In the latter case—what we refer to as "the aggregate"—claims held by banks on other banks wash out. Accordingly, interbank transactions do not appear on the banking system balance sheet, and sectoral balance sheets generally will lack items found on individual balance sheets.

The Government Sector

The government is the historical prime mover in the monetary system. The previous chapter emphasized the necessity of an authority in establishing money. The government's role in the monetary system shrinks as the banking system grows, but it remains the issuer of the ultimate settlement media in the economy: cash and bank reserves. Hence, we begin our tour of the system of monetary claims with the government.

We present an idealized version of the government's balance sheet in three steps. First, we draw up the balance sheet of a fiscal authority which, in the absence of a monetary authority, issues notes and coins directly to the public, as was typically the case in the pre-modern era. Second, we introduce a monetary authority which takes over the issuance of cash and transacts with the banking system as the supplier of a settlement medium and as a lender of last resort. Finally, we consolidate the fiscal and monetary authorities to show how the presence of the monetary authority affects the government's finances.

The Fiscal Authority

One typically imagines the fiscal operations of the government as first collecting money and then spending it, much as a household does. Money is transferred to the Treasury or the finance ministry (we refer to the relevant organ as the "fiscal authority") through tax payments or in connection with bond issues. Government expenditures on labor, finished goods, services, and interest then draw down the balance of the fiscal authority.

What distinguishes the fiat system based on gold from the fiat system based on central banking is *the ordering of taxation and spending*. Under the gold standard, governments were obliged to collect money prior to spending it. Under central banking, government *spends money into existence*, while taxes and debt issuance *take money out of circulation*. With central banking, there is no physical restraint on monetary production by governments. Constraints on monetary production arise entirely from the government's ability to balance its budget and finance deficits in debt markets. The problem the government faces in balancing its budget is not whether it collects enough revenue to support its spending, but *whether it pulls enough money out of circulation to sterilize the monetary consequences of its spending.*[2]

In developed countries, the finances of the fiscal authority include not only those of the finance ministry, but also the finances of agencies of the government, contingent obligations vis-a-vis government-sponsored entities (GSEs), and the finances of state-owned enterprises (SOEs). Though we adopt a simplified picture here, the presence of multiple actors is important for discussions of recent history and policy. In the United States, for example, the actions and obligations of agencies and GSEs like the Federal National Mortgage Association (FNMA or "Fannie Mae"), the Federal Home Loan Mortgage Corporation (FHLMC or "Freddie Mac"), the Government National Mortgage Association (GNMA or "Ginnie Mae"), and the Federal Home Loan Banks (FHLBs) expand the footprint of the United States government in international capital markets and have a material impact on monetary conditions.

The primary asset of the fiscal authority is its claim on tax revenue from households and firms under its jurisdiction. Its liabilities include its expenditure commitments, debt issued to the public, and the notes and coins used by the public as money.

One of the public's primary reasons for holding the fiscal authority's money is the need to discharge tax claims denominated and payable in that money. The denomination of the tax claim in the local currency is essential in establishing the local money as the unit of account. To be able to settle the tax claim in the local currency establishes money's place in the redemption of claims and a mechanism for the subsequent destruction of money.

The abbreviation "PV" in Table 3.1 refers to the *present value* of streams of revenue and expenditure that extend into the future. Future revenues and expenditures are discounted at a rate of interest appropriate for the government's obligations, which can be discovered as the market interest rate for government debt.

Table 3.1 Fiscal authority balance sheet.

Fiscal Authority	
PV of Tax Revenue	PV of Expenditure
	Government Debt
	Notes and Coins

Table 3.2 Simplified fiscal authority balance sheet.

Fiscal Authority	
PV of Primary Budget Balances	Government Debt
	Notes and Coins

The expenditure on the liability side of the fiscal authority's balance sheet can be divided into debts requiring service and everything else. We can clean up the balance sheet by consolidating revenue and expenditure not requiring debt service into the fiscal authority's *primary budget balance*.

The primary budget balance in Table 3.2 is the difference between tax revenue and expenditure, excluding interest on government debt. The market value of government debt captures all principal and interest obligations of the government. Though increases in these obligations are connected to the timing of primary deficits, the scheduling of government debt obligations can generally be managed to decouple the maturity structure of government debt from the pattern of primary deficits adding to the stock of debt.[3]

The government's ability to discharge its debt obligations depends on its ability to maintain a sequence of primary budget balances with a large, positive present value. We analyze these conditions at greater length in Chapter 9. A secondary source of financing comes from the government's ability to issue notes and coins as liabilities, which earn no interest and have no maturity date.

The Monetary Authority

The monetary authority is a branch of the government that exchanges government debt for currency on behalf of the nonbank public and the banking system. In what follows, we assume the monetary authority is a central bank.

Central banks issue two forms of currency. The currency issued to the banking system is known as *reserve money* (or just reserves) and circulates exclusively *within* the banking system. The purpose of reserve money is to allow banks to settle transactions with each other in a common form. The currency issued to the nonbank public is *cash* (notes and coins), which serves the same purpose of settling transactions *outside* the banking system.[4]

We underline the role of the monetary authority as the *fiscal agent* by creating an explicit current account for the fiscal authority at the monetary authority. The government current account creates a buffer between government expenditures, taxes, and debt issuance.

In Tables 3.3 and 3.4, we introduce the convention of identifying the sector counterpart of each item in parentheses. The two liabilities of the central bank,

Table 3.3 Fiscal authority balance sheet with a fiscal agent.

Fiscal Authority	
PV of Primary Budget Balances (Public)	Government Debt (Public)
FA Current Account (Monetary Authority)	Government Debt (Monetary Authority)

Table 3.4 Monetary authority balance sheet.

Monetary Authority	
Government Debt (Fiscal Authority)	Reserves (Commercial Banks)
	Notes and Coins (Public)
	FA Current Account (Fiscal Authority)

reserves and cash, comprise the *monetary base* and are assured *convertibility* into one another at par. Cash deposited at a bank can be held in the bank's vault as cash, where it is treated as part of the bank's reserve balance, or returned to the central bank in exchange for credit to the bank's reserve account. The converse is true as well, allowing banks to meet customer demands for cash by exchanging reserves with the central bank.

Until the Global Financial Crisis (GFC), central banks' cash liabilities were historically much larger than the quantity of bank reserves. Despite the enormous volume of payments settled within the banking system, banks economized reserve balances because they were a non-interest-earning asset. A consequence of central bank balance sheet expansion (quantitative easing) since the GFC has been to expand the amount of reserves held by commercial banks.

The Consolidated Government

The monetary authority is generally owned by the fiscal authority. Thus, a complete picture of government finances requires consolidation of their accounts. We combine balance sheets and eliminate internal claims, one step at a time.

In Table 3.5, government debt held by the monetary authority is an obligation payable by the fiscal authority to itself. From the perspective of the government's consolidated finances, the monetary authority's purchase of government debt with reserves and cash is an effective *cancellation* of the debt while it is held by the monetary authority. The principal and interest paid by the fiscal authority to the monetary authority is a wash for the government. Substantial holdings of government debt at the monetary authority significantly reduce the gross debt numbers typically reported by government statistical agencies and the press.[5] Governments seeking to erase debt burdens can put immense pressure on central banks to purchase government debt, which may not otherwise find a buyer on the open market.[6]

The other item appearing on both sides of the ledger in Table 3.5 is the government's current account. It signals that the government's money balances are not a net asset for the economy, but rather an expedient for predictable debt management.

Eliminating the government debt held by the monetary authority and the fiscal authority's current account in Table 3.6 reduces consolidated government liabilities to debt in the hands of the public, bank reserves, and cash. Reserves and cash can offer the government a financial advantage relative to debt because no interest is payable on cash. Bank reserves may earn interest at a below-market rate, or no interest at all. The interest savings enjoyed by government on its monetary liabilities is known as seigniorage, and the present value of those savings may be capitalized as a seigniorage asset (Table 3.7). The term "seigniorage" has feudal echoes, referring to the privilege enjoyed by a lord over his domain. The potential to earn seigniorage generally makes the monetary authority a valuable asset and a profit center for the government. To the extent that the monetary authority monetizes the fiscal authority's debt—either benignly by maintaining a robust

Table 3.5 Combined government balance sheet.

Combined Government	
PV of Primary Budget Balances (Public)	Government Debt (Public)
FA Current Account (Monetary Authority)	*Government Debt (Monetary Authority)*
Government Debt (Fiscal Authority)	Reserves (Commercial Banks)
	Notes and Coins (Public)
	FA Current Account (Fiscal Authority)

Table 3.6 Consolidated government balance sheet.

Consolidated Government	
PV of Primary Budget Balances (Public)	Government Debt (Public)
	Reserves (Commercial Banks)
	Notes and Coins (Public)

Table 3.7 Consolidated government balance sheet with seigniorage.

Consolidated Government	
PV of Primary Budget Balances (Public)	Government Debt (Public)
PV of Seigniorage (Monetary Authority)	Reserves (Commercial Banks)
	Notes and Coins (Public)

issue of base money or egregiously by force—the monetary authority creates further "fiscal space" for the government.[7]

Thus the two assets supporting the government's liabilities are the government's ability to generate primary budget surpluses—the "full faith and credit" of the government, as Federal Reserve notes say—and seigniorage. Were the government's balance sheet the beginning and the end of the monetary system, capitalized net tax collections would have to equal or exceed the value of government liabilities if they were to maintain the value of the government's liabilities and the monetary standard. Otherwise, the government would need recourse to seigniorage through a forced monetization of the government's debt. Many developing countries have faced this "unpleasant monetarist arithmetic."[8] However, in the modern economy, the set of monetary liabilities is much larger, and the system of assets supporting those liabilities is far more diverse, embedding the value of fiat money in a network of claims extending well beyond the government.

Monetary authority purchases of government bonds have a downstream impact on the monetary base which is generally confined to the reserve market, outside of the broad money supply. Its aggregate effect on money in the hands of the public comes from the exchange of reserve money for bonds. The reserve money is credited to the deposit accounts of bond sellers via their banks.

In Chapter 9, we consider the contribution of the government budget to the money supply on a disaggregated basis. The benefits of government monetary production fall unevenly on those subject to its taxation powers. More so than the overall impact on money supply, the distributional impact of the government's contribution to the money supply can be overwhelming and decisive.

The Commercial Banking System

We now turn to the commercial banking system. We emphasize *commercial* banking because most of the institutions that immediately spring to mind in discussions of "banks"—JPMorgan Chase, Goldman Sachs, Bank of America, and so on—are *hybrid* institutions that combine a commercial bank with various financial intermediation and capital markets functions traditionally called "investment banking" or "merchant banking." It is analytically necessary to separate the banking and capital markets business of such universal banks (or "Bank Holding Companies" or "Financial Holding Companies") because they perform different economic functions.

In Table 3.8, commercial banks hold reserves at the monetary authority, government debt, and loans to the nonbank public as assets. Bank liabilities comprise deposits. Deposits are segmented according to their liquidity, from those available immediately (demand deposits) to those available at the end of a fixed

Table 3.8 Consolidated banking system balance sheet.

Commercial Banking System

Reserves (Monetary Authority)	Demand Deposits (Nonbank Public)
Government Debt (Fiscal Authority)	Savings Deposits (Nonbank Public)
Loans (Nonbank Public)	Time Deposits (Nonbank Public)
	Equity

term (time deposits). The difference between the value of assets and liabilities is the equity of the banking system.

The core of any commercial bank's balance sheet is loans and deposits, and the same is true for the system at large. The primary function of commercial banks in the monetary system is to lend money against *credible claims to future savings*—what we later call "bankable projects" in Chapter 5—and to create deposit money as the counterpart to their lending activity. This deposit money constitutes the bulk of what functions as money in the developed world. Its prudent expansion is a ready index of the banking system's productivity.

Most monetary transactions in a fiat system take place in deposit money. Workers receive the direct deposit of their wages and salaries into bank accounts from the bank accounts of their employers. Households have rent and mortgage payments debited from their bank accounts and make other purchases on debit and credit cards, which are ultimately settled through transfers of deposit money from the household to the card-issuing bank. The purchase and sale of financial assets, payment of taxes and receipt of refunds, and myriad other material transactions are all settled through bank accounts with deposit money. Banks settle the transactions on their own books when both parties are customers, or by sending reserve money to accounts held at other banks via public and private payment systems. In both cases, settlement results in the cancellation of claims on the books of the bank or the clearinghouse.

All commercial banks hold reserve balances because reserves are the settlement medium for payments between banks. Transactions in reserves, cleared through the monetary authority, settle claims on behalf of bank customers and make the deposit money issued by any bank fungible with the deposit money of other banks in the system.

Although it is not evident in a consolidated balance sheet for the system, an interbank market between banks for reserves is extremely important in allowing banks to manage their reserve balances economically. Reserves, like cash, usually earn less return than other assets available to the bank. To avoid idle balances, banks with surplus reserve balances lend to banks with reserve deficits. When the financial condition of interbank market participants is not in question, the interbank market clears at an equilibrium interbank rate. In cases where a bank's financial condition is doubtful, however, it may be unable to borrow in the interbank market.[9] One reason to regulate banks is to ensure confidence in interbank transactions, preserving confidence in the fungibility of deposits issued by all banks.

As the monopoly supplier of reserve money, the monetary authority exerts considerable weight in the interbank market. Its efforts to align the interbank rate with its target policy rate are the bread and butter of central bank policy. We explain the conduct of interest rate policy and reserve market conditions in Chapter 10.

Banks hold government debt and a small list of other acceptable debt securities. These holdings are a way for banks to invest excess reserves and earn a higher rate of return without sacrificing liquidity. Should the bank find itself in need of reserves, government debt is readily liquidated into reserve balances or, in extreme cases, swapped with the monetary authority for a loan of reserve money. The latter case involves the monetary authority's "lender of last resort" powers.

The equity of the banking system, unlike the deposit balances created by the banking system, is funded by aggregate savings. In addition to funding bank operations, bank equity shields depositors from losses on the bank's assets, ensuring that deposits can be redeemed at par. When the claims on future savings underlying a bank loan are not redeemed, the bank redeems the claim out of its own equity, charging the unrecoverable principal balance of the defaulted loan to its own account.[10] In this case the bank, rather than the borrower, destroys money equal to the principal balance of the loan. Bank equity can account for a substantial share of current savings. At the end of 2023, the Bank for International Settlements (BIS) estimates the book value of equity for the global banking system is $6.5 trillion.[11] The market capitalization of banks further accounts for a large share of the publicly traded equity in many countries. Equity is costly and banks seek to economize it by making safe loans and maintaining adequate loan loss reserves.

The desire to protect bank depositors from the consequences of *loan defaults* and losses on bank securities portfolios should be distinguished from the desire to buffer them from losses arising as a result of other risky activities taking place in financial holding companies outside of the banking subsidiary. We unpack this distinction through the course of the book.

Deposit Creation by Individual Banks

Commercial banks create deposits whenever they make a loan or advance to a customer. The creation of the deposit balance occurs by simple book entry, where an increase in a deposit liability balances the principal amount of the loan or advance recognized as a bank asset. No funds must be in place as a precondition for the deposit balance. When loans and advances are made by banks, new money is indeed created out of nothing.[12]

The economic salience of deposit money creation by banks is the emergence of new purchasing power which requires no previous act of saving by anyone in the economy. No economic resources need to be produced or intermediated between borrowers and savers in order for banks to create deposit money. The creation of deposit money through bank credit allows the supply of money to expand without requiring anyone in the economy to forego consumption.[13] By *monetizing credible claims to future savings*, the banking system makes purchasing power available to finance investment, over and above the investment that may be funded from aggregate savings.

Ordinary language gets in the way of understanding how bank money comes into being. The word "deposit" is left over from the days of the metallic standards, when customers would open an account by depositing coinage with a bank. Afterwards, it would be more convenient for depositors to exchange bank balances rather than transport metal, which is bulky and subject to theft. Of course, an individual can now bring cash to a bank and exchange it for a bank deposit or withdraw from his deposit account in the form of cash, but this is not how the supply of money grows and shrinks. Both transactions are settled via exchanges of cash for reserves within the bank's reserve balance. What the bank customer truly has is a *bank balance* which can be transferred to settle obligations or redeemed for cash.

Similarly, the word "loan" suggests a bank is temporarily parting company with something it already has in favor of a "borrower" who takes possession. It would be more correct to say that banks extend credit, and that the owner of the newly created bank balance (the debtor) has had his account credited. As the Latin root *credere* (belief) of the word "credit" suggests, the basis of the credit is not an existing resource, but the bank's *underwritten belief* that the extension of credit will be retired on schedule by the debtor as the surpluses promised by the debtor emerge. In fact, the core of a bank's balance sheet consists of *extensions of credit* on the asset side and *customer balances* on the liability side. Though we will continue to speak of loans, borrowers, and deposits for the sake of brevity, the reader should bear in mind the correct senses of these words.

It is hard to be over-impressed with the fact of money creation by individual banks because the consequences of this fact for monetary economics, the analysis of the business cycle, and the understanding of financial crisis are so utterly fundamental. *The purpose of this book is largely to explain the economic consequences of this fact.*

Fallacious Accounts of Bank Funding and Deposit Creation

The ability of individual commercial banks to create deposit money out of nothing is one of the great forgotten facts of monetary economics, banished to a memory hole for most of the twentieth century.[14] Over the latter half of the twentieth century, the view that banks are merely intermediaries of funds became so dominant that the majority of academic economists think of banks as entities that "invest" in loans using deposit "funding" raised in the open market.[15] Independently of trends in academic research, undergraduate textbooks generally teach that banks collectively create money through a reserve multiplier model. Both of these alternative stories are false characterizations of where deposit money comes from, which fail to understand the economic function of banks, the dynamics of money supply, and the differences between credit creation and the intermediation of savings.

Collective deposit creation in a fractional reserve system. According to the reserve multiplier model, money creation begins with a customer deposit of funds, of which a fractional reserve is retained and the balance loaned to another customer. That customer makes a deposit, and the process repeats. Some clever geometric series math then argues the amount of money created is the size of the original deposit divided by the reserve fraction.[16] Though no one bank creates money in the deposit multiplier story, the daisy-chaining of fractionally-reserved loans across institutions allows the collective expansion of deposit balances beyond the supply of cash that ultimately supports them.

The falsity of the deposit multiplier story is evident from the complete absence of relationship between the level of the bank reserve requirement and the ratio of deposit balances to the stock of currency. If the deposit multiplier theory were true, the reserve requirement would be the most powerful tool of monetary policy, with small changes leading to massive changes in the supply of deposit money. Adjustments within the banking system would be violent. A small increase in the requirement would trigger a vicious unwinding of the loan-deposit daisy chain, as all banks scramble to put their hands on adequate cash at the same time.

In fact, reserve requirements are small and apply to only a fraction of the deposit base. Where they are used as a tool of policy, they are rarely changed, and treated as a tool of bank regulation more so than as an instrument of monetary policy. In 2020, the Federal Reserve eliminated reserve requirements completely for banks in the United States. Under the multiplier theory, deposits should explode to infinity. Clearly they have not, and the Fed has delivered the *reductio ad absurdam* for the multiplier theory empirically.

Bank funding and financial intermediation. That banks are not financial intermediaries is clear from the mechanics of the loan origination process, the fixed price and (limited) redeemability of deposit liabilities, and legal differences distinguishing deposit liabilities from other customer claims on financial institutions. Distinguishing banks from financial intermediaries anticipates our discussion of financial intermediary balance sheets and business models, so it may be worth returning to this section after reading the remainder of the chapter and Chapter 4.

The mechanics of the loan origination process make clear that no intermediation of funds occurs.[17] The coincidence of loan assets and deposit liabilities is a direct consequence of double-entry bookkeeping. In the most basic sense, a deposit balance is precisely what a customer receives when a loan is granted, not a bundle of cash. If the customer decides to transfer that balance to a customer at another bank or to withdraw the balance as cash, the lending bank must be prepared to swap reserve balances with other banks or the central bank. If the bank lacks reserves, they can always be borrowed in the interbank market, where interbank rates signal their relative scarcity.[18] But this weak dependence on reserve money flows does not somehow anchor lending to the quantity of reserve money.

Transfer of the deposit balance to other bank account holders is the most likely outcome following the receipt of loan proceeds. We cannot point to a difference between deposit growth and savings rates as evidence against the intermediation view, however. The recipient of a loan receives a bank balance that, at that very instant, is savings for them. When they transfer the balance to purchase goods and services from others, those savings are *then* "intermediated" from a "saver" to a "borrower."[19] The quantity of deposit money in the banking system remains unchanged after the loan is made. The loan proceeds become income and savings for somebody *ex post*, despite no savings being needed *ex ante*. Bank lending pulls credible expectations of savings forward in time, to function as savings now.

The price and redeemability of bank liabilities distinguishes them from funding raised in capital markets by financial intermediaries. When a financial intermediary issues debt or equity liabilities in exchange for funds, the supply of such liabilities is fixed unless the issuer redeems or repurchases them. Because the economy cannot collectively rid itself of these liabilities, market prices must be discovered at which someone is willing to hold the entire stock of outstanding debt and equity. For some securities, that market price may be zero, indicating default or bankruptcy. Deposit liabilities, by contrast, have a fixed price of par that cannot be changed during secondary exchange. Unable to adjust the price of money, the economy adjusts by changing the prices of everything else. Though not every holder of deposits may redeem deposit liabilities, they are redeemable for those in the economy who owe loan balances to banks. The need to repay loan principal maintains a basic demand for deposit balances, which are destroyed whenever loan principal is repaid. Hence, the economy has a limited capacity to rid itself of excess money balances by repaying loan principal, whereas debt and equity securities generally cannot be tendered at par to the firms issuing them.

There are also important legal differences between bank deposits and liabilities funded with savings. One might compare bank "funding" to the funding raised by mutual funds to invest in debt and equity securities on their customers' behalf. Money market mutual funds (MMFs), which offer money-like claims on a portfolio of low-risk, short-term money market assets, are an important case in point. Mutual funds offer their customers daily liquidity at a net asset value determined by the market prices of assets held in their portfolios. However, mutual funds are required to segregate customer funds, similar to broker-dealers managing brokerage accounts; funds on deposit with a mutual fund or a broker-dealer never cease to be the property of each particular customer. Bank deposits, on the other hand, are a general unsecured claim of the account holder on the bank.[20] While every customer is entitled to their bank balance, these balances do not exist in separate "boxes" labeled with each depositor's name. This distinction mirrors the fungibility of deposit balances and the bank's active creation of its own deposit funding, as opposed to the limited fungibility of fund shares and brokerage account balances and the passive receipt of funds by mutual funds and broker-dealers.

Bank deposits as claims on reserve money. Individual creation of deposit money by banks provides the only coherent story for the dynamics of bank money. Some economists will grant this view, but maintain that deposit money is not money proper, but a claim on reserve money, the only token worthy of the name.

Our reply is: deposits spend like money. The fact that a smaller supply of reserve money is sufficient to settle transactions in deposit money across banks does not lessen the moneyness of deposits. It merely illustrates that delayed clearinghouse settlement with netting across institutions requires smaller flows than real-time settlement in gross terms. Deposit money pays taxes, retires loans, and pays for almost all legitimate commerce. Deposits are convertible to legal tender cash at par. There can be no doubt that bank deposits are money, and rather than use settlement media to distinguish deposits from money, we should be intensely interested in how the mechanisms of settlement constitute and reinforce the status of bank money as money.

That all deposit balances cannot be redeemed for cash at once is well-appreciated. Government-provided deposit insurance further ensures the convertibility of deposit claims at par. When deposit insurance premiums are assessed from banks according to the quality of their management, they help to discourage behaviors that would undermine confidence in the bank's deposit liabilities. Deposit insurance is an essential component of modern fiat money systems, not because banking is an inherently fragile intermediation enterprise, but because it takes government's guarantee of the convertibility of bank balances to its logical conclusion.[21]

Financial Intermediaries

The financial intermediation sector is the segment of the economy responsible for connecting savings to investment. Savings are accumulated and invested in the household and nonfinancial business sectors of the economy, which we will describe in the next sections.

Firms in the financial and nonfinancial business sectors raise funds and access savings by issuing financial claims on themselves, which can take the form of debt, equity, or hybrids of the two. To the limited extent that households can access savings through financial intermediaries, they can only do so by issuing debt claims. Claims on firms often take the form of securities. Claims on households take the form of loans. These financial claims may be held by nonfinancial firms, households, or financial intermediaries.

We will adopt the fiction that households and nonfinancial businesses hold all their financial claims (apart from money balances) through financial intermediaries. This is not so different from reality. Even households that trade individual stocks and bonds hold them in a brokerage account, rather than in certificated form, while investment holdings through pension funds, insurance policies, mutual funds, private equity, venture capital, and other more obviously intermediated forms are common.

In focusing on the economic impact of financial intermediation, we are interested in the moment that claims on firms and households are created, and not in the subsequent trading of those claims. Primary offerings of securities occur when savings encounter investment opportunities in venture capital funding rounds, initial public offerings of exchange-traded stock, and new debt issues. The secondary trading of debt and equity securities does nothing to reallocate savings among investment opportunities, however much professional portfolio managers and traders speak of "allocating capital." Secondary trading merely transfers the ownership of the financial claim, with no meaningful changes in the aggregate. Funds change hands between the old owner and the new owner of the security, but no new funds are extended to business.

For purposes of exposition, we divide the financial intermediation sector into three subsectors. *Asset managers* buy and sell debt and equity securities and offer investors claims on their securities holdings. We include broker-dealers, mutual funds, insurance companies, and pension funds within the asset management subsector. *Money market funds* specialize in the production of money-like liabilities from public and private securities, which we have previously called "store-of-value money." Finally, *asset-backed securities* are like asset managers that run on autopilot according to detailed agreements with their investors, holding a pool of assets in a special purpose vehicle (SPV) funded mostly by debt claims. The trading of *financial derivatives* which reallocates risk between agents is also critically important but not covered here.[22] We will return to derivatives trading in Chapter 6.

Asset Managers

The asset management industry holds financial claims on behalf of households and firms. In many cases, the claim held on the asset manager is simply a pass-through claim to assets held by the manager: brokerage accounts, mutual funds, family offices, hedge funds, and private equity funds work this way. In other cases, a significant amount of risk transformation takes place between the manager's asset holdings and the payoff realized by the claimholder: pension benefits, insurance policies, and structured notes are a few examples of the latter.

The asset side of Table 3.9 again conceals more than it reveals, given the variety of debt, equity, and hybrid securities issued by firms. The holding of money fund balances by asset managers is discussed in the following subsection. In addition, we note that a substantial portion of government debt is held by the public through mutual funds, pension funds, and insurance policies, if not directly.

On the liability side of Table 3.9, we note the presence of loans from the commercial banking sector. Banks lend against financial asset holdings just as they lend against capital projects and physical assets. Yet such loans are not claims on future surpluses and do not necessarily support investment. For households,

Table 3.9 Simplified asset manager balance sheet.

Asset Managers	
Government Debt (Fiscal Authority)	Loans Payable (Commercial Banks)
Corporate Debt (Financial, Nonfinancial Business)	Claims held by households (Households)
Equities (Financial, Nonfinancial Business)	Claims held by business (Nonfinancial business)
Store-of-Value Money (Money Funds)	
Deposits (Commercial Banks)	Equity: Claims on fees

borrowing against appreciated financial assets monetizes capital gains without triggering capital gains taxation. The disposition of funds by the household may fund consumption or investment depending on household behavior and restrictions from the lending bank. Similarly, when banks lend to financial intermediaries against financial asset collateral, they are either monetizing a fully funded investment in securities or a loan underwritten by a third party. In the first case, the bank keeps the term of the loan short so the value of the security can be updated continuously. In the second case, the bank delegates underwriting to another entity, ceding its control over the pricing and terms of the loan. These activities stretch the banking system's balance sheet beyond the funding of investment and expose the banking system to market risks not otherwise encountered in asset-based lending.

Households and firms hold claims on the assets held in the asset manager's portfolio. The asset manager's claims on fees constitute its equity proper. A certain amount of equity capital is also needed for equity manager operations. But in general there is no equity buffer that would absorb portfolio losses—these are passed through completely to the clients of the asset manager and the managers themselves.

Money Market Funds

In a world with large financial intermediaries, the ability to keep large quantities of funds in cash becomes a problem.[23] Consider BlackRock, which manages some $10 trillion in customer funds. If even 1% of those funds is to be kept in cash to meet anticipated investor redemptions or to preserve the option to buy assets at a bargain price, BlackRock must carry $100 billion in cash. The banking system is one option, but it is not ideal at this scale. Most of BlackRock's deposit balance would not be insured, and large movements in the balance could create serious liquidity management problems for the bank. BlackRock would want to earn something close to the market rate of interest on its deposit balance, but without sacrificing liquidity in a savings or time deposit. Finally, BlackRock wants to account for its liquid funds as cash equivalents to avoid complexity in the valuation and disclosure of its liquid asset holdings.

Accordingly, there is an opening for a specialized type of intermediary called a money market fund to offer customers a money-like liability with which they can maintain larger balances with minimal risk. The balance carried at the money fund can be reasonably expected to maintain a value of par. At the same time, customers enjoy the earnings on a portfolio of risk-free and low-risk assets, net of the money fund manager's fee.

Table 3.10 Money market fund balance sheet.

Money Funds	
Government Debt (Fiscal Authority)	Store-of-value Money (Asset Managers, Public)
Corporate Debt (Business)	Equity: Claims on fees

What the customer sacrifices, relative to a bank deposit, is possession of a balance that is useful as final settlement. Though a customer can write a check on their money market fund balance, the store-of-value money issued by money funds must be converted into deposit money for settlement within the banking system. Because money market funds typically hold a deposit money balance to meet normal redemptions, this distinction only matters in situations where money market fund balances are redeemed on a large scale.

What we have summarized as "government debt" and "corporate debt" in Table 3.10, in fact, comprises a wide array of short-term money market instruments. Government debt includes short-term Treasury bills as well as repurchase agreements, which are sales of government debt for cash with the agreement to repurchase the debt on a future date. One can think of repurchase agreements as short-term loans of government debt collateralized by money.[24] Government debt can also include debt securities issued by government agencies and municipal (sub-national) governments. Among short-term corporate debt, commercial paper is the most common instrument. The liabilities of a money fund exhaust its net asset value (NAV); any equity in the fund is negligible.

The ability of money fund customers to convert their store-of-value money into deposit money depends closely on market conditions for their asset holdings. Following the GFC, revisions were made in 2014 to the list of permissible assets for money funds, with the goal of assuring money fund investors that their balances can always be realized at par in certain money funds. Money funds may either hold the permitted assets (essentially government debt) and maintain an NAV of par, or invest in a wider set of assets and calculate a daily NAV based on the market value of their holdings. Investors appear to favor a fixed NAV by about 5:1. The 2014 reforms resulted in a shift of some $1 trillion from money market fund investments in short-term private obligations to short-term government obligations.[25]

Asset-backed Securities

We single out asset-backed securities (ABS) due to their role in shadow banking, which we discuss in Chapter 6. ABS are issued by SPVs, or companies that have

Table 3.11 Stylized ABS balance sheet.

Asset-backed Securities	
Claims on Households	Claims on Cash flows
Claims on Nonfinancial Business	Equity: Residual claims on cash flows

no other operations besides holding the assets which generate the cash flows to pay investors in the asset-backed securities. Such assets are claims on households and nonfinancial business which would typically be held by the banking system or a nonfinancial firm (Table 3.11). Mortgage, auto, and credit card loans are some of the most common household asset types held by ABS, whereas common claims on nonfinancial business include leveraged loans for corporate buyouts, commercial mortgages, and loans to support the purchase of large- and small-ticket capital equipment.

In some markets, private-label issuers of ABS compete with ABS issued by government agencies and GSEs. The presence of agencies and GSEs in the U.S. residential and commercial mortgage credit market is well-appreciated and significant.

The degree of asset management in an ABS SPV varies widely. ABS backed by residential mortgages, auto loans, and equipment loans run essentially on autopilot, with a fixed pool of assets running off according to the terms of the underlying loans and borrowers' propensity to prepay their loan obligations.[26] Credit card ABS receivables are continuously refreshed by their issuers, owing to the short-term nature of the obligations.[27] The composition of commercial mortgage pools does not change, but special servicers have significant discretion over the modification and resolution of problematic loans.[28] Leveraged loans are actively managed in collateralized loan obligations (CLOs).[29]

Asset-backed securities vehicles achieve risk transformation by establishing a priority of payments among various classes of investors and by availing themselves of third-party credit enhancements like guarantees and insurance. In Chapter 6, we will highlight the role of credit enhancements in creating conditions for ABS markets to flourish. Strictly speaking, the residual claims on ABS cash flows constitute the "equity" of the sector, which is owned by the ABS sponsor and transformed through liability structures. The claims on cash flows of an ABS will mostly exhaust the cash flows generated by the assets, leaving a small residual interest. The residual may be quite valuable to the ABS sponsor, but it is not significant in the aggregate.

Consolidated Financial Intermediation Sector

We now put the pieces together to obtain a consolidated view of the financial intermediation sector. In Table 3.12, we reinforce our discussion above by distinguishing between the debt and equity claims held by the nonbank public and the debt and equity of the financial intermediation sector proper.

The piece we call "claims held by households, nonfinancial firms" in Table 3.12 passes through the value of debt and equity investments held at intermediaries. You can think of this component as the value of the fictional brokerage accounts we introduced at the beginning of the section, combined with the ABS holdings of households and nonfinancial firms. The financial intermediation sector also produces a stratum of the money supply that we call store-of-value money, which is held by asset managers and the nonbank public as a risk-free destination for savings. Store-of-value money issued by MMFs differs from bank money because it is fully funded by existing savings and not immediately available to settle payment obligations. Though it is a substantial portion of the money supply, it is smaller than the component produced by banks.

We have divided the equity of the financial intermediation sector into three pieces. The piece we call "Equity 1" capitalizes the fees earned by asset managers. "Equity 2" comprises residual claims on ABS. The ability of ABS to channel loanable funds from the capital market to the household sector is unique and motivates our decision to distinguish them. That leaves "buffer equity" as the equity proper of the financial intermediation sector, or the value of financial intermediaries' own account. This last equity component is consolidated with the equity of a commercial bank in a universal banking institution.

Table 3.12 Consolidated financial intermediation sector balance sheet.

Financial Intermediation Sector	
Government Debt (Fiscal Authority)	Claims held by households, nonfinancial firms
Corporate Debt (Financial, Nonfinancial Business)	Store-of-value Money (Asset Managers)
Equities (Financial, Nonfinancial Business)	Store-of-value Money (Nonbank Public)
Claims on Households	Loans Payable (Commercial Banks)
Claims on Nonfinancial Business	Equity 1: Claims on fees
Store-of-value Money (Money Funds)	Equity 2: Claims on residual cash flows
Deposits (Commercial Banks)	Buffer equity

It bears repeating that much of this financial intermediation sector lives in the institutions we call banks: universal banks combine financial intermediation business with commercial banking business. We distinguish between the two analytically in this chapter to emphasize that one side of the business uses savings and intermediates loanable funds (the financial intermediation side) while the other side of the business creates credit without being constrained by available savings (the commercial banking side). Claims about the business of "banking," its risks, and the use of leverage are muddied when the distinction is not maintained. In Chapter 6, we will present a universal bank balance sheet which consolidates the two functions.

The Nonbank Public: Nonfinancial Firms and Households

Economic theory has almost no role for the sectors we have discussed up to this point. Government financial policy and monetary policy are taken to be neutral, financial intermediation is a maze of dispensable institutional arrangements that obscure the equality of savings and investment, and banking is a pesky subspecies of financial intermediation worthy of attention only because it is used more pervasively by households than the rest of the capital markets. What matters most for economic theory are the activities of households and nonfinancial business, which constitute the "real" economy underlying the inessential, frictional, and redundant monetary economy. Indeed, many economists will argue it is artificial even to separate the household and nonfinancial business sectors, as nonfinancial business is ultimately owned and managed by households to suit their own purposes.

Our reasons for dissenting from this conventional view will become more clear in this section, as we map the connections between households, nonfinancial business, and the financial side of the economy. Financial intermediation plays an important role in mobilizing savings and positioning equity in investable projects within the nonfinancial business sector.[30] Meanwhile, conditions in the household and nonfinancial business sectors establish the set of bankable projects available to the commercial banking sector. These activities of generating *investable* and *bankable projects* make productive investment and money creation possible.

Nonfinancial Business

The business sector includes all firms. The *nonfinancial* business sector excludes commercial banking and financial intermediation. While flow-of-funds accounting distinguishes between corporate and non-corporate forms of business, we

Table 3.13 Nonfinancial business sector balance sheet.

Nonfinancial Business Sector

Claims held by business (Asset Managers)	Accounts Payable
Store-of-value Money (Asset Managers)	Loans Payable (Commercial Banks)
Deposits (Commercial Banks)	Corporate Debt (Asset Managers)
Real Estate	Equity (Asset Managers)
Fixed Assets	
Working Capital	
Intangible Assets	

adopt the simplifying fiction that all firms are corporations, and all ownership interests in business are held in security form through financial intermediaries, rather than partnership interests or sole proprietorships directly owned by households.

The analytical salience of separating the nonfinancial business sector from the household sector in Table 3.13 is to emphasize the control over productive assets by professional management in firms. Assets operated by professional managers are more valuable than those owned by households. The way that firms use their control over the asset base of the economy need not correspond to households' optimizing activity, throwing a wrench into representative agent models.

Balance sheets on the "real" side of the economy include assets that are not claims on other sectors. The buck stops here: such assets underpin the network of financial claims we have spun up to this point. The value of financial assets depends, in large part, on the value realized from the asset base controlled by the real economy.

The ability of the banking sector to create credit can support the expansion of the nonfinancial business sector over and above what capital markets will support in the form of debt and equity. Not all the assets held by the nonfinancial business sector are able to serve as security for a bank loan, however.[31] As we explain further in Chapter 5, banks overwhelmingly prefer loans to be *secured* by tangible assets as collateral. Real estate and fixed assets are ideal in this regard, as they are durable and readily marketable in secondary markets. Working capital assets like inventories and accounts receivable are less suitable as collateral; they can be liquidated for cash, but with much greater effort. Intangible assets like patents, trademarks, know-how, a cohesive workforce, customer lists, and so on are generally not suitable as collateral for bank lending, so their construction must usually be funded with equity or debt. However, once firms demonstrate the value of their intangible assets in generating free cash flow, borrowing on an unsecured basis can become possible.

Households

In capitalist society, the household sector is the ultimate owner of all productive assets. Much of these assets are owned through financial intermediaries as debt and equity claims on nonfinancial and financial businesses; we have adopted the fiction that *all* debt and equity are owned this way. Outside of the business sector, households accumulate assets of their own that include real estate and consumer durables (cars, large appliances, etc.). Households also manage their earning potential, a key intangible asset, by investing in education, training, and other activities that sacrifice current income for increases in expected future income. The claims owned by the household sector are summarized in Table 3.14.

As in the nonfinancial business sector, not all the assets held by the household sector are equally suitable as collateral for bank lending. Real estate and consumer durables generally make good collateral. Yet consumer loans are ultimately repaid with surpluses generated by household earning potential, an intangible asset, as the household's primary residence and durables do not generate surplus cash flow in normal circumstances.[32] That is not to say that investments in earning potential are fully bankable. Loans are available for education, within certain boundaries but are often supported by a co-signer with established assets and earning potential. The characteristics of bankable projects are discussed in Chapter 5.

In addition to assets ultimately owned by the household sector, the net worth of the household sector—or household *wealth*—is not subject to external claims. It is not possible, in general, for households to issue debt or equity that makes claims on their wealth available to other households. As a result, loanable funds flow *from* households, but do not generally flow *to* households except through ABS. Of course, *credit* flows to households—and if you have been paying attention, you now know the difference between credit and loanable funds.

Table 3.14 Household sector balance sheet.

Household Sector	
Claims of Households (Asset Managers)	Loans Payable (Commercial Banks)
Real Estate	Loans Payable (Asset-backed Securities)
Consumer Durables	
Earning Potential	
Deposits (Commercial Banks)	Net Worth/Wealth

The ability of the banking sector to create credit has supported the ability of the household sector to accumulate assets over and above what their existing savings (net worth) would support, particularly in real estate assets. A shift in banking sector focus from commercial to consumer lending, combined with withdrawals of savings from the nonfinancial business sector by the household sector, has produced a significant drag on economic growth, debilitated the commercial banking system, and shifted burdens onto capital markets they are not prepared to manage, while exacerbating inequality in the distribution of wealth. We will unpack this thesis over the remainder of the book, especially in Chapters 6, 7, 8, and 13.

The Rest of the World

The balance sheet schema we have presented thus far is *closed* in the sense that all financial claims are traceable to another sector of the economy. When each sector is defined to comprise those entities that are *resident* in the economy, the schema lacks claims that non-resident entities hold on the domestic economy, as well as claims issued to residents by non-resident entities. These two categories of claims can be gathered into a consolidated balance sheet for the *rest of the world* (ROW).

Integrating the ROW into the flow-of-funds schema shows that no one economy is strictly limited to its own financial resources. Banks lend across borders, creating credit for non-residents. Global savings may be invested outside their economy of origin. The flows of claims captured on the ROW balance sheet are captured in *balance of payments* accounting as *foreign direct investment* when they represent offshore capital expenditures, and as *portfolio investment* when they involve foreign capital market or lending transactions.[33] The balance of payments is the obverse of an economy's balance of trade in goods and services and can often be a more insightful way in for those seeking to explain the origin of persistent trade imbalances.

We have not included the ROW in our balance sheet schema because doubling each of the entries to distinguish between residents' and non-residents' claims would clutter the presentation, and because our focus on the developed world involves economies with robust domestic financial systems. Nevertheless, transactions with the ROW are essential for a complete analysis of monetary and financial conditions precisely because they can permit imbalances to persist for so long. They are also key to the analysis of exchange rates, which are the crucial degree of freedom for adjustment when networks of international claims cannot be easily unwound. In Chapter 10, we will observe how the Federal Reserve has taken measures since the GFC to facilitate flows of international dollar liquidity, and in Chapter 13, we will consider the role persistent global savings inflows have played in generating financial system imbalances in the United States.

The Money Supply and Its Connections to the Nonbank Public

Our balance sheet schema has clarified the origins of the money supply as claims on various economic sectors underpinned by various assets. To aggregate the money supply in Table 3.15, we consolidate the balance sheets of the government, the banking system, and financial intermediaries and isolate the monetary liabilities issued by each. Reserves issued by the central bank and held by the banking system are netted. Government debt is netted, leaving government debt in the hands of the nonfinancial public on the liability side. Similarly, we net out the money market fund and deposit holdings of financial intermediaries, as well as loans from banks to financial intermediaries.

We highlight the liabilities with a price of par that may potentially be counted as part of the money supply in italics. While government debt and claims on corporate debt and equity can be liquid, their prices are less certain except for very short-term debt obligations. The assets backing monetary claims include not only the present value of primary government budget balances and seigniorage, as traditionally acknowledged by economists but also loans to the nonbank public and

Table 3.15 Consolidated monetary system balance sheet.

Consolidated Monetary System	
PV of Primary Budget Balances (Public)	Government Debt (Nonfinancial Public)
PV of Seigniorage (Monetary Authority)	*Notes and Coins (Public)*
Loans (Nonbank Public)	*Demand Deposits (Nonbank Public)*
	Savings Deposits (Nonbank Public)
	Time Deposits (Nonbank Public)
Corporate Debt (Financial, Nonfinancial Business)	*Claims held by households, nonfinancial firms*
Equities (Financial, Nonfinancial Business)	*Store-of-value Money (Nonbank Public)*
Claims on Households	Claims on financial intermediaries
Claims on Nonfinancial Business	Equity 1: Claims on fees
	Equity 2: Claims on residual cash flows
	Buffer equity

claims on the nonfinancial public supporting the issuance of store-of-value money. *In an economy with a large financial system, the enterprise of fiat money extends beyond the government, and fiat money's value is underwritten by more than the government's own finances.*

We are now ready to set out a taxonomy of the financial claims that comprise the money supply in advanced economies. These instruments appear as liabilities of the government, commercial banks, corporations, and financial institutions, but in compressed form. Taken together, they comprise aggregates called "broad money." We use the definitions of aggregates formulated by William Barnett and collaborators at the Center for Financial Stability (CFS).[34]

Broad money is held by the nonbank public, which excludes banks and all levels of government. The components of broad money listed in Table 3.16 are ordered according to how readily they can be converted to a liquid, spendable form. The most obvious component of broad money is cash, the stock of notes and coins issued by the central bank. Cash is immediately ready to spend and settles a transaction immediately. No conversions are necessary to make cash acceptable as a means of payment. For a transaction to be settled means the value that has been promised has been delivered.

Table 3.16 Sources of broad money.

Aggregate	Instrument	Source
M1	Cash	Monetary authority
M1	Demand deposits	Commercial banks
M1	Other current deposits	Commercial banks
M2	Savings deposits	Commercial banks
M2	Money market deposit accounts	Commercial banks
M2	Savings deposits	Commercial banks
M2	Retail money market funds	Financial intermediaries
M2	Small time deposits	Commercial banks
M3	Institutional money market funds	Financial intermediaries
M3	Large time deposits	Commercial banks
M3	Repurchase agreements	Financial intermediaries
M4-	Commercial paper	Nonfinancial corporations
M4	Treasury bills	Government

Notes: Higher-order aggregates like M3 include all of the items in lower aggregates like M1 and M2. Demand deposits and other current deposits (OCDs) are adjusted for sweeps, as further explained in the main text. The CFS aggregates distinguish between deposits at commercial banks and thrift institutions to capture differences in interest rates, but we suppress the difference in the table for simplicity. The balances of store-of-value money held by money market funds are not eliminated from computation of the higher-order aggregates.

At the other end of the spectrum are MMF balances, Treasury bills, repurchase agreements, and commercial paper, which take some time to convert to a final form of payment and involve a small degree of price risk. Broad monetary aggregates like M3, M4-, and M4 begin to incorporate such liabilities. We have referred to many of these liabilities as "store-of-value money" possessing the qualities of par valuations and relatively easy convertibility to bank money. What these instruments share is the ability to be accounted for as cash equivalents.[35]

The production of broad money falls most squarely on the commercial banking system. Commercial banks are dominant in issuing the M1 and M2 aggregates, which capture all but the largest time deposits of the banking system. Cash from the monetary authority and retail money market funds issued by financial intermediaries make relatively small contributions in the developed world. As a result, *any inquiry into the evolution of monetary conditions must focus squarely on the conditions facing the commercial banking system.*

In addition, there is a clear sense in which the productivity of the commercial banking system consists in its ability to produce monetary liabilities. An expanding supply of bank money is emblematic of a growing supply of *credible claims to future surpluses*. While the growth of such claims may be exogenous or unrelated to the activity of the banking system, they may also be endogenous to the banking system, reflecting an improved ability within the banking system to *discover* and *credit* claims to future surpluses which were previously inadequate for loan underwriting. We elaborate on this distinction in Chapter 5.

The System of Claims as a Foundation for Monetary Theory

Our balance sheet schema shows the system of claims that supports the creation of the broad money supply. The value of claims rests ultimately on the value of aggregate savings and credible claims to future savings. These claims are credited by the government, the banking system, and financial intermediaries. We have also connected several monetary and financial variables to the real economy. These connections show that monetary values are backstopped by the realization of value from assets held by the household and nonfinancial business sectors. Our schema begins to loosen up the tight connection between the value of physical capital assets and financial claims that is taken for granted in economics.

Like the connection between physical capital and financial claims, our schema loosens the connection between savings and investment. We have focused on stocks of assets rather than flows. Economics is generally concerned with flows and tends to define income in terms of flows. The flows in which we are most interested are those of savings and investment.

The stocks shown in our schema can be reconciled with flows by taking differences and making a few adjustments. Between two balance sheet dates a certain volume of claims is recognized at a certain domestic currency value and a certain exchange rate. The difference in claims between two balance sheet dates, therefore, consists of the change in the volume of claims at their original valuation, the revaluation of those claims due to changes in prices and exchange rates, and adjustments to volumes due to defaults and losses of assets.

The balance sheet schema thus generates a consistent set of stocks and flows between sectors of the economy that serves as a starting point for macroeconomic and monetary theory. While it is not our project in this book to elaborate a rigorous system of macroeconomic theory, the connections between sectors of the economy displayed in this chapter aid in maintaining a general equilibrium orientation as we proceed through our exposition.

At the same time, flow-of-funds accounting has led to some wrong turns in the development of monetary theory, as the interconnected schema encourages the symmetric treatment of all actors in the financial system.[36] Morris Copeland himself, the originator of the flow-of-funds approach, began to view money as just one asset among many.[37] Gurley and Shaw[38] suppressed the specialness of the commercial banking system, though they recognized the uniqueness of bank credit creation when criticized for not highlighting it in their other work.[39] But perhaps more importantly James Tobin denied banks' ability to create money.[40] Tobin later formalized the system of financial claims in matrix form and presented restrictions on changes in the matrix as equilibrium conditions for money and financial markets.[41] In doing so, he assumed equilibrium where equilibrium is not in evidence, failed to recognize the autonomy of money creation and destruction within the banking system, and reduced the determination of the quantity of money to merely one portfolio decision among many made by actors in the real economy. Through Tobin's lens, the quantity of money would sort itself out once interest rates were set and portfolio allocations were revised in response. We seek to correct this perspective and improve the conduct of banking, capital markets business, and monetary policy.

Notes

1. Flow-of-funds accounts are published in most major economies. In the United States, the Federal Reserve publishes them as the Z1 statistical release. We are indebted to Wynne Godley and Marc Lavoie for emphasizing the "stock-flow consistency" afforded by flow-of-funds accounts as a prerequisite for coherent monetary theory. See Godley, W. and Lavoie, M. (2007). *Monetary*

Economics, 2e. Palgrave-Macmillan. For the pioneering work on flow-of-funds accounting, see Copeland, M. (1952). *A Study of Moneyflows in the United States.* National Bureau of Economic Research.

2. Nangle, T. (2016). How helicopter money works. *Columbia Threadneedle Investments*, May. The government's ability to sterilize the monetary consequences of its spending depends on its capacity to collect taxes and issue debt denominated in its own currency. Where much of the economy is informal or conducted outside of markets in households or similar social arrangements, there is little opportunity for governments to collect taxes (and, admittedly, little demand for money); a deficit of coercive power over parts of the population similarly makes tax collection difficult. Marketing debt presumes a segment of the population holding ample money balances and willing to part with purchasing power for a length of time at a reasonable price for the government's promise to pay in local currency. Less economically developed countries often lack these capacities, and as a result their government spending tends to increase the money supply (via the central bank) without a corresponding increase in output.

3. Some monetary theorists argue the fiscal authority's balance sheet can be simplified further. If all government debt is outstanding for one period, the public can meet all its obligations—taxes and otherwise—with government debt. No incentive remains for the public to use cash which, unlike government debt, does not earn interest. Hence, the only variable that matters for the value of the money supply and the price level in the economy—according to these theorists—is the evolution of government debt; cash is just a frictional residue of no importance.

4. Central bank digital currencies (CBDCs) would allow the public to hold reserve money directly with the central bank. Reserve money is already a kind of digital currency because it exists in book entry form at the central bank. Hence, CBDCs do not necessarily involve any technological change, though they potentially create a vehicle for the nonbank public to hold current accounts directly at the central bank, rather than through a commercial bank. For a review and critique of CBDCs, see Dowd, K. (2024). So far, Central Bank Digital Currencies have failed. *Economic Affairs* 44: 71–94.

5. The Federal Reserve's holdings of government debt are not the only important reductions of gross debt in the United States because other government agencies also hold Treasuries. See Buiter, W. (2021). *Central Banks as Fiscal Players.* Cambridge University Press for gross/net debt in the United States, the Eurozone, and Japan.

6. The postwar world is replete with examples of governments that could not resist the temptation to abuse their money creation powers. Almost any amount of spending could be rationalized by placing bonds at the central bank to augment the balance of the fiscal authority. Such transactions are mere bookkeeping to account for the government's promises to pay, however worthless they may be. Where the rule of law prevails, government spending is kept to finite levels by the requirement for spending to be appropriated by the legislature, or whatever body is empowered to make appropriations. Limits on the production of money by government are as good as the appropriations process.
7. Buiter, W. (2021). *Central Banks as Fiscal Players.* Cambridge University Press.
8. Sargent, T.J. and Wallace, N. (1981). Some unpleasant monetarist arithmetic. *Quarterly Review of the Federal Reserve Bank of Minneapolis* 5: 1–17.
9. Freixas, X. and Jorge, J. (2008). The role of interbank markets in monetary policy: A model with rationing. *Journal of Money, Credit and Banking* 40 (6): 1151–1176.
10. Generally banks reserve for expected losses, so that charges to equity occur only when losses are greater than expected.
11. See the consolidated banking statistics available at https://data.bis.org/topics/CBS/tables-and-dashboards/BIS,CBS_B1,1.0?time_period=2023-Q4.
12. This view is increasingly embraced by economists and others including (for example) Godley, W. and Lavoie, M. (2007). *Monetary Economics*, 2e. Palgrave-Macmillan, Werner, R.A. (2014a). Can banks individually create money out of nothing? – The theories and the empirical evidence. *International Review of Financial Analysis* 36: 1–19, McLeay, M., Radia, A., and Thomas, R. (2014a). Money in the modern economy: An introduction. *Bank of England Quarterly Bulletin* 2014 Q1: 4–13, McLeay, M., Radia, A., and Thomas, R. (2014b). Money creation in the modern economy. *Bank of England Quarterly Bulletin* 2014 Q1: 14–27, Jakab, Z. and Kumhof, M. (2015). Banks are not intermediaries of loanable funds – And why this matters. *Bank of England Working Paper 529*, May, Ricks, M. (2016). *The Money Problem: Rethinking Financial Regulation.* University of Chicago Press.
13. Jakab, Z. and Kumhof, M. (2015). Banks are not intermediaries of loanable funds – And why this matters. *Bank of England Working Paper 529*, May.
14. Werner, R.A. (2016). A lost century in economics: Three theories of banking and the conclusive evidence. *International Review of Financial Analysis* 46: 361–379.
15. For example, Diamond, D.W. and Rajan, R.G. (2001). Liquidity risk, liquidity creation, and financial fragility: A theory of banking. *Journal of Political Economy*

109 (2): 287–327 and Kashyap, A.K., Rajan, R., and Stein, J.C. (2002). Banks as liquidity providers: An explanation for the coexistence of lending and deposit-taking. *Journal of Finance* 57: 33–73.

16. Let the reserve fraction be r. The initial deposit of $1 yields a loanable balance of $1 - r$. That money is deposited and enables another bank to lend $(1 - r)(1 - r) = (1 - r)^2$. If we let $s = 1 - r$, the total amount of money generated by the initial deposit is $1 + s + s^2 + s^3 + \cdots$. If $S = 1 + s + s^2 + s^3 + \cdots$, then $sS = s + s^2 + s^3 + s^4 + \cdots$, so $S - sS = (1 - s)S = 1$, from which we conclude $S = \frac{1}{1-s} = \frac{1}{r}$.
17. Werner, R.A. (2014a). Can banks individually create money out of nothing? – The theories and the empirical evidence. *International Review of Financial Analysis* 36: 1–19. Jakab, Z. and Kumhof, M. (2019). Banks are not intermediaries of loanable funds – Facts, theory and evidence. *Bank of England Working Paper 761*, June also point out that no savings-based mechanism can explain the observed volatility of the banking system balance sheet, leaving credit creation as the only reasonable cause.
18. Disyatat, P. (2008). Monetary policy implementation: Misconceptions and their consequences. *BIS Working Paper No. 269*: 15 describes how private bank deposit creation attracts reserve creation by the central bank. 'The banking system creates deposits as they are demanded by the private sector, and the central bank's main liquidity management task is to ensure a sufficient supply of balances for the system as a whole to maintain reserve requirements, if any, associated with those deposits. It is the amount of deposits that the banking sector can attract that determines the level of reserves not the other way around.'
19. Incidentally, this is what allows factors of production to be hired before revenues and profits are realized.
20. Werner, R.A. (2014b). How do banks create money, and why can other firms not do the same? An explanation for the coexistence of lending and deposit-taking. *International Review of Financial Analysis* 36: 71–77.
21. The paradigmatic model of inherently fragile banking is Diamond, D.W. and Dybvig, P.H. (1983). Bank runs, deposit insurance, and liquidity. *Journal of Political Economy* 91 (3): 401–419. We do not agree with it because the premises of the model do not agree with the structure of commercial banking. We will return to government deposit insurance in Chapters 8 and 9.
22. The current market value of derivatives can appear on either side of the asset manager or ABS balance sheets considered here.
23. In this section, we are indebted to Poszar, Z. (2014). Shadow banking: The money view. *Office of Financial Research Working Paper 14-04* and Ricks, M.

(2016). *The Money Problem: Rethinking Financial Regulation*. University of Chicago Press. Similar considerations apply to wealthier households who wish to hold cash in excess of deposit insurance ceilings.

24. Reverse repurchase agreements switch the roles of government debt and cash; they are short-term loans of cash collateralized by government debt.
25. Gissler, S., Macchiavelli, M., and Narajabad, B. (2023). Providing safety in a rush: How did shadow banks respond to a $1 trillion shock? *Working paper*, August 2.
26. Fabozzi, F.J. (ed.) (2006). *The Handbook of Mortgage-Backed Securities*, 6e. McGraw-Hill.
27. Furletti, M. (2002). An overview of credit card asset-backed securities. *Federal Reserve Bank of Philadelphia Discussion Paper*, December.
28. Fabozzi, F.J. and Jacob, D.P. (eds.) (1998). *The Handbook of Commercial Mortgage-Backed Securities*, 2e. Wiley.
29. Lucas, D.J., Goodman, L.S., and Fabozzi, F.J. (2006). *Collateralized Debt Obligations: Structures and Analysis*, 2e. John Wiley & Sons, Inc.
30. Equity investment in financial business is also important and has the ability to improve productivity in credit creation and the allocation of savings to investment.
31. Hemmendinger, T.S. (2012). *Hillman on Commercial Loan Documentation*, 5e. Practising Law Institute: Chapter 10.
32. "Earning potential" also includes the potential to receive transfers from family and is not strictly a function of personal productivity for individual households.
33. International Monetary Fund. (2013). *Balance of Payments and International Investment Position Manual*, 6e. International Monetary Fund.
34. Barnett, W.A., Liu, J., Mattson, R.S. et al. (2013). The new CFS Divisia monetary aggregates: Design, construction, and data sources. *Open Economies Review* 24: 101–124.
35. Ricks, M. (2016). *The Money Problem: Rethinking Financial Regulation*. University of Chicago Press.
36. Cohen, J. (1972). Copeland's moneyflows after twenty-five years: A survey. *Journal of Economic Literature* 10 (1): 1–25: 14 writes Morris Copeland's 'thesis that banks act as financial intermediaries in the same fashion as other financial institutions has received wide currency' through works by Gurley and Shaw, Tobin, and Gramley and Chase. We discuss Gurley and Shaw and Tobin below.
37. "The cash-balance holder in Copeland advances funds in the same way as the holder of other financial assets. ... Copeland's view of moneyflows as a "cash-or-equivalent" accounts system leads him to downgrade the role of

money and to view its "scorekeeping role" as similar to the role of other "loan-fund balances" (financial claims)." Cohen, J. (1972). Copeland's money-flows after twenty-five years: A survey. *Journal of Economic Literature* 10 (1): 1–25: 14.

38. Gurley, J.G. and Shaw, E.S. (1960). *Money in a Theory of Finance.* Brookings Institution Press.
39. Culbertson, J.M. (1958). Intermediaries and monetary theory: A criticism of the Gurley-Shaw theory. *American Economic Review* 48 (1): 119–131: 119–20 criticizes Gurley, J.G. and Shaw, E.S. (1955). Financial aspects of economic development. *American Economic Review* 45: 515–538, Gurley, J.G. and Shaw, E.S. (1956). Financial intermediaries and the saving-investment process. *Journal of Finance* 11: 257–276 for treating commercial banks as if they are not unique in their ability to create credit. Gurley and Shaw responded, 'First, [banks] create money. We have to agree with that. Second, they create loanable funds, while other financial intermediaries are mere middlemen in this respect.' Gurley, J.G. and Shaw, E.S. (1958). Intermediaries and monetary theory: A criticism of the Gurley-Shaw theory: Reply. *American Economic Review* 48 (1): 132–138: 135). Nevertheless, though they acknowledge the uniqueness of money and banking, Gurley, J.G. and Shaw, E.S. (1958). Intermediaries and monetary theory: A criticism of the Gurley-Shaw theory: Reply. *American Economic Review* 48 (1): 132–138 appear unimpressed by their implications for the theory of money and finance.
40. Tobin, J. (1963). Commercial banks as creators of 'money.' *Cowles Commission Discussion Papers No. 159.*
41. Tobin, J. (1969). A general equilibrium approach to monetary theory. *Journal of Money, Credit and Banking* 1 (1): 15–29.

Chapter 4

Financial Intermediation in the Capital Markets

The financing of business investment draws on funds from the commercial banking sector and the financial intermediation sector. Bank funds and intermediated finance are distinguished by their dependence on savings. Intermediation requires pre-existing savings, whereas bank finance does not. This potential for bank credit creation to relax the constraint of aggregate savings in a growing economy is the primary axis on which our macroeconomic analysis turns.

The dominant trend in macroeconomic thinking and modeling does not recognize a distinction between bank credit creation and financing from loanable funds. In the standard story, the path of investment and economic growth are determined entirely by decisions about consumption, leaving savings as the unconsumed residue of current production. In fact, bank credit creation pulls future savings forward, making funds available today before loanable surpluses come into existence. Bank credit creation also competes with future financial intermediation, pre-allocating future savings to the amortization of credit claims. *Future* capital markets are constrained by *past* bank lending.

To bring out the macroeconomic consequences of the flexibility afforded by bank credit creation, we begin with a picture of the aggregate economy where intermediated savings—loanable funds—are the only source of funds available to entrepreneurs for investment.[1] In Chapter 5, we will characterize the constraints on aggregate credit creation, which include the configuration of intermediated savings, and consider the consequences for aggregate investment.

After reviewing the aggregate picture as it is implemented in standard economic models, we turn to the microeconomics of savings formation, the demand for loanable funds in investment, and the process by which savings are matched to investment opportunities. We emphasize that the capital market in which savings are matched to investment opportunities *does not clear at the market interest rate*, leaving some otherwise feasible and profitable investment projects unfunded and a residue of loanable funds in search of a suitable use.[2] The resulting capital markets equilibrium is more complicated and nuanced than the standard view, rendering the proliferation of safe investment vehicles problematic and further undermining standard models of economic growth.

The microeconomics of capital markets suggests that financial intermediaries have an important role to play in discovering and authenticating information about investment projects. Such activity by intermediaries partitions potential investment projects into investable and non-investable sets, and stratifies investable projects according to their *monitoring intensity*—the amount and frequency of effort needed to supply adequate information to maintain the investability of the project.[3] Financial intermediation makes the greatest contribution to economic growth when it can sustain a large set of investable projects, including those with significant monitoring intensity.

In Chapter 5, we will describe how the set of *investable projects* delimited by financial intermediation configures the possibilities for *bankable projects* available to the commercial banking system, in tandem with other conditions that support credible claims to future savings. Investable and bankable projects are the ultimate constraint on financial intermediation and credit creation. Their supply fluctuates with the state of technology, entrepreneurial activity, and financial market conditions. Though unobservable, the supply of bankable and investable projects determines the productivity and efficiency of the banking and capital markets sectors.

Savings and Investment: The Standard Macroeconomic Story

The capacity of an economy to accumulate savings and invest them to expand production possibilities is one of the single most important determinants of its growth potential, rivaling technical change in importance. One of the many ways in which economists demonstrate the truth of economic propositions is to construct a model in which behaviors, accounting identities, and equilibrium conditions are carefully specified. Such models allow us to check that outcomes follow causally from identifiable variations in external conditions when actors are economically rational. In this section, we walk through a benchmark model of economic growth that connects growth to decisions about saving and investment.

The modern theory of economic growth boils down to a few simple propositions.[4] Decision-makers in the economy face a fundamental choice between using the economy's productive capacity to make goods for current consumption, or to make goods that will produce consumption goods in the future. The second category of unconsumed production is called investment. On one hand, decision-makers want to reduce investment because they prefer having goods today versus having goods later. On the other hand, producing goods later allows economic actors to take advantage of improvements in productivity to produce more output than what is possible today.[5] The optimizing decision-maker strikes a balance between these considerations to choose a profile of consumption and investment (non-consumption) that maximizes the expected utility of consumption over a long horizon.

Over time, investment accumulates as the *capital stock* available to the economy for production, which is identical with social wealth.[6] Production combines capital and labor to produce output. The capital stock loses value over time as processes dependent on it become less productive relative to new investment, which we account for as depreciation.[7] For the economy to maintain a constant capital stock, new investment must offset depreciation to constantly renew the capital stock. Investment must exceed depreciation for the economy to increase its capital stock and grow more quickly than the rate at which productivity increases.

In the standard model, decisions about the time profile of consumption determine a time profile of savings, which in turn results in a time profile of investment. The accumulation of investment, net of depreciation, according to that time profile determines the value of the capital stock for all relevant times in the economy's planning horizon. Assuming households work as much as they can, the supply of labor is given for all relevant times as well. Thus, the path of output for the economy is determined as a function of these capital and labor input profiles, as well as the state of productivity. Consumption decisions determine the economy's productive capacity, and decisions that maximize the value of consumption maximize the value of the economy's productive capacity. Only unanticipated changes in the state of productivity disrupt the economy from its path.

The previous analysis in terms of production, namely that output equals production for current consumption plus production for investment, or $Y = C + I$,[8] can also be interpreted from the perspective of incomes, where aggregate income is equal to the wages paid to labor plus the payments made to capital. Under standard assumptions, the addition to output from a marginal hour of labor is paid to every hour of labor, and the addition to output from an additional increment of capital is paid to every increment of capital in equilibrium. Accordingly, all output is distributed to the economy as income. Competitive payments are made to the factors of production, labor and capital, and no surplus remains that can be earned by an economic actor as profit.

Shifting our perspective from production to income, let us interpret Y as both aggregate output and aggregate income. We can write a new accounting identity for Y in terms of expenditure: $Y = C + S$, where C is expenditure on consumption and S is non-consumption or savings. Comparing the identities for production and expenditure, it becomes obvious that $S = I$: savings is equal to investment. The equality of savings and investment is a bedrock identity of dynamic economic modeling, connecting economic outcomes through time ("intertemporally") via the accumulation of capital.

As is common elsewhere in economics, capital and investment in this benchmark equilibrium model are real things: the actual stuff produced in order to support and augment future production. Financial capital enters the picture as a claim on stuff: title to an asset, which is to say, entitlement to the remuneration paid to the asset as it yields its marginal product over time in a production process. The financing of investment is an exchange of these asset-based claims for savings.

Because all investments are ultimately financed from savings in the benchmark model, intermediation between savers and borrowers exhausts the possibilities for finance in this benchmark growth model. The only way investment can increase is if someone foregoes consumption.[9] Intermediation is a simple process, taking place at a market-clearing interest rate which is driven by savings decisions and the rate of technical progress. Accordingly, no genuine decisions are made concerning *which* projects to finance. Those that are sufficiently productive are waved through, while those that are not, are abandoned. The simple model thus implies a simple capital market in which all relevant information is given and intermediation is immediate.

Savings and Investment: The Microeconomic Foundations

Does the standard macroeconomic story about savings and investment survive scrutiny at the microeconomic level? To explore this question, we investigate the supply of loanable funds, which accumulate in the household and nonfinancial business sectors, and the demand for loanable funds from entrepreneurs. We then ask what kind of equilibrium prevails when supply and demand encounter each other in the capital market. We continue to operate under the usual economic fiction that all decisions are made in terms of real resources rather than in money terms.

A household accumulates savings when income exceeds expenditures. A business accumulates savings when revenues exceed costs. Business sector savings may be redistributed to the household sector in the form of interest, dividends, or share repurchases, or kept within the business sector as retained earnings. Savings become loanable funds when mobilized in a capital market. In general, capital markets cannot grow faster than unconsumed income, and if some share of savings fails to be mobilized as loanable funds, capital markets will grow slower than savings.

The economic problem of the capital markets is to match loanable funds to investments. Ideally, the matching will be done in some rank order of importance, exhausting the supply of available savings on the best available investment projects. Supply and demand schedules achieve such an ordering.

For purposes of building a demand schedule for loanable funds, we assume that available investment opportunities can be quantized into discrete projects. We further assume that investment projects are common knowledge based on the state of technology and exist independently of entrepreneurs. In the context of each project, the economic question at hand is whether initial commitments of resources that produce no current output can be justified by the increase in future output the commitment affords. We assume that the required resources can be enumerated and priced, and that future output and prices are known today. The supply schedule traces the willingness of households and firms to forego a marginal unit of consumption to earn a rate of return on an investment project.

The NPV Criterion

Weighing the future returns against current commitments is an exercise in putting current costs and future revenues on common footing despite differences in their timing. The price of future resources in terms of current resources is an interest rate.[10] Its inverse is a discount rate.[11] We can assume interest rates are given by the equilibrium path of savings for the current state of the economy, as discussed in the previous section. Interest rates are the shadow price of an additional unit of savings when the economy is in intertemporal equilibrium.[12] Discounting future revenues at a given interest rate prices future resources in terms of current resources (their "present value"), putting them on equal footing with costs by showing how much consumption must be given up today to realize another unit of future output. Subtracting costs from discounted revenues yields the net present value (NPV) of the project. Because projects with positive NPVs yield a surplus of resources when evaluated at current prices, it is rational to invest in them. We refer to the NPV criterion as a shorthand for making decisions on this basis.[13]

The NPV criterion reduces the analysis of projects to resource flows and prices at different times in the future. With the NPV criterion, we can construct a demand schedule for loanable funds with projects ordered in descending order of NPV per unit of investment. That is, given the current state of technology, a set of feasible investment projects may be analyzed into sets of potential resource flow profiles, subjected to a common discount schedule, and sorted from greatest to least NPV. Projects with positive NPVs are "investable" under the NPV criterion given the current state of technology and interest rates. If capital markets clear, investable projects are funded in order of descending NPV until the supply of loanable funds is exhausted at the equilibrium interest rate. As loanable funds are matched to investment projects, savings flow from the household and business sectors into the business sector. The investment equilibrium is disturbed when changes in technology affect the tradeoff between current and deferred output, leading to changes in the time pattern of desired consumption, the supply of savings, and the structure of interest rates. Adjustments in interest rates change the number and character of projects with positive NPVs, creating changes in the volume and allocation of savings to investments.

Is it reasonable to expect that capital markets do, in fact, clear? Do the conditions of competitive equilibrium prevail in the market for loanable funds? The microeconomic model we have developed so far has depended on several assumptions. First, all feasible investment projects are simply given. All project ideas are public goods and entrepreneurs are just a specialized form of labor that pilots projects when funds are available. Second, the future resource flows associated with projects are common knowledge for entrepreneurs and investors alike. The entrepreneur is no better informed about the prospects of the project than a potential investor. Third, the volume and allocation of investment are determined entirely by the structure of interest rates (discount rates) and the time pattern of a project's resource flows, which determine the project's NPV.

Information Asymmetry

Acknowledging a gap in knowledge has far-reaching consequences. When investors are less well-informed than an entrepreneur about the prospects of an investment because entrepreneurs propose unfamiliar projects with uncertain results, ranking projects in order of expected return is no longer straightforward. The problem is complicated further when investors recognize that entrepreneurs are not mere handmaidens of technological change and begin to analyze the entrepreneur's own motivations.

Entrepreneurial motivations depend on how the entrepreneur is compensated, which will also determine how the rewards of an investment project are shared between the entrepreneur and investors. The entrepreneur earns a "rent" corresponding to the specific knowledge they bring to the projects about the prospective investment projects and their execution. The split of this "entrepreneurial rent" between the entrepreneur and potential investors determines the entrepreneur's participation and effort, as well as the investors' expected return.[14]

Assume that all transfers of loanable funds are made in exchange for equity.[15] In exchange for the funds provided, an entrepreneur agrees to pay an investor a share of all profits. The residual share of profits not pledged to investors is retained by the entrepreneur. Assume further that investments are made through limited-liability enterprises. If the venture fails, the entrepreneur does not have to make investors whole using funds not invested in the business. Limited liability puts a floor under the entrepreneur's payoff from the venture: Their upside is unlimited, while their downside is limited.

Limited liability raises an entrepreneur's expected return from a risky venture relative to a situation of *unlimited* liability. Suppose the entrepreneur had equal chances of making $1 million and losing $1 million. The expected payoff to the entrepreneur—the probability-weighted average of the two equally likely scenarios—is zero. Under limited liability, however, the entrepreneur's potential loss in the downside scenario is truncated to the amount of their own investment—say, $100,000. Thus, the expected payoff to the entrepreneur under limited liability is the probability-weighted average of −$100,000 and $1 million, or $450,000.

Equity investors anticipate the entrepreneur's expected payoff calculations. Indeed, their own payoffs will be determined by the same considerations. Suppose an investor is offered a 50% stake in a venture for $100,000, so that the investor's expected payoffs are the same as the entrepreneur's. The investor knows the expected payoff is $450,000, but does not know whether that arises from equally likely scenarios of $1 million and total failure (loss of $100,000), as in the example above, or from equally likely scenarios of $400,000 and $500,000. That is, the expected payoff (NPV) does not tell the investor anything about the *risk* of the venture because the high-risk venture with widely dispersed outcomes has the same expected payoff as the low-risk venture with a narrow range of outcomes—they are "observationally equivalent" in terms of expected returns. If investors make funds available based on expected returns, entrepreneurs will raise funds for high-risk projects on the same terms as they would for low-risk projects. There is an *informational asymmetry* between the investor and the entrepreneur: the entrepreneur knows how risky the project is, while the investor does not.

Equity Rationing

While the entrepreneur generally cannot fully communicate the risk of a project to an investor, they can send a signal about project risk. Entrepreneurs offering low-risk projects have an incentive to speak up and differentiate themselves. In our low-risk project example, the entrepreneur could assure the return of the investor's principal because the project's NPV exceeds $100,000 in both possible outcomes ($400,000 or $500,000). The high-risk entrepreneur could not keep such a promise because they have a 50% chance of losing everything. The low-risk entrepreneur, therefore, signals the low risk of their project by offering the investor a bond which pays 20% interest and gives control of the company to the investor if a payment is missed. But now the low-risk entrepreneur is offering a different kind of security with downside protection. Investors now have the choice between debt and equity securities, with the offer of debt signaling the entrepreneur's knowledge that the project is low-risk.

The fact that an entrepreneur is trying to raise equity is thus taken to be a negative signal about the project being pursued by the entrepreneur. Where equity is being offered, substantial risk is present. Debt is a more positive signal. The most positive signal of all is an entrepreneur who funds projects out of their own funds or retained earnings.[16] The presence of the entrepreneur in the capital market and the terms on which they are seeking funds communicate information to investors *over and above the NPV of the project*. Evidently, complications for investment arise because project ideas are particular to entrepreneurs, and because entrepreneurs demand compensation for carrying projects through. Entrepreneurs earn informational rents because they know something investors do not know about project risk.[17]

Investors are unable to completely overcome the information asymmetry between themselves and fundraising entrepreneurs. A random sampling of potential projects at any expected payout rate will tend to turn up more of the high-risk variety, reducing investors' risk-adjusted returns. Investors, therefore, commit fewer funds at any potential payout rate. As a result, many entrepreneurs that are observationally identical to entrepreneurs who raise funds successfully will remain unfunded.[18] Only a subset of projects meeting a given NPV threshold will ultimately be *investable*. We say that equity is *rationed* in equilibrium. A rationed capital markets equilibrium means that entrepreneurs will have an *excess, unsatisfied demand for loanable funds* regardless of the structure of interest rates. Positive NPV projects will remain unfunded, and the allocation of funds to projects will be resolved according to non-price criteria.[19]

Equity rationing leaves investors with an *excess supply of loanable funds*, because the reduced set of investable projects available to investors is not sufficient to absorb available savings. The same dynamic that reduces the set of investable projects creates a demand for a "default investment option" earning a return with minimal risk. A prime example is government debt. Another is land. Meeting this demand for a default option requires a kind of entrepreneurship in proffering low-risk investment vehicles to absorb uninvested savings. Such vehicles overwhelmingly take the form of debt securities.

The degree of equity market rationing thus establishes a movable boundary in the capital markets between the set of equity and debt investments made available to investors. Greater information asymmetry between entrepreneurs and investors results in lower volumes of *ex post* equity investment and a proliferation of safe investment options. Risky projects have poor prospects of obtaining funds, even with very high expected rates of return.

Revising the Growth Model

Equity rationing undermines the benchmark economic growth model. The microeconomic foundations necessary to generate balance between savings and investment at a market-clearing interest rate involve unrealistic assumptions about the discovery of investment projects, the motivations of entrepreneurs, and the distribution of information about project risks. While balance is eventually achieved by introducing a safe option in which funds are risklessly "parked," the balance fails to allocate funds to projects based on productivity and interest rates.

Though the result of equity rationing is fundamental, we have been led to it by excluding basic features of capital markets like security design, information disclosures, and the presence of informed intermediaries. These exclusions do not falsify the model. Instead, they point us toward capital market institutions which may mitigate or eliminate the informational asymmetry that drives our result.

Financial Intermediation and Project Stratification

Financial intermediaries discover and disseminate information about investment projects which aids investors in achieving an efficient allocation of savings. Much of this information is only produced in the context of intermediation, for intermediaries' own use in matching savings to investment opportunities. Intermediaries are not redundant and costly middlemen, but crucial nexuses of information that enable exchange.[20] The information produced by intermediaries reduces the asymmetry between entrepreneur and investor, allowing investors to form reasonable expectations about an investment's prospects and an entrepreneur's ability to realize them. Information mitigates the tendency toward equity rationing.

On the supply side of the market for loanable funds, intermediaries identify sources of funds by getting to know wealthy households, asset managers, and other institutional investors. Intermediaries are interested not only in the amount of resources an investor can supply, but also the investor's risk tolerance and capacity for independently processing information about various categories of investment projects.[21] Investors' risk tolerance tends to increase with information processing capacity. When an investor lacks that capacity, they can effectively delegate information processing to the intermediary, who takes on the responsibility directly or offers investments that are more suitable for the investor.

On the demand side, intermediaries qualify potential uses of funds. Both entrepreneurs and projects must be identified and qualified. The due diligence undertaken by an underwriting team in connection with an initial public offering of stock is an excellent example.[22] Underwriters meet extensively with company management to understand the nature of the firm's business and the competence of the firm's managers. Company results are benchmarked against similar firms. Financial and technical information is gathered, subjected to critical review, and disseminated to potential investors.

In order to match potential investments to investors with various risk tolerances, intermediaries must stratify investment projects according to their risk and monitoring intensity. We conceive of the hierarchy as a simple three-way classification into high-, low-, and no-risk investment opportunities. The division of investment opportunities into high- and low-risk projects corresponds roughly to the decision between equity and debt funding. Risky investment projects can be segmented into equity-fundable projects, debt-fundable projects, projects which can be funded either way, and projects which are rationed from both debt and equity markets.[23] Debt investments have simple payoffs and may be offered to investors with limited monitoring capacity. The value of equity investments is more sensitive to information flows, making them more suitable for investors with more monitoring capacity. Beyond debt investments one can imagine a limiting case of a security that is completely insensitive to information. Such an investment would have a value that is assured to prevail in every state of the world and would thus require no monitoring. In this regard, it would approach the status of money, with an invariant value of par.[24]

Intermediaries realize matches between investors and entrepreneurs not only by coordinating issues of debt and equity but also by designing debt and equity investment products tailored to specific clienteles. Such products are designed to meet the risk tolerance and monitoring capacities of investor groups based on their competence or the requirements imposed on them by law. Products may pool similar investments to reduce the importance of issuer-specific information, partition risks into specific segments, and so on. This productization by intermediaries gathers wide universes of investment opportunities into marketable funds, asset-backed securities (ABS), and other well-recognized structures, facilitating investor uptake. Further structuring enhances secondary market liquidity.

In segmenting the universe of investors and investments according to risk and monitoring intensity, financial intermediaries are a kind of platform business that trades in monitoring and risk transformation services.[25] The intermediary's production of a stratified menu of investment opportunities involves an allocation of due diligence among potential entrepreneurs and investment projects. When an intermediary creates an investment opportunity with less monitoring intensity for an investor, the intermediary must allocate more resources to underwriting the reduced range of possible outcomes. Opportunities with greater monitoring intensity require ongoing updates and recalibrations. The intermediary's effort allocation is constrained by the prevailing set of entrepreneurs and technically feasible projects and reweights fixed and variable costs in the intermediary's production function. Thus, we can summarize the optimization problem being solved by intermediaries as maximizing profits from matching savers to investment opportunities, subject to investor risk tolerances, the characteristics of current ventures, and the intermediary's fixed and variable costs of producing information sufficient to sustain a stratified product offering.

Intermediaries have little control over the supply of would-be entrepreneurs and the set of feasible investment projects, which generally reflect the prevailing state of technology. Financial intermediaries thus *screen* entrepreneurs and their projects. While screening cannot eliminate information asymmetries, it can make stronger inferences possible about an entrepreneur's competence and the potential payoffs of a given venture.

On the other hand, intermediaries have some influence over the composition of investment opportunities they make available to investors. By deciding how to allocate their efforts to screening and the production of relatively safe investment vehicles, intermediaries influence the distribution between debt- and equity-like investments and define the "risky frontier" at which projects become investable. Some examples include venture capital funds dealing with entrepreneurs even before they have investment projects defined, middle-market private equity funds that buy and sell the equity of small- and mid-size firms, venture debt firms that offer bond finance to small firms, nonbank financial institutions structuring and selling consumer ABS, and investment banks with debt and equity capital markets divisions that prepare companies to issue securities publicly on exchanges or privately to institutions. Nor should we neglect the internal capital markets of nonfinancial firms with surplus funds, who rely on specialized internal managers to identify investable projects.

In Chapter 5, we will explain how the distribution of equity capital generated with the aid of the capital markets affects the lending opportunity set available to the banking system. Financial intermediaries' production of safe financial assets will be discussed in Chapter 6.

Notes

1. Our exposition owes much to Jakab, Z. and Kumhof, M. (2015). Banks are not intermediaries of loanable funds – And why this matters. *Bank of England Working Paper 529*, May.
2. On this point, our exposition is indebted to the work of Joseph Stiglitz.
3. Our notion of monitoring intensity owes much to Gary Gorton's notion of information-insensitive security creation. Monitoring intensity increases with sensitivity to information.
4. For the standard theory, see Barro, R. and Sala-i-Martin, X. (2003). *Economic Growth*, 2e. MIT Press and Acemoglu, D. (2009). *Introduction to Modern Economic Growth*. Princeton University Press.
5. These are often subsumed under the notions of "technology," "technical progress," or "total factor productivity." Assuming continuous technical progress may seem ideological or at least overly optimistic. However, the assumption amounts to the observation that processes become more efficient as sustained attention is devoted to them. Outside of completely apathetic environments, the assumption seems to be a safe one.
6. Consider the real assets on household and nonfinancial business balance sheets in Chapter 3.
7. This interpretation of depreciation in terms of value and relative productivity is somewhat nonstandard, as economists are wont to identify depreciation with physical wear and tear.
8. This can be expanded into other familiar identities. Dividing consumption between the private sector and the government yields $Y = C + I + G$. Allowing output to be exported or imported gives $Y = C + I + G + (X - M)$. The latter is a fundamental identity in accounting for gross domestic product (GDP). We can suppress the government and transactions with the rest of the world without fundamentally altering the basic economic story about saving and investment.
9. As emphasized by Jakab, Z. and Kumhof, M. (2015). Banks are not intermediaries of loanable funds – And why this matters. *Bank of England Working Paper 529*, May.

10. In this case, a gross interest rate R is greater than one. Subtracting one yields a net interest rate r on a familiar scale. Thus $R = 1 + r$. Each gross and net interest rate has an associated time span.
11. That is, $1/R$ or $1/(1 + r)$.
12. Cox, J.C., Ingersoll, J.E., and Ross, S.A. (1985a). An intertemporal general equilibrium model of asset prices. *Econometrica* 53 (2): 363–384.
13. The NPV criterion is not the only possible criterion. Dixit, A. and Pindyck, R. (1994). *Investment Under Uncertainty.* Princeton University Press pioneer the analysis of investments in terms of real options.
14. Holmström, B. and Tirole, J. (2011). *Inside and Outside Liquidity.* MIT Press.
15. The famous Modigliani-Miller theorem of corporate finance states conditions under which the division of funding into debt and equity does not matter. While those conditions are regularly violated in the real world, they allow us to treat the division of corporate finance into debt and equity as a mostly idiosyncratic, firm-level problem rather than a problem for capital market equilibrium. Nevertheless, the analysis can be extended to situations with multiple securities. The main result still holds, but substitutions between different kinds of securities can become intricate. See Hellman, T. and Stiglitz, J.E. (2000). Credit and equity rationing in markets with adverse selection. *European Economic Review* 44: 281–304.
16. This result is known as the pecking-order hypothesis in corporate finance. See Myers, S.C. and Majluf, N.S. (1984). Corporate financing and investment when firms have information that investors do not have. *Journal of Financial Economics* 13 (2): 187–221. Of course, self-funding is not possible for all entrepreneurs.
17. See Bolton, P. and Dewatripont, M. (2004). *Contract Theory.* MIT Press on the idea of informational rents.
18. Myers, S.C. and Majluf, N.S. (1984). Corporate financing and investment when firms have information that investors do not have. *Journal of Financial Economics* 13 (2): 187–221, Greenwald, B., Stiglitz, J.E., and Weiss, A. (1984). Informational imperfections in the capital markets and macro-economic fluctuations. *American Economic Review* 74 (1): 194–199.
19. These other criteria are not necessarily economic. Other social considerations may step into the void to determine allocations.
20. This is the Achilles' heel of "decentralized finance," in our view. Putting the burden of information discovery on every investor will tend to support disintermediation, not more efficient intermediation.

21. For retail investors and many institutional investors, standards of risk tolerance and diligence are prescribed by law. Those standards are beyond the scope of this book but are instrumental in generating the imbalances we discuss in Part Three.
22. See, for example, Corwin, S.A. and Schultz, P. (2005). The role of IPO underwriting syndicates: Pricing, information production, and underwriter competition. *Journal of Finance* 60 (1): 443–486.
23. Hellman, T. and Stiglitz, J.E. (2000). Credit and equity rationing in markets with adverse selection. *European Economic Review* 44: 281–304.
24. Gorton, G. and Ordoñez, G. (2014). Collateral crises. *American Economic Review* 104 (2): 343–378.
25. Platform businesses bring together distinct clienteles who often have different elasticities of demand for the platform's services. We discuss platform competition further in Chapter 12.

Chapter 5

Credit Creation by the Commercial Banking System

Chapter 4 outlined the financial possibilities of a system of intermediated savings. In this chapter, we examine how the banking system allows the economy to go beyond the constraint of currently existing savings.

In the first chapters of the book we have emphasized that bank credit creation is not constrained by pre-existing financial resources in the way that financial intermediation is. What limits bank credit creation is the prudential management of the bank and the supply of credible claims to *future* savings. Just as in the case of investable projects in Chapter 4, a claim to future savings involves the existence of a surplus that will emerge over time. In addition, the emergence of that surplus must be sufficiently credible and reinforced by other assurances for it to be *underwritten* by the bank. Because many investable projects lack these additional assurances, relatively few of them qualify as *bankable projects*, so credit is rationed in equilibrium just as equity is.

In light of the conditions that generate credit rationing, banks have developed mechanisms that mitigate asymmetric information. We focus on the role of well-defined underwriting domains, borrower equity, and marketable collateral in supporting claims to future savings. These additional elements often make a claim to future savings credible and an investable project bankable.

Prudential bank management results in additional constraints on credit creation. In conjunction with their lending and money-creation activity, banks expose themselves to risks. While it is typical to treat credit, interest rate, and liquidity risks as random events that can be treated from a statistical standpoint, we offer an economic interpretation of banking risk and the measures taken by banks to mitigate risk. In addition to its impact on individual banks, bank risk management can have non-trivial macroeconomic consequences.

Borrower equity links capital markets and credit creation. A poor allocation of equity to investable projects limits the set that can potentially become bankable and support money creation. The linkage also runs in the other direction. As claims on future savings are redeemed and loan principal is amortized, money is taken out of circulation rather than entering the supply of loanable funds. In this sense, bank credit creation allows future savings to be pulled forward in time. Interest earned by the bank represents the bank's portion of the surplus generated. It becomes part of the bank's capital and the supply of aggregate savings.

In Chapters 6, 8, and 12, we will consider whether competition between banking and capital markets is a zero-sum game or a sphere in which meaningful complementarities exist.

Savings and Investment: Expanding the Standard Story

Whereas the intermediation of loanable funds involves allocating the *current* stock of savings to *investable* projects, credit creation by the banking system generates new funding for *bankable* projects *without drawing on existing savings*. Instead, the credit created by the banking system is supported by claims on the future savings of the economic actor receiving funding. These future surpluses are the source of value that will ultimately amortize the principal of the bank loan.

As the bank loan is amortized, the funds initially created by the lending bank are destroyed. Payments of loan principal reduce the asset balance of the bank. The balancing item for this reduction is the retirement of the deposit balance transferred to make the principal payment. Because funds are regularly destroyed in the banking system, the supply of bank money must be constantly renewed with new loans.

From the perspective of the general equilibrium of the economy, the creation of credit by the banking system decouples consumption and investment from the current flow of income and savings.[1] Consumption is funded not only by current production, but also by underwritten claims on future income. Aggregate investment is funded not only by existing savings, but also by underwritten claims on future savings. Credit creation by the banking system brings savings forward in time, allowing the economy to consume and invest beyond the constraints of its current resources. From the perspective of an optimizing agent, the choice of consumption over time now involves a tradeoff between consumption and investment from current production, bank-funded consumption and investment, and "loan service"—the schedule of principal amortization and interest in which bank credit may be contracted.² Choices about bank-funded investment and loan service are linked and constrained by the terms on which banks make credit available. At this point it becomes difficult to maintain that a single decision-maker simultaneously chooses production, consumption, and credit creation plans to maximize intertemporal utility. Equilibrium involves interactions between banks and other economic actors.

We are now in a world in which households, banks, financial firms, and nonfinancial firms each make multiperiod plans, according to expectations about the behavior of other actors and constraints imposed by other actors through labor, credit, capital, and product markets. *The need to coordinate independent plans requires a certain amount of slack in the economy, a relaxation of standard economic assumptions about perfectly competitive and fully clearing markets, and, of course, the ability to hold short-term balances in money* to mitigate the risk of events that are contrary to expectations.

On the production side of the economy, production does not take place at an output-maximizing locus of a technological frontier. If any genuine decisions may be made about levels of current output and current investment, then the economy cannot always be operating at its full productive capacity. As a result, output in any period generally falls short of *potential output*, the amount of output that would be produced if productive capacity were fully utilized. Producing below full capacity also decouples the remuneration of productive factors (labor, capital, entrepreneurship) from their marginal products at potential output.

On the consumption side of the economy, bank credit allows consumption and saving plans to be partially decoupled from the production and investment plans of the nonfinancial business sector. Investment can increase in the short term without a sacrifice of current consumption, but the savings commitments that support bank credit creation impose upper bounds on future consumption and residual savings. That is not to say that future savings commitments are binding for future consumption. Nevertheless, it is easy to imagine circumstances in which aggregate indebtedness to the banking system begins to weigh on aggregate consumption and the formation of new savings.

The commercial banking system stands in between production and consumption plans, and between the economy's present and future. Credit creation opens space between aggregate savings and investment. The space created expands as additional commitments are underwritten and closes as savings commitments are met or exceeded. The commercial banking system can keep the space open for longer periods by lending for very long terms or refinancing loans as principal payments come due. It is also possible to shrink the space rapidly when loans are made for short terms, subject to the bank's option to roll the loan over to a new term.

We have already noted how non-clearing markets separate wages and the cost of capital from their marginal products at maximum output. The insight extends to other prices in the economy as well. The slack between production and consumption plans introduced by credit creation removes some of the pressure placed on prices to ensure markets clear in all periods. Instead, prices ensure market balance over the longer horizon spanned by production and consumption plans and temporary imbalances are absorbed in inventories.[3]

Money and banking thus transform the basic economic growth problem by making investment choices distinct from consumption choices, and by untethering investment decisions from the fund of existing savings. Money allows payments of income to factors of production to be decoupled from the production of current output.[4] Money and banking fit uneasily into standard macroeconomic models. Their presence transforms our model of the economy from the behavior of a "representative household" in perfectly competitive markets to the interactions of multiple actors in non-clearing markets with the coordination of prices, expectations, and mutual restraint. Excluding money and banking makes economic modeling easier, at the price of removing a significant and perhaps decisive feature of capitalist society.

In addition to transforming aggregate macroeconomic analysis, money and banking introduce distributional consequences. The ability to create monetizable claims to futures surpluses is not evenly distributed in the economy among households or firms, and within households and firms some projects are more bankable than others. As a result, credit creation is not neutral, and its non-neutrality channels the growth prospects of the economy in some directions, while presenting resistance in others.

The ability of an economy to invest beyond what its current endowment of savings will permit allows it to grow at an accelerated rate.[5] The rapid postwar economic development of East Asia owes much to bank finance.[6] But the mere possibility of banks financing productive investment does not ensure that all lending will be channeled to productive asset creation. Lending can also finance consumption and the transfer of existing assets at appreciated values, with no obvious contribution to economic growth, and at the cost of exposing banks to excessive risk.[7]

What constrains the banking system's capacity for credit creation? What risks does the banking system face when bridging current investment and future savings? And how might the banking system's profit maximization and risk management activities influence activity in the wider economy?

First, we are interested in the conditions under which future savings commitments can be underwritten. What determines the set of *bankable projects* in the economy, and what prevents the banking sector from underwriting future savings without limit?

Second, we are interested in the risks that exist while the redemption of savings commitments is pending, and the role of the banking system in managing and mitigating these risks. The "maturity transformation" achieved by the banking system is not an undesirable and unintended consequence of credit creation; rather, maturity transformation is one of its primary functions. Nevertheless, maturity transformation comes with risks, and it is evident that deferring loan amortization and the realization of savings commitments indefinitely creates significant risks for the banking sector and the economy.[8]

Finally, we summarize how conditions in capital markets and the banking sector affect the growth of the economy. The productivity of financial intermediaries and banks in carrying out their economic purpose weighs directly on the productivity of the "real" economy.

The Set of Bankable Projects

The asymmetry of information between a potential borrower and a bank creates the necessary conditions for credit demands to be rationed, just as demand for loanable funds is rationed in capital markets.[9] Credit rationing is a fact of everyday experience. Most people and firms have less access to credit than they would like, even if they could afford the associated loan service. Banks have little interest in speculative projects, leaving entrepreneurs to seek funding for risky projects in the capital markets. Credit markets thus fail to clear at market interest rates.

When a bank offers to lend money at a given interest rate, it faces two risks. First, the bank cannot see what the borrower ultimately does with the money. As a result, the lender—borrower relationship is one of asymmetric information: the borrower knows more about the likely outcomes of the project than the bank does. The potential for the borrower to take hidden, value-destroying actions is known as *moral hazard*. Second, the advertised loan rate will attract both reliable and risky borrowers. On average, the risky borrower will earn enough of a return to repay the loan, but there are many potential scenarios in which the risky borrower will fall far short of repaying the loan principal, let alone interest. This tendency of posted prices to elicit demand from risky customers is known as *adverse selection*.

The key difference between credit rationing and equity rationing lies on the supply side of the market. Because banks create funding on demand by issuing deposit money, credit rationing does not leave a residual pool of excess funds like that observed in the capital market.[10] The extent of credit rationing is challenging to observe.[11]

Banks rely on several devices to mitigate information asymmetry. These devices define the boundaries of loan markets and set an economic limit on the growth of the banking sector and the expansion of bank money.

Credit is only available to those who can contribute adequate funds of their own to the project. A potential residential mortgage borrower making a 50% down payment has better prospects for obtaining a loan than one offering 10%, just as a company with substantial retained earnings (equity) will have better prospects obtaining a revolving line of credit for working capital than a company that has just begun operating on a shoestring.

The presence of borrower equity in a bankable project serves two functions. First, it shows the borrower has an independent reason to devote effort to the project, aligning the borrower's incentive to preserve and increase their equity with the bank's desire to be repaid. Second, borrower equity cushions the bank against project risk. If the project underperforms expectations, losses will be absorbed first by the borrower, whose equity is subordinated to the bank's claim on project earnings.

The importance of borrower equity in lending means that the distribution of credit will tend to follow the distribution of net worth. These net worth constraints on lending create a locus for the interaction of bank credit markets and capital markets. When net worth is concentrated in a small universe of firms or households, the universe of potential borrowers will also be small. The mobilization of savings by capital markets can reallocate net worth to firms with good investment prospects. The equity raised by such firms improves the firm's borrowing prospects.[12]

Credit is more readily available to borrowers who can pledge adequate collateral. In addition to the subordination offered by borrower equity, most bank lending is *secured* by assets the bank can seize and liquidate in the event of borrower non-payment. Reliable valuation and liquidation of collateral depend on well-organized, transparent secondary asset markets in which comparable transactions may be readily observed and sales executed with reasonable transaction costs. For example, the residential mortgage market in the United States benefits from the relatively rapid turnover of homes and the data captured from those transactions, which are available from several public and private sources. From the bank's perspective, the sale of collateral involves finding another actor willing to destroy a money balance to acquire the collateral asset. Liquidation transfers ownership of the asset while redeeming the money created by the bank loan.

Unsecured lending is usually available only to the largest firms on the commercial side, while credit cards and personal loans are the most important forms of unsecured credit on the consumer side. In those cases, substantial surplus income is needed to overcome the lack of security.

Credit is generally only available within standard lending domains. Banks prefer to operate in domains in which they are equally well-informed as their borrowers, if not more so. After making an initial commitment to lend in a particular domain, the bank's accumulated experience with hundreds or thousands of loans eventually generates sufficient information to rival that of any borrower.

By operating in well-defined lending domains, banks become familiar with risks in classes of bankable projects. They can intelligently demand borrower equity contributions which are sufficient to reduce the remaining project risk, and reliably value collateral offered as security. Further, they can write restrictions on the use of funds into loan contracts which increase the odds that the project will be carried through as expected: conditioning the release of funds on receiving proof of transactions, directly distributing funds to known suppliers, setting the term and amortization schedule of the loan, and so on.

Formally, we can imagine banks as constructing loan production functions $L_i(E, C, A) \rightarrow \{r, M, T\}$ for projects of class i which outputs offered interest rates r, loan amounts M, and time to maturity T given equity E, collateral C, and domain-specific restrictions A. An informational investment is needed to construct each L_i, and the return on that investment depends on defining A such that available endowments of E and C produce enough non-zero offers of M.

As a result of banks' measures to tip the balance of informational asymmetry in their own favor, the potential for credit creation is limited and confined to certain well-defined domains. One can obtain a loan for a home or a car, and a business can borrow to finance inventories or a new production plant. It is much more difficult for a business to finance the purchase of a patent portfolio. Limited transaction volumes offer less information about project values and a smaller sample of *ex post* borrower performance. The bank knows less about the recovery it may realize if it is forced to seize and liquidate the patent portfolio. Secondary markets for such assets may be fragmented and expensive to access. This is not to say an innovative bank could not establish itself as a lender in one of these domains. The bank would incur the fixed cost of aggregating the relevant information and putting appropriate risk-mitigation practices in place. Such investments expand the lending market.

Collecting these economic constraints on lending, we say that the availability of collateral, the prevailing set of lending domains, and the distribution of net worth among firms and households at a point in time together define a set of *bankable projects*. Formally, the set of bankable projects is the set of all classes i such that the expected value of M output by $L_i(E, C, A)$ is sufficient to support a bank's investment in domain-specific information. The set of bankable projects defines the short-run frontier for bank lending and the creation of new bank money by the banking system. While we cannot observe the set of bankable projects *per se*, it is useful to consider where the state of bank lending is relative to this frontier in the short run and the long run. Slack relative to the frontier in the short run creates potential for credit expansion, while tightness at any horizon limits the amount of investment that can be financed through the banking system.

We tend to think that variations in the set of bankable projects are driven primarily by changes in interest rates, as well as by changes in A captured bluntly by surveys of senior loan officer underwriting standards. While changes in underwriting standards undoubtedly contribute, we wish to highlight the structural constraints of equity and collateral which tie credit creation to the distribution of equity capital and the nature of the assets being constructed.[13] They serve to anchor credit creation by the banking system to savings formation, savings allocation, and the state of technology, rather than the risk appetites of bankers which are emphasized in boom-bust credit cycle theories.

Maturity Transformation and Bank Risk Management

From the moment a bank credits a borrower with new funds until all loan principal is amortized, the bank is exposed to the risk that the borrower will fail to repay principal and interest, that movements in interest rates will reduce the value of the loan contract, and that reserve outflows from the bank prompted by the borrower's transfer of the newly created funds will not be replaced by other inflows. These credit, interest rate, and liquidity risks are the core risks of the banking business.

While it is common to describe and manage these risks in terms of statistical distributions of outcomes or scenarios without inquiring into their root causes, we want to highlight the economic origins of credit, interest rate, and liquidity risk. Similarly, we want to explore the economic consequences of their management. While individual banks may manage core risks by transferring them, it is generally not feasible for the banking system as a whole to transfer its credit, interest rate, or liquidity risk to other sectors of the economy. Hence, we must be concerned with the prospects for managing risk within the banking sector and individual banks.

Credit Risk Management

Credit risk is the risk that a borrower will fail to pay loan service on schedule. The failure to pay loan principal or interest generally results in the default of the borrower on the loan. In the event of default, the bank has recourse to assets pledged as collateral to secure the loan. The bank may seize and liquidate the collateral of a defaulting borrower.[14] If the proceeds from liquidation are insufficient to pay the outstanding principal balance of the defaulted loan, the bank realizes a loss, which is charged against the bank's equity, canceling the bank's own funds.

From the perspective of monetary economics, a defaulted loan is the collapse of a claim on future savings. The money created by the bank in extending the loan is redeemed not by the emergence of a new surplus, but by collateral pledged by the borrower and the bank's own equity. The transfer of existing capital via the repossessing bank from the borrower to a new owner has no impact on the amount of capital available to the aggregate economy. Instead, it is the reduction of bank equity that compensates for the unredeemed money creation by destroying savings held in the banking sector. Bank equity is the final stop for redeeming claims on future savings.[15]

To protect its equity, a bank uses risk-based loan pricing, crafts contractual terms carefully, limits its exposure to the value of the investment project, and evaluates the quality of collateral assets pledged by the borrower.

In risk-based loan pricing, borrowers are charged a markup over the risk-free rate corresponding to the term of the loan. The premium, known as a credit spread, accumulates in the equity of the bank while borrowers are making interest payments. For a large pool of similar borrowers, the accumulated premium serves as a fund to pay off the credit losses of a defaulted borrower. For example, if 2% of borrowers in a certain domain are expected to default on their loans each year, resulting in a loss of 50% of their outstanding principal balance, charging a credit spread of $0.02 \times 0.5 = 0.01 = 1\%$ per annum to all borrowers in the pool will offset the bank's expected losses in that domain.

Expected loan losses depend on the difference between the principal balance of the loan and the value of pledged collateral at the time of default. The above example assumed the value of collateral would be 50% less than the outstanding principal balance upon default. In the exceptional case that the pledged collateral's realizable value declines exactly in line with the repayment schedule for loan principal, the bank would face no loss in the event of borrower default. In reality, scheduled principal payments rarely align with the economic depreciation of the collateral asset, and there is substantial uncertainty about the evolution of collateral values after a loan is underwritten.

To protect itself against uncertain collateral values, a bank requires the value of collateral assets to exceed the value of the loan at the time of underwriting. The difference is the borrower's equity contribution. Potential gaps between outstanding principal and collateral values are eliminated by shifting the schedule of loan principal downward—that is, requiring more equity.

Risk-based pricing, collateral, and borrower equity thus serve to limit defaults and expected loan losses based on observable characteristics of the borrower, the investment project, and the pledged collateral. Risk premiums charged to borrowers can be accumulated as a reserve against expected credit losses.[16] After the loan is underwritten, however, unobservable characteristics of the borrower, the project, and the collateral emerge. While strong underwriting processes may help to discover some of these unobservable characteristics so they may be incorporated in pricing, the emergence of adverse unobservable characteristics of the borrower and the investment project generally results in *unexpected* losses for the bank. These unexpected losses threaten bank capital.

To create adequate capital buffers for unexpected loan losses, a bank must evaluate the relative importance of observable and unobservable characteristics in determining borrower outcomes.[17] Imagining that we begin from a position where all characteristics are unobservable, how effectively does the bank's underwriting process discover observable characteristics to reduce the variance of unobservable borrower characteristics?[18] And given that residual variance, what are the potential losses to the bank if the borrower pool is *adversely selected*?

Because banks compete with all other enterprises for savings, additional equity comes at a price. Accordingly, banks must weigh the contribution margin from new lending business against the cost of holding sufficient equity to protect against adverse selection. Such considerations lead to the concentration of bank lending in particular domains, as we have emphasized previously. Bankable projects exist when credit risk can be controlled through underwriting, pricing, adequate collateralization, and reasonably sized bank equity backstops.

Credit risk evaluations are inescapably subjective because they depend on expectations about the future. Though such expectations may be formalized as credit risk models, the modelability of credit risk does not eliminate its subjectivity. Accordingly, we would expect banks to come to different conclusions about the bankability of various projects and borrowers, and to some extent, a borrower's search for credit is a search for the bank that believes in them and/or their project. The bankability of a project is a hypothesis of the bank.

Inevitably, some banks' hypotheses about bankability will be falsified. Commercial bankers know this. They tend to be cautious rather than bold with their hypotheses, to spread their bets among multiple hypotheses, and to hold capital based on worst-case scenarios—which is to say, they are conservative. Nevertheless, outsiders can question whether bankers are conservative enough. Fears about the adequacy of a bank's capital can lead to bank runs, as depositors begin to doubt the bank's ability to redeem their claims at par.[19] We discuss bank capital regulation in Chapter 8 and bankers' incentives in Chapter 12.

Interest Rate Risk Management

Interest rate risk arises when banks extend loans at fixed interest rates for long terms, and when banks hold securities with fixed interest rates.[20] When a borrower fixes an interest rate, they transfer the risk of renegotiating interest rates to the bank. The risk that arises from fixing interest rates over a longer period, generally commands a premium in the market above the risk-free rate known as a *term premium*, which is distinct from the credit spread discussed in the previous section. The term premium charged by a bank gives the bank a budget to spend on mitigating interest rate risk. In principle, markets should discover a price for the term premium that equals the cost of interest rate risk management, so that the bank's risk management "budget" is just adequate.[21] In practice, banks offer different lending contracts and vary in their internal interest rate risk management capacity, so they have some ability to compete in loan pricing on the basis of the term premium.

Interest rates change due to changes in the market for savings. We tend to think about interest rates in terms of a benchmark risk-free yield curve, which shows the interest rates that apply to risk-free projects of different lengths. Each point on the yield curve is an equilibrium price for savings, showing what borrowers will pay for a risk-free investment and what compensation investors demand for a risk-free investment.[22] The yield curve also implies prices for savings at different points in the future—say, for one-year risk-free investments made one, two, or three years from now, which are called *forward* one-year rates. Changes in forward interest rates therefore arise from expected changes in the market balance for savings at different points in the future. Declining forward rates imply an excess of savings and/or reduced investment demand. Conversely, rising forward rates suggest reduced savings and/or increased investment demand. The balance is struck in the capital markets.

Movements in the market for risk-free savings depend not only on the balance between savings flows and investment plans but also on the success of capital markets in steering savings to risky projects in the form of equity. If more savings inflows are seeking risk-free destinations, the risk-free yield curve will shift downward and bank loan values will increase. If, on the other hand, there is a shortfall in the formation of savings, the yield curve will rise and bank loan values will decline. Capital market conditions thus feed back to credit market conditions via the channel of interest rate risk. Four decades of consistently declining risk-free rates in the United States have largely absolved U.S. banks of managing interest rate risk as an economic matter. The rapid pace of interest rate increases beginning in 2022 was a rude awakening for some, with poorly managed interest rate risk leading to the failure of Silicon Valley Bank and other institutions.[23]

Banks have several tools available for mitigating interest rate risk internally. A bank's primary tool is not accepting interest rate risk in the first place, a contracting decision. Floating-rate loans and securities carry interest rates that reset periodically, aligning them with prevailing market rates. Such instruments are exposed to interest rate risk only for the length of the reset period.[24]

Banks can also mitigate interest rate risk through their deposit liabilities, which serve as an internal hedge.[25] A bank's exposure to fixed interest rates on deposits is favorable and opposite to its exposure on fixed-rate loans. When interest rates rise, the bank benefits from having previously contracted deposits at a lower rate, as well as its ability to raise its deposit rates at a slower pace than market interest rates.[26] The interest rate risk benefit of deposit liabilities to a bank increases with their average lifetime. Though any individual depositor can demand redemption of their deposit balance within days, the overall mass of deposits remains with a bank for a relatively long term and turns over slowly. The behavioral maturity of deposits far exceeds their legal maturity.

Depositor behavior is motivated by any number of individual circumstances, but banks enjoy a certain amount of influence. Depositors have an incentive to maintain deposits with the same bank to become a "known quantity" and enjoy better borrowing terms. Access to more and better payment services via the bank make a deposit balance more money-like and increases borrowers' willingness to accept below-market rates of interest. When these non-pecuniary incentives are not enough, the bank can increase deposit rates to further discourage deposit turnover. Interest rates on savings and time deposits (certificates of deposit) are particularly important in motivating depositors to hold balances for longer terms.[27]

The residual interest rate risk faced by a bank after contracting, investing in liquid securities, and setting deposit rates may be transferred to another party using interest rate derivatives. Such transfers may operate within the banking system or transfer interest rate risk outside of the banking system. We discuss interest rate derivatives at greater length in Chapter 6. A bank may also decide not to manage its residual interest rate risk, tolerating the effect such risk has on the volatility of earnings.

Liquidity Risk Management

Without systems to achieve rapid, reliable, and final payments, the funding created by banks would lose its character as money. A breakdown in these functions would not only harm banks' lending business but also the substantial business enjoyed by banks in facilitating payments. Good liquidity management is thus a central responsibility of a bank to its customers and part of the "table stakes" for every bank.

The primary concern of bank liquidity management is the evolution of its reserve balance.[28] The bank's reserve balance consists of notes and coins kept on hand (its "vault cash") and its account balance held at the central bank, sometimes called the "nostro" account. The bank's ability to maintain adequate reserve balances is generally referred to as the bank's liquidity. Unlikely the supply of bankable projects, the management of liquidity is a constraint that falls more squarely on individual banks, though the availability of liquidity on a system-wide basis can be an important constraint in times of stress.

Over time, a bank's assets will produce reserve inflows, while its liabilities will lead to reserve outflows. Inflows are highly visible, spaced out in time, and generally long-term. Outflows are more difficult to predict and operate on multiple time scales. Some transactions between customers of the same bank can be settled entirely on the bank's books, with no movement of reserves. Otherwise, inflows and outflows move through the central bank's payment system to settle transactions with customers at other banks, where they may be netted off (or not) before affecting the bank's nostro account balance.

The creation of money in a loan transaction will be accompanied by a transfer of the loan proceeds to the customer of another bank in most cases. As a result, lending can be expected to generate reserve outflows almost immediately. If the lending bank is not in a surplus reserve position, the outflows can be financed by borrowing reserves in the interbank market. The bank earns the difference between the loan interest rate and the interbank rate. However, the question remains whether the reserve outflows generated by lending can be expected to reverse themselves in the short term, rather than leaving the bank in a deficit.

Three sources of funds tend to increase a bank's liquidity position. First, the bank earns a net interest margin, or the difference between interest earned on its assets and interest paid to depositors and lenders. Net interest margins are stable and positive, generating consistent reserve flows for the bank. Second, depositors tend to grow their account balances. While the net flow of customer payments will vary widely from day to day, one can expect a rational bank customer with a deposit account to maintain or increase their balance over time by spending no more than they receive in income, though this can change in the event of unemployment or when making a large purchase. Overall, a bank expects that a solid base of deposit customers transacting on their accounts will tend to improve the liquidity of the bank. And as we pointed out in our discussion of interest rate risk management above, banks can influence the turnover of their deposit base by changing the rates of interest they offer to depositors.[29] By offering an incentive for customers to maintain and accumulate deposit balances, banks encourage them to hold the outstanding stock of money, while limiting the demand for reserve outflows created by deposit outflows. Third, the bank's own customers will sometimes be the beneficiaries of other banks' lending, resulting in reserve inflows. When banks are growing their loan portfolios at similar rates, the net liquidity impact of new lending will be less important for individual banks.[30]

Forecasting payments and balance sheet-driven flows allows the bank to anticipate the evolution of its reserve balance over some horizon by accumulating net inflows and outflows, starting from the initial balance. The bank's anticipated lending, existing balance sheet, and banking system trends aid in forecasting the bank's nostro balance. To the extent that the forecasted balance is unsatisfactory, the bank can take actions in the money market to offload excess liquidity or finance a liquidity deficit. To raise liquidity, the bank can sell securities or offer them as collateral in a repurchase ("repo") agreement, issue commercial paper, or borrow reserves in the interbank market. Banks and bank customers with surplus liquidity are often the counterparties for these transactions, allowing liquidity risk to be managed largely within the banking system.

Running out of liquidity is more consequential for a bank than holding a surplus, so bank management tends to be hyper-focused on maintaining a level of liquidity that will allow the bank to withstand any conceivable outflow scenario, within the bounds of its current resources and those that can be mobilized on short notice. Much of liquidity risk management is concerned with making precise the notions of "any conceivable outflow scenario" and "resources that can be mobilized on short notice," particularly in situations where other banks are also seeking liquidity.

Maintaining liquidity resources is costly for banks, just as it is for the nonbank public. Reserves earn a below-market return, creating a tradeoff between liquidity and profit maximization. Some of the opportunity cost of reserve holding can be offset by investing surplus reserves in liquid securities. However, reserve balances will be a scarce resource for most banks, most of the time. An abundance of liquidity cannot be taken for granted, and system-wide demands for borrowed reserves put upward pressure on short-term interest rates if the central bank does not supply additional reserves in response. If the expected cost of borrowing short-term funds exceeds the interest rate on new lending, extending new loans makes little sense. It is in this economic sense that liquidity constrains the growth of the banking system.

Even responsible liquidity management by banks can be compromised when all banks are trying to increase their liquidity at the same time. Those who normally have surpluses to lend, stop; those who have deficits find themselves with greater deficits. To ensure that the liquidity of the banking system can be increased rapidly in such situations, central banks stand ready to lend, as a "lender of last resort," to banks against high-quality securities. Many further measures exist, and the details of the lender of last resort arrangement deserve further comment. We shall have more to say about both in Chapters 8 and 14.

For the moment, however, we can imagine a banking system in which certain institutions tend to accumulate liquidity and others tend to consume liquidity. But because these institutions are connected to each other in an essentially closed system, the system as a whole tends to balance. So long as borrowers and lenders can find each other in the interbank market and the money markets, individual banks need not be self-sufficient in managing their liquidity. There may even be room for banks to specialize in being sources of liquidity (by running a robust deposit business) and users of liquidity (by originating many loans), and trading the resulting assets and liabilities alongside the trade in reserves.

We have devoted so much discussion to bank risk management in an effort to identify and elucidate the *economic* constraints on bank lending and bank money creation. It is our experience that these considerations receive relatively little attention in our era of regulation, in which risk management has transformed into a compliance exercise. When we discuss *regulatory* constraints on bank liquidity and capital in Part Two, it will be helpful to bear in mind the economic constraints on bank liquidity and capital that arise in the normal course of bank risk management. While all banks must *comply* with regulatory constraints on bank liquidity and capital, the regulatory constraints do not necessarily *bind* from an economic perspective if bank management would ordinarily choose to hold greater levels. Whether economic or regulatory constraints bind bank credit expansion is a crucial question for evaluating monetary conditions. Banks are quick to blame regulation for disappointing results, with little pushback based on the economics of the business. Binding regulatory constraints imply a loss of output from the banking system, some of which may be justified as a prudent limitation of bank- and system-level risk, but which eventually must be weighed in terms of its impact on real output.

Economic Growth with Credit and Capital Markets

At this point, we can make an initial sketch connecting the activities of banks and financial intermediaries to the productivity of the economy.

The distribution of income generates a distribution of savings in the household and business sectors.[31] Such savings are potentially available as equity to finance new capital projects in the personal realm (building homes) or the commercial realm (investing in businesses). The financial sector mobilizes these savings, redirecting them from where they were accumulated to a different set of ventures. The flows of importance are not those in which savers transfer the ownership of claims in the secondary market—the trading of shares and debt that most people identify with "investing"—but those in which new funds are devoted to business ventures.

Thus, the capital markets reconfigure the distribution of available savings into a distribution of equity, by which we mean unencumbered funds put at the disposal of an entrepreneur in a business venture, regardless of the form of security offered to the investor. Ideally, the distribution of equity ensures that savings are put to their best (most productive) use as entrepreneurs compete with each other for resources on equal footing. In truth, the gap in information between entrepreneurs and investors, which is controlled and attenuated imperfectly by financial intermediaries, reduces the amount of funds distributed to business ventures and results in non-price allocation of funds among projects. Misallocations of savings represent a first drag on the productivity of the economy because too few ventures are financed, and those that are financed are not necessarily the best. A more productive financial intermediation sector minimizes such distortions and makes more projects investable.

The distribution of equity achieved with the aid of the capital markets conditions the set of bankable projects that may be financed by the banking system. Credit creation to support new bankable projects is the jet fuel of the financial system: an opportunity to create funding for a venture over and above what can be sourced from aggregate savings in the capital markets. Credit creation amplifies equity. An investable project with a positive NPV is essential, but collateral and/or equity are needed to make the project *bankable*. Were banks able to identify and finance all opportunities in which equity, collateral, and adequate expected returns are in place, the only relevant rationing and loss of efficiency would be that attributable to the capital markets. However, additional rationing of credit takes place in the banking system, as the presence of equity is necessary but not sufficient to make projects bankable. A lack of collateral pledgeable as security or significant uncertainty regarding outcomes will still ration a well-capitalized firm from the credit markets. A more productive banking sector accumulates information in multiple domains to make more investable projects bankable. A less productive sector relies on the transfer of existing assets at increased valuations to grow the aggregate balance sheet.

Efficiency losses in financial intermediation and credit creation—equity and credit rationing—result in some margin of technologically feasible investments failing to emerge into the marketplace. They also weigh on the banking system's ability to create deposit money. We emphasize that these outcomes are expected even in the absence of regulation. Discussions of regulation so completely dominate the financial press and academic publishing that one easily loses sight of the economic incentives and purposes that animate financial activity. We want to establish an analytical benchmark against which the outcomes of a regulated financial sector can be measured, at least in theory. Even in the absence of regulation, equity and credit rationing would leave some set of technologically feasible projects unfunded though adequate financial resources are in place.

Knowledge of the selection performed in funding markets undoubtedly results in self-selection among entrepreneurs, affecting both their decision to participate as entrepreneurs and the operating model they select when entering the market. We might therefore distinguish a third layer of rationing in which entrepreneurial talent selects in or out of entrepreneurship based on the expected availability of funds and the match between fundable operating models and those that are accessible to the entrepreneur.

Banking, capital markets, and entrepreneurship engage in a delicate dance to generate new investment opportunities. The economic equilibrium that emerges is not so much a necessary consequence of the state of technology as it is an art of the possible—even in a world free of regulation. The stakes of these monetary outcomes are measurable in terms of the economy's capacity to invest effectively and grow. Elastic money creation by the banking system allows the economy to grow faster when the claims backing new money are well-derisked bets on productive investment projects.

Our inquiry into the operative constraints on the banking system rests on the suspicion that forces restraining bank lending are also restraining the economy's ability to grow. With bank lending shifting toward household credit and consumption smoothing, the burden falls on capital markets to select and incubate new firms. In the absence of bank finance—by choice or by necessity—what emerges is a curious set of ventures with a characteristic operating model. Initial investments are kept small, capital services are rented in business-to-business markets, employees finance the firm through lower wages and vesting equity, and initial customers swallow high prices to subsidize later expansion. Ventures that do not match this asset-light template struggle to get off the drawing board, let alone gain traction in the market. The role and culpability of a broken financial system in these perverse economic outcomes is one of the animating concerns of this work.

Notes

1. This coupling is characteristic of general equilibrium models in macroeconomics. It is typical to think of all production as involving a single good that can either be saved or consumed. This collapses distinctions between production and income, as well as complications arising from matching supplies of multiple goods to the needs of current production.
2. We say "loan service" to distinguish these payments from "debt service" paid against debt contracted in the capital markets.
3. This observation is important for the analysis of inflation. If prices are set to achieve balance in multiple periods, the evolution of the price level will tend to be smoother than it would be if balance were achieved in every period, because current imbalances are averaged with those of other periods. Accordingly, we can conjecture that long, durable, and credible loan commitments help to create conditions for low and stable inflation rates.
4. The Swedish economist Knut Wicksell produced some of the most extraordinary mental gymnastics trying to show how productive factors would be paid their marginal product when the product arrives later than the next pay period. At the same time, Wicksell grasped the importance of the money created by bank finance in bridging the period in which workers labor at a productivity-enhancing production plan and the period in which the fruits of that labor are realized. See Wicksell, K. (1977 [1934]). *Lectures on Political Economy, Volume One: General Theory* (A.M. Kelley), Wicksell, K. (1978 [1934]). *Lectures on Political Economy, Volume Two: Money* (A.M. Kelley).
5. Beck, T., Döttling, R., Lambert, T. et al. (2023). Liquidity creation, investment, and growth. *Journal of Economic Growth* 28: 297–336.
6. See Frankel, J.A. (1991). Japanese finance in the 1980s: A survey. In: *Trade with Japan: Has the Door Opened Wider?* (ed. P. Krugman), 225–270. University of

Chicago Press: 230–232, 256–262), Fry, M. (1995). *Money, Interest, and Banking in Economic Development*, 2e. Johns Hopkins University Press, Yoshioka, S. and Kawasaki, H. (2016). Japan's high-growth postwar period: The role of economic plans. *ESRI Research Note No. 27*: 27–29), and Park, Y.C., Kim, J-K., and Park, H. (2021). *Financial Liberalization and Economic Development in Korea, 1980–2020*. Harvard University Press.

7. Müller, K. and Verner, E. (2024). Credit allocation and macroeconomic fluctuations. *Review of Economic Studies* 91 (6): 3645–3676.
8. An important recent example is the "extend and pretend" treatment given to commercial real estate mortgages. Banks roll over doubtful mortgages to avoid writing off their capital, creating credit misallocations, crowding out new credit, and building up fragility. See Crosignani, M. and Prazad, S. (2024). Extend-and-Pretend in the U.S. CRE market. *Federal Reserve Bank of New York Staff Report No. 1130*, October for an analysis.
9. Stiglitz, J.E. and Weiss, A. (1981). Credit rationing in markets with imperfect information. *American Economic Review* 71 (3): 393–410. See also Smith, V.L. 2007. *Rationality in Economics: Constructivist and Ecological Forms*. Cambridge University Press: Chapter 5 and Yeager, L. and Hanke, S.H. (2024). *Capital, Interest, and Waiting: Controversies, Puzzles, and New Additions to Capital Theory*. Palgrave-Macmillan, who stress that "credit rationing is common" and "waiting, by its very nature, cannot be rationed by price alone."
10. Banks are, in fact, part of the solution for excess savings, as deposit accounts serve as excellent risk-free sinks for uninvested savings.
11. For a study of credit rationing in the U.S. mortgage market, see Ambrose, B.W., Pennington-Cross, A., and Yezer, A.M. (2002). Credit rationing in the U.S. mortgage market: Evidence from variation in FHA market shares. *Journal of Urban Economics* 51: 272–294.
12. Some, like de Meza, D. and Webb, D.C. (2006. Credit rationing: Something's gotta give. *Economica* 73 (292): 563–578, argue that credit rationing is unimportant because one can always wait to accumulate more equity. Accordingly, we stress that projects are dated, and one is indeed rationed if unable to obtain funds as of that date.
13. On the latter point, see the interesting discussion in Pistor, K. (2019). *The Code of Capital: How the Law Creates Wealth and Inequality*. Princeton University Press.
14. For the sake of simplicity we ignore questions related to the bankruptcy process which require the bank to bargain with other creditors of the defaulted borrower.
15. Put differently, bank equity is insurance on the money supply, but not a component of the money supply.

16. As we continue to confine ourselves to the economics of the matter, we do not discuss the extensive accounting rules that apply to loan loss reserves, which are properly considered to be a form of bank regulation.
17. We refer to "borrower" outcomes only to avoid repeating borrower, project, and collateral.
18. The variance due to unobservable borrower characteristics could be measured, in principle, with a statistical underwriting model. Such a measurement would, of course, depend on the quality and stability of the model. However, the impact of unobservable characteristics is ultimately bounded by loan size, which is under the control of the bank, so unexpected losses are bounded as well.
19. We are unorthodox in connecting runs to solvency rather than liquidity. We explain further in Part Two.
20. Banks hold liquid securities to generate revenue from excess reserve balances. A bank's securities holdings thus connect its interest rate risk management with its liquidity risk management, as discussed in the following section.
21. This is the fundamental principle underneath interest rate term structure modeling – see, for example, Cox, J.C., Ingersoll, J.E., and Ross, S.A. (1985b). A theory of the term structure of interest rates. *Econometrica* 53 (2): 385–408. Other risk premiums may exist to compensate investors for other uncertainties in the evolution of interest rates, such as their correlation with the state of the economy.
22. The existence of an equilibrium rate does not mean that the market clears, as discussed in Chapter 3.
23. See Metrick, A. (2024). The failure of Silicon Valley Bank and the panic of 2023. *Journal of Economic Perspectives* 38 (1): 133–152.
24. Floating-rate loans are more common outside of the United States.
25. Drechsler, I., Savov, A., and Schabl, P. (2018). Banking on deposits: Maturity transformation without interest-rate risk. *NBER Working Paper 24582*, May.
26. The increment of deposit rate increase per unit of market rate increase is known as "deposit beta."
27. Drechsler, I., Savov, A., and Schabl, P. (2018). Banking on deposits: Maturity transformation without interest-rate risk. *NBER Working Paper 24582*, May incline toward market power as an explanation for banks' low deposit beta. While deposits are indeed concentrated in a few large American banks, we do not believe the authors have proven their case, as their arguments about market power assume that deposit rates should align with risk-free interest rates in the capital markets. As a result, they do not account for the difference in moneyness between deposits and other risk-free instruments like Treasury bills.

28. We follow the discussion in Fiedler, R. (2011). *Liquidity Modeling*. Risk Books.
29. Demand deposits tend to offer the least interest because a bank must give the customer access to such deposits immediately, without questions or recourse. In a savings account, the bank obtains the right—at least in principle—to delay the withdrawal requested by the customer. This right comes at a price, paid to the customer as a somewhat higher interest rate. Finally, in a certificate of deposit (a "time deposit"), a depositor agrees to leave money on account at one bank for a fixed period of time (months or years) in exchange for a much higher rate of interest. The depositor pays a penalty or forfeits the interest accumulated on the deposit if they withdraw it before the end of the term.
30. A point emphasized by Keynes, J.M. (1930). *A Treatise on Money*, 2 vols. Macmillan.
31. Though we take the distribution of income as given, further inquiry into the informational frictions that generate wage dispersion is an interesting research question in its own right which creates the conditions under which capital markets operate.

Chapter 6

Universal Banks and the Banking–Capital Markets Boundary

What we commonly call "banks" are not only banks. Most of them are hybrid institutions combining commercial banking with financial intermediation activity. In the United States, such "banks" are legally designated Bank Holding Companies (BHCs) or Financial Holding Companies (FHCs) housing multiple financial businesses, in which the commercial bank is one subsidiary among many. Further blurring the boundaries of banking activity, BHCs and FHCs are actively engaged in "shadow banking" activities that involve financial institutions outside of regulated holding company structures and further shift the balance of activities between banking and capital markets. The colocation of economically distinct functions in a single firm and their further distribution outside the banking system creates confusion about what banks actually do.

More importantly, such "universal banks" put the delicate questions of balance and boundaries between banking and capital markets under the control of unified management. Universal bank managers answer to a single group of shareholders who do not particularly care which side of the business profit comes from. Thus, the financial landscape of advanced economies is ordered not only by the microeconomic considerations about entrepreneurship and investment which we have unpacked in Chapters 4 and 5, but also by institutions with discretion over the form and quantity in which funding is offered to entrepreneurs and the ability to steer bankable projects to either side of their hybrid business.

We propose to compartmentalize the business of universal banks (BHCs, FHCs) according to the functions of money creation (commercial banking), financial intermediation within the holding company structure (capital markets), and services provided to financial intermediaries outside of any holding company structure (shadow banking). The commercial banking business consists of transaction banking and trade finance, as well as loans, settlement balances, a restricted set of securities holdings, and the corresponding deposit funding. The financial intermediation business consists of securities underwriting and market-making activities, as well as dealing in exchange-traded and over-the-counter (OTC) derivatives. These activities give rise to securities holdings for market-making inventory and the BHC's own account, corresponding to the broker and dealer functions of the business. Securities holdings are financed with wholesale funding from repo, commercial paper, and other money markets. The shadow banking business encroaches on commercial banking business from the side of capital markets, and resides mostly off-balance sheet as derivatives, securitizations, and other commitments and obligations. The risks of "banking" that have gathered the most attention since the GFC are not evenly distributed across the three functional areas. A great deal of subprime mortgage lending, for example, took place through unregulated shadow banks, and BHCs held large, risky positions for their own accounts on the capital markets side of the business, relying on wholesale funding and backstopped, ultimately, by the banking business' ability to create credit.

The balance sheet of a universal bank (Table 6.1) combines elements of the commercial banking system and financial intermediation system balance sheets introduced in Chapter 3. We have partitioned the assets and liabilities of the commercial banking business from those of the financial intermediation business, which we refer to in this chapter as a universal bank's "capital markets" business. Shadow bank commitments generally reside off-balance sheet as commitments to lend, as we discuss in the following sections. Earnings for the combined business come primarily from net interest income on the banking side, non-interest income (fees) and gains/losses on securities holdings on the capital markets side, and contingent fees and interest income from shadow banking commitments.

Putting all of these institutions together in a single firm creates problems because each draws from a common capital base and relies on integrated liquidity management. We have placed the universal bank's reserve balance and equity at the bottom to highlight this dependence. Capital that is adequate for the commercial banking business may not be sufficient to absorb losses from the financial intermediation and shadow banking businesses in times of market stress. This, in one sentence, is the story of the GFC.

Table 6.1 Balance sheet of a universal bank.

Universal Bank Balance Sheet

Loans (Nonbank Public)	Demand Deposits (Nonbank Public)
Government Debt (Fiscal Authority)	Savings Deposits (Nonbank Public)
Asset-backed Securities (Fiscal Authority, FinCos)	Time Deposits (Nonbank Public)
Corporate Debt (Financial, Nonfinancial Business)	Claims held by households, nonfinancial firms
Equities (Financial, Nonfinancial Business)	Store-of-value Money (Asset Managers)
Claims on Households	Store-of-value Money (Nonbank Public)
Claims on Nonfinancial Business	Wholesale Funding
Derivative Assets	Derivative Liabilities
Reserves (Monetary Authority)	Equity

While the continuity of "banks" was threatened by overexposure to real estate and mortgage markets during the GFC, the threatening exposures did not arise primarily from loans retained in the commercial banking business. Though most mortgage loans were originated through the commercial banking system according to underwriting criteria specified by government agencies (Fannie Mae, Freddie Mac, Ginnie Mae) or shadow banks (securitization SPVs), much loan risk was transferred from banks so that the most badly affected institutions were not banks at all. The GFC was initially touched off by MMF failures. Bear Stearns, Lehman Brothers, Merrill Lynch, Goldman Sachs, and Morgan Stanley were all broker-dealers: financial intermediaries operating in the capital markets. Bear Stearns and Merrill Lynch only became banks after being acquired by JPMorgan Chase and Bank of America, respectively, and Goldman Sachs and Morgan Stanley were compelled by the Federal Reserve to convert to FHCs to participate legally in crisis-era lending facilities. AIG Financial was a subsidiary of AIG, an insurance company; its excesses spilled over to markets via derivatives transactions rather than banking relationships. Both the GSEs and private label securitizers of mortgages were active in the capital markets. Many smaller commercial banks did fail due to overexposure to real estate, of which Washington Mutual was the largest. But these failures would not have been enough, on their own, to precipitate the GFC.

The intermingling of banking and capital markets business has muddied debates about reforms to the banking system. We need greater clarity on what we are talking about when we talk about bank regulation. Much of the time, the intended impact of regulation is directed not at commercial banking business, but at large complex holding companies, which include commercial banking subsidiaries. Recent trends in regulation weigh most heavily on the activities of universal banks *outside of* the commercial banking sphere, in an area described as the "trading book."

Because we reserve discussions of regulation for Part Two, the focus of the present chapter is the management of universal banking institutions. What are the consequences of placing the banking-capital markets boundary under the control of a single firm, rather than leaving it to be determined by market forces? And in what way do the risks of banking and capital markets businesses diversify or reinforce each other, supporting or challenging arguments for capitalizing a combined entity with common risk capital?

In between these bookend questions, we discuss securitization, risk transfers through credit enhancement and derivatives, and loans from banks to financial intermediaries. Each of these activities blurs the boundaries between banking and capital markets, which moved in crucial ways prior to the GFC. The derivatives and securitization operations of universal banks were highly efficient in transferring interest rate and credit risk from commercial banks to the capital markets, while transferring liquidity risk from the capital markets to the banking system. Lending from banks to in-house financial intermediaries artificially lowered their cost of funds, while loans to external financial intermediaries allow banks to participate in forbidden activities. Either way, such lending amplifies market risks, potentially at the banking system's expense.

A final section on the risk management of universal banking institutions forms a bridge to Part Two. Contemporary bank regulation is ultimately the problem of regulating universal banks, which creates unintended consequences for the commercial banking side of the house. And contemporary central banks must grapple with the noise created by non-banking business in the transmission mechanism between monetary policy and commercial bank credit creation. The path from monetary policy to credit creation is more complicated and meandering than ever, with adverse consequences for economic growth and the control of inflation.

Complementarities and Competition in Banking and Capital Markets Business

In Chapters 4 and 5, we introduced objectives and constraints for financial intermediaries and commercial banks as means of characterizing their behavior. The constraints are the interesting part because the objectives (maximize profit) are simple. They define the nature of each institution's opportunity set and actions that each must take to remain viable. Now we want to understand what happens when those objectives and constraints are combined in a single entity. Combining the constraints is the more difficult question. If each of the constraints were independent, we could simply aggregate them and see where the combined constraints lead us. In this case, however, some of the constraints depend on each other.

Previously, we considered the distribution of equity achieved by financial intermediaries in the capital markets to be *given* when commercial banks considered their opportunity set. Before a project could be bankable, it had to be investable. With a universal bank actor, investability and bankability can be achieved simultaneously. And indeed, it is not unusual to see capital raising transactions combined with the approval of new credit lines.

In addition, we assumed that financial intermediaries and commercial banks were operating in essentially different spheres. If an intermediary connected an investment project to savings, that would not affect a commercial bank's ability to connect the same project to bank credit. In a universal bank, however, there are multiple near-equivalent ways in which a project may be funded. Consider a few examples. Corporate borrowers are relatively indifferent between a covenant-light term loan from a bank and privately placed debt. A mortgage can be carried on the balance sheet of a bank or sold to a special purpose vehicle (SPV) funded by debt investors. The interest rate risk of the mortgage can be managed by the bank or transferred to the capital markets with an amortizing interest rate swap. The ability to create near-equivalent investment exposures through the discipline of *financial engineering* allows project funding and risk to shift between banks and capital markets according to their relative profitability for universal banks.

Interactions between the banking and capital markets sides of universal banks can be complementary or competitive in the determination of investable and bankable projects. Banking and intermediation are both information businesses. Because relevant information is dispersed, costly to obtain, and private once discovered, synergies may exist between the information gathering operations of banking and capital markets businesses. When they do, a project becomes investable and bankable at the same time because of information spillovers, and not because of a universal bank's own motivations to create a bankable or investable project with the help of the other side of the house. At the same time, however, legal restrictions on information sharing across business lines limit potential synergy.

The competitive perspective emphasizes financial engineering. Through that lens, the universe of investable and bankable projects is mostly given and highly overlapping. Thus, whether a project is funded by bank money or savings is largely a question of the relative pricing offered by commercial banks and financial intermediaries. When these functions are united in a universal bank, each side of the house cannibalizes some opportunities for the other side.

In a system of universal banks, aggregate constraints on loanable funds and credible claims on savings apply. An economist's job is to identify the price signals (or other coordination mechanisms) that will lead individual profit-maximizing universal banks to achieve an aggregate outcome which efficiently creates deposit money and allocates aggregate savings. If the pricing of funding alternatives is common knowledge and the sets of investable and bankable projects overlap, then we would expect funding to be drawn from capital markets or bank credit creation according to risk-adjusted prices. An inefficient allocation would occur only if prices or risk assessments were unreliable. However, it is also possible that bankable and investable projects do not overlap. The conditions leading to equity and credit rationing are quite different, as we pointed out in Chapters 4 and 5, and to conceive of banks as just another investor armed with cheap deposit funding is to miss banks' special role and the nature of bankable projects.

For us, an efficient allocation of aggregate savings boils down to a simple question. Are the savings forming the equity of the commercial banking system being used to subordinate risks taken by firms and households in asset and capital markets, or is the equity of firms and households being used to subordinate the risks underwritten by the commercial banking system? Efficiency in the allocation of aggregate savings depends on the desired allocation of risk between the banking system and the "real" economy. In our view, keeping risk in the real economy is the better option from the perspective of monetary production and economic growth.[1] In recent years, the tendency has been rather to use the equity of the banking system to absorb risk taking in the real economy.

In the next three sections we describe three mechanisms for shifting risk between banks and capital markets which blur the boundaries between their businesses and distort the allocation of aggregate savings. We also explain what we mean by subordination.

Risk Transformation in Securitization Markets

Beginning in the 1990s and gaining momentum in the 2000s, capital market savings were increasingly used to purchase loans originated by banks in a process known as securitization. In a securitization, a sponsor sets up a firm for the sole purpose of purchasing financial assets. The firm, known as an SPV, is funded by issuing debt to investors, while a minimal amount of equity is contributed and retained by the sponsor. The SPV uses its funds to purchase credit assets like mortgage loans, credit card receivables, loans financing mergers, and so on, which become the sole sources of cash flow supporting the payments due on its debt. Hence, the debt is known as an "asset-backed security," or under similar names like collateralized loan obligations (CLOs) or commercial- and residential mortgage-backed securities (CMBS and RMBS).

Securitization appears to contradict our foundational claims. When capital markets funding entails real resource costs (drawing from a finite pool of savings) and bank funding is created out of nothing, why would it ever be more efficient to fund loans in the capital markets? Without appealing to regulatory constraints, we see two potential explanations. First, the *risk transformation potential* of securitization might create opportunities for banks to selectively shed and retain certain lending risks, or to hedge the risk of fully funded loans on their balance sheets. Second, a wave of excessive credit creation elsewhere in the world may have created a surplus of *ex post* savings, making the opportunity cost of using savings artificially low.[2] Given the role of capital markets in segmenting investment opportunities into high, low, and no-risk savings products, an inflow of savings that outruns the ability of intermediaries to identify risky investment opportunities could spike demand for low- and no-risk savings products. We focus on risk transformation in the following sections and defer our discussion of artificially cheap savings to Chapter 13.

Securitization generally results in risk transformation. Individual loan assets purchased by SPVs produce streams of principal and interest payments which are pooled in an asset-backed security.[3] While these payments may simply be passed through to investors on a pro-rata basis (creating a "passthrough security"), the sponsor of a securitization can alternatively exercise discretion in distributing those streams to investors by designing debt claims whose principal and interest flows differ from those of the underlying assets.[4] For example, claims on a $100 million pool of credit risk-free loans paying fixed interest of 6% can be split into two equally sized sets of bonds, with set A receiving a floating interest rate per some reference index and set B receiving 6% *plus* the difference between 6% and the reference index. If the reference index is 5%, then set A earns 5% and set B earns 7%. The total amount of interest paid by the loan pool is equal to the total amount of interest distributed to investors, but the two sets of investors now have opposite exposures to the reference rate. By simply changing the definition of the interest rate earned by investors, the sponsor of the securitization has transformed the interest rate risk of the loan pool, transferring risk from one group of investors to the other.[5]

A common and more general technique for risk transformation in securitization is the assignment of payment priorities among investors. A priority of payments establishes a sequence in which investors are paid, with each payment in the sequence occurring only if previous claims in the sequence have been paid in full. An investor is "senior" in the payment priority if they are further ahead in the sequence than other investors, who are "junior." Junior investors are said to *subordinate* their payment rights to those of senior investors. Separate payment priorities can be defined for principal and interest payments.

By assigning priorities to the receipt of principal, securitizations can shorten or extend the time frame over which investors realize cash flows from their investments. Changing the period over which payments are received changes investors' exposure to interest rates. Investments which wait longer to receive principal are more sensitive to movements in interest rates. Thus, interest rate risk is transferred from senior to junior investors.

Principal payment priorities also transfer credit risk from senior investors to junior investors. When credit losses on pooled loans occur, they are charged against investors' principal claims in reverse order of priority, so that exposure to credit risk runs contrary to the priority of payments. Senior investments in securitizations thus amplify the credit risk faced by junior investors, which must be compensated by higher expected rates of return.

The risk transformation achieved by securitization allows the sponsor to serve multiple investor clienteles. Residuals and junior tranches offer higher returns and higher risk, making them high-monitoring intensity investments suitable for well-informed investors.[6] Low-risk inner tranches are comparable to other corporate debt securities in terms of information intensity. And at the senior end, where information-insensitive tranches have vanishingly small risk, the most senior tranches can be sold to MMFs and become the basis for money-like claims.[7] Because securitized assets are generally secured loans, a securitization produces a very high proportion of low- and no-risk savings vehicles with minimal high-risk counterparts. The sponsor, for their part, usually retain a small "residual" investment in the securitization which is paid only after all other investors have been paid in full.[8]

Such financial engineering allowed securitization to become an influence on the money supply. Senior securitization tranches can be designed to have the characteristics of other money market instruments, with standard payment schedules, short maturities, and a bit of extra interest as sweetener to compete for a place in an MMF portfolio. Entire warehouses of loans ready for securitization can be funded with short-term money market instruments ("asset-backed commercial paper") which are also ultimately funded by MMF investors.

Risk Transfer Contracts

As an alternative or a complement to subordination, guarantees from a third party may significantly reduce investors' credit risk in a securitization. Such guarantees are generically known as credit enhancements. The availability of a credit enhancement depends on the ability of an entity with superior credit to take on the obligations of another entity when the latter entity defaults. When credit enhancement contracts can be written, credit risk is transferred from the holder of the enhancement to the guarantee provider.

Credit enhancements come from the government or from entities believed to enjoy government-like creditworthiness. The government's ability to pay is never in doubt due to its money creation powers. Private providers of credit enhancements rely on the judgment of credit rating agencies to bolster their claims of superior creditworthiness. However, because all credit risk evaluations involve an irreducible amount of subjectivity, and the ability of private entities to raise funds from asset liquidations may be compromised, private credit enhancements lack the ironclad quality of a government guarantee.

For an investor, a credit-enhanced structure makes an investment claim—or some part of it—equivalent to a claim on the government, at least with respect to the risk of non-payment. Assets with this quality are monetizable in that the payment of the claim is not in doubt. Accordingly, a credit enhancement monetizes a claim which would otherwise be risky and subject to all restrictions pertaining to the domain of investability.

The force of credit enhancements is felt most fully in the U.S. system of housing finance. Residential mortgage-backed securities (RMBS) are issued by the Federal National Mortgage Association ("Fannie Mae") and the Federal Home Loan Mortgage Corporation ("Freddie Mac"), so-called Government-Sponsored Enterprises (GSEs) that have been under the conservatorship of the Federal Housing Finance Authority (FHFA) since 2008, as well as the Government National Mortgage Association ("Ginnie Mae"), an agency of the U.S. government. Fannie Mae, Freddie Mac, and Ginnie Mae make a large subset of mortgages—"conforming" mortgages—monetizable as agency mortgage pass-through bonds and more complex mortgage derivatives collectively known as agency RMBS. The Federal Home Loan Bank (FHLB) system issues bonds to fund lending to banks with high concentrations of residential mortgage loans. The bonds are not obligations of the U.S. government, but it is believed that the government would ultimately guarantee FHLB bonds, allowing the FHLBs to lend freely and act as a shadow lender of last resort. The Federal Housing Administration, Veterans Administration, and Department of Agriculture issue further guarantees to "government" mortgage borrowers with less initial capital of their own. Government flood and disaster insurance programs guarantee the value of housing collateral. Each guarantee severely reduces or eliminates the credit risk of investing in agency RMBS, based on the presumption or legislative requirement that the government will create whatever money is necessary to redeem the claim. The only risks that remain for agency RMBS are related to changes in interest rates and the borrowers' right to prepay mortgage principal.

Non-agency RMBS grew rapidly prior to the GFC. An important factor in that rapid growth was the availability of credit enhancements for "non-conforming" mortgages provided in the private mortgage insurance (PMI) market. For an insurance premium, PMI or "credit wrap" providers known as monolines would stand ready to pay shortfalls of principal and interest.[9] Such firms failed, of course, because they underpriced the risk of non-payment. However, their AAA credit ratings allowed them to act for a time as if they had government-like financial strength and were instrumental in allowing more mortgage lending to migrate from bank balance sheets to capital markets, accelerating the trend created by government agency and GSE credit enhancements.

To an important but lesser extent, government guarantees also paved the way for capital market investment in student loans (through Sallie Mae, now Navient) and small business lending (through the Small Business Administration). More recently, the tax incentives provided for investment in residential solar installations have enabled the issuance of solar asset-backed securities.

This thaumaturgical touch of the government moves lending business from the domain of banking to the domain of the capital markets. We are unaware of similar opportunities for banks to transfer loan-level credit risk to an outside insurance provider.[10] The peculiar residence of credit enhancements in the capital markets may explain the rapid growth of securitization markets, despite their costliness in terms of savings. The question has unfortunately received little attention. On the one hand, such guarantees support demands for risk-free savings vehicles. On the other hand, they displace banks as providers of risk-free savings vehicles and providers of credit over and above the pool of existing savings. We would expect such guarantees to operate in a world with surplus savings or, at any rate, a world in which savings fail to find risky projects with greater net present value (NPV).

Though securitizations create opportunities to transform and reallocate credit and interest rate risk, they introduce a liquidity management problem. When payments on the underlying assets are delayed but still expected, the payments must be advanced to the SPV so that principal and interest on bonds can be paid on schedule.[11] Because SPVs usually do not have excess cash laying around to cover such contingencies, they rely on banks as advancing agents, availing the SPV and its investors of banks' credit creation powers.[12] In effect, investors in a securitization transfer their liquidity risk to the banking system.

More broadly, the banking side of a universal bank generally stands ready to support its capital markets business with short-term lines of credit. Such credit lines finance "warehouses" where loans and leases await securitization, finance the purchase of an initial public offering of securities from an issuer before it is distributed to investors, and offer "daylight overdrafts" to repo markets while overnight repurchase agreements are renewed for the following day. Each of these operations transfers liquidity risk from capital markets to banks.

Derivatives are a more general form of contracting risk transfer. A derivative is a contract between two parties to exchange a pre-defined payoff, where the payoff is derived from the price of another asset. Most derivatives are made up of smaller building blocks known as forwards and options. In a forward contract, two parties agree to exchange an asset at a future date at a fixed price. The payoff of the forward depends on the difference between the fixed price and the realized price of the asset on the future date. In an option contract, one party grants the other party the right (but not the obligation) to buy or sell an asset on a future date at a fixed price in exchange for a premium. The payoff of the option depends on whether the right is valuable on that future date, and if so, the difference between the fixed price and the realized price of the asset.

Interest rate swaps are bundles of forward contracts where parties agree to exchange floating interest rate payments for fixed interest rate payments on a series of future (usually evenly spaced) dates. They are usually rationalized by asserting that some market participants have a comparative advantage in borrowing at fixed or floating interest rates. We might modify this slightly to say that some market participants are better at hedging interest rate risk than others. For our purposes, an interest rate swap transfers fixed interest rate risk to another party. It can be a mechanism for modifying the interest rate risk faced by banks, or for matching fixed-rate collateral to floating-rate bonds in a securitization, among other applications.

Despite their name, credit default swaps (CDS) are more like options and bear more than a passing resemblance to insurance contracts. In exchange for a premium, the protection buyer in a CDS obtains the right to receive the difference between a bond's par value and its defaulted value, in the event of default by a specified borrower.[13] A CDS thus transfers credit risk from the protection buyer to a protection seller. Its zone of application depends on the extent of the bond market. CDS may be written on corporate bonds and the bonds issued in securitizations. Securitized credit risk is transferrable credit risk—not only for the sponsor of the securitization but also for the investor.

Derivatives transfer risks within and across economic sectors. With derivatives, the ultimate holder of an economic risk need not be the entity that originated the risk. Derivatives are capital markets business because the risk management of derivative positions depends on the ability to trade efficiently in markets for the assets underlying the payoffs of the derivatives. Such trading generally leads to an accumulation of positions in the underlying asset.

Like securitizations, derivative contracts trade interest rate and credit risk for market and liquidity risk. Derivative contracts are revalued from day to day, leading to interim settlements of the contract. These interim settlements reduce the exposure of the holder of a valuable derivative to the risk of non-payment by their counterparty. The parties to the contract exchange margin money to mitigate counterparty credit risk. The need to exchange margin creates liquidity risk for holders of derivatives with negative market values. In volatile markets, temporary demands for liquidity can be considerable. A dealer bank's access to on-demand liquidity from the commercial banking business can once again lead to complacency about the liquidity risks assumed in derivatives trading.

Bank Lending to Nonbank Financial Institutions

A third activity blurring the boundary between banks and capital markets is the extension of bank credit from commercial banks to financial intermediaries. Such bank loans may be intercompany loans within a universal bank, or loans from a universal bank to a nonbank financial intermediary not housed in a BHC or FHC structure.

In our discussion of bank lending, we emphasized the existence of a credible claim to future surpluses. For a nonbank financial institution, such future surpluses may arise from a reorganization of the institution's business—investing in information technology, say, or opening new locations closer to the institution's clientele. Such investments can be analyzed under normal rubrics, applying the NPV criterion or similar frameworks. However, we are concerned with loans to nonbank financial institutions where the future surplus arises from the revaluation of investments in financial assets.

The financial intermediary balance sheet presented in Chapter 3 portrayed the intermediation business as a collection of assets funded by household and corporate savings. The profit available to the intermediary arises from the ability to collect fees on the appreciation of assets held on behalf of savings providers. Intermediaries usually invest on a fully funded basis. The money used to purchase shares of stock for a mutual fund, for example, comes entirely from savings placed with the intermediary.

Bank lending to financial intermediaries allows the intermediary to purchase more assets than their funding will permit by augmenting their resources with bank credit. Since the returns on the investment made by the intermediary will repay the bank loan, the bank effectively underwrites the same investment. Banks are willing to do this if the other claimholders on the intermediary will subordinate themselves to the bank's claim, reducing the risk of the bank loan and amplifying the risk held by the other investors. The intermediary favors this situation because amplified risk creates the potential for greater fee earnings, while the downside from failure remains the same.

Bank loans to intermediaries are risky. First, they assume that some return on investment is sufficiently assured to support the loan, which means that the risk of loss is bounded from below. Second, the bank may already be lending to the issuer of the security to be purchased by the intermediary. A loan to the intermediary would then be junior to the bank's original loan.

Nevertheless, a great deal of lending takes place between banks and financial intermediaries. At the time of writing, private equity (PE) firms are drawing "NAV loans" secured by the value of their investments in portfolio companies. PE firms also draw from subscription credit facilities backed by the funding commitments of their limited partners. Firms that took over subprime credit card lending from banks when it was banned by the Dodd-Frank Act have funded their businesses from bank credit. Any number of financial technology ("fintech") companies has attempted to replicate some part of bank lending business without actually being a bank, but while benefitting from bank credit. And of course universal banks themselves extend loans from the banking side of the house to the capital markets side for multiple purposes.

It is not particularly easy to see the growth of lending to all financial intermediaries in official statistics. Because PE and venture capital (VC) vehicles are organized predominantly as partnerships, lending to PE and VC funds appears as loans to the non-corporate nonfinancial business sector, where it is lumped in with all other lending to non-corporate, nonfinancial business.[14] However, we can see that bank lending to the sector grew from 20% of all commercial loans in the early 1990s to 30% in the early 2000s and 40% by 2005. Since then, the sector has accounted for roughly 35–45% of all commercial loans. Similarly, family offices, which can invest like PE, VC, and/or hedge funds, are likely mixed in with the household sector. The household sector quickly grew from about 5% of all commercial loans to roughly 10% in 2009 and has remained at that level ever since. Discerning a trend in lending to finance companies and broker-dealers is more difficult.[15]

The problems of lending to financial intermediaries are compounded when they take place within universal banks. As with other intercompany transactions, intercompany loans do not benefit from market pricing, but some kind of transfer pricing is generally required for managerial control and tax purposes.[16] While funds transfer prices are scrutinized by regulators, there is no guarantee that such pricing will recognize all the risk factors implicated in the loan, or that unpriced risk factors will be observable to regulators.

Risk Management in Universal Banks

Why should we care about the financing of bankable projects wandering from banks to capital markets? The theme we have emphasized from the beginning is the economic salience of the difference between bank credit creation and financial intermediation. Bank credit is bounded only by the existence of bankable projects, whereas financial intermediation and capital market activity are bounded by the existence of investable projects and the finiteness of aggregate savings. In the presence of a bankable project, the funding source that is not subject to a resource limitation should be the less expensive, more efficient option—every time. Either some sleight of hand is at work in securitization, or its presence is a sign that bank credit has become costly for reasons unrelated to the usual constraints on bankability.

If savings are scarce, securitization creates additional uses for savings that compete with and potentially crowd out other uses of savings, especially those for which bank financing is ill-suited. Another way of saying this is that low-risk securitization, like government borrowing, crowds out risky capital projects that would otherwise be financed in capital markets. Securitization is a more expensive way of doing what banks do because the choice between bank lending and capital markets lending is not merely a choice between intermediaries. Accordingly, it falls afoul of Occam's razor—it is vain to do with more what can be done with less—at first blush. We tend to think that agency MBS fall into this category.

If, on the other hand, savings are not scarce—there is actually too much savings chasing too few investment opportunities—securitization may play a deflationary role for financial asset prices. Were an immense quantity of savings competing for limited investment opportunities, asset prices would be bid up, real interest rates would fall, and risk premiums on risky assets would be compressed. Absorbing those extra savings in purpose-made low-risk assets would keep real interest rates, expected returns, and asset prices in line. At the limit, nearly riskless assets support the production of more money from savings. This dynamic seems to have operated well in the late 1990s and early 2000s, before riskier mortgage structures and loans proliferated in 2004–2006 to keep the party going.

Somewhat more subtly, large securitization markets signal the cannibalization of bankable projects by the capital markets. When bankable projects are funded in securitizations, the banking system loses some of the base against which it can lend and grow the money supply. Lending opportunities must be found elsewhere, and the availability of enough subordination from equity investors can make at least some segment of a risky project bankable. We believe this dynamic is at work in the growth of lending to nonbank financial intermediaries.

The impact of securitization on banking will thus be very context-specific, and we will offer thoughts on this later in the book. Either way, though, we have brought into relief the macroeconomic salience of the moving boundary between banking and capital markets. Movements in the boundary distort the sets of bankable and investable projects available to the economy. They potentially sequester investable funds in low-risk projects that would otherwise be bankable and challenge banks to engineer bankable projects from riskier stuff.

The blurring of the boundaries between banks and capital markets also raises the question of risk management in universal banks and the ultimate distribution of risk in the economy. Risk in a universal bank, as in the economy at large, is like air in a balloon—you can move it around by squeezing, but you cannot get rid of it. You can change its form, turning interest rate and credit risk into market risk, market risk into liquidity risk, and so on. And ultimately, all these risks reduce to risks to capital or liquidity risk in universal banks and risks to household wealth in the aggregate.

In Chapter 5, we discussed the economic origins of credit and liquidity risk in the banking business, and the role of capital in absorbing credit risk and preventing its metamorphosis into liquidity risk via a potential bank run. A commercial bank holds capital and liquidity not only to assure its continued existence, but also to preserve the moneyness of its liabilities. The money supply, which is predominantly issued by banks, depends closely on the adequacy of bank risk management.

Putting a commercial bank in a holding company with a capital markets business makes bank capital and liquidity available to the capital markets business, potentially on preferential terms through favorable transfer pricing. To avoid disrupting bank risk management in the service of the money supply, bank capital and liquidity must now be adequate to manage the risks imposed on the bank by the capital markets side of the business. The international system of bank regulation developed through the Basel Committee on Banking Supervision is focused on ensuring that capital markets businesses—what they call the "trading book" of a universal bank—are sufficiently well-capitalized to avoid jeopardizing the liabilities of the "banking book" managed by the commercial bank.

While we will examine the merits of the current bank regulatory regime in some detail in Chapter 8, it is worth asking at this point whether it is most sensible to regulate universal banks as universal banks. Would it not make sense to have one corporate form and regulatory regime for the banking book, and separate ones for the trading book, where the resources of one would not be available to ensure the compliance of the other? Indeed, before passage of the Gramm-Leach-Bliley Act (GLBA) in 1999, much of banks' current trading book business could not reside within a Bank Holding Company structure in the United States. Passage of the GLBA was bolstered by arguments about the complementarity of information discovered within banks and capital markets. Now, however, the experience of universal banking, the complexity of regulating such institutions, and—in what we see as our primary contribution to the debate—the questionable efficiency with which universal banks allocate global savings each offer counterpoints to these arguments. We may need to break up large banks not only because they are large, and not only because they are too big to fail, but also because they are two fundamentally different businesses which transform and distort financial risk without mitigating it. It may be that no combination of governance, competition, and regulation can simultaneously achieve the outcomes we want in the monetary sphere, the banking system, and the capital markets.

Notes

1. "One frequent objection to higher bank capital requirements is that some risky lending and trading activities will migrate to nonbanks—such as brokers, mutual funds and insurers—without making the financial system safer. However, not all these activities are best funded by bank deposits that are subject to runs and panics, so some of these shifts do make the overall system safer." Stephen Cecchetti and Kim Schoenholtz, "Ignore the bank lobby, regulators. It's high time for banking reform," *Washington Post*, 10 January 2024. We completely agree that risky lending and trading activities should move

outside the banking system, but the confusion about what "banks" do and the locus of bank capital is plain from the quotation.

2. The opportunity cost of savings is the real interest rate. We know that real interest rates were close to zero throughout the 2000s.
3. It is also possible to distinguish scheduled principal from unscheduled or "voluntarily prepaid" principal.
4. The process is generally known as financial engineering.
5. The transfer of risk is even more obvious when the tranches are defined to be "interest-only," yielding "IO" and "inverse-IO" bonds. The same idea applies when dividing claims over prepaid principal. The sponsor creates a "planned amortization class" with predictable amortization characteristics and a "companion bond" which absorbs unscheduled principal receipts that do not conform to the planned amortization schedule. See Fabozzi, F.J. (ed.) (2006). *The Handbook of Mortgage-Backed Securities*, 6e. McGraw-Hill for more of these typical structures.
6. The investors may even have the ability to intervene in the management of the loan pool. For example, the special servicers in commercial mortgage-backed securitizations have wide discretion in extending and restructuring loans to troubled borrowers.
7. Gorton, G. and Ordoñez, G. (2014). Collateral crises. *American Economic Review* 104 (2): 343–378.
8. Section 941 of the Dodd-Frank Act requires the sponsor to retain risk in the securitization, pursuant to rulemaking by the Securities and Exchange Commission.
9. The major players included FGIC, MGIC, and Radian.
10. However, synthetic risk transfers allow credit risk to be transferred on a portfolio basis.
11. If principal and interest are not paid on schedule, the bond is in default, which can trigger the default of other bonds in the same securitization. The decision to make advances is based on the belief that the underlying credit is good but temporarily off schedule for benign reasons. If the underlying credit were in doubt, the loan or lease would be considered defaulted and no advances would be made.
12. Securitization also depends on the banking system for underwriting and loan servicing. All the roles played by a bank in a securitization would normally be performed by a bank in garden-variety lending, without the need for further contracting, intermediate legal entities, or further coordination among disparate parties. Securitization may be said to reduce the aspects of lending that depend on credit creation to a minimum, while supporting

lending as much as possible from available savings. Securitization appears to proceed on the assumption that it is relatively expensive to use commercial bank balance sheet space and thus does so sparingly.
13. Technical complications: senior unsecured obligation, named obligor, etc.
14. The Flow of Funds statistics do not have a non-corporate financial sector.
15. Flow of Funds, Table L.215.
16. Tax authorities want to be sure that profits are not being shifted from high- to low-tax activities and jurisdictions without an underlying business purpose. The fitness of transfer pricing for this purpose or the effectiveness of authorities' enforcement are a separate question.

Part Two

A BROADER VIEW OF MONETARY POLICY

Where Part One of the book has been concerned with the microeconomic incentives underlying the creation of money and the financing of investment, as well as the macroeconomic salience of these forces in the aggregate, Part Two is devoted to understanding how official policy intervenes in the process of money creation to change incentives and outcomes. We refer to such policies as "monetary policy," though the name foreshortens the impact such interventions have on the financing of investment, the distribution of income and wealth, and economic growth in general. It would be more correct to speak of official interventions in the monetary economy.

Monetary policy is undertaken by multiple actors. Our account emphasizes the role of banking regulators and the government budget in creating monetary policy, alongside the central bank, the institution which is most usually credited with the mandate and wherewithal to regulate monetary conditions. A lack of attention to bank regulations and fiscal action leads to unrealistic expectations for what central bank policy can achieve and dissimulates the monetary impact of other official policies.

Our analysis of monetary policy in Part Two prepares the ground for proposals to reform the rules of the financial system in Part Three. The current mix of fiscal policy, central bank policy, and bank regulation being deployed in the United States is not sustainable. We will show in Part Two how the growth of bank credit has slowed, reducing the contribution of bank money to the aggregate money supply. The government is now left in the role of default liquidity provider, at considerable fiscal expense and risk to the government debt burden.

As we transition to discussions of policy and control in Part Two, it will be helpful to have some vocabulary outlining the elements of official action.[1]

The ultimate goals of monetary policy are achieved through a *monetary policy strategy*. A strategy entails a theoretical framework that connects *final target variables* like inflation, unemployment, and output to an economic variable over which the authorities can exert control. A monetary policy strategy thus depends on a *transmission mechanism* linking one or more control variables to final target variables. The transmission mechanism is generally elaborated with the aid of economic theory and observation. Given initial conditions and a theory of the transmission mechanism, policymakers can, in principle, adjust the control variables in a way that induces final target variables to move toward their desired values.

The control variables connected by the transmission mechanism to final target variables may not be directly accessible to manipulation by the authorities. Thus, we distinguish between cases in which control may be achieved directly through an authority's *operational target*, and those where it is achieved indirectly by the operational target's influence on an *intermediate target*. In the latter case, additional knowledge is needed to articulate the relationship between the operational and intermediate targets. The distinguishing feature of the operational target is its direct controllability by the authorities, with a minimum of noise or dependency on outside forces.

The authorities exert control over their operational target through an *operational framework*. Such a framework includes the *instruments* and *facilities* through which the authorities transact in order to implement policy. Instruments have their values set directly at the discretion of the authorities, while facilities operate passively at the option of counterparts, according to standing rules set by the authorities. *Monetary policy implementation* concerns the design of appropriate instruments and facilities and their use with a relevant population of counterparts comprising the monetary system to achieve the authorities' operational target.

We can easily fit the received wisdom about monetary policy into this framework. The relevant authority setting monetary policy strategy and implementing monetary policy is the central bank. The central bank's enabling legislation defines the final targets of monetary policy, but it is the remit of the independent central bank to articulate the theory linking those final targets to operational targets and to choose an operational framework to achieve its targets.

The preferred operational target for central bank policy is the overnight rate of interest on loans of reserves supplied by the central bank, known as the *interbank rate* or the Fed funds rate in the United States. This overnight rate is designated as the *policy rate*. Nearly, every major central bank describes the stance of monetary policy in terms of the target level for the policy rate. Control is exerted through *standing facilities* which allow banks to transact with the central bank at their initiative, *open market operations* in which the central bank buys and sells government debt at its own initiative to change the supply of reserves, and direct control over the *market for reserves* via reserve requirements and other non-price allocation rules. Each of these instruments allows the central bank to exert control over the policy rate by encouraging the market for reserve money to clear at the targeted value for the policy rate.

The dominant target of central bank policy is the rate of change in the price level, also known as the rate of *inflation*. For many central banks, there is little doubt that inflation is the *final* target—the European Central Bank (ECB), for example, has an inflation target written into its legislation. For other central banks like the Federal Reserve, a tension between prevailing economic orthodoxy favoring inflation targeting and enabling legislation which names multiple final targets produces ambiguity about whether inflation is an *intermediate* or a final target. This ambiguity is negotiated by more or less *ad hoc* claims by central banks about why moderate inflation is instrumental in achieving the central bank's other goals with respect to growth, unemployment, and so on.

Theories linking the short-term interest rate to inflation and other target variables are always evolving, but current monetary policy is informed in large part by neo-Keynesian extensions of DSGE models like those discussed in Chapter 1.[2] A crucial component of such models is the *reaction function* of the central bank, which describes how the central bank will adjust the policy rate in response to deviations of target variables from their targeted values. The presence of the reaction function is necessary for interest rates to be determined in such models. If interest rates were determined by other forces, the central bank's reaction function would be redundant.

The fundamental indeterminacy of interest rates in the absence of central bank policy is actually a very bold claim that flies in the face of our intuition about asset pricing. If the causality of neo-Keynesian models is to be taken seriously, asset prices follow central bank policy. When bond prices fail to fall into line with central bank policy, it is viewed by central bankers as an aberration—a lack of "credibility" on the part of the central bank—rather than a sign that bond markets discover interest rates all by themselves. As a result, new models allow for a splitting of the interest rate in which markets determine a *natural* rate of interest ("r-star") and the position of the central bank's policy rate relative to the natural rate reflects the stance of monetary policy.

In one very influential version of the central bank reaction function known as the *Taylor rule*, changes in the policy rate are a weighted sum of the deviations of inflation and output from their targets.[3] The equilibrium of the model requires economic agents to know how the central bank will react, so considerable effort is expended by the central bank in communicating its target values and providing guidance about how they will respond to future data. Indeed, such "forward guidance" can amount to a verbal interpolation of the reaction function when the central bank is less sure about how policy will react to the state of the economy, or when the central bank is less sure about how to measure the state of the economy. The proliferation of central bank verbiage and the resources expended to parse it suggest that the reaction function has become an unstable and diffuse construct.

Even so, the exact transmission mechanism(s) linking the policy rate to the wider economy are mostly unspecified in the models used by central banks to formulate policy decisions and therefore hotly debated by policymakers and researchers. Some of the leading candidates include the effects of interest rates on investment, consumption and international trade on one hand, and effects of net worth and bank lending on the other hand.[4] But when forced to make decisions, central bankers fall back on simpler models. One of the hangers-on from earlier times is the notion, captured in the Philips curve, that inflation arises from an excessive increase in wage demands. Through this lens, interest rate policy is transmitted to inflation outcomes via its impact on labor markets, putting central banks in the awkward position of stamping out any increase in the labor share of income not justified by recent productivity gains.

The received wisdom on monetary policy frames the strategy and implementation of monetary policy narrowly: monetary policy is what central banks do with certain instruments to force the policy rate to a desired level each day. Its purpose is to control the rate of growth in the price level through a mysterious and eclectic combination of guiding expectations, influencing credit conditions, and constraining nominal wage growth.

We would like to construe monetary policy more broadly, according to our view that the money supply is an effective intermediate target around which a coherent monetary policy strategy can be constructed. The exceedingly simple transmission mechanism linking the money supply to aggregate output is given by the equation of exchange, in which the main complication is to account for factors that affect money demand. The equation of exchange and related theories of money demand are the first analytical frameworks we present in Chapter 7.

The equation of exchange may also be disaggregated to account for differences in monetary conditions across sectors and strata of the economy, an area in which interest-rate based models struggle. Exerting control over the money supply implicates more authorities than the central bank and requires more instruments of control than those through which the central bank adjusts the quantity of reserve money. However, adjustments within a quantity-based operating framework are infrequent and easy to understand.

Targeting the supply of money focuses attention on the banking system. In a well-functioning monetary system, the banking system produces most of the money supply, broadly measured, and the growth rate of deposit money is the dominant influence in the supply of broad money. Previous attempts to control the quantity of deposit money focused on narrow monetary aggregates and relied on changes in the quantity of bank reserves to connect central bank operations to the balance sheet of the consolidated banking system.[5] These attempts were unsuccessful because many forms of deposit money were not subject to reserve requirements, and bank customers switched to these other forms aggressively in an environment of very high interest rates. Clearly, a better measure of the money supply and more instruments than the quantity of reserves are needed to regulate monetary growth.[6] In Chapter 7, we discuss improvements to the measurement of broad money.

Interest rate policy does not achieve control of broad money by other means, and theoretical attempts to link interest rate policy to the banking system are unconvincing. In one view, the supply of reserve money directly affects banks' propensity to lend, which only makes sense if you believe banks are intermediaries of loanable funds or otherwise constrained by the supply of reserve money.[7] Another view posits that interest rates change the net worth of banks by revaluing their asset portfolios.[8] While net worth is a more compelling candidate for constraining banks' lending activity, the so-called "bank capital" channel ignores the impact interest rates may have on bank liabilities, which are longer-lived than their contractual maturity suggests. In any event, we invite the reader to reconcile the noisy growth rates in the broad money supply presented in Chapter 7 to the persistent, low-frequency movements in the central bank policy rate from the 1980s to the present.

Because most of the money supply is produced by the banking system, the greatest current influence on the expansion of the money supply is the regime of bank regulation, which we discuss in Chapter 8. The principal features of contemporary bank regulation are (a) requirements to hold a minimum level of equity capital against the bank's risk-weighted assets, (b) to hold a minimum supply of liquid assets against a bank's worst-case outflows, and (c) to hold a collection of liabilities which is not overly vulnerable to run risks. We refer to (a) as capital requirements and (b) and (c) as liquidity requirements. Under the prevailing regime, the limiting factors for bank balance sheet growth are not reserve balances but the supply of equity capital and the composition of bank portfolios. Bank balance sheet growth is limited not only by the regulatory risk weights constraining their capital budgets but also by pressures to hold significant liquidity portfolios and limits on their unweighted leverage.[9]

The constraints of the regulatory regime directly affect deposit money growth. Each accounting period, banks' net profits are partially retained as equity and otherwise distributed to investors. Retained earnings add to the bank's capital, giving the bank a budget which can be allocated among multiple categories of risk-weighted assets, subject to other regulatory and economic constraints (including the availability of bankable projects). To the extent that the banking system "spends" the additions to its regulatory capital by underwriting new loans, deposit money grows. New lending competes with other potential additions to risk-weighted assets based on their relative returns on regulatory capital.

Whereas bank regulation is a dominant influence on the rate at which the money supply expands, fiscal policy is a substantial influence on how that growth is distributed. As we explain in Chapter 9, fiscal policy puts money into circulation according to the government's pattern of expenditures and takes money out of circulation according to tax policy and the contribution of various sectors to funding the government budget deficit. Though the aggregate impact of fiscal policy is flat, its uneven impact across sectors and strata of the economy reallocates the money supply between sectors in a meaningful way. We will show how the pattern of financial claims within and across sectors modulates the impulse of government spending to determine its sectoral impact.

Bank regulation and fiscal policy thus play important roles in controlling the growth and distribution of the money supply. Adjustments to regulatory and fiscal parameters thus qualify as potential instruments of monetary policy. The received wisdom disqualifies such instruments from the domain of monetary policy by definition because they are not controlled by the central bank, and because they change infrequently and irregularly compared to the daily transactions of a central bank. We think it is a mistake to restrict the domain of monetary policy to what a central bank can achieve through control of its own balance sheet. Instead, we want to examine the influence the central bank may exert on a tactical basis, subject to the strategic constraints imposed by the bank regulatory regime and the impact of fiscal policy.

In Chapter 10, our discussion of central bank policy will focus on the destruction of central banks' longstanding operational framework by the expansion of GFC lending facilities and the post-crisis practice of quantitative easing. Having created a world in which reserves were no longer scarce, central banks have needed a new operational framework to re-establish control over short-term interest rates.

In Chapter 10, we suggest that an underappreciated feature of post-crisis monetary policy was the steady rate of broad money growth realized from 2011 to 2019. Consistent broad money growth was achieved through a combination of large-scale asset purchases by the central bank and the recovery of bank lending, particularly in real estate and consumer-focused areas. Large-scale asset purchases put money directly into the hands of the nonbank public by monetizing government debt and agency RMBS, while the recovery in bank lending was engineered through restrictions on banks' ability to distribute their earnings to shareholders.

There can be no doubt that repeated post-crisis interventions to reduce interest rates have severely distorted the prices of real and financial assets while entrenching fierce resistance to rate increases, delaying the return of policy rates to prudent levels. In combination with quantitative easing, post-GFC interest rate policy has led to the deterioration of interbank lending markets. It has also become extremely expensive, as central banks lose money on every unit of their enormous balance sheets. Thus our task in Chapter 10 and Part Three is to plan, as much as possible, an exit from the post-QE interest rate targeting regime and a transition to a policy based on targets for the growth and distribution of the money supply.

The success realized by inadvertently using bank capital as an instrument of monetary policy during and after the period of QE suggests its more general usefulness as an instrument of control in a quantity-based policy framework. We can imagine a model in which bounds on the distribution of bank earnings work in concert with regulatory risk weights to control the rate at which the broad money supply expands. In Part Three, we will elaborate such a framework, as well as structural reforms to bank lending and capital markets to ensure that broad money growth is as economically neutral as possible.

Notes

1. We draw on the framework in Bindseil, U. (2004). *Monetary Policy Implementation: Theory – Past – Present.* Oxford University Press: Chapter 1.
2. For example, Christiano, L.J., Eichenbaum, M., and Evans, C.L. (2005). Nominal rigidities and the dynamic effects of a shock on monetary policy. *Journal of Political Economy* 113 (1): 1–45 and Smets, F. and Wouters, R. (2007). Shocks and frictions in US business cycles: A Bayesian DSGE approach. *American Economic Review* 97 (3): 586–606.

3. Woodford, M. (2001). The Taylor rule and optimal monetary policy. *American Economic Review* 91 (2): 232–237 elevated Taylor, J.B. (1993). Discretion versus policy rules in practice. *Carnegie-Rochester Conference Series on Public Policy* 39: 195–214 to the status of a rule.
4. Boivin, J., Kiley, M.T., and Mishkin, F.S. (2011). How has the monetary transmission mechanism evolved over time? In: *Friedman and Woodford 2011*: 369–422.
5. We will discuss this idea of the "money multiplier" in Chapter 14.
6. Components of the money supply produced outside the banking system only complicate the matter further.
7. Bernanke, B.S. and Gertler, M. (1995). Inside the black box: The credit channel of monetary policy transmission. *Journal of Economic Perspectives* 9 (4): 27–48, Peek, J. and Rosengren, E. (1995) Is bank lending important for the transmission of monetary policy? An overview. *New England Economic Review* (November): 3–11.
8. Van den Heuvel, S. (2002). Does bank capital matter for monetary transmission? *Economic Policy Review* 8 (1), May, Peek, J. and Rosengren, E. (2010). The role of banks in the transmission of monetary policy. In: *The Oxford Handbook of Banking* (eds. A. Berger, P. Molyneux, and J. Wilson). Oxford University Press.
9. Limits on a bank's unweighted leverage limit the amount of assets with zero regulatory risk weight a bank can hold. Reserves and government bonds are two important examples.

Chapter 7

Analytical Frameworks and Basic Monetary Facts

This chapter is devoted to understanding the composition and measurement of the money supply and the connections between the quantity of money and aggregate economic activity. We will also review some data on the key postwar monetary developments in the United States.

We present two basic frameworks. First, the *equation of exchange* connects the supply of money to nominal expenditure in the economy over a given period, with the "velocity" of money indicating how many times the money supply turns over in facilitating the relevant quantity of expenditure. In the Cambridge expansion of the equation of exchange, the velocity of money is replaced with other factors determining the demand for money as a proportion of overall economic activity. Their directness and simplicity are virtues.

The second basic framework concerns the methodology for measuring the quantity of money. Drawing on research by William A. Barnett and his collaborators, we show how to construct an index of *aggregate monetary services* by properly aggregating the monetary liabilities issued by the central bank, the banking system, and nonbank financial intermediaries. Because different forms of money have different prices or "user costs," we cannot simply add them up to obtain a useful measure of the aggregate money supply. Instead, it is better to construct a Divisia quantity index of monetary services. When "simple sum" monetary aggregates are replaced with Divisia quantity indices, the demand for money is seen to be stable over long periods.[1] When money demand is stable, policy based on regulating the money supply can be successful.

In Chapter 3, we proposed a taxonomy of the components of money supply according to their sector of origin, i.e., the government, the commercial banking system, and "nonbank" sources including the financial system and the nonfinancial business sector. In this chapter, we decompose the Divisia indices to measure the relative contribution of each sector to the evolution of the money supply and to provide an initial orientation toward explaining the origins of important monetary developments. We will see that demand deposits and other liquid deposits dominate in explaining the evolution of monetary services, even in very large aggregates encompassing store-of-value money. We believe this evidence justifies our focus on banking regulation as the most important locus of monetary policy.

An advantage of the equation of exchange is the ability to disaggregate the identity in any way desired to capture money demand at the level of individual economic sectors and/or strata of income and wealth. To show the heterogeneity of money demand and supply within these smaller units, we construct Divisia monetary aggregates for sectors and strata of the United States economy. The analysis further motivates our interest in the distributional character of monetary conditions and indicates that neutrality across sectors and strata is a non-trivial goal for policy based on the quantity of money.

Because the banking system is overwhelmingly responsible for creating the aggregate money supply, we conclude the chapter by reviewing how commercial bank balance sheets have evolved over the past 75 years. We are interested in the growth rate and distribution of bank lending and the relative importance of bank lending in financing the household and nonfinancial business sectors. The data show that bank lending has been steadily displaced by capital markets funding, that the set of bankable projects against which the banking system creates the money supply has undergone a pronounced shift, and that lending is losing ground to securities and liquidity portfolios on bank balance sheets. Chapter 8 argues that changes in bank regulation are largely responsible for the secular trends observed in banking system data.

The Equation of Exchange and the Demand for Money

At the beginning of the twentieth century, economists were revisiting the classical quantity theory of money.[2] Though these theorists found the connection between the quantity of money and the price level conjectured by classical economists to be appealing, they sought a theory of the price level which was more attentive to agents' choices about holding money and less in thrall to the cost of producing gold. In addition, they sought to incorporate money circulating within the banking system into their theories, as bank money had become a significant medium for transacting business in the Anglo-American world.

We take as our starting point the "truism" presented by American economist Irving Fisher in his 1911 book *The Purchasing Power of Money*.[3] The truism, styled as the "equation of exchange," relates the quantity of money and its rate of turnover to the total value of transactions taking place in an accounting period:

$$MV = \sum pQ = PT$$

Here, M is the stock of money, p and Q are the prices and quantities of transactions taking place within the period, and V is the velocity of money, or its rate of turnover in exchange. Both p and Q can be aggregated into indices P and T capturing the aggregate price level and the real quantity of transactions.[4]

Importantly, Fisher recognized that bank deposits circulate in exchange for goods and services just as cash does. Writing M and M' for cash and deposits and V and V' for their respective velocities, Fisher expanded the equation of exchange to read

$$MV + M'V' = PT$$

Fisher's self-imposed task was to allocate recent changes in the price level to changes in transactional volumes, cash, deposits, and their respective velocities.

An advantage of starting from Fisher's accounting identity is to see that the equation of exchange can be disaggregated by economic sectors and income/wealth strata with straightforward redefinitions of the key terms. Thus, analyses based on the quantity of money can be adapted to study distributional aspects of money supply, so long as money, prices, and transaction quantities can be measured for each unit in a disaggregated schema. A disadvantage is that transaction quantities are not easily observed, leading many economists to replace T with real income Y.

The equation of exchange has been criticized on the grounds that the quantity of money is insufficiently defined, which makes velocity a noisy and unstable plug.[5] We take up the measurement of money aggregates in the next section. As for velocity, the relevant question is whether factors may be discovered that account for the demand for money, in addition to the price level and the volume of commerce transacted.

The Cambridge Equation

Contemporaneously with Fisher, the great Cambridge economists Alfred Marshall and A.C. Pigou had begun to think of the demand for money in terms of a variant of the equation of exchange

$$M^D = kPY$$

Here, aggregate income Y replaces the quantity index T, while the proportionality constant k may be interpreted as $1/V$. This "Cambridge equation" developed into a more fully fledged theory of the demand for real money balances when k was parameterized to depend on interest rates and expected inflation, for example, not least in the work of Keynes.[6]

The Cambridge equation shares with the equation of exchange the ambiguity of measuring M and introduces new ambiguity about Y. Marshall and Pigou vacillated between defining Y as income or wealth; Keynes implicitly used both. In the United States, Y is routinely interpreted as GDP, though it could just as easily be defined as gross output or expanded to account more explicitly for the offshore use of the dollar and other open economy transactions.

An issue faced by the Cambridge equation is the unobservability of M^D. Fisher worked with the money supply M^S. Thus, besides the complications created by the distinction between observable money supply and unobservable money demand for empirical work, the Cambridge framework must grapple with the possibility of disequilibrium ($M^D \neq M^S$) over various horizons, as well as the process by which equilibrium is approached. Progress on these questions is of a more recent vintage.

The Equation of Exchange in Economic Theory

Let us suppose that the equation of exchange represents a stable, long-run relationship between money demand, velocity, the price level, and real output. We work in logs so that changes in the variables can be interpreted as approximate percentage changes.

$$\ln M^D = \ln P + \ln Y - \ln V$$

Given our concerns about the stability of velocity, we parameterize velocity to depend on prices, output, and auxiliary variables $x_1, \ldots, x_n$. Then we can write a more general function for money demand as

$$\ln M^D = f(\ln P, \ \ln Y, \ x_1, \ldots, x_n)$$

We observe money supply M^S, not money demand. If the difference $\ln M^S - \ln M^D = \varepsilon$, then

$$\ln M^S = f(\ln P, \ \ln Y, \ x_1, \ldots, x_n) + \varepsilon$$

which is a relationship between observable variables we can conceivably estimate from data and test for stability.[7] Though we are interested in the money demand function f in its own right, we are perhaps *more* interested in what accurate, stable estimates of f can tell us about $\{\varepsilon_t\}$, a time series of deviations between money supply and money demand.

We would like to know how short-term deviations between money supply and demand affect changes in the money supply, the price level, and real output. Given a form for f and estimates $\{\hat{\varepsilon}_t\}$, we are interested in the system[8]

$$\Delta \ln M^S_t = \alpha_M \hat{\varepsilon}_t + \sum_{l=1}^{N} \beta_{Ml} \Delta \ln M^S_{t-l} + \sum_{l=1}^{N} \gamma_{Ml} \Delta \ln P_{t-l} + \sum_{l=1}^{N} \delta_{Ml} \Delta \ln Y_{t-l} + \cdots$$

$$\Delta \ln P_t = \alpha_P \hat{\varepsilon}_t + \sum_{l=1}^{N} \beta_{Pl} \Delta \ln M^S_{t-l} + \sum_{l=1}^{N} \gamma_{Pl} \Delta \ln P_{t-l} + \sum_{l=1}^{N} \delta_{Pl} \Delta \ln Y_{t-l} + \cdots$$

$$\Delta \ln Y_t = \alpha_Y \hat{\varepsilon}_t + \sum_{l=1}^{N} \beta_{Yl} \Delta \ln M^S_{t-l} + \sum_{l=1}^{N} \gamma_{Yl} \Delta \ln P_{t-l} + \sum_{l=1}^{N} \delta_{Yl} \Delta \ln Y_{t-l} + \cdots$$

The coefficients α_M, α_P, and α_Y show how money, prices, and output, respectively, react to short-term deviations of money supply from long-run money demand. The other coefficients $\{\beta, \gamma, \delta\}$ are distributed over lagged changes in money, prices, and output. Summing them over N lags gives the reaction of the dependent variable to a change in the independent variable after N periods. For example, $\beta_{P1} + \cdots + \beta_{PN}$ is the cumulative effect of a 1% change in money supply on the price level after N periods.

Within this system, we can entertain three conjectures about the causal ordering of money, prices, and output:

1. *Monetary growth* ($\Delta \ln M^S$) *causes changes in prices and output.* We expect $\sum \beta_{Pl} > 0$ and $\sum \beta_{Yl} > 0$, with output reacting more strongly to recent changes in money supply, while prices react after a longer delay. If monetary policy aims to correct past errors in money supply, we would further expect $\alpha_M < 0$. To eliminate feedback effects from prices and output to money supply, we would expect $\sum \gamma_{Ml}$ and $\sum \delta_{Ml}$ to be insignificant.

2. *Inflation* (Δ ln P) *causes changes in output and money demand.* Autonomous increases in prices originating in wage bargains (for example) lead to adjustments in real output via unemployment ($\sum \gamma_{YI} < 0$) and adjustments in the money supply motivated by a desire to stabilize real money holdings relative to income ($\sum \gamma_{MI} > 0$). Policy seeks to limit aggregate wage increases to the rate of labor productivity growth plus a target rate of inflation ($\sum \gamma_{PI} < 0$).
3. *Real economic growth* (Δ ln Y) *causes changes in money and prices.* Expansions and recessions are driven by the state of technology. People adjust their demand for real money balances to keep pace with real activity ($\sum \delta_{MI} > 0$), with inflation resulting from short-term mismatches between the supply and demand for money ($\alpha_P > 0$) and overheating pressures from output growth ($\sum \delta_{PI}$).

While these theoretical statements are crude, they illustrate the variety of interpretations that can be attached to the key variables in an accounting identity and serve to distinguish—albeit equally crudely—orientations to monetary theory which may be called (old) monetarist, neo-Keynesian, and neoclassical. The latter two varieties constitute the current mainstream in monetary economics.

It is not easy to settle the debate between alternative theories empirically. Tests about causality depend on the form of the money demand function f, the auxiliary variables $x_1, \ldots, x_n$, and the lag length employed. They require errors in the money supply to be zero on average, which depends in part on the conduct of monetary policy. Researchers have experimented with nonlinear forms for f, as well as methods that acknowledge uncertainty about f, for example.[9]

Our own view is a variant of the monetarist view, with three important twists. First, we question whether the GDP deflator and real GDP are the most reliable metrics for prices and output. Nominal GDP measures expenditure on value added in the economy. However, the economic transactions in an accounting period also include purchases of intermediate products which are sold from one firm to another for further processing before final sale. These inter- and intra-industry transactions are captured in the broader measure gross output (GO). Gross output also lends itself easily to disaggregation by industry, allowing the distribution of monetary conditions to be analyzed at the industry level. The relevant price indices would then be industry-level producer price indices.

Second, we allow the drivers of real output more causal heft in determining monetary production. In addition to being demanded for transactional purposes, money is demanded for financing purposes, as we argued in Chapter 5. Technological change lies at the root of investment demand as well as real output. Changes in financial system technology can also change the calculus of credit rationing, expanding the supply of bankable projects and enabling the money supply to grow.

Divisia Broad Money

The third twist we propose to the old monetarist view is to represent M as a *quantity index*. The components of broad money aggregates are clearly heterogeneous: holding currency or demand deposits has a larger opportunity cost in terms of foregone interest than a time deposit or a money market fund balance. Further, the prices and quantities of money supply components are easily observable. An aggregation method that accounts for differences in price across components of the money supply can potentially improve measurements of the quantity of money versus a method that merely sums nominal quantities.[10] Specifically, we propose to measure M using the Divisia broad money indices published at the Center for Financial Stability (CFS) by William A. Barnett, who has done more than anyone else to ground the indexation of monetary services in economic theory and make the corresponding index calculations operational.[11]

The Divisia broad money indices are named after Francois Divisia, an engineer and economist whose contribution to index number theory appeared in a remarkable series of articles published in 1925 and 1926.[12] Divisia elaborated his methodology in terms of an integral of changes over continuous time. The discrete-time counterpart to Divisia's line integral method, which better aligns with the periodic release of economic data, was rediscovered later and is known as a Törnqvist index. We will use the two names interchangeably.

Divisia's index number methods were first applied to the computation of monetary aggregates by William A. Barnett in a seminal 1980 paper, which applied the concept of a user cost price for durable goods developed by Dale Jorgenson.[13] Divisia quantity indices weight the percentage changes (or growth rates) in their components by their shares in expenditure to compute the percentage change (or growth rate) in aggregate quantity. Expenditure on a component of the money supply is a user cost price times a quantity. The quantity is the outstanding amount of each component in terms of the unit of account. The price is less obvious, but easy to grasp.

Economists have long pointed out that holding money is costly because the same balance could be earning a risk-free rate of return.[14] The existence of such "frictions" has led economists to question why people hold money at all, and to attribute the stubborn persistence of money balances to canny bankers or poorly informed users of money. By contrast, Divisia aggregation interprets the interest foregone on monetary liabilities as the price paid by users for their monetary services. Forms of money that are more acceptable as final payment and more liquid provide more monetary services and thus command higher prices: users give up more interest to hold them. Monetary liabilities with higher prices (greater moneyness) weigh more heavily in Divisia indices.

The Divisia indices define the price of each component of the money supply as the difference between a reference interest rate—the return earned by a risk-free investment with negligible liquidity—and the interest rate earned on the money balance. They measure the quantity of money that is *used for transactions*, separating it from the quantity of money held for short-term investment purposes.[15] Using a Divisia index in the equation of exchange answers the common criticism of the quantity theory that money need not exchange against the flow of goods and services measured by nominal expenditure. When Divisia money is used to represent the quantity of money in the equation of exchange, it reflects only that portion of the money supply that is held for transactional purposes or liquidity.

Divisia indexation also implies a subtle revision to the monetarist interpretation of the equation of exchange. Inflation is not caused by "too much money chasing too few goods and services," as Milton Friedman's pithy phrase tells us, but by the production of monetary services outrunning the flow of economic transactions. Because demand deposits and other liquid deposits contribute the predominant share of monetary services, their quantity and price are the prime suspects for inflation in a monetarist theory. However, it is not immediately obvious why deposits would be overproduced by the banking system, or why bank customers would not shift their balances to forms of money with lower user costs when carrying surplus balances.

Constructing Divisia Indices

Let us introduce some notation to fix ideas. Enumerate the components of a monetary aggregate A with indices (labels) i. Each component has a quantity q_i measured in the current unit of account and a price $p_i = R - r_i$, where R is the reference interest rate and r_i is the interest earned on balances.[16] Prices and quantities are dated at each period t, so we work in terms of p_{it} and q_{it}. In theory, R is the rate of return on pure capital. A good proxy for most countries is the rate on short-term bank loans.

Expenditure on the monetary services of a component in any period is the product $p_{it} q_{it}$. The *expenditure share* of that component in the monetary aggregate is

$$s_{it} = p_{it} q_{it} / \sum_{j \in A} p_{jt} q_{jt}$$

The large sigma with the set inclusion $j \in A$ means to sum over all the components j in the aggregate A. The denominator is indexed over j to avoid confusing *all* of the components in the denominator with the *selected* component *i* in the numerator. Clearly, $\sum_{i \in A} s_{it} = 1$ for any definition of A. However, different aggregates A will assign different expenditure shares to any component that is common to both aggregates. For computations, we use averages of expenditure shares in the current period and the immediately preceding period, denoted $\bar{s}_{it} = \frac{1}{2}(s_{it} + s_{i,t-1})$.[17]

Define growth factors $\ln f_{it} = \ln q_{it} - \ln q_{i,t-1}$ capturing changes in the natural logarithm of the quantity. Using the expenditure shares as weights, we obtain the *aggregate growth factor*

$$\ln g_t = \sum_{i \in A} \bar{s}_{it} \ln f_{it}$$

That is, the *growth of the monetary aggregate* in any period can be decomposed into a *weighted sum of nominal component growth factors*, where the weights represent the share of monetary services provided by the component. A component of the money supply contributes more to the growth of aggregate monetary services if it is large, grows more in nominal terms, and carries a greater user cost relative to other components in the aggregate.

If we define an initial date or "base period" $\tau = 0$ where the quantity of money is set to $M_0^A = 100$, the quantity index of the broad money aggregate A on date T, M_T^A, is obtained by summing growth over all dates $\tau = 1, \ldots, T$:

$$\ln M_T^A = \ln M_0^A + \sum_{\tau=1}^{T} \sum_{i \in A} \bar{s}_{i\tau} \ln f_{i\tau}$$

Applying the exponential function to both sides of the equation undoes the natural logarithm and turns sums into products, yielding the Törnqvist index

$$M_T^A = M_0^A \prod_{\tau=1}^{T} \prod_{i \in A} f_{i\tau}^{\bar{s}_{i\tau}}$$

as in Barnett (1980). The CFS Divisia broad money indices can be computed using the latter formula, with $M_0^A = 100$ in January 1967.[18]

A corresponding user cost price index may be derived from the quantity index and aggregate expenditure on monetary services using Fisher's factor reversal test formula, which defines the price index as $\Pi_t^A = \sum_{j \in A} p_{jt} q_{jt} / M_t^A$. Declining user costs of money would suggest that holders of monetary balances are better compensated for them over time.[19]

Comparing Divisia and Simple Sum Aggregates

The best way to grasp the consequences of Divisia aggregation is to look at the money supply data for some tangible aggregates. We examine three broader aggregates known as M2-ALL, M3, and M4M. Recalling the taxonomy of Chapter 3, Table 7.1 shows which monetary liabilities are included in each of the aggregates and the sector which is the source of each liability.[20]

Each of the aggregates considered includes cash, the universe of demandable and small savings deposits, and the universe of money market funds. An advantage of using broader indices is avoiding noise from the once-common practice of banks "sweeping" liquid deposit balances into savings and money market accounts overnight to reduce their reserve requirements.[21] Another is to show that trends in aggregate monetary services are reasonably robust to different definitions of broad money, so long as the aggregate is reasonably inclusive. The M3 aggregate adds large time deposits and repurchase agreements to M2-ALL, while M4M ("M4-minus") adds commercial paper but excludes Treasury bills, which are part of the M4 aggregate.

We would like to compare simple sum analogues of the Divisia aggregates to the Divisia quantity indices to evaluate their usefulness in characterizing monetary conditions. Though the Divisia aggregates largely correspond to simple sum aggregates previously defined by the Fed, the Fed has, since March 2006, ceased publication of aggregates broader than M2. As a result, we are forced to compute our own simple sum aggregates from the underlying data. Adding up quantities runs into one principal problem: MMFs and money

Table 7.1 Composition of selected Divisia broad money aggregates.

	M2-ALL	M3	M4M	Source
Cash	X	X	X	Government
Demand Deposits	X	X	X	Banks
Other Liquid/Checkable Deposits	X	X	X	Banks
Savings Deposits	X	X	X	Banks
Money Market Deposit Accounts	X	X	X	Banks
Retail Money Market Funds	X	X	X	Nonbanks
Small Time Deposits	X	X	X	Banks
Institutional Money Market Funds	X	X	X	Nonbanks
Large Time Deposits		X	X	Banks
Repurchase Agreements		X	X	Government
Commercial Paper			X	Nonbanks
Treasury Bills				Government

Table 7.2 Changes in Divisia and simple sum broad money aggregates, 1967–2023.

Time Period		Divisia Aggregates			Simple Sum Aggregates		
Beginning	End	M2-ALL	M3	M4M	M2-ALL	M3	M4M
1967:1	1973:12	6.4%	7.0%	7.1%	8.6%	10.2%	10.3%
1974:1	1991:12	5.1%	5.3%	5.7%	8.3%	8.5%	8.9%
1992:1	2007:9	5.6%	6.1%	6.0%	6.2%	7.5%	7.6%
2007:10	2010:12	3.8%	0.7%	−0.5%	4.9%	1.6%	−0.2%
2011:1	2019:12	5.5%	4.4%	4.2%	5.7%	4.5%	4.3%

market deposit accounts (MMDAs) hold large time deposits, repurchase agreements, commercial paper, and Treasury bills as part of their assets, but we do not have enough information on MMF holdings to eliminate those balances. Some degree of double-counting will be present in all of the simple sum aggregates, though it is probably lowest for M2-ALL, which includes only retail MMFs.

The Divisia weighting scheme makes an enormous difference relative to simple sum aggregation. Table 7.2 compares compound annual growth rates for Divisia and simple sum M2-ALL, M3, and M4M from the beginning of the Divisia data series in January 1967 through December 2019. (Though we generally consider data through the end of 2023, we have excluded the 2020–2023 period from these comparisons due to the volatility of post-COVID developments. We discuss our choice of periodization later.) It is immediately apparent that aggregate monetary services grow less rapidly than aggregate monetary balances for all definitions of broad money and all time periods. They also tend to be less volatile than their simple sum counterparts.

The reduction in growth rates from Divisia aggregation is more pronounced for broader monetary aggregates. Simple sum aggregates will erroneously attribute weights $s_{it}^{SS} = q_{it}/\sum_{j \in A} q_{jt}$ to each component of a monetary aggregate, which does not account for differences in user cost and weights each component according to its nominal balance. Increases in transactional balances like demand deposits will contribute more to the growth of Divisia aggregates, while store-of-value money like money market fund balances will receive less weight. Because broader monetary aggregates include more store-of-value money, the adjustment from Divisia aggregation is more material.

We further note the slowdown in monetary growth during the period of the GFC (2007:10–2010:12) for the broadest aggregates and the limited recovery thereafter. The growth of M2-ALL after the GFC is comparable to its pre-crisis rate, but the large time deposits, repurchase agreements, and commercial paper included in M3 and M4M have clearly contributed less to the growth of those aggregates than they did before the GFC. Notice also that the differences between Divisia and simple sum aggregates are smallest in the post-GFC period. In an era of uniformly low interest rates, differences in the user cost of various forms of money mattered much less than they have historically.

Compound annual growth rates mask the variability in the aggregates. Figure 7.1 compares the historical year-over-year growth rates of Divisia M2-ALL and simple sum M2-ALL over the 1968–2019 period. There are evident periods of divergence between the growth rates of the aggregates. The most obvious one occurs in 1978–1984, spanning the period of the Volcker Fed and the recession of the early 1980s. While the simple sum broad money aggregates grew at an average annual rate of 9.3%, the growth rates of the Divisia aggregate averaged 2.9% and occasionally wandered into negative territory. Since Fed officials were monitoring simple sum instead of Divisia aggregates, their tightening measures were excessive and produced recessions in 1980 and 1982. The Volcker Fed clearly overshot its target while attempting to rein inflation in.[22] On the other hand, the differences between the two aggregates are understandably negligible during the period of sustained low interest rates prevailing after the GFC.

Thus, we can see that by isolating the transactional services associated with the money supply, Divisia aggregation has a significant impact on the measurement of

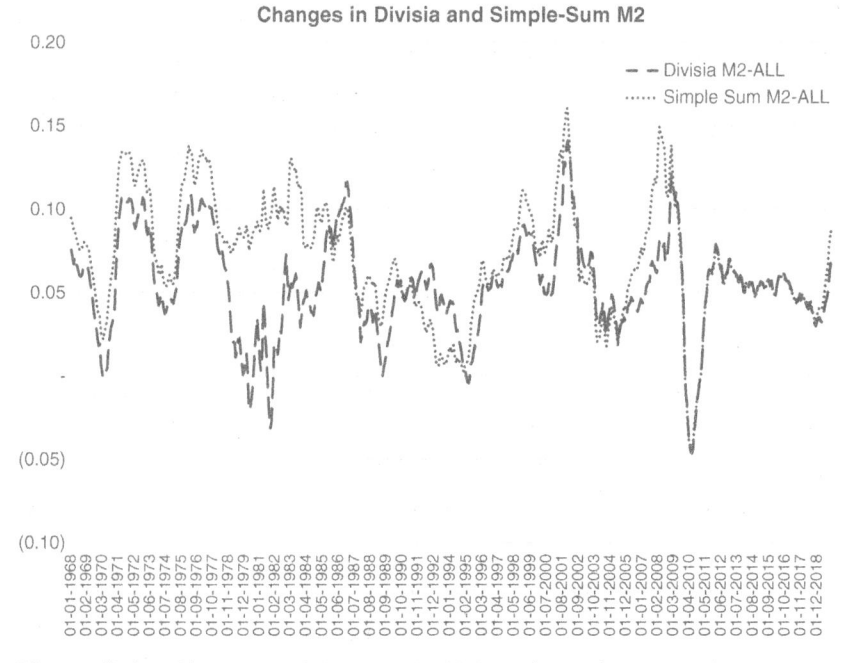

Figure 7.1 Changes in Divisia M2-ALL and simple sum M2-ALL, 1968–2023.

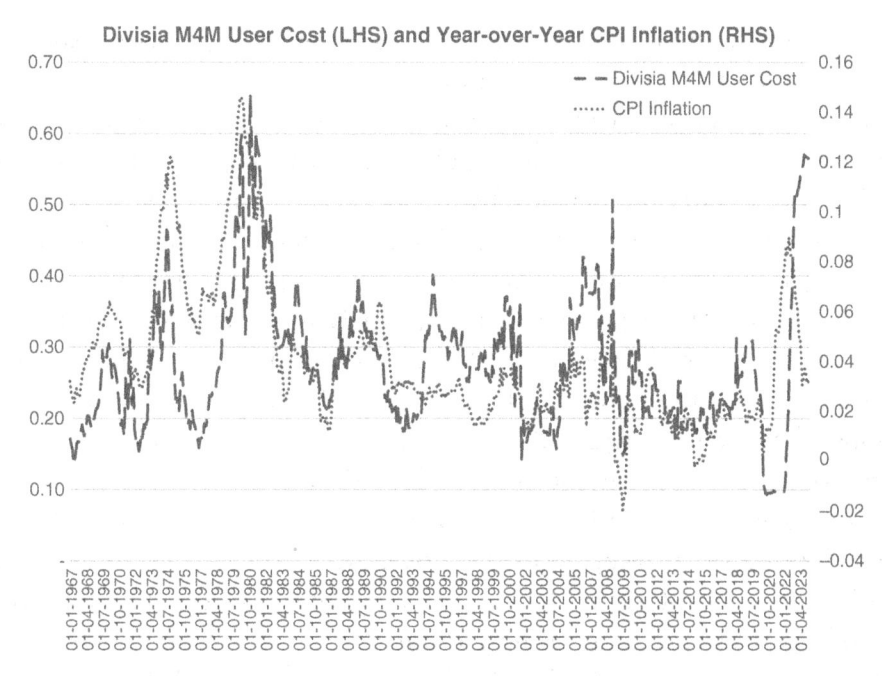

Figure 7.2 Divisia M4M user cost index and consumer price inflation, 1968–2023.

monetary conditions when considering broader aggregates and in periods of elevated interest rates. *When measured with Divisia aggregates, money demand is stable and can serve as a basis for monetary policy.*[23]

It is also instructive to look at the evolution of a user cost price index. Figure 7.2 shows the user cost price index for M4M (LHS, dashed line) overlaid with year-over-year changes in the consumer price index for all urban consumers (RHS, dotted line).[24] Though the series are in different scales and movements are not exactly in sync, it appears that variations in the user cost of money are a fairly good proxy for inflation, with inflation slightly leading user cost.

Sources of Divisia Money

Table 7.1 noted the institutional source of each form of money. The government is the source of cash and Treasury bills. We also consider the government to be the source of repurchase agreements because Treasury and agency securities are the collateral for most repo transactions. Banks supply a variety of deposit accounts. Money market funds are issued by nonbank financial institutions, while commercial paper is issued by nonbank financial institutions and nonfinancial corporations. We lump them together as nonbank sources of money.

Though we have already asserted that banks are the primary issuers of the money supply, we would like to measure the relative contributions of banks, nonbanks, and the government to monetary growth more precisely. In addition, we are curious whether there is meaningful variation in how the money supply is sourced over different time periods. To answer these questions, we decompose the monthly growth factors $\ln g_t$ into contributions from each of the three sources and accumulate them in three separate indices beginning in January 1967.

Using the same time periods from our analysis of average growth rates, we examine the sources of M2-ALL and M4M. The first three columns of Tables 7.3 and 7.4 decompose the compound annual growth rate for the period into contributions from each institutional source. The final three columns normalize the contributions as a percentage of the total growth rate.

We begin with M2-ALL, the narrower of the two aggregates (Table 7.3). Before 1974, money market funds did not exist, so there is no contribution to M2-ALL from nonbank sources. The banking system was responsible for roughly six out of every seven dollars of new monetary services created, while government supplied the seventh. As the banking system weathered the oil embargoes, historically high inflation and interest rates, a Latin American credit crisis, and the

Table 7.3 Sources of Divisia M2-ALL growth by institution, 1967–2023.

Period		Contribution to M2-ALL Growth			Share in M2-ALL		
Beginning	End	Banks	Govt.	Nonbanks	Banks	Govt.	Nonbanks
1967:1	1973:12	5.4%	0.9%	0.0%	86%	14%	0%
1974:1	1991:12	3.1%	1.3%	0.6%	61%	27%	12%
1992:1	2007:9	3.7%	1.0%	0.7%	68%	19%	13%
2007:10	2010:12	5.0%	0.6%	−1.7%	129%	15%	−44%
2011:1	2019:12	4.8%	0.7%	0.0%	87%	13%	1%

Table 7.4 Sources of Divisia M4M growth by institution, 1967–2023.

Period		Contribution to M4M Growth			Share in M4M		
Beginning	End	Banks	Govt.	Nonbanks	Banks	Govt.	Nonbanks
1967:1	1973:12	5.7%	1.0%	0.3%	82%	15%	4%
1974:1	1991:12	3.0%	1.5%	1.0%	54%	28%	19%
1992:1	2007:9	3.3%	1.6%	1.0%	56%	27%	17%
2007:10	2010:12	3.5%	−1.5%	−2.4%	NM	NM	NM
2011:1	2019:12	3.8%	0.3%	0.0%	91%	8%	1%

savings-and-loan debacle from 1974 to 1991, government and nonbank sources stepped in to supply the monetary services demanded by the nonbank public. Government support in M2-ALL comes completely from currency, which likely reflects international demand for dollar cash and substitution away from local currencies following the end of the Bretton Woods system. It is also remarkable that money market funds, a product first introduced in this period, supplied 12% of aggregate monetary services during the period. From 1992 until the beginning of the GFC, banks regained some of their dominance as suppliers of liquidity to the economy from the government, while nonbanks continued to produce roughly one of every eight dollars of monetary services.

During the GFC, balances held in nonbank store-of-value money collapsed as the public came to doubt the value of assets held by money market funds, the collateral backing repurchase agreements, and the financial capacity of commercial paper issuers. In the decade after the GFC, nonbank contributions to the money supply were negligible. Though overall growth in monetary services slowed, the destruction of nonbank monetary services was well-compensated by growth in bank-issued deposit money. Six of every seven new dollars of monetary services were coming from the banking system, though the growth rate of M2-ALL was a full percentage point lower than in the pre-1974 period. However, bank lending was not consistently the source of those deposits. Quantitative easing by the Fed put new deposits into circulation as the Fed purchased Treasury and agency securities from the nonbank public with newly created reserves.[25] In Europe and Japan, similar attempts at quantitative easing failed because those central banks purchased government securities from the banking system and no new deposits were created.[26]

A parallel analysis of M4M lets us see the consequences of including repurchase agreements and commercial paper among government and nonbank sources of money, respectively. The contribution of government and nonbank sources is clearly more important to the growth of M4M from 1967 to 2007. It is interesting to note that the pullback in the market for repurchase agreements during the GFC meant that the government's contribution to M4M growth was negative, while the impact from the collapse of nonbank money is even more pronounced when commercial paper is considered. Growth shares are not meaningful ("NM") in this period because the overall growth rate for M4M was negative.

After the GFC, the banking system is even more dominant in the supply of M4M, suggesting a lack of growth in the repo and commercial paper markets. It appears that MMFs have emerged as the most important nonbank supplier of monetary services.

Divisia Money by Sectors and Strata

We can now use Divisia aggregation to explore the dynamics of money supply in smaller cells of economic activity. We construct Divisia aggregates for sectors of the economy and strata of the income and wealth distributions of the U.S. economy. They reveal substantial differences in the growth rates and user costs of money across economic groups.

We face data limitations when disaggregating, as official sources do not provide money balances at the same level of granularity at the sector or strata levels. We also lack data on sector- and stratum-specific user costs, as the CFS data distinguish interest rates by the liability-issuing institution, not by the holder of the balance. We proceed as best as we can with the data at hand, and hope that the results of our exploration will spur interest in the collection and dissemination of more granular data to enable and refine such analyses.

The Flow of Funds instrument tables show currency and checkable deposits, time and savings deposits, money market fund shares, repo agreements, and commercial paper held as assets by the household and nonfinancial business sectors.[27] These five categories blanket the coverage of the M4M index reasonably well, though they are chunkier than those underlying the CFS indices. Nonfinancial business is divided into corporate and non-corporate business. Though the distinction is based on legal form rather than size, we use it as a proxy for large and small business. Corporate business is the only holder of repo and commercial paper, limiting the household and non-corporate business sector aggregates to three of the five available instrument series. We match pricing data from the CFS indices to each instrument and proceed to compute Divisia and simple sum aggregates at the sector level for the period 1967–2023.

Figures 7.3 and 7.4 show the year-over-year growth rates of simple sum (Figure 7.3) and Divisia (Figure 7.4) aggregates for the household (solid line), nonfinancial corporate (dotted line), and nonfinancial, non-corporate (dashed line) sectors. We first notice the extreme volatility of Divisia money growth rates relative to those for the simple sum aggregates, which shows the impact of accounting for user costs. Volatility is particularly pronounced in the corporate sector, where oscillations in the Divisia quantity index correspond quite neatly with cyclical turns in the aggregate economy. The enormous reduction in corporate sector monetary services during the Volcker disinflation suggests that the burden of policy fell disproportionately on corporate business, which was less able to shift money balances into higher-yielding forms of cash.[28]

The heterogeneity of monetary conditions across sectors is also striking. During the 1990s, for example, there is little growth in household money

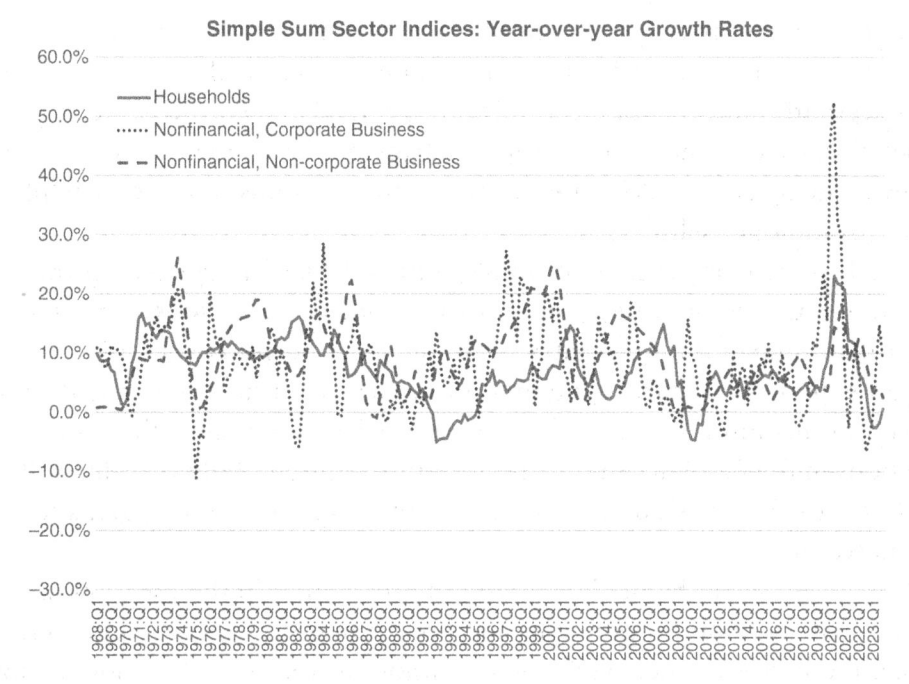

Figure 7.3 Growth of simple sum monetary aggregates by sector, 1968–2023.

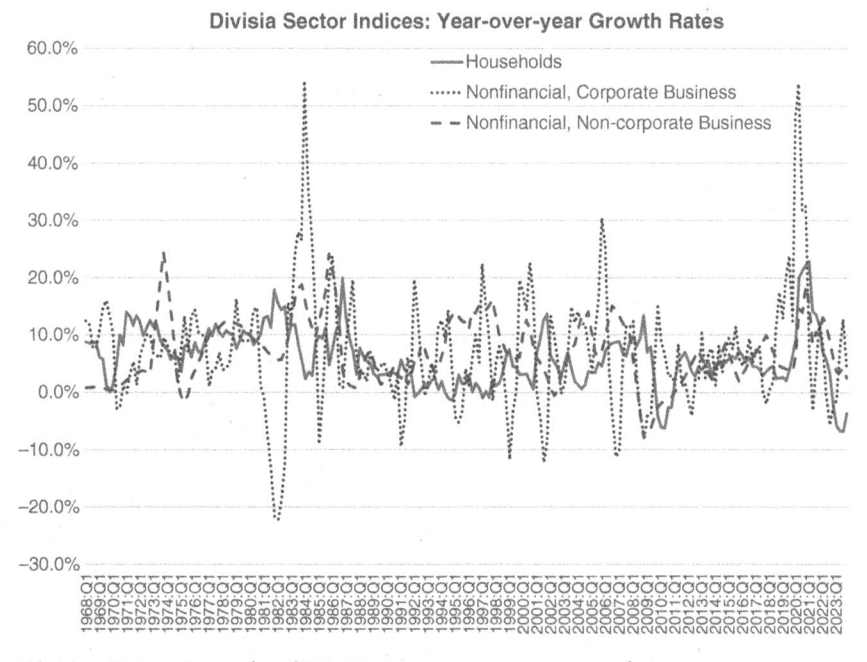

Figure 7.4 Growth of Divisia monetary aggregates by sector, 1968–2023.

demand, while non-corporate business is comparatively awash in liquidity. Broad money grew at 8.6% and 4.6% compound annual growth rates in the non-corporate and corporate sectors, respectively, versus 2.0% per year for households. At the end of the sample period in 2023, we can also see broad money growing at a modest rate in the nonfinancial business sector while contracting among households.

Side-by-side comparisons of simple sum and Divisia aggregate growth rates by sector (not presented here) show that monetary conditions were frequently tighter than simple sum aggregates would suggest. Corporate and non-corporate business experienced sharp tightening in monetary services not only during the Volcker disinflation but also at the end of the 1990s and after the GFC, despite reductions in the Fed Funds rate. The downturn in household liquidity following the 1991–1992 recession is less severe than simple sum aggregation suggests, however.

We can also see in Figure 7.5 a significant reduction in the user cost of money for corporate and non-corporate business beginning in the 1990s and continuing through the post-GFC period.[29] The expansion of store-of-value money supplied by the shadow banking system gave the nonfinancial business sector better-remunerated options for holding cash balances. Reduced long-term interest rates reduced user costs for all sectors from 2011 to 2017.

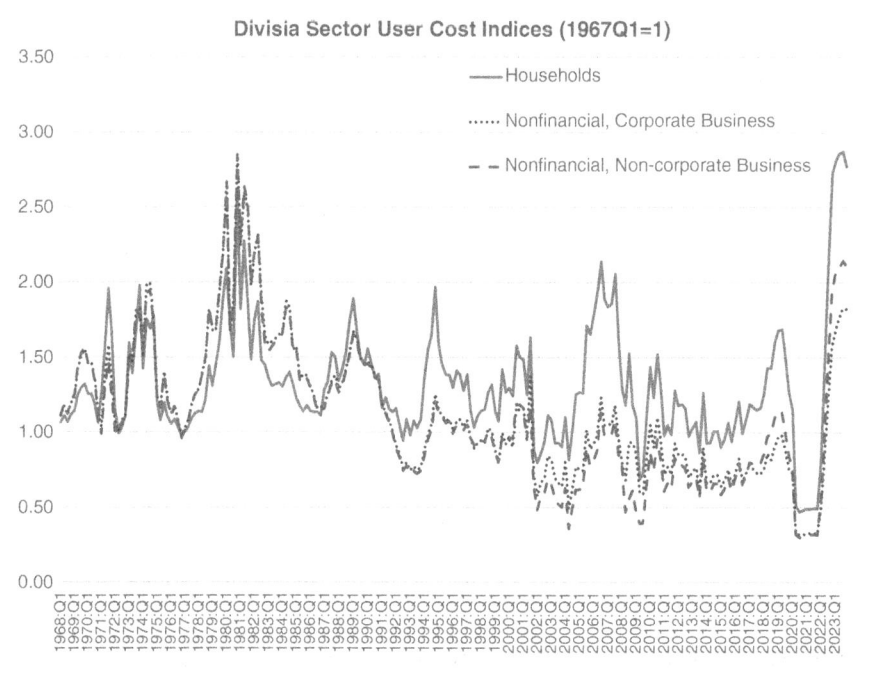

Figure 7.5 User cost indices for Divisia monetary aggregates by sector, 1968–2023.

Disaggregating money demand by sector is likely to give us greater insight into the nature and stability of money demand than we can obtain with a single broad money aggregate. However, it would take us too far from our purpose to pursue this question fully here.[30]

We now turn to constructing Divisia monetary indices by income and wealth strata. The experimental Distributional Financial Accounts compiled by the Federal Reserve permit money demand to be disaggregated according to percentiles of the income and wealth distributions, among other stratifications of household level economic outcomes.[31] Unfortunately, the money balance detail is even chunkier in these data, which run from 1989:Q3 to 2023:Q4. Money holdings are broken into deposits and MMFs. Household income levels are broken into quintiles, with the top quintile separated into the top 1% and the 19% immediately below. Household net worth levels are divided by the bottom 50%, the next 40%, the next 9%, and the top 1%. An additional category breaks out the top 0.1%.

Apart from the additional detail on the bottom of the distribution provided in the income accounts, the income and wealth-based indices produce broadly similar results, as income and wealth are highly correlated. Hence, in Figure 7.6 we focus on the stratification by income. The lowest earners (dashed line) realized significant boosts to their use of monetary services from 1997 to 1998,

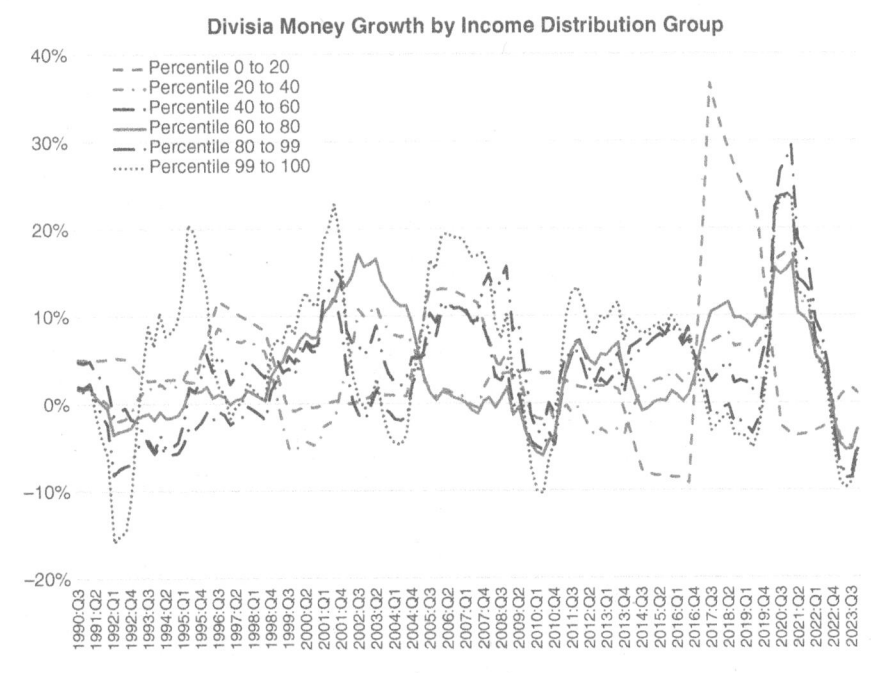

Figure 7.6 Divisia monetary aggregates by income stratum, 1968–2023.

from 2005 to 2008, and from 2017 to 2020. At the other end of the distribution, earners in the top 1% (dotted line) grew their consumption of monetary services significantly from 1993 to 1996, 1999 to 2001, 2005 to 2008, and 2011 to 2016. Overall, the correlation coefficient between money growth rates in the top and bottom income groups is −0.24, while that between the bottom 20% and the 80th to 99th percentile is −0.11. Within the extremes, however, the degree of correlation is positive and generally quite high. The first and second quintiles (excluding the top 1%) have a positive correlation coefficient of 0.84, for example.

What is perhaps more surprising is the increase in user costs as one moves up the income distribution, as shown in Figure 7.7. To make these user cost indices strictly comparable to one another, we would have to multiply by a corresponding true cost of living index and discount to the beginning of each quarterly period. These cost of living indices are necessary to deflate all nominal quantities to real quantities in the computation of user cost.[32] In the absence of such indices by income group, we are unsure whether the data show that higher earners simply spend more on monetary services and have less interest-elastic demand for deposit money, or if higher earners have faced smaller increases in the cost of living than those with smaller incomes.

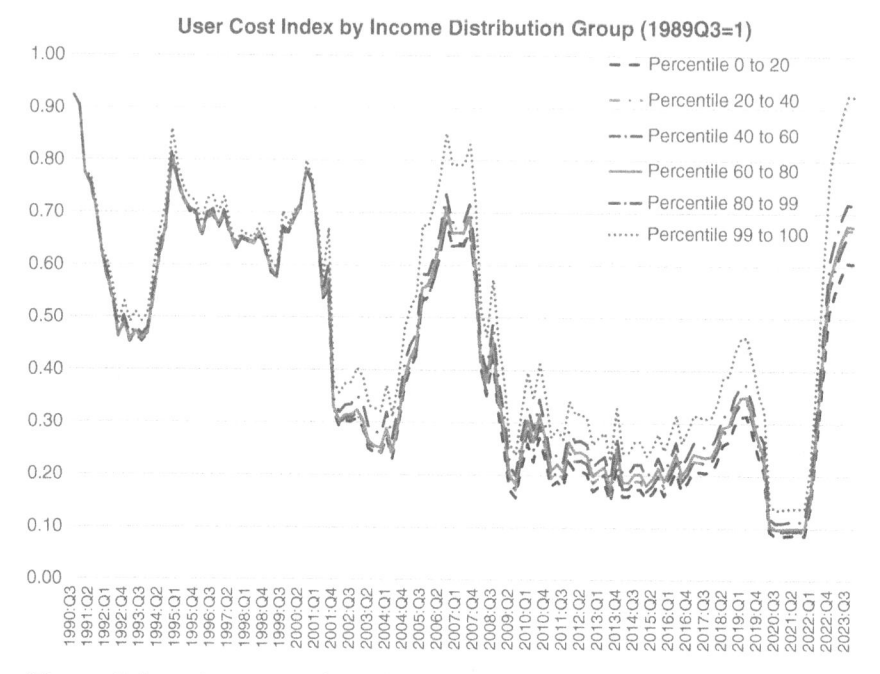

Figure 7.7 User cost indices for Divisia monetary aggregates by income stratum, 1968–2023.

Evolution of Bank Balance Sheets from 1945 to 2023

Part Two is devoted to understanding official control of the money production process, or what we call "monetary policy" in a more capacious sense than usual. We argue that because most of the production of monetary services takes place in the commercial banking system, the most important monetary policy actions take place through changes in banking sector regulations. Such adjustments are slow-moving and structural. They lack the news-cycle cachet of eight annual FOMC meetings, but have a far greater impact on monetary conditions.

To see how banking regulation and other developments in the financial sector affect monetary policy requires a wider view of the data than the path of short-term interest rates. One must consider the growth and composition of the consolidated balance sheet for the commercial banking system, the interplay of bank credit expansion with capital markets funding, and the sources and uses of savings. Long-term developments in each series may be traced to official policy actions. The prevailing mix of bank credit and capital markets funding, as well as constraints imposed by banking regulations, have profound consequences for the efficiency and composition of investment and the growth and composition of the money supply.

Thus, it is helpful to begin with a long-term tour of the relevant data. We draw on the Flow of Funds data for the United States, available quarterly from 1951Q4 to 2023Q4. The data trace balance sheet levels of financial assets and liabilities at the sectoral level, animating the framework we introduced in Chapter 2. For many instruments, levels are reasonably close to accumulated flows, but in some cases, such as the holdings of corporate equities (which are measured at market values), levels are a function of inflows and substantial revaluations.

It is worth dwelling for a bit on the impact of revaluations because they matter for the growth rate of lending. If mortgage lending grows by 10% in a year, for example, it makes a difference whether the same housing stock is re-mortgaged at 10% higher prices, or if 10% more houses are mortgaged at constant prices. If PQ is the product of asset values P and loan volumes Q,

$$\Delta(PQ) = P\Delta Q + Q\Delta P + \Delta P \Delta Q$$

The first term is new loan originations at beginning-of-period prices, the second is the revaluation of beginning-of-period loan volumes, and the third is usually small enough to ignore. Existing loan volumes are not revalued on bank balance sheets, but revaluation will occur if an existing loan is refinanced at the new valuation. For brevity, we consider only $\Delta(PQ)$ below.

Table 7.5 Periodization of U.S. banking regimes, 1945–2023.

Beginning	End	Description
1945	1956	**Postwar transition**
1957	1973	**Bretton Woods, expansion, and Bank Holding Company regime**
1974	1987	**Post-Bretton Woods internationalization**
1974	1979	*Oil embargoes and inflation*
1979	1982	*Volcker monetarism, recession, Latin American lending boom*
1982	1987	*Disinflation and financialization*
1987	1991	**Bank failures and recovery from 1980s mini financial crisis**
1992	2007	**Basel I era**
1992	1999	*Expansion and government borrowing "peace dividend"*
1999	2004	*First housing expansion, Gramm-Leach-Bliley, foreign reserve buildup*
2004	2007	*Subprime mortgage expansion*
2007	2010	**Global Financial Crisis (GFC) and recessionary aftermath**
2011	2019	**Basel III era**
2020		**COVID-19 interventions and transition to Basel III endgame**

In reviewing the data, we adopt a rough periodization of recent monetary history within which we can discern meaningful turning points and changes in trends. We have already begun to use these periods in our discussion of Divisia money developments in the previous sections. The key phases are sketched in Table 7.5. Subperiods in italics are distinguished from longer periods in bold.

In broader terms, we might group the periods into a Bretton Woods regime running from 1945 to 1973, a transitional period from 1974 to 1991, and a Basel regime running from 1992 to the present, as indicated by the shading in the table. The synchronization of monetary policy brought about by the Basel regime—particularly after Basel III—is a development with international consequences that rival those of the Bretton Woods era. The extent to which monetary policy has been standardized by the Basel regime has not yet been properly appreciated. The usefulness of our periodization will become more apparent over the remainder of this chapter and the next.

Broad Trends

We begin by focusing on the evolution of the commercial banking system's balance sheet from the end of World War II to 2023. After considering the overall growth rate of the system balance sheet, we consider broad trends in the composition of banking system assets.

The commercial banking system captured in the Flow of Funds data aggregates the banking subsidiaries of bank holding companies and other standalone banking institutions. Accordingly, it captures only the purely banking business operations of a universal banking institution. The capital markets side appears elsewhere in the Flow of Funds data, such as the tables for Holding Companies and Security Brokers and Dealers.[33]

Table 7.6 presents the level of financial assets in the banking system at the end of each period and the compound annual growth rate (CAGR) of financial assets for the period. The CAGRs indicate the trend rate of asset growth within each period. For more than 60 years prior to the GFC, the financial assets of the banking system grew at roughly 7%–8% per year. Since the GFC, the average rate has been 4.4% per year. The apparent recovery from 2020 to 2023 reflects the massive quantitative easing and government transfers related to the COVID pandemic, which flooded the banking system with reserves created by the Federal Reserve and transferred from the government's Federal Reserve account. The 6.8% CAGR for that period breaks down into 16.9% growth in 2020, 9.2% in 2021, −0.1% in 2022, and 2.1% in 2023. The break in the long-term trend rate of bank asset growth is traceable to changes in bank regulations, as we will argue in Chapter 8. Reduced growth may also betray weakness in the supply of bankable projects, as we will argue in Chapters 12 and 13.

The consolidated banking system includes depository institutions chartered in the United States, U.S. branches of foreign bank organizations, banks in U.S.-affiliated areas, and credit unions. Following we will focus on U.S.-chartered depositories, which encompass most banking system assets. Before proceeding, we check trends in financial asset growth for the subsector in Table 7.7. When foreign bank and credit union assets are excluded, asset growth rates are somewhat slower,

Table 7.6 Assets of the United States commercial banking system, 1945–2023.

Beginning	End	Assets (Mn)	CAGR
1945:Q4	1956:Q4	269,571	7.2%
1957:Q1	1973:Q4	1,138,963	8.8%
1974:Q1	1991:Q4	4,639,543	8.1%
1992:Q1	2007:Q3	12,872,556	6.7%
2007:Q4	2010:Q4	13,654,067	1.8%
2011:Q1	2019:Q4	20,088,991	4.4%
2020:Q1	2023:Q4	26,159,401	6.8%

Table 7.7 Assets of U.S.-chartered depository institutions, 1945–2023.

Beginning	End	Assets (Mn)	CAGR
1945:Q4	1956:Q4	263,945	7.0%
1957:Q1	1973:Q4	1,093,182	8.7%
1974:Q1	1991:Q4	3,976,070	7.4%
1992:Q1	2007:Q3	10,755,975	6.5%
2007:Q4	2010:Q4	11,452,763	2.0%
2011:Q1	2019:Q4	16,339,455	4.0%
2020:Q1	2023:Q4	20,967,057	6.4%

Table 7.8 Asset allocations of U.S. depository institutions, 1945–2023.

Period		Average Share of Balance Sheet			
Beginning	End	Liquidity	Securities	Loans	Other
1945:Q4	1956:Q4	10.2%	44.3%	43.5%	2.0%
1957:Q1	1973:Q4	6.1%	26.7%	64.9%	2.3%
1974:Q1	1991:Q4	6.0%	22.2%	67.7%	4.1%
1992:Q1	2007:Q3	5.0%	22.4%	64.3%	8.3%
2007:Q4	2010:Q4	7.6%	20.1%	61.1%	11.2%
2011:Q1	2019:Q4	10.0%	23.8%	57.9%	8.3%
2020:Q1	2023:Q4	12.4%	27.2%	53.4%	7.0%

but the same break in trend is evident following the GFC, as well as the burst of growth from COVID policy.[34]

We consider the composition of bank balance sheet growth in Table 7.8. The balance sheets of U.S.-chartered depository institutions are restricted to a relatively short list of assets. We can divide this list broadly into loans, a securities portfolio, a liquidity portfolio, and everything else.

Loans have long dominated the U.S. banking system balance sheet, as one would expect. During World War II the banking system absorbed Treasury bonds, supporting the war effort. As their Treasury holdings ran off after the war, loans grew from roughly 44% of bank assets to 65% in 1973. From then until the beginning of the GFC, loans accounted for roughly two-thirds of bank assets, trending somewhat downward but maintaining a central position. Following the GFC, loans have been shrinking as a component of bank balance sheets, averaging only 58% of financial assets in the following decade and falling to 53.4% in the 2020–2023 period.

Since 1957, banks' securities holdings have consistently accounted for 18%–27% of commercial bank assets, with a noticeable uptick following the GFC. Securities are purchased for a bank's own account and do not involve credit creation. Banks are motivated to hold securities when lending opportunities are scarce, to manage interest rate and liquidity risk, and to adjust their risk-weighted assets for regulatory capital compliance.[35] Federally chartered banks are permitted to hold obligations of the Treasury and agencies of the U.S. government, municipal bonds, agency and private-label mortgage-related securities, and investment-grade corporate debt. Holdings of corporate debt are limited to a percentage of the bank's equity capital, while Treasuries, agency debt, and agency MBS may be held in unlimited amounts. Other "mortgage-related securities" may be held in unlimited amounts if they are covered by the Secondary Mortgage Market Enhancement Act of 1984.[36]

We refer to banks' holdings of reserves, vault cash, Fed Funds, and repurchase agreements as their liquidity portfolio.[37] Until 2020, U.S. banks were required to hold a minimum level of reserves as a percentage of their demandable deposits, but even without requirements, a reserve balance is necessary for interbank payments. Reserves and Fed Funds may be owned outright or borrowed.[38] Repurchase agreements are short-term borrowings of funds collateralized by liquid securities. The fact that they are not legally loans but sales with an agreement to repurchase has been salient at times when restrictions on loan interest rates have been binding on the banking system.

The expansion of the banking system's liquidity portfolio during and after the GFC has been notable. As we will discuss at greater length in Chapter 10, the increase in liquidity was triggered by the expansion of the Federal Reserve's emergency lending facilities and its policy of quantitative easing. It has subsequently been reinforced by the liquidity regulations of Basel III and certain technical features of the interbank market. An overhang of liquidity is not easily resolved within the banking system. It must be drained by the central bank, which requires a reduction of the central bank balance sheet.

The remainder of banking system assets comprises more traditional financial investments in the banking enterprise itself. Progressive liberalization of banking from the 1960s allowed banks to invest in subsidiaries handling certain kinds of business including securities custody, brokerage, and some securities underwriting activities.[39] And as banking became a globalized business, U.S. banks invested directly abroad, opening branches outside of the United States. By the advent of the GFC, these enterprise-level investments and others accounted for some 12% of banking system assets. They have trended downward since then.

Finer Details

Having traced the broad outlines of bank asset allocations, we now consider changes within those broad categories. There is considerably more action here.

We consider the composition of lending, followed by the allocation of securities portfolios.

The Flow of Funds data classify bank loans as mortgages, consumer credit, other loans and advances, and loans not elsewhere classified (n.e.c.). These categories are further disaggregated in Flow of Funds instrument tables. Mortgages are separated into residential and commercial mortgages; consumer credit is classified into revolving balances (mostly credit card loans), auto loans, and student loans; and loans n.e.c. generally cover the extension of credit to the nonfinancial business sector.[40] Within the Flow of Funds instrument tables, one can see the share of funding that is created in the banking system versus funding intermediated from capital market sources, a question we explore in the following subsection.

Table 7.9 shows most bank lending in the United States is mortgage lending secured by real estate collateral. The average share of mortgages in bank lending portfolios trended steadily upward from the end of World War II through the end of the GFC, accounting for a clear majority of all bank lending. Though mortgage lending retreated somewhat after the GFC, it continued to account for more than half of all bank lending. By contrast, the share of commercial lending (loans n.e.c.) had been steadily shrinking until the GFC.[41] It appears that almost all growth in mortgage lending came at the expense of commercial lending. Consumer credit has long been some 14%–15% of bank lending, and its uptick after the GFC is notable. The observed shifts in the composition of post-GFC lending should be discounted somewhat by the overall reduction of bank lending in bank assets, however.

The composition of bank securities holdings has also undergone substantial shifts in the postwar period. The broadest trend visible in Table 7.10 has been the consistent replacement of Treasury and municipal securities with higher-yielding

Table 7.9 Composition of U.S. depository institution lending, 1945–2023.

Period		Average Share of Bank Lending			
Beginning	End	Mortgages	Loans NEC	Consumer	Other
1945:Q4	1956:Q4	50.4%	35.4%	13.8%	0.4%
1957:Q1	1973:Q4	56.0%	29.4%	13.9%	0.8%
1974:Q1	1991:Q4	56.5%	27.2%	14.6%	1.7%
1992:Q1	2007:Q3	59.7%	24.7%	15.4%	0.2%
2007:Q4	2010:Q4	63.9%	21.8%	14.3%	0.0%
2011:Q1	2019:Q4	54.5%	28.0%	17.4%	0.1%
2020:Q1	2023:Q4	49.8%	32.9%	17.1%	0.2%

government agency securities and corporate debt. Agency and GSE securities have come to dominate bank security holdings.

Breaking the agency/GSE and corporate securities categories down further in Tables 7.11 and 7.12 shows that bank securities holdings have also been dominated by mortgage-related finance. During the Basel era agency passthrough and structured RMBS issued by Fannie Mae, Freddie Mac, and Ginnie Mae have accounted for more than two-thirds of the agency and GSE securities held by commercial banks, and nearly half of banks' overall securities holdings.[42] Private-label RMBS were an important supplement to agency RMBS during the Basel I era but have almost completely run off since the GFC. Other corporate bond debt has taken its place. It does not appear that CMBS have made comparable inroads in bank portfolios, suggesting that banks prefer to hold their commercial real estate exposure in loan form.

Table 7.10 Composition of U.S. depository institution securities portfolios, 1945–2023.

Period		Average Share of Bank Securities Portfolio				
Beginning	End	Treasuries	Munis	Agency/GSE	Corporate	Paper
1945:Q4	1956:Q4	80.6%	11.5%	2.5%	5.0%	0.5%
1957:Q1	1973:Q4	55.7%	29.2%	8.0%	5.6%	1.5%
1974:Q1	1991:Q4	27.7%	28.0%	31.4%	10.7%	2.2%
1992:Q1	2007:Q3	13.4%	8.9%	58.2%	19.4%	0.2%
2007:Q4	2010:Q4	5.1%	9.7%	56.1%	28.7%	0.4%
2011:Q1	2019:Q4	11.4%	13.7%	58.7%	16.2%	0.0%
2020:Q1	2023:Q4	22.2%	10.5%	54.9%	12.3%	0.1%

Table 7.11 U.S. depository institution securities portfolios: agency MBS, 1945–2023.

Period		Average Share of Bank Securities Portfolio (Agency/GSE)				
		Agency RMBS		Agency CMBS		
Beginning	End	Passthrough	Structured	Passthrough	Structured	Other
1945:Q4	1956:Q4	0.1%	0.0%	0.0%	0.0%	2.4%
1957:Q1	1973:Q4	0.9%	0.0%	0.0%	0.0%	7.1%
1974:Q1	1991:Q4	17.0%	0.7%	0.0%	0.0%	13.7%
1992:Q1	2007:Q3	33.0%	10.1%	0.0%	0.0%	15.0%
2007:Q4	2010:Q4	34.6%	10.6%	0.1%	0.1%	10.7%
2011:Q1	2019:Q4	34.4%	13.6%	1.8%	2.7%	6.3%
2020:Q1	2023:Q4	35.7%	9.2%	3.5%	3.8%	2.7%

Table 7.12 U.S. depository institution securities portfolios: corporate bonds, 1945–2023.

Period		Average Share of Bank Securities Portfolio (Corporate)				
		Private RMBS		Private CMBS		
Beginning	End	Passthrough	Structured	Passthrough	Structured	Other
1945:Q4	1956:Q4	0.0%	0.0%	0.0%	0.0%	5.0%
1957:Q1	1973:Q4	0.0%	0.0%	0.0%	0.0%	5.6%
1974:Q1	1991:Q4	0.7%	0.2%	0.0%	0.0%	9.8%
1992:Q1	2007:Q3	2.1%	4.7%	0.0%	0.0%	12.6%
2007:Q4	2010:Q4	1.2%	10.5%	0.3%	0.6%	16.1%
2011:Q1	2019:Q4	0.4%	2.1%	0.2%	1.2%	12.3%
2020:Q1	2023:Q4	0.1%	0.9%	0.1%	0.9%	10.3%

Clearly, bank loan and securities portfolios are both tightly bound to the fate of real estate collateral. In Chapter 13, we will consider economic reasons why commercial banking and real estate are so inseparable, and why we believe the relationship is a fatal attraction in need of reform.

Since the GFC, bank analysts have also paid attention to the accounting treatment elected by banks for their securities holdings. Securities that are "available for sale" are marked to market, and unrealized gains and losses on them pass through the value of bank equity. Securities deemed "held to maturity" are carried at amortized cost and have no accounting effect on equity. As interest rates have risen sharply since 2022, concerns about unrealized losses on held to maturity securities remain elevated. Such losses were instrumental in the failure of Silicon Valley Bank and continue to be monitored by U.S. regulators.[43]

Bank Lending Versus Capital Market Finance

We now investigate how capital markets funding competes with bank credit in the lending business. Drawing on aggregate savings to fund bankable projects seems inefficient when the funding could just as well be created by the banking system. Does the presence of more capital markets funding in lending markets suggest increased risk in lending, or a cannibalization of bank business by the capital markets?[44]

Figure 7.8 shows the universe of outstanding mortgage credit comprises single-family loans on one- to four-family properties (about 60%–70% of the total), loans on multifamily properties (10%), mortgages on commercial property like offices, retail space, and hotels (20%), and mortgages secured by farms and farmland (1%–2%).[45]

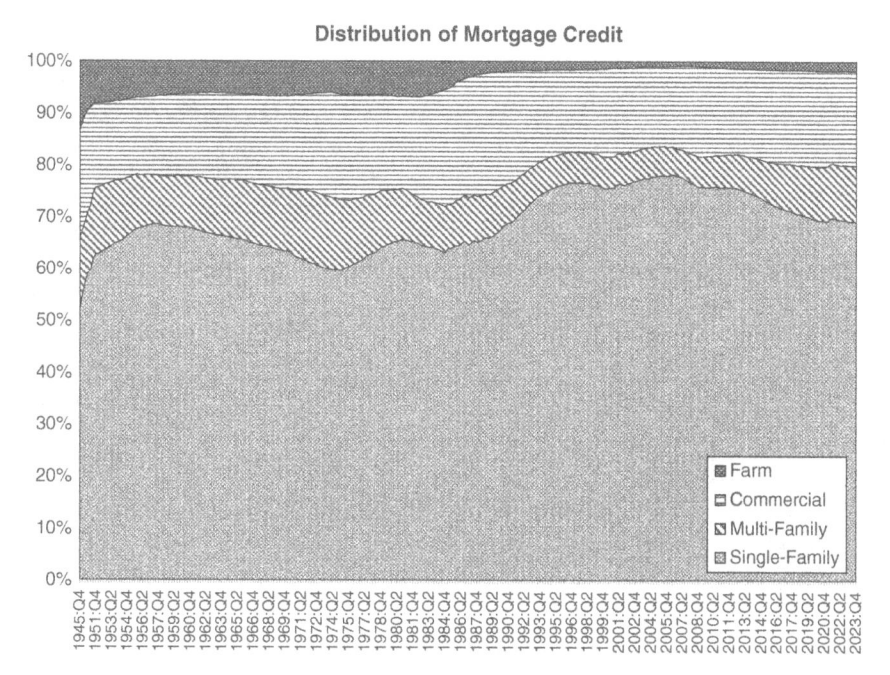

Figure 7.8 Composition of U.S. mortgage credit, 1951–2023.

Mortgage market shares are presented in Figure 7.9. Banks' share of the mortgage credit market grew steadily from 40% at the end of World War II to about 60% in the late 1970s.[46] Life insurance companies were also significant providers of mortgage credit through the 1960s. Since then, government agencies and GSEs have dominated the nonbank mortgage market. Though private issuers of RMBS and CMBS grew from nothing to almost 20% of the mortgage market in the Basel I era, they have largely ceded their gains to agency/GSE mortgage finance since the GFC. At the end of 2023, GSEs and government agencies accounted for 51% of the overall mortgage market.[47] Figure 7.10 breaks the government-related contribution down further into agency and GSE sources.

Beginning from the bottom of Figure 7.10, Fannie Mae and Freddie Mac account for roughly 20% and 15% of the U.S. mortgage market, respectively. Thus, more than one-third of all mortgage credit has been purchased and guaranteed by institutions under the conservatorship of the Federal Housing Finance Agency since the GFC. Ginnie Mae, a government-sponsored enterprise, is responsible for another 10%–12% of the mortgage market. The remainder can be traced to various farm agencies, the Federal Home Loan Banks, the Veterans Administration, and others.

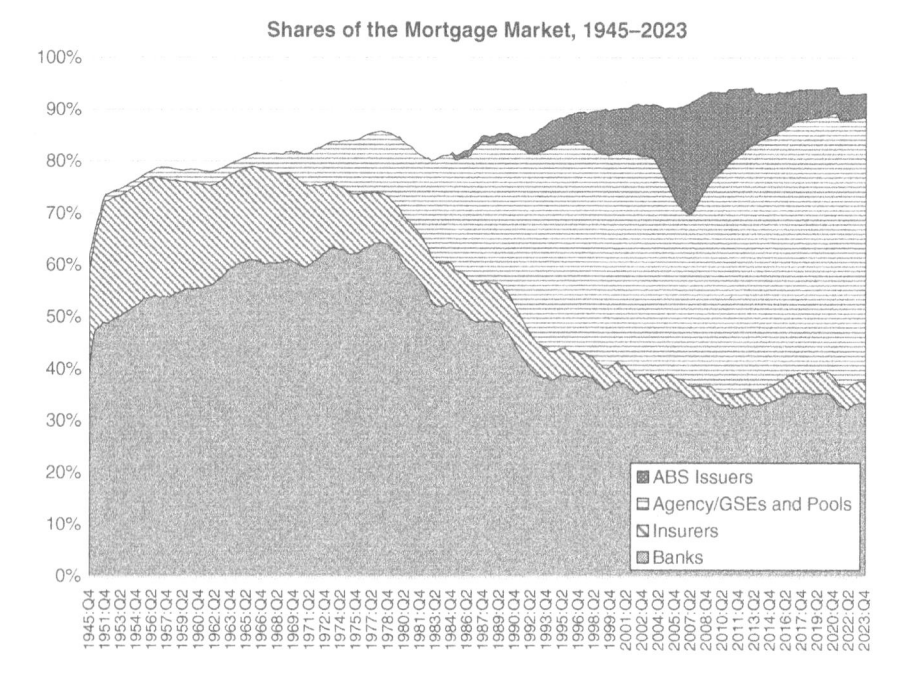

Figure 7.9 Shares of U.S. mortgage credit issued by institution type, 1951–2023.

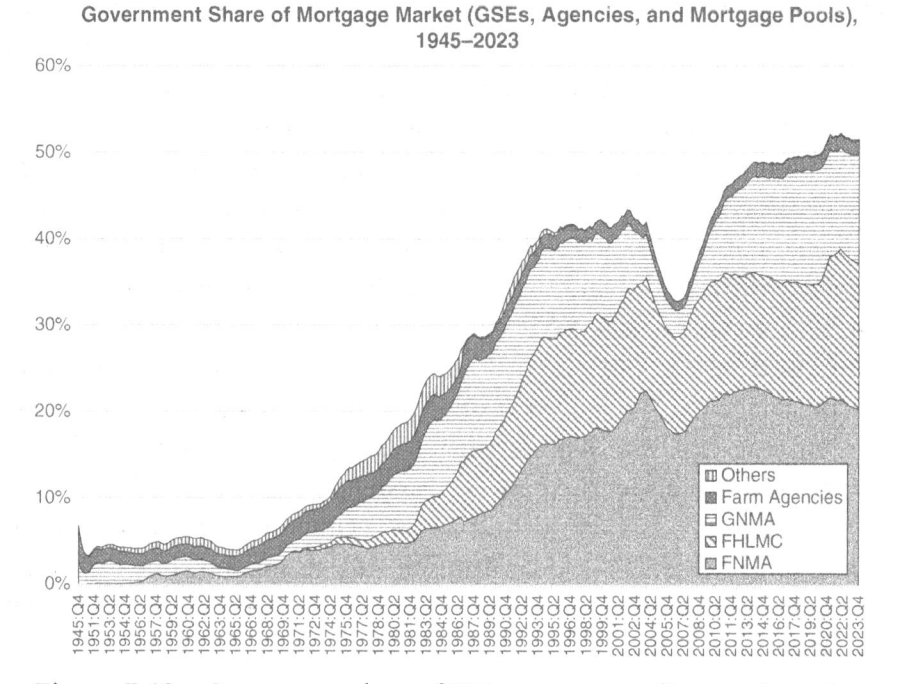

Figure 7.10 Government share of U.S. mortgage credit: agencies and GSEs, 1951–2023.

We can see in Figure 7.9 that the agency and GSE takeover of the mortgage market took off in the late 1960s and reached an initial peak in the 1990s. Fannie Mae was chartered during the Great Depression to make mortgages more available. In 1968, President Johnson spun it off like a privatized company, but Fannie Mae retained its public mission and implicit government backing. A similar, abbreviated process created Freddie Mac in 1970. Free of banks' capital requirements and enjoying the sponsorship of the U.S. government, Fannie Mae and Freddie Mac grew rapidly and made their shareholders wealthy.[48] The government-supported share held steady at roughly 40% of the market during the 1990s. After giving some ground to the private MBS market in the mid-2000s, the agencies and GSEs pressed on to grow their share further, becoming the marginal source of mortgage funding for most of the post-GFC era.

The residential, commercial, and multifamily components of the mortgage market each tell a somewhat different story. As the largest of the mortgage markets, the residential mortgage market (Figure 7.11) largely mirrors the trend of mortgages as a whole.[49] The ground lost by the banking system is even more visible here, however. Banks' share of residential mortgages fell below 30% at the beginning of the GFC and has not recovered. Government-sponsored enterprises, government agencies, and their mortgage pools now account for a staggering 65% of all residential mortgage lending. Private RMBS peaked at about 21% in 2007, but now make up less than 2% of all residential mortgage loans.

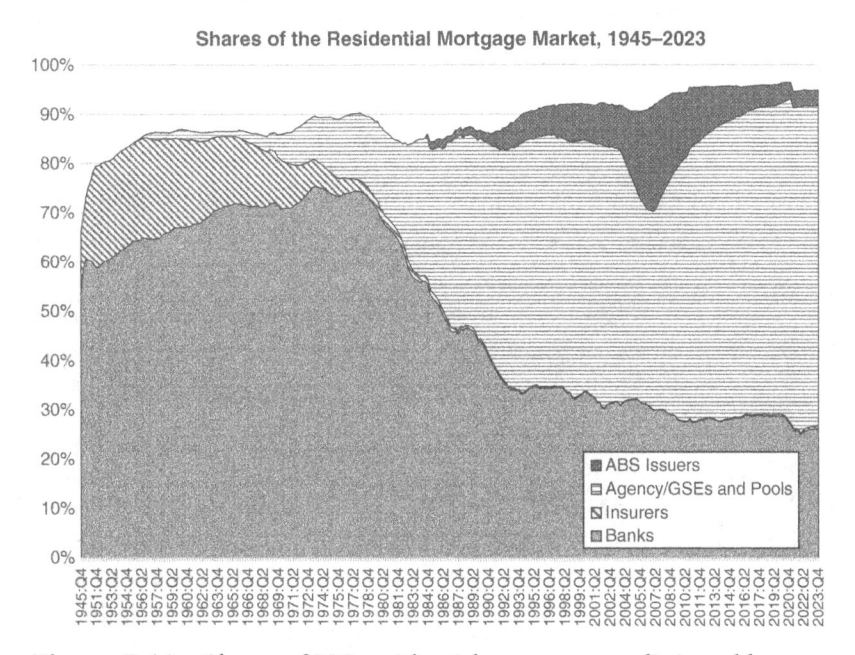

Figure 7.11 Shares of U.S. residential mortgage credit issued by institution type, 1951–2023.

We should also briefly mention residential home equity lending, in which the owner of a home draws a revolving line of credit using their home as collateral, possibly in a second lien position behind a residential mortgage.[50] Such lending grew from $215 billion in 1990Q4 (when data are first available) to a peak of $1.14 trillion in 2008Q2 (9.8% CAGR), making it larger than the multifamily mortgage market and roughly one-half the size of the commercial mortgage market at the time. Banks consistently made 75%–80% of home equity loans. Since the GFC, the market for home equity lending has contracted by more than 50%, and credit unions and nonbank financial institution have taken share from banks. In a low-interest rate environment, one can more easily monetize home equity through a cash-out refinancing of one's first-lien mortgage.

Banks are better situated in the commercial mortgage market (Figure 7.12), currently making more than 60% of all commercial mortgages.[51] Life insurance companies and private CMBS are major players as well, combining for a current share of about 25%.

GSEs and government agencies make nearly one-half of all multifamily mortgages (Figure 7.13).[52] In addition to banks (one-third), state and local governments have been lenders for 5%–15% of multifamily mortgages since the early 1970s. Overall, the government's footprint in the mortgage market is considerable, though not evenly distributed. Commercial mortgages have been left largely to the

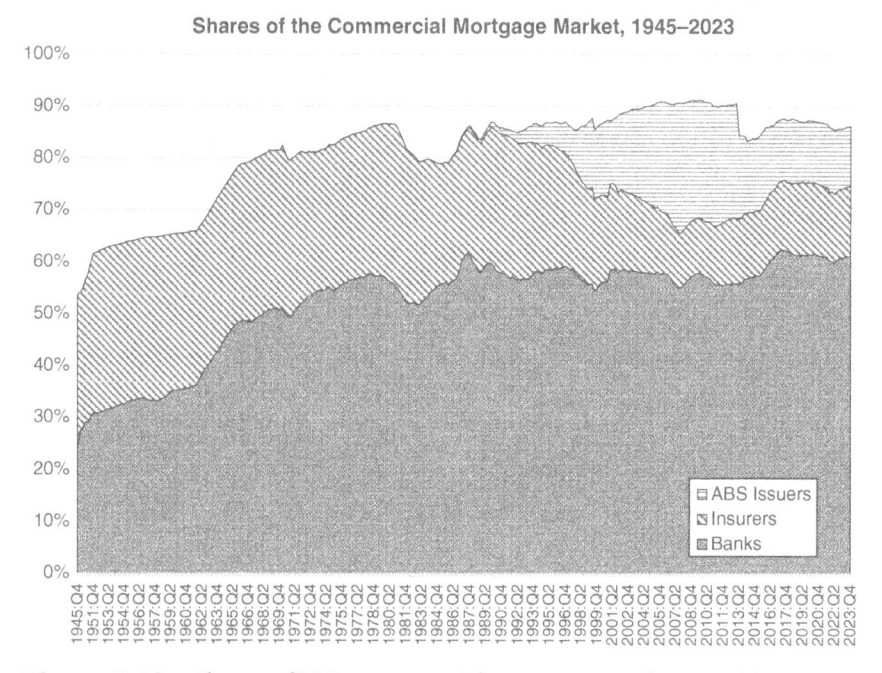

Figure 7.12 Shares of U.S. commercial mortgage credit issued by institution type, 1951–2023.

Shares of the Multifamily Mortgage Market, 1945–2023

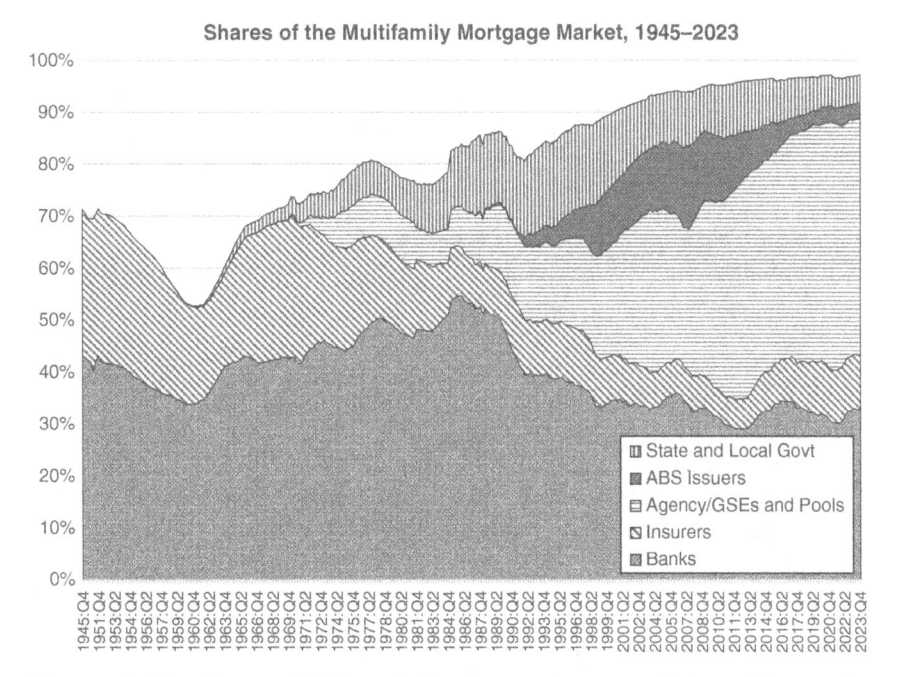

Figure 7.13 Shares of U.S. multifamily mortgage credit issued by institution type, 1951–2023.

banking system and other private players. Government presence has catalyzed capital markets funding into securitized mortgages and paved the way for securitized mortgages to be held by banks as if they were mere intermediaries.

Consumer credit (Figure 7.14) comprises revolving credit card balances, personal loans, auto lending, and student loans.[53] Though consumer lending is heavily favored in banking regulations, the banking system currently accounts for only half of all consumer credit. Much auto lending comes through captive finance companies operated by automakers. These assets appear in the top segment of the graph. Student loan asset-backed securities (ABS) were once a significant part of the consumer credit market, but ABS and the private student loans underneath them have been overtaken by direct loans from the Department of Education. The field is largely open to banks for credit card lending and personal loans, which have grown to become a $1.7 trillion market.[54] Unsecured consumer credit has mostly replaced the secured home equity loan credit which receded after the GFC. In 2021, both began to grow rapidly, with a 9.6% CAGR from 2020Q4 to 2023Q4.[55]

"Loans not elsewhere classified" are the last important category of bank lending and are, by definition, reserved to commercial banks.[56] Figure 7.15 shows that about 80% of such loans come from U.S. banks, while the other 20% comes from U.S. branches of foreign banking organizations. The Figure 7.15 shows which

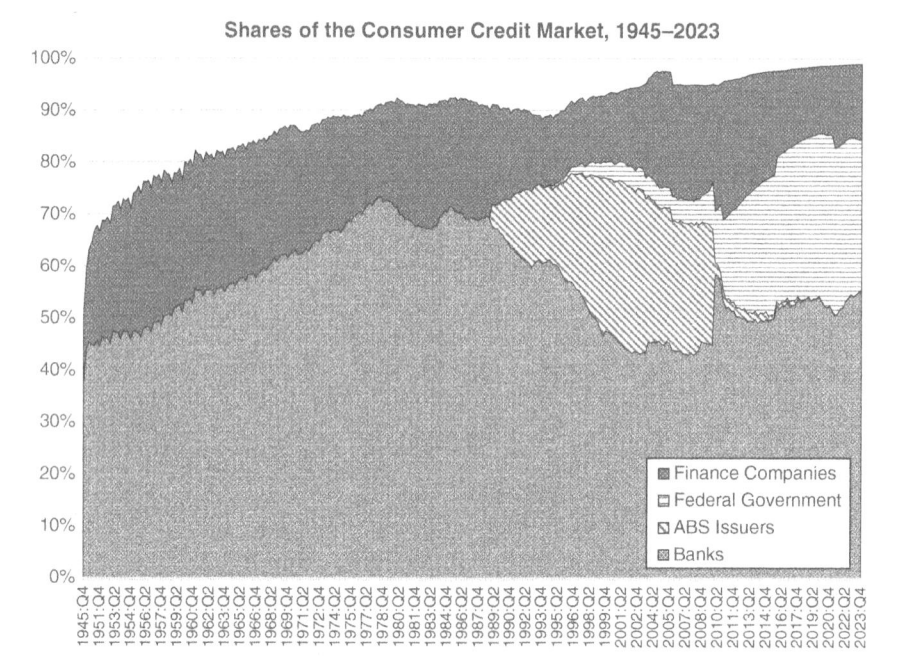

Figure 7.14 Shares of U.S. consumer credit issued by institution type, 1951–2023.

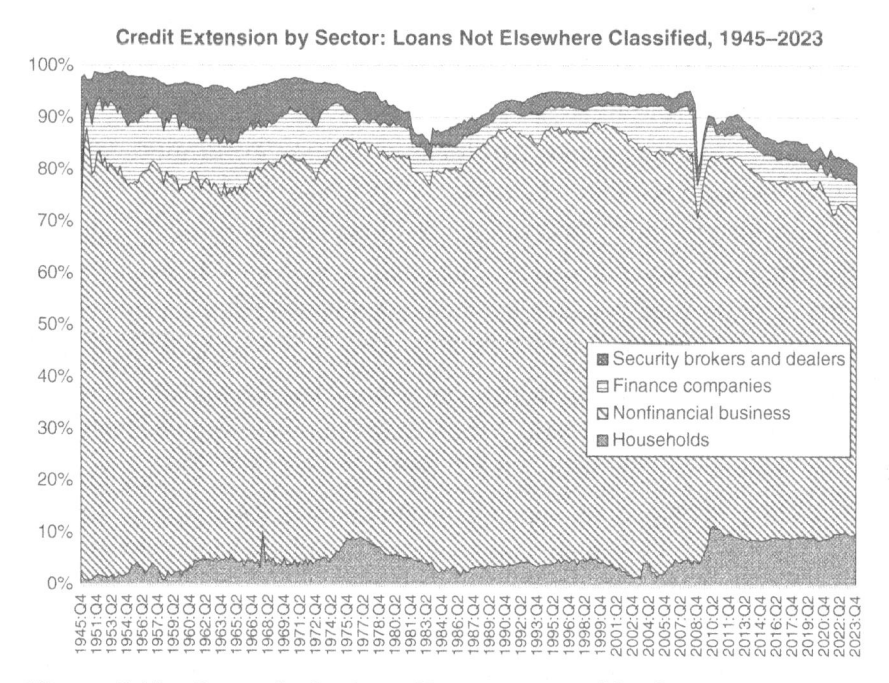

Figure 7.15 Sector destination of U.S. commercial lending, 1951–2023.

sectors receive bank credit that is not otherwise classified as mortgage credit or consumer credit. The majority of banks' other lending is directed to the nonfinancial business sector, shown in the second segment from the bottom. Notably, lending to non-corporate business overtook lending to corporate business in 2005. This trend may reflect expanded lending to private equity funds, which are organized as partnerships. Another 10% goes to the household and nonprofit sector (bottom), which is comparable to the share of lending to finance companies (second from top) and securities brokers and dealers (top). Almost all the unfilled space above the graph is lending to foreign borrowers, which likely reflects U.S. branches of foreign banks lending dollars to foreign borrowers, especially foreign nonbank financial institutions.[57]

But before we conclude that some $4 trillion in corporate lending by U.S. depositories faces no external competition, we note that collateralized loan obligations (CLOs) have issued nearly $1 trillion in corporate loans, often for leveraged buyouts of companies.[58] In addition, nonfinancial corporate business had $7.4 trillion in bonded corporate debt outstanding as of the end of 2023. Corporate bond issuance grew at a 4%–5% annual rate through the GFC and accelerated in the low-interest rate period that followed.[59] In Chapter 8, we will see that capital markets issuers benefit from several bank regulations that make corporate lending more costly than other banking book business. Nevertheless, it is notable that the banking system has not kept pace with the capital markets in providing debt finance to the nonfinancial business sector.

Three Big Questions

This chapter has covered a lot of ground. We began with Fisher's equation of exchange, which connects the use of money to output and the price level. In the hands of Cambridge economists, the equation of exchange became a theory of the demand for money. We then explored how deviations of the money supply from long-run equilibrium money demand can affect output and prices, and stressed that our analysis could be reproduced at the level of economic subsystems within institutional sectors and income strata.

Historically, a weak link in the quantity theory of money developed by Fisher and at Cambridge has been the measurement of the aggregate quantity of money. We showed how Barnett's Divisia indices of broad money based on the user costs of monetary liabilities provide a rigorous answer, isolating monetary services from the investment component of money balances. The resulting quantity indices give considerable weight to growth in demand deposit liabilities, while down-weighting MMF holdings and better-remunerated store-of-value moneys in determining the overall trend of monetary growth. Such indices support the notion that money demand is stable and behaves differently in cyclical downturns when compared to the simple sum aggregates historically tracked and disseminated by the Federal Reserve.

We then constructed Divisia quantity and user cost indices for selected sectors and strata of the U.S. economy. Our analysis showed marked differences in the demand for monetary services across households, corporate business, and non-corporate business, as well as across income strata. This heterogeneity in money demand is not an issue in a world of perfect capital markets, where money is frictionlessly reallocated from those with surpluses to those with deficits. But when obstacles to the reallocation of balances exist, changes in the dynamics of money supply can have skewed impacts. As a result, our analysis motivates our interest in designing monetary policy around the goal of neutrality, such that policy interventions do not systematically favor or disfavor selected sectors or strata of the economy. We describe our vision of neutral monetary policy more fully in Chapter 11.

Our exploration of Divisia broad money focused attention on the banking system as the primary source of monetary services. Throughout Part One, we emphasized that the banking system creates new deposit money by underwriting and originating loans. To understand the growth of monetary services over recent history, we reviewed data from the Flow of Funds statistics on the growth and composition of bank lending. We are particularly interested in the composition of bank lending as it highlights which bankable projects are the dominant bases for money creation.

Flow of Funds data show that the banking system has become dominated by mortgage credit. At least half the volume of bank loans in the postwar era were residential and commercial mortgages. While mortgage lending has pulled back since the GFC, the securities portfolios of banks remain concentrated in MBS issued by government-sponsored enterprises. For a time, mortgage lending crowded out corporate lending, though the latter has made a comeback of late. Consumer credit has also accelerated, perhaps picking up where pre-GFC home equity lending left off, albeit on an unsecured basis.

Overall, however, the growth rate of bank lending has been slowing. Bank balance sheets are growing at a reduced pace, and a smaller share of them is dedicated to lending. The share of loans in bank balance sheets has declined from a peak of two-thirds at the beginning of the Basel era to just over one-half. Balance sheet space has been consumed instead by securities holdings (especially MBS) and, since the GFC and COVID, by reserves and liquidity portfolios.

We have also shown that bank lending increasingly takes place against a backdrop of competition from the capital markets. Mortgage lending is dominated by the GSEs. The government is also a major player in consumer credit, along with captive auto finance companies. Corporate debt markets have grown much more quickly than corporate lending. Each of these entities sources funds from capital markets, drawing on savings rather than using the banking system's power of credit creation to finance projects which—at first blush—are bankable. Hence, we are interested in three big questions. First, are capital markets cannibalizing bankable projects which would otherwise support money creation by the banking system? Second, are savings no longer scarce, such that intermediating funds in the capital markets is not more costly than creating funding in the banking system? And third, if the base of bankable projects is eroding, how will the banking system safely meet the demand for money?

We believe that capital markets have been cannibalizing bankable projects. The mortgages, consumer credit, and commercial credit funded in capital markets is not uniformly more risky than similar projects funded by banks. Much of the mortgage credit securitized by the GSEs has long been underwritten to high standards and extended to prime borrowers. While exceptions undoubtedly exist—and existed in quantity before the GFC—one cannot argue, outside of the subprime debacle, that mortgage credit funded in the capital markets has served a different kind of borrower and a different sort of mortgage lending than bank credit has over more than five decades. Similarly, any company that can issue debt in the capital markets should be able to draw a commercial loan from the banking system. If corporate lending is not keeping pace with corporate debt, is leverage on the rise? If so, why can't bank credit contribute to that expanded debt stack in some proportional amount?

We believe that this pattern of cannibalization is symptomatic of an abundance of global savings flowing to the United States from the 1990s forward, as well as concentrations of savings within wealthy households and large business. We will explore these secular changes in the dynamics of saving in Chapter 13. However, we also see an important role for universal banks in fostering the cannibalization dynamic. In an entity with separate commercial banking and capital markets divisions, decisions about how to fund a project are not made based on whether the project is an efficient use of global savings. Instead, one decides based on risk-adjusted returns on regulatory capital on each side of the house. For much of the Basel I era, regulatory capital rules for the capital markets side were consistently more favorable for returns on equity than on the commercial banking side. We explore these rules in Chapter 8. However, even in a regime of regulatory parity between the divisions—if we can imagine one—incentives would still strongly favor the transactional approach of matching savings to investment for fees versus creating credit for a stream of interest payments. In Chapter 12, we express our doubts about whether a balance may be struck between the economic purposes of banking and financial intermediation within a universal banking firm through any mix of competition, corporate governance, and regulation.

In the context of monetary policy, our focus for Part Two, the big takeaway is our answer to the third question: the banking system has struggled to meet the demand for money since the GFC. This deficiency has been masked by waves of "quantitative easing" deployed from 2010 to 2014 and from 2020 to 2021. As we explain in Chapter 10, these interventions resulted in the Federal Reserve's balance sheet ballooning to nearly $9 trillion, as the Fed monetized trillions in government debt and agency MBS. The interventions have come at considerable fiscal cost and collateral damage to interbank markets and the conduct of central bank policy itself. They have also distorted asset prices, the income distribution, and capital formation.

If the banking system is to regain its position as the engine of aggregate money supply, we will have to attend to the obstacles in the way of bank credit creation. In the next chapter, we explore the incentives for bank credit creation stemming from the current global system of bank regulation. Much more ground concerning obstacles to bank credit creation will be covered in Part Three. There is some urgency in finding a solution, as abundant global savings cannot be taken for granted now as they have been in the past.

Notes

1. Because so many design choices are involved in measuring the demand for money, we do not put forward a preferred specification here. Some evidence is available in Barnett, W.A. (1980). Economic monetary aggregates: An application of index number and aggregation theory. *Journal of Econometrics* 14: 11–48; Janssen, N. (1996). The demand for Divisia money by the personal sector and by industrial and commercial companies. *Bank of England Quarterly Bulletin* (November): 405–411; Barnett, W.A. (2012). *Getting It Wrong: How Faulty Monetary Statistics Undermine the Fed* (MIT Press); and Barnett, W.A., Ghosh, T., and Adil, M.H. (2022). Is money demand really unstable? Evidence from Divisia monetary aggregates. *Economic Analysis and Policy* 74: 606–622.
2. In this section, we follow the historical account of Laidler, D. (1991). *The Golden Age of the Quantity Theory.* Princeton University Press. We thank David Laidler for his helpful comments on this chapter.

3. Fisher was not the first to write down the equation of exchange. He points to Simon Newcomb, a distinguished Professor of Mathematics at Johns Hopkins University and director of an autonomous branch of the United States Naval Observatory, as an important predecessor. Humphrey, T.M. (1984). Algebraic quantity equations before Fisher and Pigou. *Federal Reserve Bank of Richmond Economic Review* (September/October): 13–22 presents Newcomb's work, along with many other antecedents of the equation of exchange in multiple research traditions.

4. The desire to measure P and T accurately motivated Fisher to undertake significant research on index numbers beginning in the appendices to *The Purchasing Power of Money* and culminating in his 1923 book *The Making of Index Numbers*. (Fisher, I. (1911). *The Purchasing Power of Money: Its Determination and Relation to Credit, Interest, and Crises*. Macmillan; Fisher, I. (1923). *The Making of Index Numbers: A Study of Their Varieties, Tests, and Reliability*, 2e rev. ed. Houghton Mifflin).

5. See, for example, Rogers, C. (1989). *Money, Interest and Capital: A Study in the Foundations of Monetary Theory*. Cambridge University Press and Stiglitz, J.E. and Greenwald, B. (2003). *Towards a New Paradigm in Monetary Economics*. Cambridge University Press.

6. The Cambridge approach was a mostly oral tradition from its early development by Marshall in the 1870s until the appearance of Pigou, A.C. (1917). The Value of Money. *Quarterly Journal of Economics* 32.

7. Engle, R.F. and Granger, C.W.J. (1987). Co-integration and error correction: Representation, estimation, and testing. *Econometrica* 55 (2): 251–276 introduce an influential method for testing the long-run stability of an equilibrium relationship between variables and using that relationship to correct dynamic estimates of economic systems. They applied their testing framework to $MV = PY$, rejecting stability for all measures of money except M2.

8. See, for example, Miller, S.M. (1991). Monetary dynamics: An application of cointegration and error-correction modeling. *Journal of Money, Credit and Banking* 23 (2): 139–154. A complete system includes lagged changes in $x_1, \ldots, x_n$ on the right-hand side, as well as equations modeling changes in $x_1, \ldots, x_n$. We suppress these for simplicity.

9. Bae, Y. and DeJong, R.M. (2007). Money demand function estimation by nonlinear cointegration. *Journal of Applied Econometrics* 22 (4): 767–793, Gefang, D. (2012). Money-output causality revisited—A Bayesian logistic smooth transition VECM perspective. *Oxford Bulletin of Economics and Statistics* 74 (1): 0305–9049.

10. Summing up nominal quantities is recognizable as a simple form of index construction in which all prices are equal to one. Balk, B. (2008). *Price and Quantity Index Numbers: Models for Measuring Aggregate Change and Difference.* Cambridge University Press: 5 notes that the method was proposed in 1738 by Dutot, so simple summation can be called a Dutot index. Representing the simple sum as an index may seem like a needless abstraction, but it facilitates testing for properties we would like indices to have. Thus, it can be proven that simple sum indices fail for heterogeneous aggregates (193–194).
11. We thank William A. Barnett for his helpful comments on this chapter, and William A. Barnett and Jeff van den Noort for granting us access to the non-public underlying data for the Divisia broad money indices, which are available to other researchers on request.
12. The story of Divisia aggregation of broad money is told with more rigor (and a generous helping of notes from the trenches) in Barnett, W.A. (2012). *Getting It Wrong: How Faulty Monetary Statistics Undermine the Fed* (MIT Press). The theory underlying the Divisia indices appears in Barnett, W.A. (1980). Economic monetary aggregates: An application of index number and aggregation theory. *Journal of Econometrics* 14: 11–48. Barnett, W.A., Offenbacher, E.K., and Spindt, P.A. (1984). The new Divisia monetary aggregates. *Journal of Political Economy* 92 (6): 1049–1085 shows how empirical results on the quantity theory change when simple sum indices are replaced with Divisia indices. Further important papers are collected in Barnett, W.A. and Serletis, A. (eds.) (2000). *The Theory of Monetary Aggregation.* Elsevier. The details of the Divisia indices published by the CFS are available in Barnett, W.A., Liu, J., Mattson, R.S. et al. (2013). The new CFS Divisia monetary aggregates: Design, construction, and data sources. *Open Economies Review* 24: 101–124.
13. Barnett, W.A. (1980). Economic monetary aggregates: An application of index number and aggregation theory. *Journal of Econometrics* 14: 11–48, Jorgenson, D.W. (1963). Capital theory and investment behavior. *American Economic Review* 53 (2): 247–259.
14. Baumol, W.J. (1952). The transactions demand for cash: An inventory theoretic approach. *Quarterly Journal of Economics* 56: 545–546; Tobin, J. (1956). The interest-elasticity of transactions demand for cash. *Review of Economics and Statistics* 38 (3): 241–247.
15. Or what Keynes might have called the speculative demand for money.
16. We assume these are measured in compatible units—i.e., per annum rates with the same compounding frequency.

17. Adding up over t with this definition of $\overline{s}_{it}$ creates a trapezoid approximation to the continuous time integral.
18. In levels we have $f_{it} = q_{it}/q_{i,t-1}$.
19. Barnett, W.A. (1980). Economic monetary aggregates: An application of index number and aggregation theory. *Journal of Econometrics* 14: 11–48. The user cost must be divided by $(1 + R)$ to discount back from the end of the discrete period and multiplied by the true cost of living index p^* to become nominal, if it is to be used in a demand for money equation. However, for purposes of computing a monetary index, the factor $p^*/(1 + R)$ cancels out of the numerator and denominator of the expenditure shares. We thank William Barnett for pointing out this difference.
20. Travelers checks are included in cash. They were discontinued as part of the CFS aggregate in 2018.
21. See Barnett, W.A., Liu, J., Mattson, R.S. et al. (2013). The new CFS Divisia monetary aggregates: Design, construction, and data sources. *Open Economies Review* 24: 101–124 for details on the sweeps adjustments.
22. This point is made by Barnett, W.A. (2012). *Getting it Wrong: How Faulty Monetary Statistics Undermine the Fed* (MIT Press): 102–107.
23. Barnett, W.A., Offenbacher, E.K., and Spindt, P.A. (1984). The new Divisia monetary aggregates. *Journal of Political Economy* 92 (6): 1049–1085; Barnett, W.A., Ghosh, T., and Adil, M.H. (2022). Is money demand really unstable? Evidence from Divisia monetary aggregates. *Economic Analysis and Policy* 74: 606–622.
24. https://fred.stlouisfed.org/series/CPIAUCSL.
25. In response to the Fed's announcement of quantitative easing, economists and financiers including John Taylor and Clifford Asness published an open letter in the *Wall Street Journal* sounding the alarm for inflation. If the signatories had been paying attention to the relative contribution of banks, nonbanks, and the government to the money supply, they would have realized their letter was a misguided false alarm.
26. See Hanke, S.H. and Sekerke, M. (2017). Bank regulation as monetary policy: Lessons from the great recession. *Cato Journal* 37: 385–405 for a more detailed analysis.
27. These are tables L.204–L.207 and L.209 in the 2023Q4 Flow of Funds data.
28. From 1978 to 1984, 88% of the corporate sector's expenditure on monetary services was allocated to checkable deposits, versus 59% for households. Non-corporate business was similarly exposed to the increased user cost of

checkable deposits, but managed to grow these deposits steadily to offset the effect of higher interest rates.

29. See the important caveats on comparing the indices made in connection with the stratification by income below.
30. For some examples of money demand estimation with sectoral Divisia indices, see Drake, L. and Chrystal, K.A. (1994). Company-sector money demand: New evidence on the existence of a stable long-run relationship for the United Kingdom. *Journal of Money, Credit, and Banking* 26 (3): 479–494, which studies industrial/commercial sector demand for British pounds, and Janssen, N. (1996). The demand for Divisia money by the personal sector and by industrial and commercial companies. *Bank of England Quarterly Bulletin* (November): 405–411, which studies the demand for the British pound in the person and industrial/commercial sectors in a more complete system.
31. Batty, M., Bricker, J., Briggs, J. et al. (2022). The distributional financial accounts of the United States. In: *Measuring Distribution and Mobility of Income and Wealth* (ed. Raj Chetty, J.N. Friedman, J.C. Gornick, B. Johnson, and A. Kennickell), 641–677. University of Chicago Press.
32. Barnett, W.A. (1980). Economic monetary aggregates: An application of index number and aggregation theory. *Journal of Econometrics* 14: 11–48: 17.
33. See Kornfeld, R.J., Lynn, L., and Yamashita, T. (2016). Expanding the integrated macroeconomics accounts' financial sector. *Survey of Current Business* 96 (January): 1–15: 4: "The [Financial Accounts of the United States] provide separate statistics for all private depository institutions and for U.S.-chartered depository institutions, credit unions, foreign banking offices in the United States, and banks in the U.S. affiliated areas.... An advantage of these data is that the boundary of depository institutions is well defined: the data cover only insured banking operations and not the operations of nondeposit taking entities."
34. The assets of banks in U.S.-affiliated areas are small enough to ignore when considering aggregate trends.
35. Vickery, J., Deng, A., and Sullivan, T. (2015). Available for sale? Understanding bank securities portfolios. *Liberty Street Economics*, February 11.
36. Office of the Comptroller of the Currency. (1990). *Comptroller's Handbook, Investment Securities (Section 203)—Narratives and Procedures*, March. After the Dodd-Frank Act additional guidance has been issued about determining what securities are "investment grade" without relying on external credit ratings.

37. The difference between reserves and Fed Funds was based on required and excess reserve balances. With the elimination of reserve requirements in 2020, the distinction no longer matters.
38. The balance of borrowed reserves for the entire banking system is non-zero because government agencies such as the Federal Home Loan Banks and the GSE mortgage lenders can be net lenders of reserves.
39. Kaufman, G.G. (1984). The securities activities of commercial banks. *Federal Reserve Bank of Chicago Staff Memoranda 84-2*; Fischer, T.G., Gram, W.H., Kaufman, G.G. et al. (1985). The securities activities of commercial banks: A legal and economic analysis. *Federal Reserve Bank of Chicago Staff Memoranda 85-2*; Grossman, R.S. (2010). *Unsettled Account: The Evolution of Banking in the Industrialized World Since 1800*. Princeton University Press: Chapter 10.
40. Other loans and advances are a grab-bag of lending activities in which banks seldom participate.
41. Draws on committed credit lines boosted commercial lending post-GFC (Ivashina, V. and Scharfstein, D. (2010). Bank lending during the financial crisis of 2008. *Journal of Financial Economics* 97: 319–338).
42. Agency multifamily mortgage securities are classified as agency CMBS but excluded from commercial mortgages in the Flow of Funds instrument tables.
43. See, for example, FDIC Quarterly Banking Profile First Quarter 2024, available at https://www.fdic.gov/news/speeches/2024/fdic-quarterly-banking-profile-first-quarter-2024.
44. Competition between commercial banks and investment banks for the same opportunities was long viewed as a reason for separating their spheres of activity. In 1984, George Kaufman of Loyola University of Chicago and the Federal Reserve Bank of Chicago wrote, "established commercial and investment banks each have secured positions in markets in which they had been sheltered by law or by regulation from competition from the other. As may be expected, some of these institutions have been reluctant to surrender these privileges peacefully, and have resisted efforts of the other to penetrate their markets through changes in laws or regulations. Indeed, the battle for turf between commercial and investment banks is being hotly contested in national and state legislatures and regulatory agencies, as well as in the marketplace." (Kaufman, G.G. (1984). The securities activities of commercial banks. *Federal Reserve Bank of Chicago Staff Memoranda 84-2*: 2–3).
45. Flow of Funds Table L.217.
46. Ibid.

47. The agency/GSE share includes balance-sheet loans and sponsored mortgage pools. Following the GFC, most GSE mortgage pools were consolidated on GSE balance sheets.
48. Blumberg, A. (2011). "Kill Them, Bury Them": The Rise of Fannie and Freddie. *All Things Considered (NPR), March 28.* See also Jaffee, D. (2008). Reregulating Fannie Mae and Freddie Mac. *Working Paper, Haas School of Business, University of California, Berkeley,* Jaffee, D. (2009). The future of Fannie Mae and Freddie Mac in the U.S. mortgage market. *Working Paper, Haas School of Business, University of California, Berkeley* on the GSEs.
49. Flow of Funds Table L. 218.
50. Ibid, lines 23–28.
51. Flow of Funds Table L. 220.
52. Flow of Funds Table L. 219.
53. Flow of Funds Table L. 222.
54. Every credit card network has either a network of commercial banks (Visa, Mastercard) or a single commercial bank (American Express, Discover—pending merger with CapitalOne) behind it. Credit card ABS remain consolidated on issuing bank balance sheets because receivables are continuously contributed and withdrawn, making the "true sale" necessary for bankruptcy remoteness an impossibility.
55. The CAGRs are 11.1% and 5.1%, respectively, for consumer credit and home equity lending.
56. Flow of Funds Table L. 215. A small portion of loans not elsewhere classified were made by the Federal Reserve during the GFC.
57. Flow of Funds Table L. 215.
58. These appear in tables L.127 and L.133 of the Flow of Funds data. The series are divided by the domicile of the issuing CLO. Loans issued by U.S.-domiciled CLOs appear in L.127 (securitized other loans and advances, about $305 billion), while those issued by CLOs domiciled outside the United States appear in the Rest of the World table L.133 (bonds—collateralized loan obligations—liability, about $660 billion).
59. Flow of Funds Table L. 213.

Chapter 8

The Regulation of Universal Banks

Bank regulation deserves a bigger place in discussions of monetary policy because most monetary services are produced by the banking system.[1] Over long periods, the conditions governing money creation by banks will dominate the tactical decisions made by central banks in determining the money supply and its impact on the economy. The money creation process is no mere "channel" through which changes in the central bank's short-term policy rate affect the wider economy.

By bank regulation we mean restrictions on the size, distribution, and content of bank balance sheets imposed by law or required by a suitably empowered government agency. The primary goal of bank regulation is to preserve the moneyness of the deposit claims created by each bank and the banking system collectively. It provides a layer of assurance that each bank is sufficiently liquid and solvent to allow nonbank holders of deposit claims to dispose of their deposit balances at par. Such assurance applies both when the bank is a going concern and when the bank has failed.

Compliance with bank regulation is necessary to maintain a bank's charter, its access to deposit insurance, and its ability to transact with the central bank. In the United States, each of these consequences is meted out by a distinct regulator. The Office of the Comptroller of the Currency (OCC), housed under the U.S. Treasury, charters national banks under the National Bank Act of 1863, revised substantially in 1864. State banks are chartered by state-level agencies. The Federal Reserve sets rules for state- and nationally chartered banks to transact with the Federal Reserve System through the Federal Reserve Act of 1913, and charters

Bank Holding Companies under the Bank Holding Companies Act of 1956. The Federal Deposit Insurance Corporation (FDIC) was created by the FDIC Act of 1933 and sets requirements for state and national banks that wish to obtain deposit insurance.[2]

Bank regulation has always been present whenever the possibility of chartering a bank as a corporate enterprise has existed. It has two basic components. First, *liquidity rules* require a bank to hold sufficient liquid assets to allow deposits to be realized as cash and to enable settlement of transactions via deposit balances within the banking system. Liquidity rules may extend beyond deposits to other existing and contingent obligations of the bank that require immediate access to funds. Second, *capital rules* require a bank to hold sufficient capital to absorb unexpected losses on assets and preserve the value of deposits. They specify what capital *is* in the context of banking—which may be quite different from other corporate finance contexts—and align its quantity with various indicia of bank risk-taking.

In Chapter 5, we argued that profit maximizing banks would maintain sufficient liquidity and capital to support the expansion of their balance sheets and the associated creation of monetary claims. The bank's economic needs for capital and liquidity constrain the expansion of its balance sheet. Bank regulation introduces regulatory analogues of the capital and liquidity constraints. The important question for analysis is which of the economic and regulatory constraints will bind, and when. To the extent that regulations require levels of liquidity and capital in excess of those the bank would choose itself—that is, when regulations are the binding constraint on bank balance sheets—they may be regarded from an economic perspective as a kind of tax on the bank.

Taxes lead to "deadweight losses," or output that is lost to society as a result of the tax. When bank regulations are the binding constraint on the sector, banks do not produce as much money (deposit liabilities) as they would in the absence of regulation, and bankable projects are not funded. The loss can be a constraint on the growth rate of the economy if it prevents money supply from keeping pace with money demand. Efforts to obtain money through other channels may shift production of money outside of the banking system into the "shadow banking" system. Another efficiency loss from regulation-based rationing of bankable projects occurs when projects that could otherwise be funded with bank money creation are funded by savings in the capital market, or not at all.

The deadweight loss of production in the banking system is, therefore, realized twice in terms of aggregate savings. When loans are not made to fund bankable projects, the project consumes savings when funded in the capital markets. And when deposit money is not created to fund the loan, some portion of aggregate savings must be rendered sufficiently safe as an investment to issue money-like claims against it. Unless savings are not scarce (in the aggregate), a diversion of risk capital to safe assets will tend to depress risk-free rates and increase risk premia for risky assets. Safe assets will increase in price, while the price of risky assets will fall.

What is unusual about the recent financial history of the United States is the coincidence of overproduction of safe assets, a secular decline in risk-free interest rates, and a compression of risk premia in the equity market. When it comes to savings, our cup runneth over. No matter how many assets our financial system produces, from government debt to private debt to securitizations to equity shares, there is foreign or domestic capital clamoring to snatch them up. On one hand, this is the realization of the "exorbitant privilege" that comes with being the issuer of dollars in a globalized and dollar-based financial system. On the other hand, the fruits of that privilege may not be durable or sustainable. If they are not, the usefulness of bank credit in economizing savings stands to become a matter of intense interest.

We shall argue in Part Three that recent developments in the world economy suggest that the profligate use of savings to reproduce the function of banks is not a wise strategy for the future. As global populations age in the rich world and central banks sit atop mountains of dollar reserves, the tide of international capital is receding for the United States. The overproduction of safe assets in the capital markets has also delivered inordinate power to the venture capitalists and growth-equity funds that supply risk capital to new enterprises, leading to waves of fragile, lookalike "unicorn" startups, cycles of dubious hype, and a corresponding dearth of new business formation and economic dynamism. From a macroeconomic perspective, savings are better used to reinforce bank capital, where they can be safely leveraged into the production of loans and deposits, and to fund risky investments that spur competition and innovation.

As a kind of tax, bank regulation also distorts incentives. Banks face a sort of "budget constraint" for their lending and investments in securities given by their capital and funding levels. The capital and liquidity constraints imposed by contemporary bank regulation apply tax rates unevenly to assets in a bank's budget set based on regulators' perceptions of their respective credit and liquidity risks. Regulation not only gives us less lending and less money creation, but also changes the set of projects funded with bank credit and the distribution of purchasing power by distorting bank budget constraints.

We have consciously posed the costs and benefits of bank regulation in terms of the production of money, rather than in terms of safety versus bank profitability. The latter framing provides political cover for bank regulation and is justified in no small part by cases of egregious conduct, compensation, and consumption by bankers before and after the GFC. However, it reduces questions of regulation to debates about discipline and punishment rather than the proper functioning of the banking sector. We believe there is an approach to regulation that is compatible with safety and soundness as well as robust production of purchasing power. We expand on this vision in Part Three.

As we present the form and recent history of bank regulation in this chapter, we begin to explain the secular trends identified in Chapter 7. We seek to explain long-term shifts in the growth and composition of bank balance sheets. In particular, we aim to explain why the distribution of debt finance toward the nonfinancial business and household sectors has tilted so profoundly against bank credit in favor of debt securities, and why households switched from being a strong source of savings to the capital markets to being large users of capital market savings. We investigate how far the incentives created by bank regulation can be held responsible for the compression of bank lending in the overall share of finance.[3]

More broadly, we worry that the tendency of bank regulation to expand in scope and specificity has transformed the business of banking from a dynamic enterprise supported by innovation and judicious risk-taking into a rote exercise in which compliance (and games to defeat it) absorb the imagination of the major players. For lack of a better idea, the regulatory regime is turning the sector into an odd sort of public utility, gravitating toward an ersatz "natural monopoly." While regulators are not to blame for the incompetence of the fintech challengers nipping at incumbents' heels, they are largely to blame for the conditions creating them.

We begin our analysis with capital rules, returning to liquidity rules afterwards. We defer discussion of deposit insurance until Chapter 9 and devote less space to it than has become customary because we are less impressed than "modern" theorists of banking by the game-theoretic dilemma that supposedly animates and requires it.

Bank Capital Regulation

The basic idea of bank capital regulation is to provide a backstop for unforeseen risks. The primary form of risk faced in banking is credit risk. Banks manage credit risk first by rejecting unsafe lending opportunities and second by attaching credit risk premia to loan interest rates. The excess interest earnings can be accumulated in a loan loss reserve and released if losses are realized. If loss reserves are inadequate, losses are charged against the bank's own account.

Capital regulation ensures that the bank's own account holds enough funds to absorb these unforeseen losses.

How much capital should banks hold? The overriding concern for regulators is to protect the value of the bank's deposit liabilities, ensuring that bank money continues to exchange for cash at par. The assets of a bank must be sufficient to redeem the deposit money it created, whether from the future surpluses underwritten by the bank or from the bank's own funds.

Defining Bank Capital

Discussions of bank capital regulation often proceed as if we know exactly what capital is, when in fact one of the ongoing tasks of bank capital regulation has been to clarify what components of a bank's balance sheet constitute capital. And it goes without saying that deposits are not part of a bank's "capital structure," in the sense that they are not just another (peculiar) sort of debt subject to the standard Modigliani-Miller analysis.[4] The determination turns on how we would like capital to *function*, which itself has been an ongoing topic of debate among regulators. Before arguing about percentages, economists and others would do well to grapple with these foundational questions.

The capital structure of a bank is what remains after eliminating deposit liabilities from the right-hand side of the balance sheet. These items decompose into debt, other borrowed funds, and equity capital. We might, as a starting point, hope to find easy agreement that equity is bank capital. However, almost all of the complications associated with analyzing the equity of a corporation are present with respect to bank equity.[5]

For much of the history of banking as a corporate enterprise, the common equity of banks has not been a limited liability instrument. Bank owners have often been liable to reimburse their banks for losses in excess of their original investment. Their commitments thus required the distinction between fully "paid-in" and "committed" equity capital.[6] In a regime of double liability, for example, paid-in equity capital would be matched by an equal amount of committed capital which had not yet been contributed to the business. Both portions would be available, in principle, to absorb losses by the bank in a situation of distress. Nevertheless, one might wonder whether bank distress would trigger personal bankruptcies if the shareholders were unable to make good on their commitments. Regimes of triple and unlimited liability have previously existed for holders of common bank shares.[7]

Additions to common equity naturally accumulate through retained earnings. Changes in the value of bank assets and liabilities pass through bank equity as Accumulated Other Comprehensive Income (AOCI). The impact of AOCI depends on the extent to which the bank's assets and liabilities are subject to mark-to-market accounting, the bank's foreign currency exposures, and dull but not irrelevant details related to pension accounting and deferred tax assets. None of the change in surplus has been realized in ready funds, but its visibility has sometimes made surplus (or at least some components of it) acceptable as capital for regulatory purposes.

Common equity also grows in acquisitions when a bank acquires intangible assets or capitalizes the purchase price premium as goodwill. As neither of these transactions results in funds that can absorb losses, goodwill and intangibles are generally deducted from equity to obtain "tangible equity" for regulatory capital purposes. An exception is sometimes made for purchased mortgage servicing rights (MSRs), which can be somewhat reliably valued based on anticipated streams of fees earned when the bank, as mortgage servicer, collects payments on mortgages owned by someone else.

One also has to worry about minority interests, especially those held by other banks. Cross-holdings of equity were (and are) a major headache among Japanese banks, for example. Preferred equity grates because of its required dividend, which comes at the expense of retained earnings. On the other hand, it, too, is usually crushed in bankruptcy and absorbs losses.

Finally, in a bank holding company, there is equity held at the bank level and equity held at the holding company level. Under the so-called "source of strength doctrine," Bank Holding Companies in the United States are meant to contribute funds to subsidiary banks in times of financial distress, partly mimicking previous regimes with weaker limits on shareholder liability.[8] Holding company funds are sometimes raised by issuing debt at the holding company level, creating additional needs for bank subsidiary dividends to the parent.

Bank loan loss reserves have had a surprisingly controversial history. On the balance sheet, they are a "contra-asset" account rather than a component of equity, but this is semantics. They are manifestly funded and available to take the pain from loan defaults so depositors do not have to. U.S. tax rules once favored the accumulation of generous loan loss reserves on a pretax basis (up to 2.4% of assets). Reforms limiting their force as a tax shield duly shrunk them. Changes in accounting rules may be bringing them back.[9] As additions to loan loss reserves offset current income, banks are not keen to use them, especially if they do not count as regulatory capital.

From there we move into the realm of debt, which is subordinated to deposits and potentially convertible to equity. Subordinated debt provides additional cushion for the value of deposits once a bank is insolvent by absorbing losses not borne by equity or loss reserves. Convertible debt is better, provided it converts to equity at a time it can function as equity. Convertible noteholders will generally not convert when they expect their equity to lose most or all of its value. Contingent convertible ("CoCo") bonds triggered by stress or bonds convertible at the option of the bank are two potential improvements.

Our purpose in this review is not so much to impress (or bore) you with our knowledge of esoteric funding instruments and their accounting as it is to point out that many aspects of a bank's balance sheet can potentially function as equity to ensure that depositors' balances are realizable at par. Banks may be better capitalized than regulatory capital ratios imply. At the same time, bankruptcy is costly and there is an obvious interest in maintaining banks as going concerns. There are tangible consequences to declaring what is and is not capital for regulatory purposes, both for the returns earned by holders of common bank equity and for the safety and soundness of the bank.

Capital Adequacy Before the Basel Era

Capital adequacy has long been evaluated through balance sheet ratios of assets to capital, risk assets to capital, risk-weighted assets to capital, and (deposit) liabilities to capital. Sometimes ratios have been used as bright-line criteria, and other times as guidelines in conjunction with other factors.[10]

The ratio of assets to capital is incredibly easy to compute and provides an immediate indication of how leveraged the bank's capital is. It does not discriminate among categories of assets, so it does not systematically favor or disfavor any of them. But it is very hard not to discriminate when certain assets like reserves and government debt are free of credit risk, for example. Hence, regulators might look at the ratio of risk assets to capital after deducting cash and government bonds from total assets, as U.S. regulators did in the post-World War II era.[11] The all-or-nothing treatment of assets can be refined into risk weights, establishing a spectrum of risk characteristics across assets but potentially boosting the attractiveness of certain categories. The Federal Reserve introduced the first system of risk-weighted assets in the United States in 1956 with its Analyzing Bank Capital framework, which provided an indication of bank soundness rather than a dispositive measurement.[12]

The scope of unexpected losses potentially extends beyond default risk to foreign exchange, interest rate, and other market risks. The international expansion of banks under the Bretton Woods system of fixed exchange rates, the development of the offshore market for U.S. dollar-denominated deposits (the "Eurodollar" market), exposure to commodities in the oil trade and elsewhere, and the disinflationary hikes in interest rates during the 1970s each pushed new risks to the forefront of regulators' thinking.[13]

As the province of bank regulators, the subject of regulatory capital has not always been viewed as an inherently economic problem. In the United States and elsewhere, the regulation of banks was driven by lawyers and accountants in its early days, and their influence on regulatory processes remains.[14] Many difficult regulatory problems are punted to legislators and government agencies for legal definitions, or to accounting bodies for accounting definitions. Consequently, criteria for bank regulations tend to prefer verifiability to insightful modeling or handwringing about incentives. This disconnect remains in current discussions on bank regulation.

Capital Adequacy After the First Basel Accord

The Basel Committee on Banking Supervision (BCBS) was established in the 1970s by the banking supervisors of the G10 group of countries as a technical working group to coordinate the regulation of banks across jurisdictions. The project of an international accord on bank capital regulation led by the BCBS was prompted by a wave of defaults on loans made by U.S. banks to firms and governments in Latin America. As the U.S. authorities contemplated a recapitalization of the banking system, they believed additional measures to preserve the international competitiveness of the U.S. would be prudent. The principle they embraced was a minimum level of capital based on the risk-weighted assets of banks.

From its first stirrings, the Basel regulatory regime sought to accommodate marked differences in the practice of banking across far-flung jurisdictions. In the United States, the activities of banks were still fairly restricted. Prohibitions on the interstate branching of banks still had not been removed, though a two-decade-long consolidation of the commercial banking system was well underway.[15] Banks were still essentially confined to lending, deposits and government securities transactions, with pseudopodia projected into a short list of other financial businesses. The European landscape, by contrast, was dominated by universal banks straddling the capital markets and traditional banking business. Meanwhile in Japan, South Korea, and Taiwan, nascent banking sectors were growing rapidly and extending their reach into all areas of finance. Industrial policy aimed at the semiconductor sector and other technologically advanced areas was supported by the aggressive expansion of bank credit.[16] U.S. firms would loudly complain about the advantageous terms on which their Japanese and Korean competitors would obtain finance, and it is not absurd to think that capital-based restraints on bank lending were—at least in part—a device meant to subdue this new Asian competition.

A first consensus on the Basel regulatory regime would also be informed by the experience of banking crises. Excessive lending against residential and commercial real estate for long, fixed terms created a wave of failures among U.S. savings and loan associations (commercial banks with a limited form of charter) beginning in 1987.[17] The Resolution Trust Corporation was set up to acquire the sector's distressed assets and liquidate them to repay depositors, with a generous assist from government funds. The sale of commercial real estate assets through securitizations launched the commercial mortgage-backed securities (CMBS) market.[18] In 1989, Japan's real estate mania collapsed, plunging banks and corporate business alike into a long hibernation in which unrealized massive losses left much of the corporate sector insolvent.[19] German banking was knocked off course during the reunification of East and West, as the inferior East German currency was converted to Deutsche marks at par, along with the assets and liabilities of the East German banking sector.

The first Basel Accord of 1988 established an international system of risk-weighted assets to evaluate capital adequacy, adopting an approach the Federal Reserve had introduced in the 1950s.[20] Banks were required to hold capital equal to at least 8% of their credit risk-weighted balance sheet exposures, the credit-equivalent amount of their off-balance sheet exposures, and their potential future exposure to over-the-counter (OTC) derivatives counterparties (collectively "risk-weighted assets" or RWAs). Capital was structured as Tier 1 and Tier 2 capital. Tier 1 capital comprised of paid-up common stock and retained earnings or surplus (net of goodwill) was intended to be "going concern" capital equal to at least 4% of RWAs. "Gone concern" capital in Tier 2 would then bring the total over 8% of RWAs using loan loss reserves, undisclosed reserves, asset revaluation reserves, hybrid capital instruments, and subordinated debt.[21] The level of 8% was chosen following a two-decade trend of declining capital/asset ratios in the United States which left banks holding capital in the range of 5%–6% of their unweighted on-balance sheet assets. The wave of bank failures in the late 1980s contributed to the perception that bank capital levels had become too low.

The classification of assets under Basel I was comparatively simple, with five categories of risks receiving credit risk weights of 0%, 10%, 20%, 50%, and 100%. The risk weights favored securities of the government and government agencies, claims on other OECD banks, and mortgages. Corporate credit, commercial real estate, and asset-based lending received the highest risk weights.[22] A simple formula pegged the potential future credit exposure of derivatives, requiring banks to recognize the converted amount plus an add-on as the risk-weighted exposure.[23]

The 1996 Market Risk Amendment

In the first Basel Accord, no provisions were made for market risk, nor were any distinctions drawn between banking book and trading book exposures. The issues had not escaped notice, but the BCBS needed another eight years to work them out. The result was the 1996 market risk amendment to the Basel Accords, which first distinguished the "trading book" from the "banking book" and established market risk weights for "trading book" exposures carried by banks at market values.[24] Significantly, banks were permitted to use internal risk models to determine the required amount of capital, defined as the 99% 10-day Value at Risk (VaR) of in-scope trading book exposures.[25] The computation acknowledged the inherent diversification of market risks as well as the difficulty of prescribing risk weights for a wide range of heterogeneous exposures. Control over the VaR modeling was established by backtesting it on historical data. If a model failed more frequently than anticipated in backtests, the required market risk capital would be scaled up through an increased multiplier coefficient.

Banks also won the right to recognize diversification in their potential future derivative exposures. The initial implementation of Basel I acted as if all of banks' derivative exposures would be in the bank's favor at the same time, which was highly unlikely. The 1996 amendment permits the netting of derivative exposures where legally enforceable netting agreements are in place. The design of such agreements under the aegis of the International Swaps and Derivatives Association was no small feat and represented a signal advance in the development of OTC derivatives markets.

Before the market risk amendment of 1996, banks already had a clear incentive to convert loan credit risk into market risk wherever possible. Following the 1996 amendment, universal banks could not shed credit risks entirely, but they remained able to evaluate their VaR-based regulatory capital requirements against the corresponding credit risk weights. In many cases, the market risk-based requirements remained much lower than the prescribed credit risk weights. And where the market-risk based capital requirements were larger, the embedded leverage banks obtained through financial engineering meant that banks' return on regulatory capital could be higher for a market risk-based transaction than it would be as a loan. Where there were borderline cases, banks freely moved exposures back and forth, changing their treatment for accounting and regulatory purposes.

The market risk amendment of 1996 was considered an embrace of the cutting edge of risk management by the Basel regime. While capital requirements could be computed according to a standardized treatment, a bank with modest sophistication in quantitative risk management could compute capital requirements using an enterprise VaR model.[26] VaR calculations consider a distribution of potential losses for the portfolio held in the trading book over a specified horizon. For Basel regulatory capital, banks were asked to compute the 99th percentile of their loss distribution over a 10-day horizon. The calculations offered benefits from the perspective of the regulator and the bank. The regulator is assured that losses will exceed VaR only 1% of the time, provided VaR is calculated reliably.[27] From the bank's perspective, the VaR calculation recognizes that not every position will lose money at the same time. In addition, the bank has discretion over the way its risks are aggregated, the risk factors defining loss scenarios, and the data used to estimate the loss distribution. If the bank's sole concern were to minimize regulatory capital, the rules for market risk prevailing from 1996 left many levers available for that purpose.

Furthermore, little in the Basel market risk regime prevented a universal bank from moving positions between the banking book and the trading book via creative financial engineering. Back-to-back derivative transactions between the banking and capital markets businesses could rapidly and synthetically transfer the risk of any position from the banking book to the trading book, or vice versa, enabling the bank to obtain the more favorable capital treatment on a position-by-position basis. With a good deal of additional work, credit risks in the banking book could be transmuted into trading book market risks by securitizing loans as mortgage- or asset-backed securities. The resulting securities traded like safe bonds, implying minimal levels of market risk.

The Monetary Policy Impact of the Basel I Era

Together, the Basel Accord of 1988 and the 1996 market risk amendment formed the core of international bank regulation for the pre-GFC period from 1992 to 2007. The initial accord was phased in over a nearly four-year transition period in the United States, and its replacement Basel II had only begun to be implemented in parallel by the largest banks when the GFC reached its peak. Implementation in Europe began in 2007, with advanced methods phasing in from 2008. Thus, the story of evolving bank regulations' impact on the global financial system is really a story about the transition from Basel I to Basel III, with the latter drawing on the perceived strengths of Basel II and unfolding in steps from 2011 to the time of writing.

Within the domain of monetary policy, our concern is how the regulatory capital incentives faced by universal banks affected the commercial banking side of the business. We saw commercial bank balance sheets reacting to the Basel Accord incentives from 1992 to 2007 in Chapter 7. The relative share of loans on bank balance sheets declined, while the share of securities expanded. Changes in the pattern of lending followed the risk weight incentives. Loan portfolios shifted away from the nonfinancial business sector to residential mortgages. Securities portfolios came to favor securitized mortgage exposures, especially collateralized mortgage obligations (CMOs). Nonfinancial business increasingly raised debt finance in the capital markets. Universal banks could hold high-rated corporate bonds in the banking book on the same terms as corporate loans, or in the trading book based on their VaR. The low volatility of corporate bond prices made it advantageous to fund commercial borrowers in capital markets rather than on bank balance sheets.

During the Basel I era, the base for commercial bank money creation shifted from the nonfinancial business sector to the household sector. Bank assets continued to grow at a 7%–8% annual rate, but the reduction of loans' share in bank assets meant that the supply of bank money was growing at a slower rate than previously. To meet the money demand of an expanding economy, nonbank sources stepped in to fill the gap. MMFs and repos based on securitized collateral supplied store-of-value money to a nonfinancial business sector hungry for cash equivalents.[28]

A drag on monetary production had already been induced by bank capital regulations in the relatively permissive era of Basel I. The drag was mitigated and obscured by shadow bank money production. But after the GFC laid bare the risks of relying on shadow banking, revisions to the bank regulatory regime did not prioritize commercial bank loan growth or bank money creation. The new standardized credit risk weights of Basel III do little to redress the distortions of Basel I. Instead of carrots for new lending, Basel III is replete with sticks for securitization, derivatives, and trading book assets. New and expansive liquidity requirements have further reduced the share of bank balance sheets devoted to lending. These constraints, coupled with increased capital requirements and supplementary leverage ratios, have further squeezed the production of bank money in the post-GFC era.

The Problem of the Trading Book

Passage of the Gramm-Leach-Bliley Act (GLBA) in the United States in 1999 completed and ratified the transformation of Bank Holding Companies into universal banks, following multiple relaxations of Glass-Steagall era restrictions on the activities of banks. The largest U.S. banks wasted no time in building or buying trading books to go with their banking books.

In a universal bank, losses can arise on the capital markets side of the business. Outside of fee-based advisory and underwriting services, the capital markets business is exposed to losses on trades for the bank's own account. The business is further exposed to loss in the event a derivative counterparty fails to pay on a contract favorable to the bank, or that the bank incurs a loss due to misconduct or error. Though such losses arise outside the sphere of the commercial banking business, they threaten the capital in place for the safety of depositors. Accordingly, the Basel regulatory regime has grown to encompass and police the capital markets business of banks, which it calls the "trading book." The trading book contains market, counterparty credit, and operational risks against which minimum levels of capital are required, over and above the capital held for credit risk in the banking book.[29]

In the trading book, market risk dominates. When market risk is measured with VaR methods, the universal bank has considerable discretion about how risks are aggregated, how risk factors are defined, and which data are used to estimate the distribution of potential losses. Basel I gave universal banks many levers that could be used to reduce the risk capital requirements of the trading book, as well as the freedom to move positions between the banking book and the trading book at will.

The porousness of the trading book regime did not escape notice. However the reaction from the BCBS was not to police the boundary between the banking book and the trading book, nor to question the methods being used to quantify market risk in the trading book. Instead, the BCBS proposed a new approach to credit risk measurement in the banking book which would permit banks more discretion. Before the sticks of Basel III, Basel II offered carrots for everyone. Basel II brought the VaR approach to banking book credit risk and allowed banks to develop their own data-driven estimates of credit risk parameters.

When the GFC came, many universal banks turned out to be seriously undercapitalized, resulting in bankruptcies or generous support from central banks and the public purse. It is not all together clear whether responsibility lay with the banks themselves—cynically and pervasively gaming the regulatory capital regime to profit from dangerously elevated leverage—or with the unprecedented decision of the Fed to deny liquidity support to Lehman Brothers for which the investment bank evidently qualified.[30]

The failure of Lehman Brothers led to a self-fulfilling spiral of market risk losses. Connected to each other through networks of derivative transactions, the major universal banks aggressively marked derivative valuations in their own favor, taking advantage of the fog of crisis, a dearth of external reference points, and the considerable discretion granted to valuation agents under standard credit support annex documents.[31] These punitive marks were used as a basis to call for immense quantities of collateral, precipitating a liquidity crisis on the back of an exaggerated crisis of market risk.[32] Activity in repo markets followed a similar pattern. Whereas dealer banks previously borrowed funds with ease by pledging bonds and asset-backed securities as collateral, the failure of Lehman Brothers blew up longstanding repo agreement terms. Collateral values were marked down, larger haircuts were applied owing to the sudden step-up in market risk, and some collateral became simply too radioactive to continue supporting loans.[33] These conditions only exacerbated the universal bank liquidity crisis. Asset sales to raise liquidity fed further paroxysms of market risk, stopped only by new emergency lending facilities, recapitalization with public funds, and regulatory forbearance.

Given the opportunity, the BCBS blamed the banks for their capital shortfalls. Their primary evidence was an exercise in which banks were asked to measure the risk of a predefined portfolio.[34] Responses from the banks showed wide dispersion in estimates across banks. Dispersion is not itself evidence of inadequacy—a widely dispersed set of estimates may still uniformly exceed the amount of capital needed to absorb an adverse shock. Nor was much inquiry devoted to reconciling the differences in estimates. Were they the result of different models, data, assumptions, aggregation choices, or something else?

Banks' discretion in measuring market risk was replaced by a highly prescriptive approach to measurement. The resulting Fundamental Review of the Trading Book (FRTB) standardizes the risk factors and correlations used to develop market risk estimates and sets a high bar for qualifying additional risk factors and parameterizations. The correlations and parameters chosen are intended to capture the conditions following the bankruptcy of Lehman Brothers, forcing capital markets businesses to act as if always in the depths of a 100-year flood.[35] The reductions in risk capital attainable through internal modeling approaches are capped, and regulators can impose the standardized measurements on the bank at any time. The possibility of making internal estimates for securitizations and complex credit risk transactions has been eliminated altogether. Strong restrictions apply to the transfer of positions between the banking book and the trading book as well.

The Fundamental Review of the Trading Book has ushered in a capital regime in which capital markets activity will be far more expensive to undertake within a regulated universal bank.[36] We do not agree with the bankers who complain that such costs necessarily spill over to the cost of consumer and commercial lending in the banking book.[37] However, if the management of a universal bank decides that the additional equity needed to support the trading book will be drawn from the same pot as the banking book, banking book lending business is likely to be capital constrained.[38] In this respect, we agree with

Anat Admati and Martin Hellwig that bankers' excuses about raising more equity are disingenuous.[39] However, Admati and Hellwig fail to distinguish the capital demand arising from the trading book from banking book capital needs. In calling for "banks" to double or triple their capital, Admati and Hellwig fail to pinpoint the source of the greatest risks in universal banking, and so they call for more capital than is really required. Splitting off well-capitalized trading books from well-capitalized banking books would make a lot of sense because the resources needed for each to be well-capitalized are much different. We return to this theme in Part Three.

The Fundamental Review of the Trading Book also reveals a depressing development in regulators' approach to risk management. Prescriptive approaches result in easily comparable and compatible results. However, they also make the financial system fragile. Just as genetic monoculture is vulnerable to extinction in the face of disease, some variation in operating models makes industries robust to unexpected developments. If highly prescriptive capital regulation fails in some way, all banks will fail together. Standardization also transforms some of the most crucial operations of a bank into compliance exercises. The muscles trained for thinking through risks, models, and measurements atrophy when such exercises are removed from the regular practice of risk management.

Regulatory Capital Under Basel III

The package of regulatory initiatives known as Basel III has truly been 20 years in the making. It begins from the Basel II regime, first published in 2004 and phasing in during the GFC years. Though we have deferred discussion of Basel II so as not to confuse the issue of pre-GFC universal bank incentives, it forms the core on which Basel III builds, as well as the source of perceived deficits against which Basel III reacts, retrenches, and revises.

Basel II was an ambitious and sweeping reform to the Basel I regime and its amendments.[40] Internal modeling was expanded from market risk in the trading book to credit risk in the banking book. Diversification of credit risk in homogenous pools of loans was recognized. New requirements for securitization exposures were introduced to recognize the special nature of such risks. The treatment of counterparty credit risk in OTC derivatives exposures was further refined, and new risk capital requirements were introduced for the operational risk of large trading organizations. Definitions of capital were refined, creating a third tier of capital responsive to market risk. And the risk capital requirements were integrated as one of the three "pillars" on which the regime of sound bank regulation was to rest, supported by proactive supervision by the authorities and informative disclosures to encourage market discipline.

For our purposes, the most relevant revisions in Basel II are those affecting the credit risk regime. Though banks can fall back on standardized risk weights, institutions may employ an advanced approach to estimating the credit risk of exposures in the banking book. Credit risks are equal to the expected loss on an exposure, given by the product of exposure at default, the probability of default, and the loss rate experienced by the bank given the event of default. Expected losses are adjusted based on the maturity of the underlying loan so that longer-maturity exposures carry more capital than short-term exposures.[41] Banks are allowed to apply their own probability of default estimates in a foundational internal ratings-based (IRB) approach, with other inputs remaining as they are in the standardized approach. The advanced IRB approach allows internal estimates for the remaining inputs, but may only be applied to sovereign, bank, and corporate exposures in Basel II.

Under the foundational IRB approach to credit risk, the risk weights applicable to retail credit and residential mortgage exposures remained significantly lower than those for corporate credit at comparable maturities, probabilities of default, and losses given default.[42] Risk weights for corporate credit could be mitigated by demonstrating lower losses given default or exposures at default.

The IRB approach of Basel II survives in Basel III in modified and elaborated form. In order to continue using internal estimates for credit risk parameters, banks must demonstrate that the estimates are used in the bank's normal operations and not only to achieve a regulatory capital result. Corporate and retail exposures are refined into six and three sub-classes, respectively, with advanced approaches being limited for specialized lending on the corporate side and expanded on the retail side.[43] However, in the United States, regulators continue to discuss the possibility of eliminating internal model-based calculations all together.[44]

Basel III has also thoroughly revised the definition of regulatory capital and raised risk-weighted capital ratios. Minimum capital levels now consist of tier one "going-concern" capital equal to at least 6% of risk-weighted assets and tier two "gone concern" capital bringing total capital to at least 8% of risk-weighted assets. Tier one common equity must be at least 4.5% of risk-weighted assets. A "capital conservation buffer" adds another dollop of capital for good measure. National authorities may add a countercyclical capital buffer on top of these requirements at their discretion. The third tier of capital previously proposed for market risk has been dropped.[45]

In addition to the new risk weights and capital requirements, Basel III adds a supplementary leverage ratio which relates tier one capital to a bank's total unweighted exposures. Banks must hold tier one capital equal to at least 3% of total exposures.[46] Because the securities and liquidity portfolios held by banks generally carry very low credit risk weights, a bank that is well-capitalized on a risk-weighted basis may find that the supplementary leverage ratio binds its growth instead.

On its own, the credit risk regime of Basel III is not so bad, though elements of the non-neutrality across sectors inherent in Basel I and II clearly survive. What weighs most on bank credit creation in the Basel III framework are the supplemental leverage ratio, the pressure exerted from the side of the trading book, and the new self-help regime of liquidity crisis management to which we now turn.

Bank Liquidity Regulation

A new feature (or bug) introduced by Basel III is a set of minimum requirements for bank liquidity. The BCBS gestures toward the "liquidity phase" of the GFC and the industry practice of maintaining liquidity "coverage ratios" as sufficient justification for the new rules.[47] Banks are now required to maintain Liquidity Coverage Ratios (LCR) and Net Stable Funding Ratios (NSFR) above 100%. The principles for computing these ratios are described below.

The new liquidity rules deal with potential liquidity needs arising from a universal bank's balance sheet, off-balance sheet commitments, and derivatives exposures. They affect both the banking book and the trading book and can have material consequences for each, though the relative stability of deposit funding tends to make the banking book's contribution to universal bank liquidity positive, and the trading book's dependence on the banking book becomes more explicit.

The rules apply a common taxonomy to the bank's assets, liabilities, contingent commitments, and derivative obligations for purposes of determining minimum funding and liquid asset needs. Each class of liability and contingent commitment is assigned a probability of run-off or potential drain on liquidity, as well as an implicit probability of renewal over the lifetime of the bank's lending and investment commitments. Liabilities are generally classified as retail or corporate deposits and secured or unsecured wholesale funding. An ample list of event-driven liquidity demands is appended to the baseline assumptions about normal turnover. Against these potential liquidity drains, the ability of assets to produce current cash flow, be sold for cash, or to mature in full is weighed to determine whether the bank has adequate liquidity and sufficiently stable funding. Assets are generally classified as loans and securities according to the Basel credit risk taxonomy, with the most preferred of them deemed High-Quality Liquid Assets (HQLA).

Together the new LCR and NSFR requirements make the banking system a significant *demander* of liquidity from government sources in a measure that is loosely related to each bank's role as a *supplier* of liquidity to the wider economy. We shall have more to say about the quality of the linkage in Part Three. Government debt and reserves issued by the monetary authority have pride of place in this new regime. When the LCR and NSFR were first introduced as part of Basel III, it was convenient that they would require the banking system to absorb the liquidity created by quantitative easing for the long term. In the minds of the Basel firefighters, inundation is the best prevention. We are skeptical of enormous bank-level buffers as a durable solution to liquidity crisis not because they do not work, but because they constrain the core lending business of banks.

Similarly, the NSFR penalize "maturity transformation," or the coincidence of long-lived assets and redeemable funding on bank balance sheets. Banks are invited to shorten the term of their lending or to seek longer-term liabilities. The logical limit of this process is for the bank to run a "matched book" where assets are connected to funding for the same term and no maturity transformation takes place. Under such arrangements, banking would be deformed into pure financial intermediation and the liquidity services supplied by the banking system would vanish. The NSFR does not go this far, but we are keenly aware of its power to discourage the creation of bank money.

The Liquidity Coverage Ratio

The first requirement of the Basel III liquidity rules demands that banks hold sufficient HQLA to fund the net cash outflow from a 30-day liquidity stress period. Net cash outflows are simulated using the current composition of the bank's liabilities, off-balance sheet commitments, and derivative positions in tandem with regulatory assumptions concerning how each will behave in a stress situation. Anticipated liquidity outflows are calculated separately for liabilities on the balance sheet, off-balance sheet commitments, and derivatives exposures. Liquidity outflows for derivatives may be netted against anticipated derivative inflows with the same counterparty where a netting agreement exists. Otherwise, liquidity inflows are limited to the receipt of scheduled principal, interest, and fees on the bank's performing assets, and subject to a cap. At the moment, there is no "advanced approach" to the LCR whereby a bank might apply its own behavioral assumptions. Nor do the BCBS's assumptions involve any evident contact with data or an explicit theoretical framework.

The bank's on-balance sheet liabilities are divided into deposits, secured wholesale funding, and unsecured wholesale funding, with various grades distinguished within each category. The LCR rule classifies retail deposits as highly stable, stable, and less stable, depending on the term of the deposit, the existence of a well-funded deposit insurance scheme, the depositor's other relationships with the bank, and other affirmative evidence that supports a judgment that the deposit is other than "less stable."[48] Uncollateralized obligations to legal entities like partnerships and corporations are treated as "unsecured wholesale funding." The deposits of small business customers are treated like retail deposits, mirroring the special treatment given to small and medium enterprise (SME) loans by the Basel credit risk weights. The deposits of larger businesses receive distinct treatment, as do deposits generated by clearing and custody arrangements, deposits in networks of cooperative banks, funding provided by sovereigns, central banks, and multilateral development banks, and funding provided by other legal entities. Secured funding is classified according to the type of collateral securing the liability.

Different run-off rates are applied to the liability balances according to the taxonomy of liabilities. The run-off rate is the percentage of the liability balance that is expected to be redeemed during the 30-day stress scenario. Lower run-off rates signal more stable funding and fewer outflows. The lowest run-off rates apply to retail and small business deposits, with rates between 0% for some deposits with terms exceeding 30 days to 10% for deposits lacking other evidence of stability. Deposits of larger nonfinancial business customers are assigned a run-off rate of 40%, however, which may be reduced to 20% if the entire amount of the deposit is covered by deposit insurance or an equivalent government guarantee. As a result, corporate deposits are heavily penalized under the LCR rule relative to retail deposits.

The same tilt in favor of retail and small business customers is seen in the treatment of committed credit and liquidity facilities which generally reside off-balance sheet for the bank. Unless the facility is unconditionally revocable by the bank—essentially an uncommitted commitment—run-off rates apply to the undrawn portion of the facility. Commitments to retail and small business customers are assigned a run-off rate of 5% versus 10% for corporate credit facilities and 30% for corporate liquidity facilities. Those extended to banks and other financial institutions face run-off rates of 40% to 100%.

As in the Basel III capital rules, the trading book weighs more heavily on universal bank liquidity requirements than the banking book. Derivative exposures and wholesale funding are recognized as particularly exposed to outflow risk.

Leaving aside a lot of technical hair, the run-off rates form a weighting scheme for the bank's on- and off-balance sheet liabilities which yield an expected 30-day outflow of funds. The expected outflow is the denominator of the LCR. The numerator is the total amount of HQLA held by the bank. Because the LCR must be at least 100%, the bank's holdings of HQLA must be at least as large as the 30-day expected outflow. Thus, the larger the run-off rate applied to a (contingent) liability, the greater the amount of HQLA that must be held against the liability. If HQLA yield less than other bank assets, they are effectively a tax on less stable funding.

An asset is HQLA if it can be easily and immediately converted to cash at a value close to its current value. Several layers of qualifications are embedded in the determination, and discretion is extended to national supervisors. In broad strokes, however, assets are classed as Level 1, Level 2A, and Level 2B assets based on specified criteria, and may be applied against the 30-day outflow hierarchically, with upper limits set for the use of Level 2B and Level 2A assets. Level 1 assets include cash, reserves, high-quality sovereign debt, and the debt of international financial institutions like the World Bank. Level 2A and 2B assets have non-zero credit risk weights under the standardized Basel credit risk approach, are subject to haircuts, and included at the discretion of national regulators. Thus, the offset to the LCR "tax" afforded by securities with greater returns is itself offset by haircuts which require a larger amount of the security to be held. For a security subject to a 25% haircut, for example, the bank must hold $1 / (1\% - 25\%) = 4/3$ as much of the security than the corresponding acceptable level of reserve money.

The LCR rule is thus a generalization of classical reserve requirements, one of the traditional pillars of monetary policy implementation. In the language of Basel III, classical reserve requirements apply a small run-off rate to demandable deposits and define HQLA to be reserve money and cash. Basel III widens the scope of the reserve requirement to nearly all of a bank's liabilities and expands the scope of HQLA to include somewhat less liquid assets on which a bank might earn better returns than reserve money and cash. The Federal Reserve recognized the redundancy of reserve requirements under the Basel III liquidity regime in 2020 by eliminating its reserve requirements under Regulation D.[49]

The generalized reserve requirements of Basel III complicate central bank management of short-term interest rates, however, because they introduce uncertainty about the banking system's demand for reserves. Even if the central bank can forecast banks' HQLA demands accurately, errors may occur in anticipating the extent to which the banking system will rely on reserves to satisfy their liquidity requirement. The current Federal Reserve regime of "abundant" reserves shields interest rate policy from the consequences of such errors, but they will become a challenge whenever reserves are in shorter supply. We discuss this issue further in Chapter 10.

The LCR "tax" is a convenient way for governments and central banks to require the banking system to absorb the consequences of quantitative easing and massive post-GFC debt issuance. The banking system has been transformed by Basel III into a sink for much of that new reserve money and debt. We have already seen the persistent post-GFC jump in banks' liquidity and securities portfolios in Chapter 7. Like other taxes, the LCR reduces output and distorts incentives facing the banking system. Though HQLA carry low credit risk weights and therefore appear to economize regulatory capital, they consume large portions of a bank's unweighted asset exposure under the supplementary leverage ratio.

The Basel III decision to tax corporate deposits at 2–10 times the rate of retail and small business deposits is particularly alarming. As a government-franchised issuer of deposit money, the banking system as a whole faces an inelastic demand for deposits.[50] While the incidence of the LCR tax is nominally on the banking system, the burden of the tax falls on depositors. Banks can pass through the cost of the HQLA tax to corporate depositors, who then face the choice of banking on poorer terms or seeking store-of-value money elsewhere outside the banking system in shadow banks. The higher rates of outflow assumed under the LCR rules are partly self-fulfilling. Worse, the HQLA tax disincentivizes corporate lending. The immediate result of a corporate loan is a corporate deposit, which persists as a corporate deposit within the banking system so long as the borrower maintains the balance or uses it to pay other corporations for inputs. If all banks maintain their pace of corporate lending, the banking system is confronted with the problem of ridding itself of these costly balances. The HQLA tax must be priced into loan rates, then, eroding the competitiveness of balance sheet lending versus the bond market and collateralized loan obligations. The current interest in private credit has roots in the punitive credit and liquidity risk treatment of commercial lending under the Basel rules.

Finally, there is no escaping the arbitrariness of the classifications, the relative size of the run-off rates, the duration of the run-off episode, or the haircuts applied to Level 2 HQLA in determining the LCR. The lack of a model-based approach to the LCR means that the arbitrariness has no remedy. It is counterintuitive that banks should be deterred by regulation from further developing their behavioral modeling around liabilities, designing more stable funding contracts, or exploring multiple avenues for meeting stressed liquidity demands. The LCR thus repeats all of the well-known design flows of Basel I's credit risk weights in the domain of liquidity risk management, with the same sorts of unintended but entirely predictable consequences.

The Net Stable Funding Ratio

Where the LCR addresses "asset liquidity" and emphasizes convertibility to cash for the settlement of payment obligations, the NSFR represents Basel III's approach to "funding liquidity," or the likelihood that funding will be available or renewable over the lifetime of the assets being financed.

To anyone who recognizes banks as creators of liquidity rather than intermediaries of funds, the NSFR will immediately appear to be ill-conceived. That long-term loans are "funded" by deposits is not an absurd funding mismatch brought about by bank "maturity transformation" and an insatiable appetite for yield-curve arbitrage, but a direct consequence of credit creation to support a bankable project. But for the NSFR, the maturity mismatch is a major problem, indeed. "The NSFR requires stable funding for some proportion of lending to the real economy in order to ensure the continuity of this type of intermediation."[51] Intermediation is not a problem to be solved by the banking system, but that will not stop the BCBS from "fixing" it.

The NSFR establishes a funding liquidity "budget" for a bank based on the bank's liability structure. The four liability time horizons that matter for the NSFR are non-maturity, less than six months remaining, six to twelve months remaining, and more than twelve months remaining to maturity. One hundred percent of equity capital and debt with more than a year to maturity is regarded as stable funding, as well as time deposits with more than one year to maturity. Term deposits with less than one year remaining to maturity and stable demand deposits from retail and small business customers are taken to be 95% stable, with less stable deposits for the same clienteles treated as 90% stable. Like the LCR, the NSFR features a cliff for nonfinancial corporate clients. For purposes of calculating the NSFR, nonfinancial corporate deposits are considered 50% stable. All other categories of funding have an available stable funding (ASF) factor of 50% or zero. These include derivative liabilities and other wholesale funding.

Available stable funding factors are multiplied by the amounts of corresponding liabilities to obtain an aggregate measure of ASF, which is the numerator of the NSFR. The denominator of the NSFR is the required amount of stable funding, obtained by multiplying segments of the asset portfolio by required stable funding (RSF) factors. Because the NSFR must not fall below 100%, the aggregate amount of RSF may not exceed ASF. The taxonomy of assets largely follows that used for the LCR and the standardized approach to credit risk, and once again the same four maturity categories apply. Assets that qualify as HQLA generally receive low RSF factors of zero to 15%, with some exceptions. Loans and securities have RSF factors between 50% and 100%. The 50% factor applies only to loans with less than one year to maturity. For longer-term loans, factors range from 65% for residential mortgages and loans with a credit risk weight of 35% or less, to 85% for loans with higher risk weights and securities with more than one year to maturity, to 100% for all other loans and securities, including defaulted loans and securities.[52]

Compliance with the NSFR thus makes any involvement in lending for terms beyond one year or longer-term securities expensive items in the bank's ASF budget. Operating within the NSFR budget will tend to discourage corporate deposits and to shift bank activity from lending and loans in security form to HQLA—i.e., cash, reserves, and sovereign debt. The NSFR thus reinforces the incentives created by the LCR—and the standardized approach to credit risk, for that matter—by nudging banks to hold more government-created liquidity and to produce fewer liquidity services themselves.

As in the LCR rule, there is no scope in the NSFR rule for banks to develop estimates of funding stability based on internal models, dulling incentives for new funding contracts, investments in behavioral modeling, or differentiation in strategies to achieve the objective of stable funding. Banks are obliged, in effect, to operate as if they were in a regime of constant distress, where no relationships may be taken for granted. The NSFR assumes a "self-help" regime for banks in the presence of funding liquidity pressures, as recourse to the central bank plays no role in its design. It acts as another constraint on the banking book, especially when a large trading book is present, and further tilts bank activity toward consumer credit and away from corporate lending.

Summing Up

The regime of bank regulation places regulatory constraints on capital and liquidity on top of the economic constraints already faced by banks. The Basel III regime intends that the regulatory constraints on capital and liquidity will bind. Whereas regulatory constraints were previously intended to converge with banks' internal modeling and economic risk management, they have now become increasingly prescriptive, turning active risk management into a compliance exercise.

Within a universal bank, a single pool of liquidity and capital resources must meet the separately defined needs of the trading and banking books. In Basel III, heightened expectations for trading book capital and liquidity are spilling over to the banking book, limiting the ability of the banking system to create new money. Further, the Basel III regime continues to favor extending credit to households over commercial borrowers. In Part Three, we will discuss reforms to bank regulation that will restore the banking system's role in the monetary system and eliminate distortions in the allocation of credit.

Notes

1. We first highlighted the importance of banking regulations for monetary policy in Hanke, S.H. and Sekerke, M. (2002). An accountancy standard for monetary authorities. In: *Accounting Standards for Central Banks* (ed. N. Courtis), 273–301. Central Banking Publications.
2. The attentive reader will notice the logical possibility of a state-chartered bank outside of a holding company which eschews Federal Reserve membership and FDIC deposit insurance as a means of avoiding most regulation. Such operations are not good for much besides shouting for new "crypto bank" regulations from Wyoming.
3. These questions have been analyzed by Buchak, G., Matvos, G., Piskorski, T. et al. (2024). The secular decline of bank balance sheet lending. *NBER Working Paper 32176*, February. We believe their analysis is misguided because it views banks and capital markets as two methods of intermediation, deposits and other financial assets as driven in the aggregate by individual portfolio choice, ignores the role of universal bank actors in determining equilibrium, and assumes that the process is driven by technology, preferences and changes in the degree of information asymmetry. If the latter is correct, why does technological change fall only on the side of the trading book? Why is it specific to the United States?
4. We view this as a particular weakness of the analysis by Admati, A. and Hellwig, M. (2024). *The Bankers' New Clothes*, new and expanded edition. Princeton University Press.
5. Goodhart, C. (2011). *The Basel Committee on Banking Supervision: A History of the Early Years*, 1974–1997. Cambridge University Press: Chapter 6 provides a comprehensive discussion.

6. Haubrich, J. (2020). A brief history of bank capital requirements in the United States. *Federal Reserve Bank of Cleveland Economic Commentary 2020-05*: 3.
7. Grossman, R.S. (2010). *Unsettled Account: The Evolution of Banking in the Industrialized World Since 1800.* Princeton University Press: 237.
8. Haubrich, J. (2020). A brief history of bank capital requirements in the United States. *Federal Reserve Bank of Cleveland Economic Commentary 2020-05*: 3 makes the connection between double liability and the source of strength doctrine. The source of strength doctrine is analyzed in Lee, P.L. (2012a). The source of strength doctrine: Revered and revisited—Part I. *Banking Law Journal* 129 (10): 771–801, Lee, P.L. (2012b). The source of strength doctrine: Revered and revisited—Part II. *Banking Law Journal* 129 (11): 867–906. We also note that the bankruptcy of Silicon Valley Bank in 2023 neglected to draw on funds available at the holding company level, leading to deposit insurance losses despite the availability of loss-absorbing capital in the parent.
9. New rules require loan loss reserves to reflect "current expected credit losses" over the lifetime of the loan for all loans, rather than only the losses expected over the next 12 months.
10. See Tufts, R. and Moloney, P. (2022a). The history of supervisory expectations for capital adequacy: Part I (1863–1983). *Moments in History: Economic Insights from the History of the Federal Banking System (OCC)*, Tufts, R. and Moloney, P. (2022b). The history of supervisory expectations for capital adequacy: Part II (1984–2021). *Moments in History: Economic Insights from the History of the Federal Banking System (OCC)*.
11. Tufts, R. and Moloney, P. (2022a). The history of supervisory expectations for capital adequacy: Part I (1863–1983). *Moments in History: Economic Insights from the History of the Federal Banking System (OCC)*.
12. Tufts, R. and Moloney, P. (2022a). The history of supervisory expectations for capital adequacy: Part I (1863–1983). *Moments in History: Economic Insights from the History of the Federal Banking System (OCC)*.
13. Goodhart, C. (2011). *The Basel Committee on Banking Supervision: A History of the Early Years, 1974–1997.* Cambridge University Press: 25–44.
14. Goodhart, C. (2011). *The Basel Committee on Banking Supervision: A History of the Early Years, 1974–1997.* Cambridge University Press: 572–580; Haubrich, J. (2020). A brief history of bank capital requirements in the United States. *Federal Reserve Bank of Cleveland Economic Commentary 2020-05*.
15. Rhoades, S.A. (1994). A summary of merger performance studies in banking, 1980–93, and an assessment of the "operating performance" and "event

study" methodologies. *Board of Governors of the Federal Reserve System Staff Study 167*, July, Rhoades, S.A. (1996). Bank mergers and industrywide structure, 1980–94. *Board of Governors of the Federal Reserve System Staff Study 169*, January.

16. Miller, C. (2022). *Chip War: The Fight for the World's Most Critical Technology.* Simon & Schuster.
17. Pyle, D.H. (1995). The U.S. savings and loan crisis. In: *Handbooks in Operations Research and Management Science, Volume 9: Finance* (eds. R. Jarrow et al.), 1105–1125. Elsevier.
18. Alexander, G. and Raburn, T. (2005). FDIC closes the books on RTC securitization program. *CMBS World* (Winter 2005): 50–53, 57.
19. Koo, R.C. (2011). *The Holy Grail of Macroeconomics: Lessons from Japan's Great Recession.* John Wiley & Sons.
20. The discussion of this section is based on Basel Committee on Banking Supervision. (1988). *International Convergence of Capital Measurement and Capital Standards.* Basel; Hull, J.C. (2018). *Risk Management and Financial Institutions*, 5e. Wiley Finance: 347–376; and Jorion, P. (2009). *Financial Risk Manager Handbook*, 5e. John Wiley & Sons: 667–697.
21. Basel Committee on Banking Supervision. (1988). *International Convergence of Capital Measurement and Capital Standards.* Basel, paragraph 44 and Annex 1. Additional limitations and caveats apply.
22. Basel Committee on Banking Supervision. (1988). *International Convergence of Capital Measurement and Capital Standards.* Basel, Annex 2.
23. Basel Committee on Banking Supervision. (1988). *International Convergence of Capital Measurement and Capital Standards.* Basel, Annex 3.
24. Basel Committee on Banking Supervision. (1996). *Amendment to the Capital Accord to Incorporate Market Risks.* Basel, especially paragraph 3: "In many banks the trading activities are carried out in quite separate units from the normal banking activities and so it is possible to identify the business which falls in the trading book. Even where this is not the case, the trading activities tend to be readily identifiable because of their intent."
25. Basel Committee on Banking Supervision. (1996). *Amendment to the Capital Accord to Incorporate Market Risks.* Basel, Part B.
26. To say that VaR represented the cutting edge of quantitative risk management is not to say that it remains so. Many criticisms have been leveled at VaR, from mathematical problems with the measure to practical problems stemming from the false sense of precision the metric communicates to senior management.

27. The Basel regime requires banks to monitor how frequently their computed VaR is exceeded. If exceedances are more frequent than expected, multipliers are applied to scale up the VaR and the required capital. The scaling factors are a blunt instrument to incentivize reliable calculations.
28. Ricks, M. (2016). *The Money Problem: Rethinking Financial Regulation.* University of Chicago Press.
29. We do not treat counterparty credit risk or operational risk in any detail as it would take us too far afield. Similarly, our discussion of market risk smooths over a great deal of detail that is well-known to specialists but at odds with a discussion focused on economic impacts. As with the rest of the material in this chapter, we have aimed for accuracy in the large rather than the small, and no bank manager should rely on this chapter as a guide to compliance with the Basel regime.
30. See Ball, L.M. (2018). *The Fed and Lehman Brothers: Setting the Record Straight on a Financial Disaster.* Cambridge University Press, who concludes that Lehman Brothers was solvent and should have qualified for the Fed's Primary Dealer Credit Facility.
31. On the latter, see Gregory, J. (2020). *The xVA Challenge: Counterparty Risk, Funding, Collateral, Capital and Initial Margin,* 4e. Wiley Finance.
32. Duffie, D. (2009). The failure mechanics of dealer banks. *Journal of Economic Perspectives* 24 (1): 51–72.
33. Gorton, G. and Metrick, A. (2009). Haircuts. *NBER Working Paper 15273,* August; Gorton, G. and Metrick, A. (2012). Securitized banking and the run on repo. *Journal of Financial Economics* 104: 425–451.
34. Basel Committee on Banking Supervision. (2013a). *Regulatory consistency assessment programme (RCAP)—Analysis of risk-weighted assets for market risk.* Bank for International Settlements: 6. "The focus of the hypothetical test portfolio exercise was to discover the design elements of internal models that have the greatest potential impact on the level of variability in [risk weighted assets based on the market risk framework]."
35. Carvalho, P.V. de, Pinheiro, C.M., and Rodrigues, M.S. (2024). The impact of the fundamental review of the trading book: Evaluation on a stylized portfolio. *Journal of Risk* 26 (3): 49–73.
36. In addition to the impact of FRTB, the Volcker Rule places restrictions on banks' proprietary trading operations within the United States, with exemptions for market making and underwriting. However, it is unclear whether the Volcker Rule has any teeth in its Version 2.0.

37. Viewed in the best possible light, raising equity for the trading book might be misinterpreted as a negative signal about the banking book, and no bank CEO wants to trigger a run on the bank.
38. Banks often find it easier to shrink risk-weighted assets than to raise more equity, as existing shareholders are not as obviously diluted, and no negative signals are sent about the capitalization of the bank.
39. Admati, A. and Hellwig, M. (2024). *The Bankers' New Clothes*, new and expanded edition. Princeton University Press.
40. Basel Committee on Banking Supervision. (2006). *International Convergence of Capital Measurement and Capital Standards: A Revised Framework, Comprehensive Edition*. Bank for International Settlements.
41. The maturity adjustment is based on an empirical estimate of how expected losses evolve over time. It is easily avoided by contracting the loan for 364 days and renewing it at the end of the term.
42. Jorion, P. (2009). *Financial Risk Manager Handbook*, 5e. John Wiley & Sons: 684–685.
43. Corporate lending is divided into project finance, object finance, commodities finance, income producing real estate, high volatility commercial real estate, and everything else (general corporate credit). Retail lending is divided into residential mortgage loans, revolving credit products, and everything else. Small business loans may also be managed as though they were retail exposures. Basel Committee on Banking Supervision. (2017). *Basel III: Finalising post-crisis reforms*. Bank for International Settlements: 53–108.
44. According to the OCC: "…the Internal Ratings-Based approaches of Basel II had fallen so far out of favor among the U.S. agencies that, as this article is written in October 2022, the agencies are considering substantially modifying or abandoning those approaches." Tufts, R. and Moloney, P. (2022b). The history of supervisory expectations for capital adequacy: Part II (1984–2021). *Moments in History: Economic Insights from the History of the Federal Banking System (OCC)*: 7.
45. Basel Committee on Banking Supervision. (2011). *Basel III: A global regulatory framework for more resilient banks and banking systems*, revised ed. Bank for International Settlements: Part I.
46. Basel Committee on Banking Supervision. (2011). *Basel III: A global regulatory framework for more resilient banks and banking systems*, revised ed. Bank for International Settlements: Part V and Basel Committee on Banking Supervision. (2017). *Basel III: Finalising post-crisis reforms*. Bank for International Settlements: 140–158.

47. Basel Committee on Banking Supervision. (2013b). *Basel III: The Liquidity Coverage Ratio and liquidity risk monitoring tools.* Bank for International Settlements, Basel Committee on Banking Supervision. (2014). *Basel III: the net stable funding ratio.* Bank for International Settlements.
48. "Highly stable" is not a term employed in the regulation. We use it to encompass the cases of term deposits that cannot be withdrawn in the next 30 days without penalty (0% runoff rate) and deposits that qualify for a 3% runoff rate rather than 5% ("stable").
49. *Federal Register* 85(82): 23445–23448 (April 28, 2020).
50. Omarova, S.T. and Steele, G.S. (2024). Banking and antitrust. *Cornell Law School research paper No. 24-03* use the franchising metaphor to describe the delegation of the state's money creation powers to the banking system.
51. Basel Committee on Banking Supervision. (2014). *Basel III: the net stable funding ratio.* Bank for International Settlements: paragraph 14a.
52. We note that interbank loans are treated particularly harshly by the LCR and NSFR, under the assumption that 100% of such loans will run off or fail to renew in a situation of liquidity stress. This treatment would dull incentives for banks to transact in interbank markets even if they were not already flush with liquidity.

Chapter 9

Monetary Aspects of the Government Budget

The government budget is the second major influence on monetary conditions overlooked in a central-bank centric conception of monetary policy. As an independent source of variation in monetary conditions, the government budget is a crucial component of monetary policy. The management of the government budget—which we term fiscal policy—weights on the monetary system in several ways. The long-term trajectory of fiscal policy is essential to the maintenance of the fiat monetary standard. Purchases and sales of government obligations by the central bank affect aggregate reserve balances and are passed through to deposit money balances when sellers lie outside of the banking system. Government-sponsored enterprises (GSEs) and financial agencies allow the credit risk of certain projects to be transferred to the government, making them bankable or investable. When savings are absorbed by government obligations, less funding is available to support the formation of bankable and investable projects as equity. Finally, the uneven distribution of net money creation by the government generates important differences in monetary conditions which are not completely offset by capital market transactions.

The monetary standard in a fiat system is underwritten by the ability of the government and the banking system to redeem the monetary claims they create. The banking system's contribution to maintaining the monetary standard is its solvency, which is achieved by underwriting credible claims to future surpluses. The same is broadly true for the government. The government respects the monetary standard when the taxes it collects from a larger economy in the future exceed the cost of new debt obligations issued today. Increases in government debt can be stabilized as long as the primary budget surplus reacts positively to the level of the debt. Whereas the rate of inflation clearly offers an extra degree of freedom to balance the government budget when growth and budget discipline will not, the long horizon of the relevant fiscal arithmetic makes the stability conditions more accommodating. We also consider the role of deposit insurance as a government backstop to the monetary standard in the sphere of banking, in contrast to its usual justification as bank run prevention.

The government budget has no net monetary impact in the aggregate. Nevertheless, we can distinguish two important classes of fiscal policy's influence on monetary conditions. The first involves indirect impacts of aggregate government operations. Central bank monetization of government obligations allows the government budget to have an aggregate impact on monetary conditions at the discretion of the central bank. The activities of government agencies and GSEs in the financial sphere goes beyond their contribution to the budget by making certain projects bankable or investable which would not be otherwise. The activities of GSEs in the mortgage finance space are the most obvious example in which the government wields a disproportionate influence on investability. The activities of the Federal Home Loan Banks are less obvious but nevertheless critical. Finally, we consider the potential for government debt obligations to crowd out other projects seeking funds in the capital markets.

Fiscal policy also has distributional impacts. The government budget distributes its monetary impact unevenly over sectors and strata of the economy in intended and unintended ways. This impact is not unwound by financial transactions between net receivers of expenditures and net payers of taxes. The uneven impact of fiscal policy creates the possibility that inflation and growth rates will move at different speeds within the economy if the fiscal impact is not compensated by private money creation. We give several examples of sectors in which fiscal policy has disproportionately eased monetary conditions, with the apparent result of faster rates of inflation. In addition, we consider the sectoral impact of quantitative easing, a set of post-GFC actions which combined a stream of government deficits with large-scale government debt purchases by the central bank. A mathematical Appendix shows how an impulse of net government spending is distributed across the economy over the long run.

Stable Government Debt Dynamics and the Monetary Standard

The years following the GFC have witnessed an unprecedented expansion of government debt in the world's major economies. Discomfort with debt levels exceeding GDP has prompted fears of spiraling inflation or the collapse of fiat money systems in general. Such fears are overblown. The obstacles to achieving debt stability and maintaining a price index-based monetary standard are driven by political dysfunction more than economic impossibility.

Stability Conditions

Debt issued by the government is a claim on future tax revenues, growing at a risk-free rate of interest. If tax revenue grows more rapidly than interest on the debt, the claim is good. Revenue may grow at prevailing tax rates because the volume of economic activity increases, or because shifts in the distribution of income move more earnings into higher tax brackets. Reductions in expenditure can also add to future net revenues.

Debt stability analysis formalizes this intuition mathematically. The analysis lets us reduce the infinite potential paths for government debt issuance to those that do not require increased inflation to close the government's budget constraint. In other words, the analysis constrains options for debt issuance to those that are compatible with the monetary standard.

To say that government debt is sustainable is to say that the fiscal authority respects its intertemporal budget constraint. Over some horizon, the government's debt burden will revert to some average level, rather than continue growing without limit. Given that the future is uncertain, the budget constraint faced by the government is an average over possible futures. Abiding by the budget constraint can involve adjusting budget strategies based on the realized path of the economy, and discount rates for the future must account for this uncertainty.[1]

We can set some of this subtlety aside to grasp the basic arithmetic around debt sustainability.[2] Writing D_t for government debt in the hands of the public, S_t for the government's primary surplus (taxes minus non-interest spending), and R_t for the interest rate on the debt, the government budget must satisfy the constraint

$$D_{t+1} = (D_t - S_t)(1 + R_{t+1})$$

in each period. That is, whatever outstanding debt is not paid down with a primary surplus will be rolled over to the next period with interest.

We want to find conditions where D_{t+k} does not grow without limit as k increases. To that end, it is convenient to normalize by income Y_t, which we take to be GDP. Multiplying the right-hand side by Y_t/Y_t and dividing both sides by Y_{t+1}, we obtain

$$\frac{D_{t+1}}{Y_{t+1}} = \left(\frac{D_t}{Y_t} - \frac{S_t}{Y_t}\right)(1 + R_{t+1})\frac{Y_t}{Y_{t+1}}$$

Writing the debt and surplus in percentages of GDP as d_t and s_t, respectively, and defining $x_{t+1} = (1 + R_{t+1})\frac{Y_t}{Y_{t+1}}$ as the effective gross interest rate, we have

$$d_{t+1} = (d_t - s_t)x_{t+1}$$

Debt as a percentage of GDP is reduced by primary surpluses, and the effective gross interest rate is deflated by the growth rate of the economy.

We can interpret x_{t+1} further by separating R_{t+1} and Y_{t+1} into real growth rates and inflation:

$$x_{t+1} = (1 + R_{t+1})\frac{Y_t}{Y_{t+1}} = (1 + r + \pi)\frac{Y_t}{Y_t(1 + g + \pi)} = \frac{1 + r + \pi}{1 + g + \pi} \approx 1 + r - g$$

When r, g, and π are small, inflation cancels out in the growth factor x_{t+1}, which is now seen to depend on the real rate of return on government debt r and the real growth rate of income (GDP), g.[3] When $g > r$, the effective interest rate on government debt is negative.

For most of the recent fiscal history of the United States, g has been larger than r.[4] As a result, debt sustainability has been consistent with a structural primary *deficit*:

$$\bar{d}\frac{1 - \bar{x}}{\bar{x}} = -\bar{s} > 0$$

To get a sense of the size of this "growth dividend," set the long-run debt/GDP ratio to 50%, $r = 0.3\%$, and $g = 2.5\%$ to obtain a long-run primary deficit of 1.1% of GDP compatible with a sustainable debt burden.[5] As $r \to g$, a balanced budget is required for stability. For $r < g$, however, the analysis seems to imply a larger $\bar{d}$ is compatible with larger structural deficits.

Hence, we consider the process for how government debt evolves. Based on previous results, we have

$$\Delta d_{t+1} = d_{t+1} - d_t = -d_t + (d_t - s_t) x_{t+1}$$

If primary surpluses depend positively on the level of debt after controlling for temporary factors μ_t affecting the surplus, we can write

$$s_t = \rho d_t + \mu_t$$

where $\rho > 0$. Now,

$$\Delta d_{t+1} = -d_t + (d_t - \rho d_t - \mu_t) x_{t+1} = -[1 - (1 - \rho) x_{t+1}] d_t - \mu_t x_{t+1}$$

This process is mean reverting so long as the coefficient on d_t is less than zero, i.e., if $(1 - \rho)\bar{x} < 1$ and temporary factors are indeed temporary. Hence, $\rho > 0$ is another mechanism for arresting the growth rate of the debt. It can complement the growth dividend when both $(1 - \rho) < 1$ and $\bar{x} < 1$. When only one mechanism is debt-stabilizing, the other may compensate for certain parameter values. If changes in the government debt revert to a mean value, then the government is respecting its budget constraint, debt is sustainable, and the monetary standard will not be threatened.

Assessing the sustainability of current debt levels in the developed world thus requires judgments about the path of long-run growth rates and expected real rates of return on government debt obligations. It requires distinguishing temporary additions to the debt burden from those that are structural. It also depends on the strength and durability of fiscal commitments to limit primary deficits in response to growing debt burdens, and judgments about which departures from responsible fiscal management are temporary when viewed on a suitable time scale.

In the United States it seems, for now, that the government will continue to enjoy a growth dividend. Much of the recent increases in debt are arguably temporary, relating to the cost of providing retirement and healthcare benefits to a large segment of the population that is now retiring. Debt capacity has been increased somewhat artificially through the holdings of the central bank and regulatory requirements for holdings in the banking system. Care is needed to ensure that structural deficits do not become entrenched. Outside the United States, increased economic growth rates are needed to swing the debt sustainability calculus more fully in favor of stability.

Deposit Insurance

The second way in which governments support the monetary standard is through deposit insurance. Deposit insurance arrangements ensure that deposit money will trade at par with the unit of account, even if the bank issuing the deposit becomes insolvent. Deposit insurance guarantees are limited, however, which makes nonbank store-of-value money competitive with a segment of bank deposit money.[6]

The government is the natural insurer of deposits because it can create money to fill any shortfall in the deposit insurance fund. Though such funds will take pains to charge banks actuarially fair insurance premiums that are sufficient to cover system losses, the question remains about who will insure the insurer, or how much equity is needed to absorb an unexpected loss. The deposit insurance premium may also be seen as a means of reappropriating some of the rents earned by banks as delegated issuers of fiat money for the sake of reinforcing the fiat money system. Both the rents and the capacity to support the deposit insurance fund depend on government's respect of the monetary standard.

Deposit insurance is better understood as a protection against bank insolvency than bank illiquidity.[7] By their nature, banks are unable to redeem their entire deposit base for cash on demand. Everyone knows this, and such demands do not arise from sources outside the banking system. Such a demand would kill the bank, so the only reason demands for complete deposit redemption arise is when the bank is already suspected to be dead. A comprehensive review of bank failures through history shows that bank runs do not create bank failures; instead, bank failures precipitate bank runs.[8] When liquidity is the problem, the deposit insurance fund is not the best or the quickest way to obtain it. Banks can obtain reserves and cash on short order by pledging securities at the discount window. As securities have traditionally been about 20% of bank assets, their ability to raise liquidity is significant. During a more recent episode of bank runs, surviving banks improved their liquidity by borrowing funds and raising their deposit rates.[9]

In the United States, deposit insurance is provided by the Federal Deposit Insurance Corporation (FDIC). The FDIC participates alongside the Federal Reserve and the Office of the Comptroller of the Currency in designing the prudential framework that governs bank capital and liquidity. So long as a bank has paid its insurance premiums and is in compliance with the prudential framework, its deposits are as good as money. The European Union has been working to harmonize and complete a deposit insurance scheme for the last 30 years. Its absence has been a weakness in the banking union and the euro itself.

Fiscal Influences on Aggregate Conditions

The government spends money into existence through its expenditures and removes it from existence with taxation.[10] If expenditure exceeds tax revenue, the government creates money on balance and has a budget deficit. Otherwise, the government has a budget surplus and destroys money on balance. The government's history of budget deficits and surpluses accumulates as the government debt balance. Deficits are financed by new debt issuance, which adds to the total of outstanding debt. Surpluses allow for the redemption of government debt. Each of these operations sterilizes the monetary impact of the government's budget balance: debt issues take the money out of circulation, while redemptions put it back in.

We adopt the fiction that all government debt is composed of zero-coupon bonds issued over a sequence of maturity dates.[11] A portion of the government debt thus matures in each period. The amount maturing turns into cash and thus implies (or requires) government expenditure, regardless of whether the maturing debt is "really" principal or interest. The maturing portion can be financed by tax revenue or the issuance of new debt. In the first case, debt is retired; in the second, it is rolled over. Thus, our expanded government budget identity is

$$T_t + I = E_t + D_t$$

where T_t is the current period's tax revenue, E_t is the current period government expenditure excluding payments related to the debt, D_t is the amount of debt maturing in the current period, and I is new issuance of government debt. In accordance with our zero-coupon bond device, D_t includes interest due on the debt in the current period as well as maturing principal. We will return to I below.

Economists generally talk about the *primary* deficit $E_t - T_t$ which ignores expenditures related to the debt. Since $E_t - T_t = I - D_t$, the primary deficit determines the *net* issuance of debt in each period. The larger, *consolidated* budget deficit $E_t + D_t - T_t$ is the most often-reported version of the government budget balance and corresponds to *gross* issuance of debt in each period.[12]

Accordingly, another way of looking at the expanded government budget identity is as a relation between the creation and destruction of purchasing power implicit in government finances. On the right-hand side of the identity, government expenditure and debt redemptions entail the creation of money. Taxation and debt issuance on the left-hand side of the identity remove money from circulation. The equation balances, so net money creation is zero in the aggregate.

Central Bank Transactions in Government Obligations

The government's contribution to the money supply need not be zero each period. Some portion of it can be allowed to turn into newly issued money via the monetary authority. Thus, we split the issuance of new debt into $I = I^M + I^P$, where I^M is debt issued to the monetary authority (the central bank) and I^P is the debt issued to the public (everyone else). When the monetary authority purchases I^M, it emits reserve money, R_t, which can accumulate in a current account for the government, circulate within the banking system as reserve money, or be converted into cash. Our identity is now

$$T_t + I^M + I^P = E_t + D_t + R_t$$

which implies that the monetary financing of a consolidated budget deficit $E_t + D_t - T_t$ reduces the government's required debt issuance to the public from I to I^P.[13] As before, the right-hand side collects emissions of money. But now I^M is effectively money paid by the government to itself via the central bank, so it has no impact on the amount of money in the hands of the public. Instead, we see that the net emission of money associated with the government budget is the amount financed by the central bank, $I^M = R_t$.

An independent central bank chooses the size and timing of government debt purchases according to its own objectives, rather than out of any desire or pressure to finance government spending.[14] The impact of central bank purchases of government debt depends on where the newly created reserve money goes. New reserves may augment the government's current account at the central bank or the supply of bank reserves, with the latter potentially increasing cash in circulation or deposit balances. It is depressingly common for central bank watchers to assume that all debt purchases turn into cash or liquid deposits at banks and immediately increase the money supply. When new reserves accumulate in government accounts or remain within the banking system, their emergence into the money supply is delayed, or may never occur.

Debt purchases by the central bank can turn into a bank balance for the government.[15] The balance is reduced whenever the government spends money or when debt held by the central bank matures. If the government spends the balance, it is converted to reserve money and transferred to the reserve balance of the bank where the recipients of government funds hold their accounts. If the balance is used to redeem debt held by the central bank, the balance is destroyed, and the central bank's balance sheet shrinks. (We will be interested in the contraction of central bank balance sheets in Chapter 14.) In effect, the government's current account at the central bank (and the use of the central bank as the fiscal agent) does two things. When it is spent, it simply runs down a buffer created when the central bank acquires debt, delaying its entry into the reserve money supply. Otherwise, it is an accounting device that allows the central bank to hold government debt to maturity.[16]

Debt purchases by the central bank can also turn into reserve money held by the banking system. As we have emphasized many times, reserve money does not add to the supply of money in circulation among the nonbank public. However, interbank interest rates typically move inversely with the supply of reserve money, and changes in the quantity and price of reserve money may have some downstream impact on money creation by the banking system. Regardless of how this transmission mechanism may ultimately work, the creation of reserve money and current account balances for the government tend to dissipate the immediate monetary impact of central bank purchases of government debt, because it takes some time for the reserve balances to catalyze expansion of the banking system's balance sheet.

Government-sponsored Enterprises and Financial Agencies

Our discussion of government's role in monetary policy would not be complete without considering the government agencies and government-sponsored enterprises (GSEs) which serve the banking system, offer credit guarantees, and create bridges between lending and capital markets. Their impact on the monetary system goes far beyond their impact on the consolidated government budget.

The importance of the Government National Mortgage Association (GNMA or Ginnie Mae) agency and GSEs Federal National Mortgage Association (FNMA or Fannie Mae) and Federal Home Loan Mortgage Corporation (FHLMC or Freddie Mac) in shifting the weight of residential mortgage lending from bank credit creation to capital markets funding cannot be overstated. (For brevity we will abuse terminology somewhat and refer to all three as the "mortgage GSEs.") Government policy sought to make housing affordable by extending 30-year financing terms to qualified borrowers at fixed interest rates. In the years before interest rate derivatives, banks hesitated to lend for such long periods for fear that the unmatched interest rate risk from such long-term exposures would put their earnings and capital excessively at risk, to say nothing about the associated credit risks. However, other financial entities like life insurance companies and pension funds—which, incidentally, had been material lenders in the mortgage market—were eager to hold long-duration assets to match their very long-duration liabilities. A market for mortgage risk transfer was thus born when the mortgage GSEs began acquiring mortgages from commercial banks with proceeds from capital market investors like insurance companies and pension funds. The mortgage GSEs set underwriting criteria for the mortgages and their documentation, which rendered the mortgages sufficiently comparable to bundle them into mortgage passthrough securities by interest rate, term, and geography. When borrowers of the underlying mortgages made their payments each month, the cash flows would be passed through to investors in the mortgage securities on a *pari passu* basis.

A crucial component in the mortgage GSEs' transformation of bank loans into capital market securities was their credit guarantee. In exchange for an upfront fee paid by the borrower, the mortgage GSEs agreed to advance any missed payments of principal and interest by the underlying mortgage borrowers. Were the borrower to default all together, the mortgage GSEs would pay 100% of the outstanding principal.[17] Investors in mortgage passthrough securities, thus, were virtually assured return of their principal plus interest, with a small risk premium attached to account for potential small shortfalls. The remaining risks are the interest rate risk inherent in holding a fixed coupon security and uncertainty about the timing of principal cash flows. The latter risk is known as prepayment risk and arises from the mortgage GSE design feature that allows borrowers to repay principal ahead of schedule without penalty. Borrowers can pay early because they wish to get out of debt, because they have sold their home, or because they have obtained a new mortgage on the same property at a lower interest rate; they may also prepay involuntarily because they default on the mortgage and the GSE advances the outstanding mortgage principal to the investor before liquidating the collateral.

The mortgage GSEs' credit guarantee catalyzed a transformation in banking and the capital markets. We have already remarked on how banks have preferred to hold mortgage risk in security form, benefiting from the credit guarantee, favorable risk capital weighting, and the newfound liquidity of their holdings. Investors have been keen to hold a long-term "fixed income" security which has the implicit support of the U.S. government behind it, but earns a healthy premium above government debt. GSE mortgage securitizations became the template for the disaggregation of bank balance sheet lending into origination (underwriting), loan servicing (collecting payment), and distribution to investors.[18] They also became building blocks for more complex securities. For investors who wanted more or less interest rate or prepayment risk than passthrough securities offered, designers of collateralized mortgage obligations (CMOs) could repackage passthrough security cash flows into newly engineered securities with the desired characteristics, while keeping some spread for themselves.[19] Almost every innovation observed in securitization markets was seen first in the "conforming" residential mortgage securitization space created by the mortgage GSEs, including those associated with subprime mortgage credit and collateralized debt obligations (CDOs).

Monetary Consequences of GSE Guarantees

The mortgage GSEs have been important catalysts in shifting mortgage funding from bank credit creation to the capital markets. Though large volumes of agency MBS end up back on bank balance sheets, they do so as fully funded securities rather than loans funded with bank credit. The shift of mortgage funding from bank balance sheets to capital markets absorbs tremendous quantities of savings. Securitizing mortgages in the capital markets also means that a substantial share of all bankable projects has not been available to support the creation of bank credit, constraining the growth of the aggregate money supply.

The mortgage GSEs collectively fund more than $10 trillion in mortgages as of end-2023. Fannie Mae and Freddie Mac fund residential mortgages on 1–4 family homes, while Ginnie Mae also funds mortgages on multifamily housing, which are usually considered commercial mortgages. GNMA securities are government agency obligations, while those of FNMA and FHLMC benefit from the implicit promise of government support.[20] Because the government supports the GSEs, bank regulators have no good argument to restrict bank holdings of agency MBS. The Fed can hold agency MBS and accept them as collateral from the banking system because government support allows the Fed to treat their credit risk as negligible. The GSE guarantee liquefies agency MBS, enhancing its status as collateral so that it may function similarly to Treasury securities in the financial system. Their footprint in capital markets is substantial.

Private securitizations came to encompass larger shares of the mortgage markets prior to the GFC, often by leveraging analogues of the GSE guarantees from private mortgage insurers. While these securitizations obviously lack the imprimatur of the government's backing, they arguably suggest that the government's involvement in mortgage markets has an associated multiplier, at least in the mortgage space.[21] At their peak, private mortgage securitizations funded some $2.35 trillion in residential mortgages.[22]

Government guarantees have catalyzed the movement of other bank lending activities into the capital markets, though not at the same scale as mortgage credit. Guarantees of Federal student loan payments through the GSE Sallie Mae supported an active market in student loan asset-backed securities (ABS) until Sallie Mae was privatized in 2006. The Department of Education has since dominated direct student lending with $1.5 trillion in loans outstanding at the end of 2023. These loans turn into money when they are forgiven by the government. Whether repeated government bailouts of U.S. automakers can be interpreted as an implicit guarantee of the ABS issued by their captive finance companies is a matter for productive speculation.

It is curious that the GSE guarantees are bundled with loan sales.[23] The guarantees could just as easily be structured as a mortgage insurance contract. Provided the guarantee fees are set at an actuarially fair level sufficient to pay out expected future losses, the mortgage GSEs could end up in the same place financially by insuring mortgages on commercial bank balance sheets. What is lost through such an arrangement is the interest rate risk transfer and the liquidity. Derivatives markets have now developed sufficiently to allow mortgage interest rate risk to be transferred synthetically, if desired. The GSEs could accept this risk separately if capital markets lacked capacity. That leaves the liquidity risk of a loan versus a security. Even that aspect could be worked around if the central bank were to accept GSE-insured mortgage loan collateral at its discount window.[24]

While this is far from a complete blueprint for reforming the mortgage GSEs, it is not so hard to see alternative designs which permit credit, interest rate, and liquidity risks to be unbundled and transferred, while shifting the funding of mortgage credit back onto bank balance sheets. The same architecture could be employed for any other government credit guarantee. We will return to these points in Part Three.

The Federal Home Loan Bank System

Twelve Federal Home Loan Banks operate in various regions of the United States. Officially, they offer loans to support banks' lending to housing markets. Unofficially, they have become a shadow lender of last resort to smaller banks in the United States. The Federal Home Loan Bank System comprises GSEs under the control of the Federal Housing Administration (FHA). Unlike Fannie Mae and Freddie Mac, they have always been solvent.

The FHLBs raise funds by issuing debt in the capital markets. Like the mortgage GSEs, they benefit from the implicit guarantee of the United States government and earn money by investing funds in mortgage-related securities. However, the majority of FHLB balance sheets are devoted to advancing capital market funds to qualified U.S. banks against a portfolio of collateral. For the FHLBs, the collateralization terms are generous; the FHLB obtains a "super lien" interest in bank collateral worth much more than the amount advanced. Interest earned on the advances pays the FHLB system bonds, FHLB expenses, and FHLB insiders.

The FHLBs are required to maintain significant liquid assets, much of which are held as reserve balances at the Federal Reserve. Unlike banks, the FHLBs do not earn interest on their reserve balances. As a result, they are content to lend reserves to other banks in the interbank market at a rate just below the lower end of the Fed's target range. After the GFC, the FHLBs have become the dominant lender of reserves in the interbank market, where little other lending takes place.[25]

For banks that lack liquidity, an advance from the FHLB system is often preferable to pledging collateral at the Federal Reserve system's discount window. Indeed, the FHLBs were originally intended as a kind of "Federal Reserve for thrifts" outside of the Federal Reserve System, though this distinction is no longer important.[26] An illiquid bank can obtain funds for a fixed term from the FHLBs below the punitive rate charged for discount window advances. The stigma of obtaining funds from the official "lender of last resort" is also avoided. And perhaps most importantly, the bank can borrow against its loan book, whereas the Federal Reserve generally requires a pledge of securities. As a lender of last resort, the FHLB system is generous and discreet. On the other hand, a bank borrowing from the FHLB system gives away a lien on its assets which subordinates the bank's other creditors and shareholders, without consequences for the calculation of regulatory capital ratios. Further, the FHLB's secured advances will be senior to the FDIC's unsecured advances in a bankruptcy. In Part Three, we will consider ways to integrate the FHLB's lender-of-last-resort role into the Fed's standing monetary policy facilities.

In 2022 and 2023, rapid increases in interest rates created unrealized losses on bank securities portfolios. The unrealized losses were large enough to prompt questions about banks' solvency and raise the possibility of bank runs. The possibility was realized in the case of Silicon Valley Bank and First Republic Bank. While the Federal Reserve created facilities to let banks realize their securities portfolios at their face value and the FDIC expanded its existing deposit guarantees, many—if not most—banks preferred to avail themselves of FHLB advances. As a result, total FHLB system advances expanded from $349.4 billion at the end of 2021 to

$827.1 billion in 2022 and $813.8 billion in 2023, a level unprecedented in the history of the FHLB system.[27] For comparison, the Fed's balance sheet increased by about $1 trillion during the GFC to accept ABS as collateral.

Together, the mortgage GSEs, the FHLBs, and other government agencies involved in various lending programs comprise a $12 trillion shadow bank on the balance sheet of the government that funds bankable projects using the resources of the capital markets.[28] GSE obligations are contingently monetized by the government when they are pledged as collateral at the central bank, when guarantees are paid out, or when defaults on agency securities are imminent. These public shadow banking commitments have vast consequences for the distribution of risk in the financial system and the production of money. They are also extremely costly in that they require $12 trillion in savings to fund what could be funded with an order of magnitude less bank capital.

Crowding-out in Capital Markets

According to the standard analysis, a large government debt competes with all other investable projects for savings.[29] In a closed economy, the market for private investable projects clears at a higher real interest rate than it would in the absence of new government debt, as a smaller pool of national savings is available to fund private investment. In an open economy with global savings flows, new government debt is a smaller share of the investment opportunity set, so real interest rate increases are less severe but government deficits are accompanied by trade deficits. However, when many governments are increasing their deficits simultaneously, the impact on global savings and investment can have a material impact on real interest rates.

At the beginning of the 21st century, the United States enjoyed the benefits of running a budget deficit in a world with abundant global savings flows. Global capital flows found their way to U.S. shores resulting in large trade deficits, but with little impact on real interest rates.[30] Since the GFC, however, the world's major economies have been running deficits simultaneously and government debt burdens have grown significantly. We would therefore expect real interest rates to rise as private investment competes with the world's major governments for global savings.

Nearly $28 trillion in Treasury debt combined with $12 trillion in agency obligations accounts for a significant share of global debt capital markets. At the end of 2023, global debt capital markets absorbed $140 trillion in global savings.[31] Though equity capital markets are valued globally at $115 trillion, much of that value reflects appreciation rather than new savings inflows. Flows into exchange-traded equities are roughly $500 billion annually, though this is only a small part of equity formation as we define it. Annual debt issuance is roughly $20–25 trillion globally, but much of this reflects the rolling over of existing obligations rather than contributions from new savings. Hence, we might peg new debt issuance very approximately at $5–10 trillion annually, and new equity formation on roughly the same scale. It is therefore plausible that trillion dollar deficits in major economies can indeed move the needle in terms of global savings flows.

We see the issue of private investment being crowded out by public debt not only in terms of rising real interest rates, but also in terms of equity rationing. Investment projects that offer greater returns are also more susceptible to adverse selection and moral hazard. Thus, as we pointed out in Chapter 4, we would expect greater investment project rationing in addition to higher real interest rates.

The government's footprint in capital markets is large enough that it can affect the formation of new ventures and be a drag on private investment. In Chapter 13, we dissect the secular shifts in global savings flows that have brought us to this point. In Chapter 14, we outline elements of a program to shrink government's capital markets footprint.

The Disaggregated Budget Arithmetic

In the previous section, we showed the aggregate government budget has no aggregate monetary impact. Now suppose that we want to split the economy up into sectors according to some schema. The sectors are indexed by $i = 1, \ldots, N$. Expenditure and taxation are particular to each sector, as are the purchase and redemption of government debt. The government budget identity becomes, trivially,

$$\sum_{i=1}^{N} T_{it} + \sum_{i=1}^{N} I_i = \sum_{i=1}^{N} E_{it} + \sum_{i=1}^{N} D_{it}$$

Equality does not imply that the government budget is simultaneously balanced across all sectors. The net creation of money in sector i is $E_{it} + D_{it} - I_i - T_{it}$, ignoring other influences and the potential for subsequent redistribution of balances. Across sectors, the net creation of money is zero, but it can be non-zero within sectors.

It is somewhat more convenient to rewrite the net creation of money as $(E_{it} - T_{it}) - (I_i - D_{it})$, which expresses sectoral money creation as net transfers from the government minus the sector's net provision of financing to the government.

The latter can also be read as the change in (the market value of) the sector's government debt holdings. A sector's money balances grow with net transfers and decline with purchases of government debt. Where transactions in government debt fail to offset the net effect of government transfers, there is a net gain or loss in the purchasing power of the sector.

Disaggregating the government budget makes it more interesting as a matter of monetary policy. Write $M_{it}^G = (E_{it} - T_{it}) - (I_i - D_{it})$ and break the money demand system of Chapter 7 into sector-level subsystems[32]:

$$\Delta \ln M_{it}^P = \alpha_i^{MP} \varepsilon_{it} + \beta_{iMPi}^{MP} \cdot \Delta \ln M_{itl}^P + \beta_{MGi}^{MP} \cdot \Delta \ln M_{itl}^G + \gamma_i^{MP} \cdot \Delta \ln P_{itl} + \delta_i^{MP} \cdot \Delta \ln Y_{i,t-l} + \cdots$$

$$\Delta \ln M_{it}^G = \alpha_i^{MG} \varepsilon_{it} + \beta_{MPi}^{MG} \cdot \Delta \ln M_{itl}^P + \beta_{MGi}^{MG} \cdot \Delta \ln M_{itl}^G + \gamma_i^{MG} \cdot \Delta \ln P_{itl} + \delta_i^{MG} \cdot \Delta \ln Y_{i,t-l} + \cdots$$

$$\Delta \ln P_{it} = \alpha_i^P \varepsilon_{it} + \beta_{MPi}^P \cdot \Delta \ln M_{itl}^P + \beta_{MGi}^P \cdot \Delta \ln M_{itl}^G + \gamma_i^P \cdot \Delta \ln P_{itl} + \delta_i^P \cdot \Delta \ln Y_{i,t-l} + \cdots$$

$$\Delta \ln Y_{it} = \alpha_i^Y \varepsilon_{it} + \beta_{MPi}^Y \cdot \Delta \ln M_{itl}^P + \beta_{MGi}^Y \cdot \Delta \ln M_{itl}^G + \gamma_i^Y \cdot \Delta \ln P_{itl} + \delta_i^Y \cdot \Delta \ln Y_{i,t-l} + \cdots$$

Imbalances in government creation of purchasing power have the potential to generate heterogeneity in expenditure, leading to sectoral differences in inflation rates ($\Delta \ln P_i$), real purchase growth ($\Delta \ln Y_i$), or both. If too many monetary services are chasing too few goods (after redistribution through intermediaries), sectors with rapid monetary growth will be sources of inflation to the rest of the economy.

At first blush, we might believe the bar is pretty high for differences in inflation to be realized. In those sectors where the fiscal impulse is positive, actors could always purchase government bonds with surplus balances, rather than overpay for goods and services that are not yet available in the desired quantities. Initial research into the possibility of heterogeneous inflation rates largely rubbished the idea.[33] While it was clear that different segments of the economy defined by income, wealth, age, or other criteria had different consumption baskets, differences in the weighting of consumption did not appear to produce materially different outcomes in the experience of inflation.

More recently, however, the availability of more granular data have renewed interest in the question. We can now see that different strata of economic actors spend their budgets on different varieties of goods, that pricing does not change uniformly across these varieties, and that the ability to substitute between different varieties and search for better prices is not evenly distributed. As a result, we can now see differences in inflation across strata of the economy that are at least as large as other biases in inflation that we care about, and if we were able to extend the measurement methodology beyond retail goods consumption to the services that account for most private consumption expenditure, the differences could be large indeed.[34]

Differences in sector-level expenditures are important features on the supply side of the economy as well. Research by Dale Jorgenson and coauthors shows that differences in growth rates across 50 industries varied widely and were largely attributable to differences in the intensity of intermediate input use.[35] Purchases from other industries that embody greater productivity increase industry and aggregate growth.

Accordingly, there are good reasons to be interested in the evolution of the money supply at the sectoral level. While our current focus is on the sectoral impact of the government budget, equal attention should be given to the supply of money from banks and nonbank financial institutions. We return to this theme in Part Three.

Some Examples of Sector-level Fiscal Influence

The benefits of monetary production by the government fall unevenly on those subject to its taxation powers. For example, government spending monetizes healthcare expenditures in the United States through Medicare and Medicaid, tax deductions for employer- and employee-paid health insurance premiums, tax deductions for health savings accounts, and a litany of other tax incentives. Annual healthcare spending through the Department of Health and Human Services was $1.875 trillion in fiscal year 2023, while medical-related tax deductions were the government's costliest tax expenditure, totaling $237.4 billion in waived taxes.[36] But because much of the health system is organized as non-profit institutions, the money created for health spending is not drained back out of the health system through taxes on system surpluses or government bond purchases by health system entities. Surpluses that would normally be recognized as profits are recharacterized as salaries for large administrative retinues, support staff, and supplements to medical professional pay. Surpluses are also spent on arm's race-like purchases of medical equipment and other devices at eye-watering markups. Government policy drives a net expansion of the money supply within the healthcare sector, which in turn generates an artificially costly production environment for healthcare. This direct, monetary explanation of healthcare price inflation has attracted little attention, perhaps because monetary conditions are rarely considered on a disaggregated basis.

Similarly, the tax system encourages the acquisition of land and improvements to land as zoned bundles of real estate through the preferential treatment of mortgage interest and the ability to defer taxes on land rent indefinitely.[37] We explore the unusual incentives of real estate markets at greater length in Chapter 13. For now, we note that government policy favors investment in real estate by taxing the benefits from real estate ownership more lightly than other investments. The lack of sterilization from tax policy results in a net increase in the money supply for residential real estate. Unsurprisingly, the prices of houses have grown more rapidly than prices of goods that are not so well-favored fiscally.

The cost of higher education has also accelerated as a result of the government's readiness to underwrite tax-favored debt to finance educations and measures that allow savings for education to grow tax-free for spending at non-profit colleges and universities. Since 2006, the government has created some $1.5 trillion in funding for tuition at institutions of higher learning.

The distributional impact of the government's contribution to the money supply can be significant. It is evident to most observers that the prices of healthcare, houses, and education have grown much faster than prices for other goods and services for the last 50 years. These impacts are mostly dissimulated by the methodologies used by government agencies to calculate consumer price inflation, which attribute such price increases to quality differences and create an artificial sense of stability in the monetary standard.[38] The uneven impact of the fiscal impulse deserves wider consideration, as well as differences in inflation rates across sectors of the economy, alongside the productivity-based explanations more often proffered by economists.[39]

Sectoral Impact of the Fiscal Impulse from Quantitative Easing

We have noted that a sector receiving a net transfer of purchasing power via the government budget can defer use of that purchasing power by purchasing government bonds. Alternatively, a money surplus sector can lend its surplus to another sector facing a deficit via a financial intermediary.[40] The intermediary will issue liabilities to recipients of the transferred funds, and the sector lending funds will receive an asset which is a claim on the borrowing sector. In fact, the intermediary may lend those surplus funds right back to the government by purchasing government debt. When surplus funds are put into a money market fund, this is effectively what happens. Capital market transactions can also intermediate surplus funds to the household and business sectors. The role of MBS in reallocating savings from international savers to U.S. households has been remarked upon; we return to this point in Part Three. Similarly, one can buy newly issued corporate bonds or equity, transferring funds to the corporate sector. Multiple sectors, intermediaries, and capital market instruments quickly overwhelm one's ability to trace transfers intuitively. We need some mathematical help. A mathematical Appendix shows how to use information on financial assets and liabilities by sector to trace the anticipated redistribution of an exogenous receipt of funds.

Pursuing the question of how surplus funds are redistributed is interesting because it tests the assumption that sector imbalances are unwound naturally. If the structure of financial intermediation leads to sectoral imbalances following an inflow of funds, it is no longer sufficient to analyze fiscal policy at the aggregate level. Of course we are also interested in finding out which sectors are favored.

Tsujimura and Tsujimura (2018) trace the sectoral impact of the Federal Reserve's quantitative easing policy, as well as the government's fiscal impulse. During quantitative easing, new deposit money was created as the Fed purchased Treasuries and agency MBS from the nonbank public. The government also ran large deficits. The authors trace the ultimate impact of those purchases using the methodology in the Appendix, augmented with analysis of changes in sector-level expenditures induced by the policy. We examine their results for the years 2010–2014, when the Federal Reserve engaged in a series of three Large-Scale Asset Purchase (LSAP) programs (described in more detail in Chapter 10).[41] We are interested in the extent to which fiscal policy, combined with the LSAP programs, succeeded in replacing flows of funds which were not being supported by banking sector credit creation.

Table 9.1 captures annual changes in induced transaction activity at the Flow of Funds sector level in billions of U.S. dollars, and is divided into three groups of columns. The first group of columns shows the change in the monetary contribution of the banking system. We can see that the banking system's contribution to flows of funds in the economy was negative in 2010 and 2013, but positive in 2012 and 2014. The impact of these overall changes was felt unevenly across sectors. Reduced flows from the banking sector fell disproportionately on financial business in 2010, while expansion in 2012 and 2014 mostly favored households and nonfinancial non-corporate business, which we recall includes private equity and venture capital partnerships.

The second group of columns captures the combined contribution of the Federal Reserve (quantitative easing) and the Federal Government (the fiscal impulse).

Table 9.1 Changes in sector-level funds from bank credit, Federal Reserve, and fiscal policy.

In USD Billions	Banking System					Federal Government + Fed					Combined				
	2010	2011	2012	2013	2014	2010	2011	2012	2013	2014	2010	2011	2012	2013	2014
Households and nonprofits	−47	−19	272	−181	157	−394	135	−37	−31	86	−441	116	235	−212	243
Nonfinancial, non-corporate business	−3	−2	46	−39	155	5	−5	15	−17	5	2	−7	61	−56	160
Nonfinancial, corporate business	−4	79	−17	−35	2	34	50	−46	−41	−19	30	129	−63	−76	−17
Nonfinancial business (subtotal)	−7	77	29	−74	157	39	45	−31	−58	−14	32	122	−2	−132	143
Private depository institutions	−214	−45	−2	−3	38	−45	2	−27	16	−7	−259	−43	−29	13	31
Insurance companies	1	12	−13	0	3	1	6	38	7	−20	2	18	25	7	−17
Pension funds	−8	11	−3	10	2	−6	13	−3	1	1	−14	24	−6	−9	3
Other financial business	−143	−43	−65	15	−63	−455	−23	−78	450	−285	−598	−66	−143	465	−348
Financial business (subtotal)	−364	−65	−83	2	−20	−505	−2	−70	474	−311	−869	−67	−153	476	−331
State and local governments	16	−10	1	−1	−1	44	−21	−63	24	3	60	−31	−62	23	2
Rest of the world	43	16	−57	−43	−9	−121	−5	−29	46	−67	−78	11	−86	3	−76
Balance (statistical discrepancy)	0	0	0	0	0	171	−208	126	123	−48	171	−208	126	123	−48
Total change in induced transactions	−359	−1	162	−297	284	−766	−56	−104	578	−351	−1125	−57	58	281	−67

Fiscal policy and QE combined to reduce fund flows overall in 2010, 2012, and 2014; in 2011 the overall contraction is comparable to the statistical discrepancy, while policy was overall stimulative in 2013.

The third group of columns combines the impact of banking system credit and the fiscal impulse. In 2010 and 2011, it appears the fiscal impulse exacerbates the reduction in fund flows originating in the banking sector. From 2012 to 2014, the fiscal impulse tends to offset the funding impulse from the banking system. The overall impact within the household sector and nonfinancial corporate business is essentially flat, while the nonfinancial, non-corporate business sector emerged from the period a net winner. On the other hand, substantially all the net reduction in fund flows was absorbed by financial business and entities outside the United States. The data thus show that the fiscal impulse combined with quantitative easing generally did not stimulate new funding flows from 2010 to 2014. Government money creation did not offset contractions in the banking system until 2013, and the impact of money creation fell unevenly across sectors, even after accounting for the redistribution of balances.

More interesting possibilities for the sectoral analysis of the government budget's monetary impact are limited by the lack of public data. Ideally, we would have information on assets and liabilities at the industry level and by income strata to allow further disaggregation of fiscal and credit impulses. A higher level of resolution is needed in empirical data to detect and monitor non-neutrality in monetary conditions.

Appendix 9.A Propagation of a Fiscal Impulse

Tsujimura and Mizoshita (2003) apply input–output analysis to flow-of-funds data in order to discover the ultimate consequences of a financial impulse when sectors are interconnected.[42] Their idea, following in the footsteps of Stone[43] and Klein,[44] is to construct a technology matrix for the economy in analogy with the commodity-by-industry approach to input–output analysis, with varieties of financial instruments playing the role of commodities and institutional sectors in the place of industries. The authors explore the consequences of changes in the balance sheet of an exogenous sector.

The commodity-by-industry approach decomposes the technology matrix into a "use" matrix B which captures the value of commodities purchased by (input into) each industry and a "make" matrix D detailing the value of commodities produced by (output from) each industry.[45] The values in the use matrix are normalized by the total value of industry output (x), whereas those in the make matrix are normalized by the total output of the commodity (q). Multiplying B, which has dimensions (commodities × industries) by D (industries × commodities) yields a matrix with dimensions (commodities × commodities) from which one can calculate a Leontief inverse relating total commodity output q to final commodity demand e:

$$q = (I - BD)^{-1} e$$

Alternatively, some straightforward matrix manipulations can determine the consequences of final commodity demand for industry-level output x:

$$x = (I - DB)^{-1} De$$

Tsujimura and Mizoshita (2003) follow this latter approach to discover the sector-level impact of changes in the asset and liability balances of an exogenous sector at the financial instrument level. The goal is to work out the consequences of a shock to the composition of an exogenous sector's balance sheet—that is, autonomous expansions of the instruments comprising the assets and liabilities of a sector. We are interested in the movements of assets and liabilities for the consolidated government sector (the fiscal authority plus the monetary authority), and one must work out the consequences of movements in assets and liabilities separately.

Tsujimura and Mizoshita pursue parallel analyses of the asset and liability sides accomplished by swapping the roles of the make and use matrices. To work out the consequences of new liabilities issued by the exogenous sector, *asset* holdings populate the use matrix and *liabilities* form the make matrix. From this perspective, *savings* are mobilized from each sector, raising funds for the exogenous sector. Conversely, downstream *investment* is induced in sectors that issue liabilities which are purchased as assets by the exogenous sector. In this case, *liabilities* form the use matrix, and *assets* populate the make matrix. In both cases, the use matrix is normalized by the total holdings of the sector (analogous to industry output), while the make matrix is normalized by the total amount of the financial instrument outstanding (analogous to the total value of commodity output). The technology matrices for induced savings and investment flows are denoted by $C = DB$ and $C^* = D^* B^*$, respectively.

We are now ready to work out the sector-level consequences of exogenous increases in the liabilities ε and assets ρ of the consolidated government sector, which are analogous to shocks to final demand. The savings induced in each sector are

$$(I - C)^{-1} D\varepsilon$$

while the induced investment is

$$(I - C^*)^{-1} D^* \rho$$

where ε and ρ are vectors with one entry per financial instrument. They may be represented in absolute amounts or as instrument-by-instrument "impulses" which increase the value of an instrument's asset or liability balance by a unit. The consequences for the exogenous sector may be ignored.[46] Thus, for a given intervention by the consolidated government sector, the net consequences for each sector may be found as the differences between induced investment and saving:

$$(I - C^*)^{-1} D^* \rho - (I - C)^{-1} D\varepsilon$$

A positive balance indicates that the sector is a net receiver (investor) of funds. Sectors that face net drains of funds (savers) have negative balances. These balances reflect the ultimate results of a fiscal impulse, after accounting for open market operations by the central bank and subsequent reintermediation of funds by each of the sectors concerned.

As in any input–output analysis, the propagation of impulses may be studied using the mathematical identity

$$(I - C)^{-1} D = (I + C + C^2 + C^3 + \cdots) D$$

This is progress. The term in parenthesis on the right-hand side may be read as the net effect of transfers received directly (ID), plus transfers received through one level of intermediation (CD), two levels of intermediation ($C^2 D$), and so on. Because the matrix C does not consist of flows over a period but stocks, the decomposition gives no indication of the amount of time needed for fund flows to propagate, but one can reasonably expect that transfers requiring less intermediation are most likely to be felt immediately.[47] In addition, changes in the composition of sectoral balance sheets over time mean that the long-term consequences of an intervention cannot be anticipated with complete confidence.

Notes

1. Bohn, H. (1995). The sustainability of budget deficits in a stochastic economy. *Journal of Money, Credit and Banking* 27 (1): 257–271.
2. Our analysis follows Bohn, H. (1998). The behavior of U.S. public debt and deficits. *Quarterly Journal of Economics* 113 (3): 949–963.
3. Time subscripts are suppressed to unclutter the notation. For reasonable values of inflation, the approximation is accurate to 2–3 decimal places.
4. A variable with a bar on top represents the steady-state value of the variable in a dynamic model. To find a steady-state value, one replaces all the dated variables in a dynamic model with their steady-state counterparts before solving algebraically.
5. Using the parameters in the example, we have $\bar{x} = 1 + 0.003 - 0.025 = 0.978$ and $-\bar{s} = 0.5 \frac{0.022}{0.0978} = 0.011$.
6. In principle, it also creates a segment of depositors who are incentivized to monitor the bank closely, but it is not clear that those depositors have the information they need to monitor effectively.
7. The standard analysis by Diamond, D.W. and Dybvig, P.H. (1983). Bank runs, deposit insurance, and liquidity. *Journal of Political Economy* 91 (3): 401–419 centers on liquidity rather than net worth.
8. Correia, S.A., Luck, S., and Verner, E. (2024). Failing Banks. *NBER Working Paper 32907*, September. The authors also find little evidence that large depositors effectively monitor bank solvency, even in the absence of deposit insurance.
9. Cipriani, M., Eisenbach, T.M., and Kovner, A. (2024). Tracing bank runs in real time. *Federal Reserve Bank of New York Staff Reports No. 1104*, May. The authors also highlight the role of coordination among institutional depositors in generating runs.
10. Our discussion applies to that stratum of the government that issues fiat money. In a federal system, it is the budget at the federal level that matters for monetary conditions. The fiscal management of state and local governments has no impact on the amount of money outstanding.
11. Coupon and principal payments can be separated to turn a coupon bond into a series of zero-coupon bonds.
12. We have written the variable I without a subscript because the government has some latitude to choose how to distribute its promises to pay over time. In effect, $I = I_{t+1} + I_{t+1} + \cdots I_{t+T}$, where T is the maximum maturity for government debt issuance. If the government finances a deficit of 100 dollars by issuing

a 5% bond with maturity T, then $I_{t+j} = 5/n$ where n is the number of periods j per year and $I_T = 100$. As we move from period to period, the amounts $I_{-}(t+1)$ turn into D_t and result in the issuance of money to redeem the debt. Thus, the financing schedule I also implies a time profile for the future creation of money.

13. This follows because $I^M = R_t$.
14. Cukierman, A. 1992. *Central Bank Strategy, Credibility, and Independence: Theory and Practice*. MIT Press.
15. In the United States, this is the Treasury General Account.
16. When government debt matures, money is transferred from the government's current account to the central bank. The government debt asset vanishes along with an equal amount of the government's deposit balance.
17. Guarantees for some programs, such as VA loans, are less complete.
18. Poszar, Z., Adrian, T., Ashcraft, A. et al. (2013). Shadow banking. *Federal Reserve Bank of New York Economic Policy Review* 19 (2): 1–16.
19. Fabozzi, F.J. (ed.) (2006). *The Handbook of Mortgage-Backed Securities*, 6e. McGraw-Hill.
20. As a result, GNMA obligations trade at narrower credit spreads than those of FNMA and FHLMC.
21. Ahnert, T. and Kunci, M. (2024). Government loan guarantees, market liquidity, and lending standards. *Management Science* 70 (7): 4502–4532.
22. Flow of Funds Table L.218, line 20.
23. Before being spun out of the government, FNMA could only buy FHA-guaranteed loans.
24. What about the insurance companies and pension funds seeking long-term liabilities? They could contract with banks through long-term instruments that might look like a kind of savings deposit. The liquidity of these instruments would be supported by banks' ability to pledge insured mortgages at the discount window.
25. See Chapter 10 for details.
26. The Office of Thrift Supervision was buried during the GFC.
27. Metrick, A. (2024). The failure of Silicon Valley Bank and the panic of 2023. *Journal of Economic Perspectives* 38 (1): 133–152. See also https://fhlb-of.com/ofweb_userWeb/resources/2023Q4CFR.pdf, Figure 10.
28. Adding $9.3 trillion in GSE financial assets and $2.8 trillion in agency- and GSE-backed mortgage pools at the end of 2023, per Tables L.125 and L.126 of the Flow of Funds data.
29. We follow Barro, R. (1989). The Ricardian approach to budget deficits. *Journal of Economic Perspectives* 3 (2): 37–54. Whereas Barro's concern is whether

aggregate demand responds to the current primary deficit or the entire path of primary deficits, we are concerned with working out the consequences of a large government debt on equilibrium in the capital market.
30. Such is the "exorbitant privilege" associated with the U.S. dollar.
31. Global capital markets data in this paragraph are from SIFMA. (2024). *2024 Capital Markets Fact Book* (SIFMA), July.
32. To unclutter the notation, we have written the sums of lags as dot products. M_{it}^P and M_{it}^G are privately and government-supplied money in sector i, respectively.
33. For example, Garner, T.I., Johnson, D.S., and Kokoski, M.F. (1996). An experimental consumer price index for the poor. *Monthly Labor Review* 119 (9): 32–42; Hobijn, B. and Lagakos, D. (2005). Inflation inequality in the United States. *Review of Income and Wealth* 51 (4): 581–606; and McGranahan, L. and Paulson, A. (2006). Constructing the Chicago Fed income based economic index – Consumer price index: Inflation experiences by demographic group: 1983–2005. *Federal Reserve Bank of Chicago Working Paper 2005-20*, November.
34. See Jaravel, X. (2021). Inflation inequality: Measurement, causes, and policy implications. *Annual Review of Economics* 13: 599–629 and sources therein. Differences of a percentage point are large. A consumer experiencing 2% annual inflation loses half of their purchasing power every 36 years, while another consumer facing 3% annual inflation loses half every 24 years.
35. Jorgenson, D.W., Gollop, F., and Fraumeni, B. (1987). *Productivity and U.S. Economic Growth*. North-Holland; Jorgenson, D.W., Ho, M.S., and Stiroh, K.J. (2005). *Information Technology and the American Growth Resurgence*. MIT Press.
36. *Financial Report of the United States Government*, Fiscal Year 2023, pp. 57, 206. This does not include the healthcare-related expenditures of the Department of Veterans Affairs or spending on health benefits for government employees.
37. For instance, 1031 exchanges allow capital gains on real estate sales to be deferred indefinitely so long as the proceeds are used to purchase more residential real estate.
38. Diewert, W.E., Greenlees, J., and Hulten, C. (2009). *Price Index Concepts and Measurement*. University of Chicago Press.
39. And indeed, it takes some heroic dissimulation in consumer price index accounting to conclude that these imbalances in money creation are not inflationary. Healthcare services inflation accounting assumes that the value of a health service is whatever one pays for it, defining inflation out of existence except for supplies, devices, and pills which have a fixed identity over

time. The effort to understand the derivation of "owner's equivalent rent" that underlies the accounting for housing inflation has frustrated the authors to no end. Meanwhile, the value of higher education is underpinned less by increased productivity and wages than by the erosion of wages for workers without degrees. For an explanation of health and education price inflation based on "cost disease," or the idea that service industries are especially prone to inflation because service workers' wages outpace productivity gains, see Helland, E. and Tabarrok, A. (2019). *Why Are the Prices So Damn High?* George Mason University Mercatus Center.

40. Because the money has already been created by the government, the transaction is genuinely a case of intermediation and not credit creation.
41. Tsujimura, K. and Tsujimura, M. (2018). A flow of funds analysis of the US quantitative easing. *Economic Systems Research* 30 (2): 137–177, Tables 11–16. We focus on the rows for the Fed, Private Depository Institutions (the banking system), and Federal Government, which show induced transactions flowing from these sectors to the sectors enumerated on the left-hand side of the table.
42. Tsujimura, K. and Mizoshita, M. (2003). Asset-liability-matrix analysis derived from the flow-of-funds accounts: The Bank of Japan's quantitative monetary policy examined. Economic Systems Research 15 (1): 51–67.
43. Stone, R. (1966). The social accounts from a consumer's point of view. *Review of Income and Wealth* 12: 1–33.
44. Klein, L.R. (1983). *Lectures in Econometrics.* North-Holland.
45. For a complete exposition of the commodity-by-industry approach to input–output analysis, see Miller, R.E. and Blair, P.D. (2022). *Input-Output Analysis: Foundations and Extensions*, 3e. Cambridge University Press, Chapter 5.
46. Tsujimura, K. and Mizoshita, M. (2003). Asset-liability-matrix analysis derived from the flow-of-funds accounts: The Bank of Japan's quantitative monetary policy examined. *Economic Systems Research* 15 (1): 51–67 delete the row and column of C and C^* corresponding to the exogenous sector, a convention we do not follow in order to keep the notation uncluttered.
47. Dorfman, R., Samuelson, P.A., and Solow, R.M. (1958). *Linear Programming and Economic Analysis.* RAND Corporation make the connection between the Leontief inverse and iteration of the technology matrix as the receipt of intersectoral flows over time.

Chapter 10

Central Bank Policy

Our message throughout Part Two has been to decenter central bank policy in discussions of monetary policy. We have focused attention on bank regulations and fiscal policy as the principal means for official interventions in the rate of money creation and its distribution across sectors of the economy. Developments in the quantity of monetary services interact with aggregate demand (expenditure) and velocity (a slow-moving variable) to generate changes in relative prices and the overall level of prices. Whether official objectives for the monetary standard and the growth of the economy are met depends closely on the production of monetary services by the government and the commercial banking system.

On the other hand, central bank policy has a way of elbowing its way back into discussions of monetary policy. For many observers (ourselves excluded) central bank policy is identical with monetary policy, and the primary motivating factor for picking up a book about money is to better understand central bank policy. But even if one is not prepared to cede the whole territory of monetary policy to the central bank, its ability to influence monetary conditions and change the rules of the game in the monetary system remains substantial and worthy of close attention. Central bank production of reserve money in normal times and in crisis guides and constrains the behavior of the commercial banking system. The design of the reserve market is crucial to the success of the banking system, even if interventions by the central bank to influence the rate at which the overnight reserve market clears are disruptive or counterproductive.

Moreover, the manner in which central banks operate has changed so completely since the GFC that standard explanations of monetary policy implementation have become all but obsolete. These changes have unintended and perverse consequences. Reserve markets have broken down, long-term interest rates have been artificially depressed, and central banks have gone from being profit centers for their governments to enormous fiscal burdens. The resources deployed to recover from the GFC and COVID have become an albatross around the necks of central bankers, who have said little about how they plan to shrink their balance sheets and transition to more orderly regimes of policy implementation.

Thus, we have a few goals for a chapter on central bank policy.[1] First, we discuss changes in how monetary policy is implemented by the Fed. Official responses to the GFC and COVID disrupted central bank operations to an unprecedented extent. We review the "unconventional policy measures" that have expanded the Fed's balance sheet to several trillions and consider their consequences for the Fed's pursuit of short-term interest rate policy using instruments besides the quantity of reserve money. We underscore the ways in which Quantitative Easing precipitated structural changes in the market for reserve money, enlarged the Fed's footprint in domestic and international money markets, and forced the Fed to find new instruments for policy implementation. Following an initial overview, we dig deeper into the Fed's preferred instruments of policy implementation. We shall see that the balance between open market operations, standing facilities, and reserve requirements has shifted in subtle but meaningful ways. Policy has become a more active affair, while the use of standing facilities has been severely diminished.

Second, we review the evidence for the efficacy of the Fed's interest rate policies under conventional and unconventional policy measures. While there is strong evidence that short-term interest rate policy and changes in the Fed's balance sheet have significant effects on asset prices and macroeconomic variables, their effects are clearly not neutral with respect to relative asset valuations and portfolio allocation decisions. A decade of near-zero interest rates following the GFC resulted in continued overinvestment in real estate and projects with no path to increased productivity or profitability over reasonable time horizons. In the process of accumulating evidence that markets heed the Fed's interest rate policy, researchers have taken for granted that interest rates are the best mechanism for central bank policy, and that interest rate policy is neutral with respect to the character of economic activity.

Third, we observe that the decade following the GFC produced an unusually stable growth rate for broad money.[2] This outcome was achieved through a combination of fiscal stimulus (monetized by the central bank), recapitalization of the banking sector, policies controlling the release of capital from the banking sector, and inducements for banks to grow their way out of their old balance sheets by pledging illiquid assets to the central bank, re-mortgaging real estate at elevated valuations, and originating new loans. The inflation that was supposed to follow the expansion of the Fed's balance sheet never materialized because balance sheet expansion had an unnoticeable impact on broad money. Inflation remained low and stable, in line with the growth of broad money. This era of tranquility was punctured by a tightening of monetary services in 2018–2019, followed by explosive growth in broad money due to monetization of the fiscal deficit caused by COVID stimulus spending. The burst of inflation that predictably followed from that spending has since been tamed by contraction in the broad money supply.

Finally, we consider the environment currently conditioning future central bank policy. Indeed, though post-GFC measures largely accomplished their goal of preventing a prolonged, Japan-type recession in the United States, they have not led to a sustainable operating model for central bank policy. The Federal Reserve has saddled itself with an enormous balance sheet and a reserve market which it controls at considerable cost to itself, the commercial banking system, and the government budget. The operating model into which the Fed has fallen, essentially by default, is complex, expensive, and prone to amplifying policy errors.

In Part Three, we will outline a quantity-based alternative to interest-rate based monetary policy, in which bank regulation, fiscal policy, and central bank policy interact to keep the supply of monetary services growing at a rate consistent with growth in money demand. Movements in interest rates following the GFC have distorted asset markets and investment worse than any other time in the modern era.

Central Bank Policy Implementation Before and After the GFC

For at least 30 years, the implementation of monetary policy has focused on the outcomes a central bank can achieve in the market for reserve money.[3] Prior to the GFC, most central banks would aim to adjust the supply of reserve money each day to align the interest rate at which the market for borrowing and lending reserves clears with a targeted policy rate. The central bank's status as the sole issuer of reserve money makes such control possible.

A baseline demand for reserve money was assured by requirements that commercial banks hold reserves equal to a percentage of their demandable liabilities, and by the need to settle interbank payments daily in reserve money.[4] Because reserves did not earn interest, banks sought to minimize excess reserve balances, including by sweeping demandable deposits to savings accounts overnight to reduce the balance of deposits subject to reserve requirements.[5] Reserves could also be drawn at commercial banks' discretion from central bank standing facilities, and flows in and out of government accounts at the central bank would also result in reserve money demands.

Central banks' ability to meet reserve demands reliably was based on their ability to forecast daily demands with a high degree of accuracy. Reserve requirements created a structural, easy-to-forecast component to the demand for reserve money. Somewhat harder to forecast were the movements in "autonomous factors" such as the use of standing facilities by commercial banks, movements in government deposit accounts, or foreign exchange flows. If the errors of the central bank's forecasts for reserve demand can be kept reasonably small, the central bank can reliably estimate the amount of reserve money to supply each day to clear the market for reserve money at the target policy rate. The central bank can issue new reserves through open market operations such as purchasing government bonds or accepting safe bond collateral in a repo transaction.[6]

The pursuit of the central bank's interest rate policy thus entailed certain adjustments to the quantity of money. However, because the quantity of money affected (reserve money) circulated only within the banking system and the required adjustments were generally small, the connection between interest rate policy and the supply of broad money was minor. In Chapter 3, we refuted the "reserve multiplier" story of how deposits respond to reserve requirement ratios, and in Chapter 14, we will refute another multiplier-based theory connecting broad money to the monetary base (reserves and cash) issued by the central bank. Thus, one should not assume that interest rate policy simultaneously implements a policy for the quantity of money, whether that policy is implemented directly by the central bank or indirectly by the banking system.

When the supply of reserve money is sufficient to clear the interbank market at the central bank's targeted rate, a growing banking system balance sheet will create new demands for reserve money and exert upward pressure on the interbank rate. Prior to the GFC, the banking system grew steadily, and the posture of policy was generally accommodative, with central banks adjusting the supply of reserve money to relieve upward pressure on interest rates and to avoid constraining the expanding balance sheet of the commercial banking system.[7]

Quantitative Easing and Its Consequences

When interest rates are the only tool that matters to the central bank, the advent of a development on the scale of the GFC creates a massive problem. The models used by the Fed and other central banks suggested that the optimal level for short-term interest rates following the GFC was well below zero. However, a central bank cannot easily pay a negative rate on required reserve balances (effectively taxing them away), and banks can avoid the negative rate by meeting their reserve requirement with vault cash. As a result, interest rate policy faces a "zero lower bound" at the overnight maturities targeted by central banks.

The Fed lowered its target rate from 5.25% in August 2007 to 0%–0.25% in December 2008. Though the Fed's target rate was as low as it could practically go, it was still too high according to its working understanding of monetary policy transmission, implying a policy error in the zero-interest rate policy. Nor was the error confined to interest rates at the overnight maturity. One can think of long-term interest rates as a time-weighted average of expected short-term rates plus a risk premium. If this averaging process includes many contributions which are too high because they are non-negative, longer-term interest rates will also be too high. The distortion will be equal to the difference between the "correct" negative rate and zero, accumulated over the time needed for the "correct" rate to return to zero. As a result, for the Fed to achieve its goals for policy, separate interventions were needed to reduce longer-term interest rates. The era of unconventional monetary policy was born in the quest to meet this need.[8]

Unconventional monetary policy at the Federal Reserve was known formally as a series of Large-Scale Asset Purchases (LSAPs). We know it as Quantitative Easing (QE). Running from November 2008 to March 2010, November 2010 to June 2011, and September 2012 to October 2014, the LSAPs expanded the Federal Reserve's balance sheet by some $3.5 trillion. The Fed purchased nearly $1.7 trillion in long-term Treasury notes and bonds and $1.7 trillion in agency mortgage-backed securities (MBS).[9] The Fed also implemented a Maturity Extension Program, which replaced its holdings of short-term Treasuries with longer-term Treasuries. The Fed's LSAPs were overwhelmingly financed by the issuance of reserve money, of which a non-trivial amount was converted to cash. The balance was financed by increases in deposits held at the Fed and reverse repurchase transactions.

A snapshot of the Fed's balance sheet before the GFC and at the end of the third LSAP in Table 10.1 reveals the enormous transformation in the supply of reserve money wrought by QE.[10] The scale of the Fed's purchases of long-term securities dwarfed that of its GFC-era credit facilities.

Quantitative Easing ended the era of "tight" reserve money and the ability to implement monetary policy through changes in the supply of reserves. The supply of reserve money at the end of December 2014 was over $2.5 trillion more than banks held prior to the GFC. To encourage banks to hold these increased balances rather than trade them for interest-bearing obligations, Congress authorized the

Table 10.1 Simplified Federal Reserve balance sheet before and after QE.

In millions USD	August 2007	October 2008	March 2010	December 2014
Assets	**911,086**	**2,005,515**	**2,354,788**	**4,553,276**
Treasuries	784,637	476,469	776,667	2,461,420
Agency MBS	–	–	1,073,800	1,747,377
Other	126,449	1,529,046	504,321	344,479
Liabilities	**876,801**	**1,965,097**	**2,301,751**	**4,496,140**
Cash	812,481	860,588	933,542	1,338,522
Reserve money	14,652	419,979	1,144,732	2,609,634
Deposits (TGA)	12,122	585,724	155,830	242,812
Other liabilities	37,546	98,806	67,647	305,172
Equity	**34,285**	**40,418**	**53,037**	**57,135**

Adapted from Factors Affecting Reserve Balances of Depository Institutions and Condition Statement of Federal Reserve Banks.

payment of interest on reserves beginning 1 October 2008.[11] The Fed is permitted to pay different interest rates on *required* reserves and *excess* reserves but has so far chosen to apply the same rate to both. These rates are now important central bank policy instruments.

Quantitative Easing also brought transactions in GSE obligations into the domain of the Federal Reserve's open market operations. Though the general level of interest rates has always impacted home prices, the Fed's $1.75 trillion participation in the agency MBS market marked a more direct intervention in the cost of mortgage finance and the state of the housing market. It also signaled that the long-suspected commitment of the government to support GSE obligations was real, as the Fed stood ready to monetize the obligations of the mortgage GSEs alongside those of the government.

The Fed's LSAPs were transactions with the nonbank public.[12] Whenever the Fed purchases a security from the nonbank public, it creates reserve money which is credited to the bank where the seller holds their deposit account. The seller may then hold their deposit balance, transfer it for consumption or a new claim on an asset, or destroy it by repaying loan principal. Once outstanding loans were repaid, the very low-interest rate environment strongly favored purchasing claims on assets rather than holding deposit balances or bonds. QE began the era of "there is no alternative" ("TINA") to stocks, with an influx of money chasing a largely static supply of equity investments. A substantial portion of the new balances were also invested in real estate, where expected returns were returning to their long-run averages following a sharp decline in prices.

Reestablishing Control Over Short-term Interest Rates

With the expansion of its balance sheet into the trillions of dollars, the Federal Reserve lost the ability to affect overnight interest rates in the interbank market through open market operations. Reserves were abundant and overnight interest rates would remain at zero even if the Fed bought or sold a half trillion dollars of Treasury debt or MBS. An artificial tightness could be created in the reserve market by raising reserve requirements, but a sharply elevated reserve ratio would simultaneously create strong incentives for banks to evade the requirement. Some other method of achieving short-term interest rate targets would be needed in this new regime.

The solution hit on by the Fed was to implement its target rate by adjusting the interest rate it would pay on required reserves (IOR) and excess reserves (IOER), converting the overnight interest rate on reserves from a market-clearing rate to an administered rate.[13] Central banks can make the short-term interest rate whatever they like, so long as they are prepared to pay the interest rate themselves. The administered rate creates a *ceiling* for the overnight rate because some important lenders in the reserve market are not eligible to earn IOR or IOER. Such lenders can earn a return just below the IOER by lending to banks, who can invest the proceeds with the central bank at the IOER, collecting a small, risk-free spread. Likewise, banks can sell any short-term instruments earning less than IOER and invest at the IOER, encouraging the alignment of other short-term interest rates with IOER.

However, it turns out that the administered rate is not enough to set the rate at which the interbank market clears. Even with IOR and IOER there are limits on the reserve balances that banks can reasonably hold. Following the GFC, the FDIC deposit insurance fee depends on the size of a bank's balance sheet, rather than the amount of its deposit liabilities. The insurance premium erodes the benefit of holding large reserve balances at the risk-free rate.[14] In addition, the Supplemental Leverage Ratio of Basel III constrains the size of bank balance sheets relative to their equity on an unweighted basis. These limitations mean that marginal lenders of reserves to banks may find less demand than expected, leading to a downward drift in the overnight lending rate.

Should the rate on reserves begin to drift significantly below the IOER, another mechanism would be needed to set a floor below the interbank rate. For such cases, the Fed would stand ready to borrow reserves at an overnight repo rate, offering high-quality securities as collateral. No lender of excess reserve balances would agree to a lower rate from a commercial bank when a higher rate could be earned by lending to the Fed. This latter arrangement has been formalized as the Overnight Reverse Repurchase Agreement Facility.[15]

Given a mechanism for controlling the policy rate, expectations about the future path of policy rates could take center stage. Accordingly, the Fed adjusted its "forward guidance" concerning its expectations for the magnitude and timing of policy rate increases. The timing of the Fed's exit from the zero lower bound was deferred until mid-2015 at the time the third LSAP was announced in September 2012.[16]

The combination of LSAPs, short-term policy rate instruments, and forward guidance gave the Fed powerful instruments with which to affect long-term interest rates, asset prices, and the overall level of economic activity.[17] The resulting corridor-based approach to interest rate control has served as the basis for the Fed's interest rate policy implementation since the Fed's first post-GFC interest rate increase in December 2015.

But as we have already suggested, the price of regaining control was a generational distortion in asset prices and expected returns. The funding created through QE was channeled into real estate, equities, and venture capital investments on a grand scale. These flows had an uneven effect on economic activity, benefiting those with access to equity and credit markets (older households, larger companies, well-connected startups) at the expense of those who faced credit and equity rationing.

The Path to Normalization and the COVID Interventions

The Federal Reserve was aware of the difficulties and risks involved in managing the expansion of its balance sheet caused by its LSAPs. Following the second LSAP, the Fed announced its intention to reduce its securities portfolio and the quantity of bank reserves "to the smallest levels that would be consistent with the efficient implementation of monetary policy."[18] The Fed's MBS holdings would be sold "over a period of three to five years, thereby minimizing the extent to which [the Fed's securities holdings] might affect the allocation of credit across sectors of the economy."[19]

The Fed's third LSAP made reversing course more difficult. In September 2014, the Fed abandoned its intention to sell MBS. Instead, the Fed would stop reinvesting principal payments on its securities portfolio. While the Fed would, "in the longer run, hold no more securities than necessary to implement monetary policy efficiently and effectively," they declined to chart a course toward a smaller balance sheet.[20] When a plan for a gradual reduction was presented in June 2017, the previous goal of reducing reserves to "the smallest levels ... consistent with the efficient implementation of monetary policy" was amended to "reducing the quantity of reserve balances, over time, to a level appreciably below

Table 10.2 Simplified Federal Reserve balance sheet before and after COVID.

In millions USD	December 2017	December 2018	December 2019	June 2020
Assets	**4,495,736**	**4,123,322**	**4,213,891**	**7,130,953**
Treasuries	2,454,219	2,240,717	2,328,862	4,197,404
Agency MBS	1,764,926	1,637,123	1,419,980	1,943,441
Other	276,591	245,482	465,049	990,108
Liabilities	**4,454,347**	**4,084,163**	**4,175,369**	**7,092,043**
Cash	1,616,323	1,716,129	1,802,362	1,963,978
Reserve money	2,176,452	1,660,932	1,648,238	2,937,657
Deposits (TGA)	268,636	456,788	464,342	1,848,380
Other liabilities	392,936	250,314	260,427	342,028
Equity	**41,388**	**39,160**	**38,522**	**38,911**

Adapted from Factors Affecting Reserve Balances of Depository Institutions and Condition Statement of Federal Reserve Banks.

that seen in recent years but larger than before the financial crisis"—a wide range, to say the least—while allowing its securities portfolio to run off at an increasing pace.[21]

The Fed's June 2017 announcement set the Fed on a path to a modest reduction in its balance sheet, as shown in Table 10.2. The Fed reduced its MBS holdings by some $350 billion from December 2017 to December 2019, while its holdings of Treasuries fell by roughly $125 billion. Reserves held by the banking system fell from $2.18 trillion to $1.65 trillion. Nevertheless, the quantity of reserves in the system remained $500 billion above their level following the first LSAP, and more than $1 trillion above their level at the end of October 2008, suggesting that a long path to normalization remained.

Years of actions and planning intended to reduce the Fed's footprint in financial markets were quickly jettisoned in the monetary policy response to COVID. By mid-March 2020, the target policy rate was dropped to zero and the Fed announced its intentions to purchase $500 billion of Treasuries and $200 billion in MBS over the coming months. A week later, the Fed stated simply that it would purchase Treasuries and MBS "in the amounts needed" and began to purchase agency CMBS. In June 2020, the FOMC announced it would purchase at least $80 billion in Treasuries and $40 billion MBS each month.[22] Table 10.2 shows that in just three months, the Federal Reserve added another $1.3 trillion to the reserve market, nearly doubling its total size, and its balance sheet ballooned to over $7 trillion.

It is notable that only $1.5 trillion of the $3 trillion balance sheet expansion was absorbed by reserves. The balance of the Fed's asset purchases were absorbed primarily by the Treasury General Account (TGA). This boost to the government's balance on current account allowed for a delayed release of government stimulus to the public via the banking system. The runoff of the TGA would transfer more than $1 trillion in reserves from the government's account to the banking system, where the nonbank public would see their accounts credited with stimulus payments.

These transfer payment flows from the government significantly increased the growth rate of broad money. From March 2020 to February 2021, the growth rate of Divisia M3 stepped up from a 6%–7% year-over-year rate to 20%–21%, an impulse which resulted in the acceleration of inflation in 2022 and 2023 (Figure 10.1).

The expansion of the Fed's balance sheet continued through the end of 2021 (Table 10.3). Following the runoff of the TGA, excess reserve balances were absorbed through the Overnight Reverse Repurchase Agreement Facility. At the time of writing, the Fed has succeeded in reducing its balance sheet from a peak size of $9 trillion to $7.1 trillion, while reducing reserve balances from more than $4 trillion to about $3.1 trillion and reducing use of the Overnight Reverse Repurchase Agreement Facility by more than $1 trillion. Yet, the Fed remains far from restoring either its balance sheet or the quantity of reserves in circulation to their pre-GFC levels.

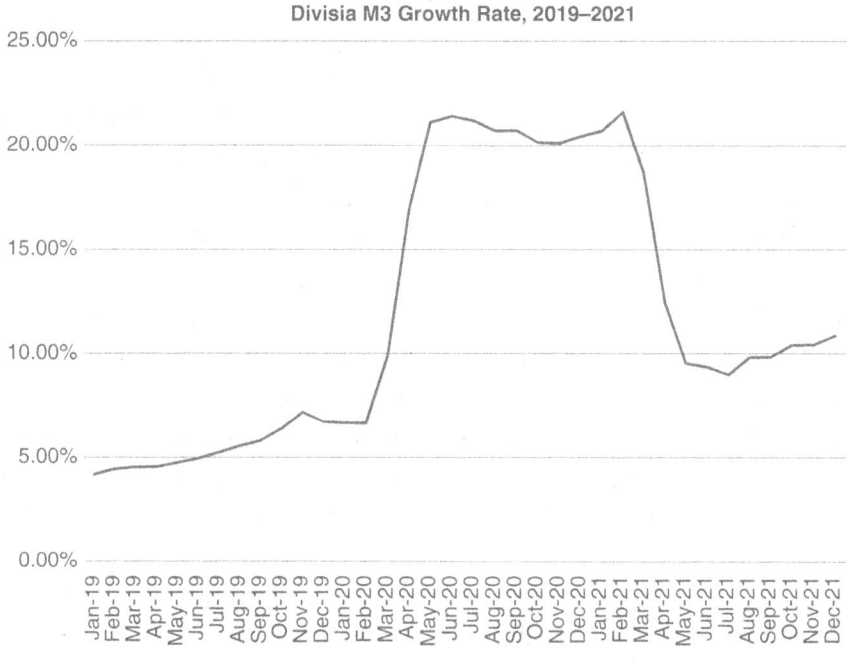

Figure 10.1 Divisia M3 growth rate, 2019–2021.

Table 10.3 Simplified Federal Reserve balance sheet, 2020–2023.

In millions USD	December 2020	December 2021	December 2022	December 2023
Assets	**7,411,465**	**8,806,581**	**8,600,805**	**7,763,508**
Treasuries	4,688,916	5,652,272	5,500,834	4,790,547
Agency MBS	2,039,468	2,615,492	2,641,402	2,431,773
Other	683,081	538,817	458,569	541,188
Liabilities	**7,372,264**	**8,765,920**	**8,559,006**	**7,720,658**
Cash	2,086,909	2,236,532	2,307,340	2,344,610
Reserve money	3,142,970	4,039,860	2,979,738	3,434,213
Deposits (TGA)	1,808,390	539,646	637,310	887,342
Other liabilities	333,995	1,949,882	2,634,618	1,054,493
Equity	**39,201**	**40,661**	**41,799**	**42,850**

Adapted from Factors Affecting Reserve Balances of Depository Institutions and Condition Statement of Federal Reserve Banks.

Reestablishing tightness in the reserve market appears no longer to be a goal of policy. On 30 January 2019, the FOMC announced, "The Committee intends to continue to implement policy in a regime in which an ample supply of reserves ensures that control over the level of the federal funds rate and other short-term interest rates is exercised primarily through the setting of the Federal Reserve's administered rates, and in which active management of the supply of reserves is not required."[23] At the same time, the Fed's estimates of reserves needed to implement monetary policy have expanded to keep pace with the growth of the Fed's balance sheet. In April 2008, the Fed estimated they would need $35 billion; as of May 2022, that figure had become $2.3 trillion.[24]

It seems that banks are content to hold reserves in vast quantities when the Fed pays them to. For much of 2023 and 2024, reserve balances were earning about 5% per year—more than long-term Treasury yields, and without any of the duration risk. And the Fed has paid. In 2023, the Fed paid $281 billion in interest to banks, resulting in a substantial fiscal loss.[25] As of October 2024, the Fed's accumulated losses exceeded $200 billion.[26] Though the Fed's current losses may be attributed to the path of interest rates from the beginning of COVID to the present, they will remain vulnerable to losses so long as its bloated balance sheet persists.[27]

Since June 2022, the Fed has sought to reduce its balance sheet at a steady pace, selling securities and declining to reinvest principal payments. Though it "intends to slow and then stop the decline in the size of the balance sheet when reserve balances are somewhat above the level ... consistent with ample reserves," it is not clear when that goal will be reached.[28]

Structural Changes in the Reserve Market

The Federal Reserve's post-crisis interventions have changed the character of the market for reserves as well as its size. An abundance of reserves has reduced the volume of interbank lending to a small fraction of its pre-GFC levels, and most of the lending that now takes place is driven by differences in regulatory treatment. Reserve demands have become more difficult to forecast, occasionally introducing ambiguity about whether reserve supply is abundant, ample, or scarce. Demand forecasting is further complicated by the presence of new participants in the reserve market, including a much larger government, securities dealers, and foreign central banks. Though the Fed has so far been able to achieve its rate targets, the structure and function of the reserve market has changed, with far-reaching consequences.

Prior to the GFC, the interbank lending market for reserves was active and vibrant. Banks with excess reserve balances lent to banks experiencing temporary deficits, making ample liquidity available at the Fed Funds rate. Federal Reserve economists have estimated the size of the pre-crisis Fed Funds market from bank and BHC call reports, FHLB financial statements, and quarterly SEC filings.[29] Those sources suggest that some $200 billion in Fed Funds were traded each day among commercial banks, which is a phenomenal amount considering that aggregate reserve balances were only $15–20 billion during the same period.[30] Interbank lending clearly relieved whatever constraints were imposed by scarce reserves, with interbank loans multiplying reserve money.

Following the GFC and the explosion of reserve supply created by Federal Reserve credit facilities and QE policy, three important changes occurred that affected reserve demand and the interbank market. First, closer supervision of banking system liquidity and new regulations (somewhat artificially) increased demand for high-quality liquid assets (HQLA), including reserves. Second, reserve demand became less certain, because HQLA can be allocated between reserves and government securities. Third, stricter regulations on bank leverage increased the cost of trading reserves between banks, because many banks found the size of their balance sheets constrained, despite the lack of risk weighting for reserves. Hence, the quantity of reserve money required by the banking system is elevated, though less certain, and reserves are not distributed efficiently in the banking system.[31]

Initial increases in the Fed's reserve balances were absorbed by the largest banks (global systematically important banks, or GSIBs) and the U.S. branches of foreign banking organizations (FBOs) from 2008 to 2012. When the third wave of QE was complete, GSIBs and FBO branches reduced their reserve holdings, while smaller banks increased their reserves. This pattern largely repeated itself after COVID, with smaller banks expanding their reserve holdings to a much greater extent than they did following QE.[32]

With reserves in ample supply, the market for interbank lending of reserve balances has largely collapsed. What remains is some artificial lending between GSEs and the U.S. branches of FBOs.[33] Daily turnover in the Fed Funds market was roughly $100 billion daily in 2009 and 2010, or about half of its pre-crisis level, and declined to $50–70 billion daily in 2011 and 2012.[34] The primary lenders in the reserve market are institutions that are not eligible to earn interest on reserves. Among such institutions, the FHLBs dominate, while FNMA and FHLMC also participate.[35] As of 2023, the FHLBs and mortgage GSEs remained responsible for more than 90% of Fed Funds lending. The main borrowers in the market are U.S. branches of FBOs, borrowing $45 to $110 billion per day, or 65%–95% of daily volume. FBO branches have liquidity-rich balance sheets with a large share of reserves, low shares of deposits, and significant positions with overseas affiliates, reflecting their role as dollar liquidity providers to the international banking system.[36] Domestic banks borrow the remaining 5%–35%, or $2.5 to $25 billion daily.[37] Hence, if we assume that FBO branches were small participants in the interbank market before the GFC, domestic bank borrowings are now one to two orders of magnitude smaller. The regular monitoring of banks by other banks encouraged by interbank lending has given way to a system in which GSEs serve as conduit lenders supporting offshore dollar liquidity.

At the beginning of the chapter, we connected central banks' ability to meet reserve demands reliably to their ability to forecast daily demands accurately. We differentiated between the easy-to-forecast component related to reserve requirements, while noting that movements in "autonomous factors" were harder to anticipate. The flood of reserve money created by the Fed during and after the GFC meant that reserve requirements were no longer binding for banks. The reserve requirement was dropped all together in 2020 after further Fed balance sheet expansion related to COVID.[38] Long before that, however, the reserve requirement had effectively been replaced by the Liquidity Coverage Ratio of Basel III, which requires banks to hold sufficient HQLA. While reserve money gets high marks under the HQLA rules, banks can satisfy their requirements by holding other, higher-earning assets as well. Banks' discretion over the form in which they hold HQLA thus introduces uncertainty about reserve demand from the central bank's core constituency.

The autonomous factors affecting balance in the reserve market have also become bigger and noisier, even after the Fed's crisis-era facilities have wound down.[39] In October 2008, the TGA moved from commercial banks to the Federal Reserve. At times, the government has sharply increased and decreased the balance of the TGA, most notably during COVID.[40]

The Fed's standing Overnight Reverse Repurchase Agreement Facility opened in September 2023. Primary dealers, MMFs, and GSEs can swap collateral for reserves, draining liquidity from the reserve market. When the Fed first began raising rates from zero, usage of the facility peaked at roughly $150 billion. Following the wave of QE associated with the COVID-19 pandemic, usage of the facility peaked at $2.5 trillion.

The Fed has also accommodated structural changes in offshore USD funding markets driven by post-crisis regulatory changes.[41] International banks have been encouraged to reduce currency mismatches and shift or curtail their geographic footprints.[42] Accordingly, the center of gravity for offshore USD funding markets has shifted from Europe to Japan and emerging markets. Banks have seen their market-making capacity in foreign exchange constrained, and nonbank intermediaries have become more important sources and uses of funding.[43]

In response to greater demand for offshore dollar liquidity, the Fed has converted its central bank USD swap lines to standing facilities, administered a larger foreign repo pool, and introduced a new standing repo facility for foreign and international monetary authorities (FIMAs). The Fed's central bank USD swap lines were established during the Bretton Woods era for FX intervention and Eurodollar liquidity management. They were redeployed and expanded in 2007 and converted to standing facilities in October 2013. Peak draws on the swap lines reached $598 billion during the GFC and $449 billion in May 2020 during COVID. The standing facilities allow foreign central banks to swap local currency for dollars at the overnight indexed swap rate plus a spread. Central banks then auction the dollars to financial institutions within their jurisdictions.[44]

Some 250 central banks, governments, and international official institutions participate in the Fed's foreign repo pool, which is managed by the Federal Reserve Bank of New York. Participating institutions can invest excess funds overnight in repurchase agreements backed by collateral in the Fed's System Open Market Account (SOMA). Balances in the foreign repo pool are regularly in the hundreds of billions, and quite volatile.[45]

U.S. branches of FBOs experienced drawdowns on their USD credit lines following the GFC and COVID shocks as their parent companies sought to access U.S. dollar funding. Foreign central banks sold USD assets in response to fund capital outflows, causing cash balances invested overnight in the foreign repo pool to spike.[46] To mitigate the volatility such sales created in the foreign repo pool, the Fed authorized the FIMA repo facility on 31 March 2020 and converted it to a standing facility on 28 July 2021. The FIMA repo facility gives foreign institutions the ability to repo Treasuries with the SOMA rather than sell them outright.[47]

The Fed's use of its primary policy instruments is complicated by the combination of enormous reserve supply and uncertain required and autonomous reserve demands. The supply of reserves relative to demand is classified by the Fed as ample, abundant, or scarce.[48] When reserves are ample or abundant, the effective Fed funds rate (EFFR) is below IOR. Banks can borrow reserves from FBOs and park them with the Fed to earn IOER.[49] When reserves are scarce, however, money market rates exceed the IOR and large banks drain their excess reserves to lend in the repo market. As a result, money market rates face downside risks when reserves are ample or abundant, and upside risks when reserves are scarce.[50]

Whether the Fed is adequately prepared for such risks depends on its ability to distinguish between the three regimes based on the elasticity of reserve demand. Apart from an episode in 2019, the elasticity of reserve demand has been statistically indistinguishable from zero since early 2012, suggesting reserves have been consistently abundant, and that the Fed Funds rate does not respond to changes in the supply of reserves.[51]

Interest Rate Policy Transmission and Asset Prices

There can be little doubt that changes in the Fed's policy rate are transmitted to the wider economy. What is less certain is how the transmission mechanism linking interest rates to ultimate outcomes like output and inflation depends on asset prices.[52] In particular, the impact of interest rate policy on real estate prices, equity prices, and long-term interest rates is diffuse and uncertain, while their implications for the distribution of wealth and the allocation of economic activity are easier to discern. To the extent that interest rate policy relies on these channels to achieve its goals, one can question the repeatability of such policy measures given current asset valuations, as well as the wisdom of exacerbating price distortions.

The current evidence that monetary policy "surprises" impact the economy is better than ever. The impact of policy rate actions and speeches by the Federal Reserve Chairman can be captured by the movements of short-term interest rate futures in a precise 30-minute window around their public release. The unpredictable component of those releases can be isolated by removing the effect of confounding announcements and movements in financial variables which otherwise contribute to forecasting the evolution of interest rates. The residual effect on short-term interest rates can be shown to have a large and long-term impact on macroeconomic and financial variables which is plausibly exogenous, causal, and specific to monetary policy.[53]

The impact of monetary policy surprises on the macroeconomic environment is seen through long, persistent effects on industrial production, the unemployment rate, and the consumer price index. As expected, raising the policy rate reduces industrial production, increases the unemployment rate, and reduces the rate of change in the consumer price index. Changes in production and employment occur relatively quickly, while the response of inflation to the policy rate phases in slowly over a longer interval. The impact of interest rate policy on Treasury yields, bond premia, and commodity prices is also presented as evidence of policy transmission to the macroeconomy, though these metrics are less obviously connected to the real economy. And increasingly, the long-term impact of monetary policy surprises on financial variables such as the entire Treasury yield curve and equity prices is proffered as evidence of monetary policy transmission.[54]

Whereas the impact of rate-based policy surprises builds on evidence accumulated over more than 30 years, evidence on the transmission of QE policy is confined to the post-GFC era and is therefore less settled. Central bankers have tended to find larger and more persistent effects from QE on output and inflation than academics have.[55] It appears that the Fed's first LSAP program successfully reduced Treasury yields, swap yields, term premia, and agency MBS yields, while strengthening the U.S. dollar.[56] However, as the effects of subsequent LSAPs were better anticipated by markets, the macroeconomic impact of later waves of QE was more muted.[57]

The impact of the first LSAP on aggregate consumption and GDP appears to have largely worked through residential housing investment. Such investment is stimulated by compression of mortgage credit spreads, or the reduction of mortgage rates relative to risk-free rates of similar maturity.[58] Each wave of QE has also had a persistent effect on equity prices.[59] The connection of equity prices to a "wealth effect" on consumption is harder to pin down, but highly plausible. More generally, evidence exists that home prices have reacted quickly to monetary policy surprises in the 2001–2019 period, and that the magnitude of their response is comparable to equity price reactions.[60]

While the Fed evidently found a way to avoid a more painful economic fallout from the GFC, it is not clear that its post-crisis mix of strategies is well-controlled, replicable, or sustainable. When much of the impact of policy on output comes from the amorphous effect of housing- and stock-based wealth on consumption, it is difficult to anticipate the timing and magnitude of policy actions. The size of monetary policy surprises is also difficult to calibrate. While their impact can be appreciated *ex post*, the central bank will have a difficult time discerning how much its actions are anticipated (or not) as they are being planned.

The persistent effects of monetary policy on asset prices leads us to worry further about relying on low interest rates and LSAPs for economic stimulus. It appears that much of the decline in real interest rates observed since the early 1980s may be attributed to the stance of monetary policy, rather than exogenous movements in real rates.[61] At the same time, return premia have been compressed in the Treasury market, money market funds, corporate bonds, and equity markets, indicating that investors have accepted less compensation for holding risky assets.[62] Presumably, much of the increase in real estate prices over the same period may be attributed to reductions in real interest rates and the compression of mortgage credit spreads. If providing future policy stimulus depends on further reducing investors' returns for bearing risk and driving asset valuations even further above their historically high levels, we may find that the monetary policy transmission mechanism that operated in the post-GFC era—whatever it may have been—quickly falls apart.

An Unintended Period of Steady Broad Money Growth

Though post-GFC central bank policy handicapped the market for bank reserves, saddled central banks with enormous balance sheets and fiscal losses, and left central bankers groping for a new policy framework, it was, nevertheless, reasonably successful in the United States. Another Great Depression was avoided, and the recession that followed was relatively brief. In the decade that followed, the United States returned to a respectable growth path and avoided the stagnation experienced by the European Union and Japan. Something about post-GFC policy was right.

We believe that post-GFC central bank policy was successful because it kept the supply of broad money growing at a consistent rate. Post-GFC policy was not advertised as a quantity-based policy, of course, but by keeping the growth rate of the money supply at roughly 3%–5% per year, the Fed supported real output growth of about 3% while keeping inflation under its 2% target (Figure 10.2). Because interest rates were at or near zero for most of the decade, the difference between the nominal quantity of money and the quantity of monetary services was negligible, making it easier to pursue a quantity-based target than during the Volcker deflation episode.[63]

Post-GFC policy took notice of the ways that banking regulation and fiscal policy impacted the growth rate of the money supply. The early phases of the

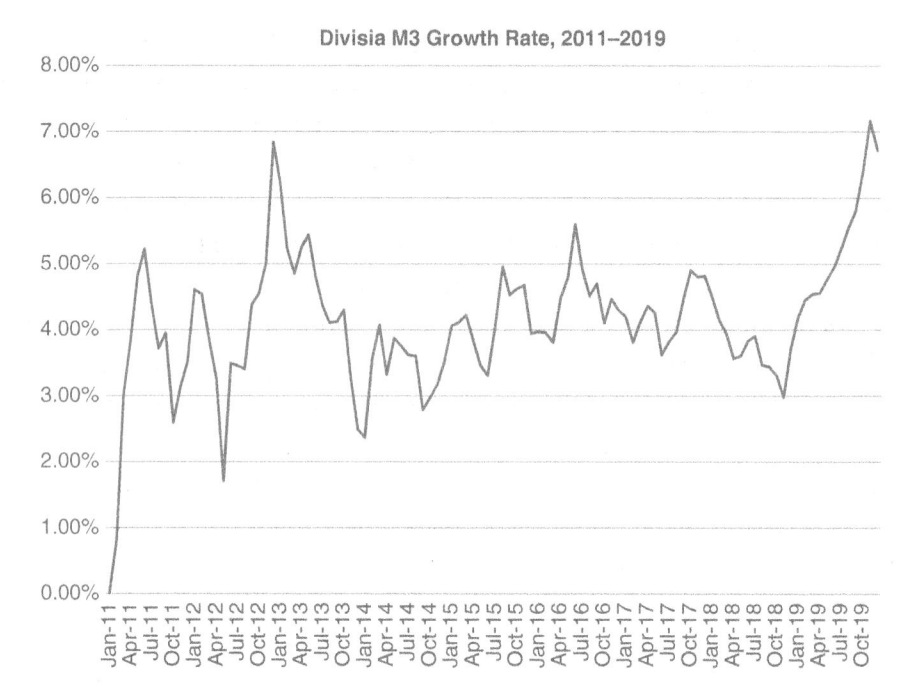

Figure 10.2 Divisia M3 growth rate, 2011–2019.

recovery were predominantly driven by monetary growth induced by the Fed's LSAPs. Deposit money grew not because banks resumed lending, but because the nonbank public traded their holdings of long-term Treasuries and agency MBS for deposit balances backed by newly created reserve money. Once bank capital levels had recovered adequately to support further lending, the Fed turned responsibility for monetary growth over to the banking system.

As we have pointed out previously, most growth in the broad money supply comes from growth in deposits in the banking system. We can re-arrange the balance sheet identity for the consolidated banking system to identify the main drivers of deposit growth.

$$\Delta Deposits = \Delta Reserves + \Delta Securities + \Delta Loans - \Delta Debt - \Delta Equity$$
$$= \Delta Reserves + \Delta Securities + (\Delta Loans(\Delta Equity) - \Delta Equity) - \Delta Debt$$
$$= (\Delta Reserves + \Delta Securities) + (\alpha - 1)\Delta Equity - \Delta Debt$$

In the second line, we group loans and equity together, emphasizing that growth in lending is connected to growth in equity. The third line observes that, because lending can grow as a multiple of equity α on the order of 10:1, we can view the deposit growth attributable to loan growth as a multiple of equity. Hence, we decompose the growth of deposits into a change in liquid assets held by the banking system (reserves and securities), the deployment of new equity into lending, and deleveraging. Though the rate of deleveraging in the banking system was impressive over this interval, debt was a relatively small component of the consolidated balance sheet, so we do not analyze it further.

Post-GFC growth in reserves and securities is dominated by reserve growth and may be seen as the consequence of QE. Significant waves of reserve increases may be seen in 2011 and 2013–2014 as Federal Reserve purchases of Treasury securities and agency MBS from the nonbank public created new deposit money. To finance their large-scale purchases of securities, the Fed created new reserve money, which was transferred to the accounts of banks where sellers held their deposit accounts. Had the Fed purchased securities from the banking system, like the European Central Bank and the Bank of Japan, the increase in reserve money would have been offset by reductions in the banking system's securities holdings, and no expansion of deposit money would have followed.[64]

By 2014, new lending began to make a substantial contribution to the growth in deposits. Corporate credit began to grow again in 2011 and consumer lending in 2012, but in 2014, bank mortgage lending also returned to growth. With the largest component of bank balance sheets once again expanding, aggregate bank lending increased from 2014 through 2016 at a roughly 7% year-over-year rate, taking over from QE as a driver of broad money growth. For the remainder of the period, lending grew at a consistent annual rate of 4%–5% per year. From 2014 to 2019, the share of loans in bank portfolios increased from a post-crisis low of 52.4% to 58.4%, while the share of cash and reserves fell by more than 7 percentage points.[65]

The renewed growth in lending observed from 2014 to 2019 may be attributed to the recovery of risk capital in the banking system. The Federal Reserve initiated a Supervisory Capital Assessment Program in 2009 to restore confidence in the 19 largest U.S. banks. These discretionary stress tests became a legal requirement with the passage of the Dodd-Frank Act. The Dodd-Frank Act stress tests were integrated into the Fed's Comprehensive Capital Analysis and Review (CCAR) framework in 2011.[66] Under the CCAR framework, banks with more than $50 billion in assets (later revised upward) are required to provide a description of all planned capital actions, including share issuances, dividend distributions, and share repurchases. Approval of a bank's capital plan is based on the results of the stress-testing exercise, which would evaluate how a bank's existing capital and ability to generate new capital through earnings would react to a severely adverse economic scenario.[67]

Facing an uncomfortable sanction of capital plan rejection, the largest U.S. banks reduced their capital payout ratios substantially. From 2000 to 2006, banks participating in the CCAR program returned an average of 76% of their net income to shareholders, of which 40% was paid out as dividends and 36% took place through share repurchases. By contrast, from 2010 to 2017, such banks' payout ratios climbed steadily from about 10% of net income, not reaching their pre-crisis average level again until 2017, the first year in which the Fed did not object to any CCAR bank capital plans. Over the post-crisis period, banks shifted to a preference for share repurchases, rather than committing to return capital to shareholders through regular dividends.[68]

In July 2019, Randall Quarles, the Federal Reserve Board's Vice Chair for Supervision, declared, "Our stress tests demonstrate that banks have now built enough capital to withstand a severe recession. The capital-building phase of the post-crisis era is now complete...."[69] After 30 June 2021, restrictions on dividends and share repurchases were removed for all large banks provided their common Tier 1 equity capital included an adequate stress capital buffer.[70]

Following the 2020–2021 burst of money creation created by the government's COVID relief programs, the trend in broad money growth reversed sharply. Over the course of 2022, the year-over-year growth rate of Divisia M3 fell from 10% to −0.4%, as shown in Figure 10.3. Divisia M3 then contracted for all of 2023. Recent data at the time of writing indicates that Divisia M3 has begun growing again at a 1% annual rate since March 2024.[71] Certainly, the excesses of the COVID years required some retrenchment afterwards. In addition, it is likely

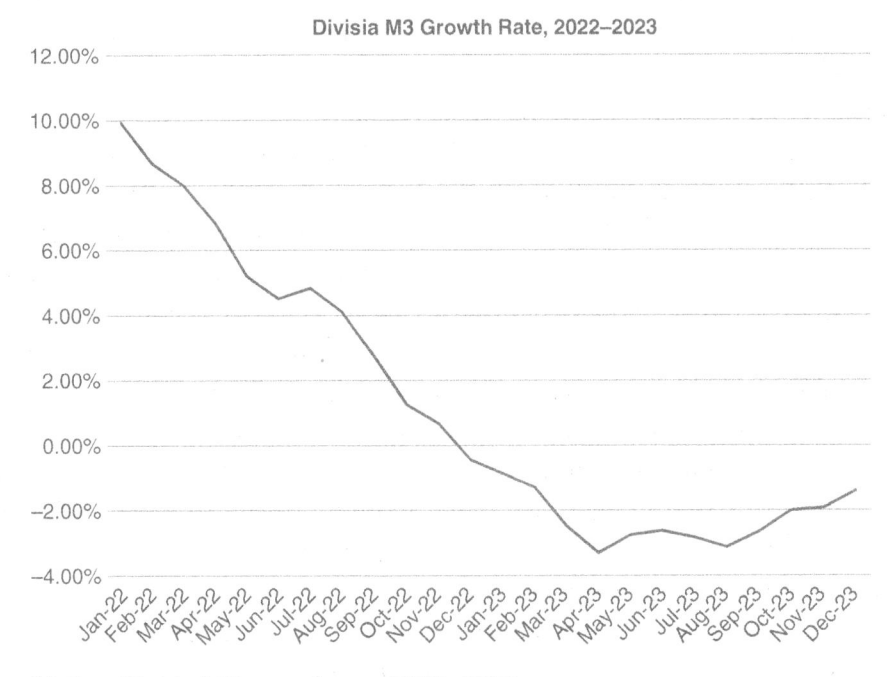

Figure 10.3   Divisia M3 growth rate, 2022–2023.

that the phasing-in of additional capital requirements affecting banks' capital markets business have once again made capital a binding constraint for universal banks. When banks are reluctant to issue new equity and potentially signal weakness, marginal dollars to support the capital markets business are most easily requisitioned from the banking book's pot.

The idea of regulating broad money growth by controlling the release of banking system capital contains the germ of the new monetary operating model we will develop in Part Three of the book. In the absence of strong evidence that other constraints are operative, it is reasonable to surmise that bank capital is the binding constraint on bank balance sheet expansion, and that a large and predictable share of bank balance sheet expansion will take the form of new lending and money creation.

Prospects for Future Interest Rate Policy

The prospects for future interest rate policy, on the other hand, do not seem very bright. The practice of interest rate policy now has weak contact with the banking system and relies on diffuse, poorly understood channels that operate through multiple asset markets. Considerable uncertainty will attend attempts to formulate and deploy policy, leading to the potential for significant policy errors.

The Fed, like other major central banks, now presides over an enormous balance sheet which holds a meaningful share of all outstanding Treasury debt and agency MBS. So many reserves have been created to finance that balance sheet expansion that interbank lending rates no longer react to changes in the quantity of reserves. And because the interest paid on those reserves now exceeds the interest earned on the Fed's portfolio, the Fed has lost hundreds of billions of dollars upon raising interest rates to tame the post-COVID wave of inflation.

The Fed will struggle to reduce its balance sheet. Large-scale sales of assets would raise long-term interest rates and depress elevated asset valuations. And indeed, at the first signs of trouble, the Fed will likely come under heavy pressure to support asset valuations with further asset purchases, exacerbating the problems it has created through its QE programs.

These doubts about the feasibility and wisdom of continuing to pursue monetary policy as interest rate policy have led to renewed interest in a quantity-based monetary framework.[72] Part Three begins to imagine what such a framework would look like in a modern financial system, including its overarching policy goals and instruments. In addition, we suggest multiple "structural reforms" to the business of banking and underlying collateral markets that are complementary to the policy framework.

Notes

1. We discuss Federal Reserve policy for concreteness, and because it is the example with which we are most familiar. There are more similarities than differences between the post-GFC policies of the Fed, the ECB, the BoJ, and other major central banks, but a full discussion covering each of these institutions is beyond our scope.
2. Because interest rates were close to zero, the distinction between the quantity of money and the quantity of monetary services makes little difference during this period.
3. Our discussion closely follows Bindseil, U. (2004). *Monetary Policy Implementation: Theory – Past – Present*. Oxford University Press and Ihrig, J.E., Meade, E.E., and Weinbach, G.C. (2015). Rewriting monetary policy 101: What's the Fed's preferred post-crisis approach to raising interest rates? *Journal of Economic Perspectives* 29 (4): 177–198.
4. Poole, W. (1968). Commercial bank reserve management in a stochastic model: Implications for monetary policy. *Journal of Finance* 23 (5): 769–791 is the *locus classicus* for models of reserve demand. The requirements were set out in Regulation D.
5. Nelson, B. (2024). How the Federal Reserve got so huge, and why and how it can shrink. *Bank Policy Institute*, February 7, Barnett, W.A.; Liu, J., Mattson, R.S. et al. (2013). The new CFS Divisia monetary aggregates: Design, construction, and data sources. *Open Economies Review* 24: 101–124.
6. Bindseil, U. (2004). *Monetary Policy Implementation: Theory – Past – Present*. Oxford University Press; Judson, R.A. and Klee, E. (2010). Whither the liquidity effect: The impact of Federal Reserve open market operations in recent years. *Journal of Macroeconomics* 32 (3): 713–731; Afonso, G., Giannone, D., La Spada, G. et al. (2024). Scarce, abundant, or ample? A time-varying model of the reserve demand curve. *Federal Reserve Bank of New York Staff Report No. 1019 (revised)*, April.
7. Disyatat, P. (2008). Monetary policy implementation: Misconceptions and their consequences. *BIS Working Paper No. 269*.
8. For a survey of the literature on unconventional monetary policy, see Bhatterai, S. and Neely, C.J. (2022). An analysis of the literature on international unconventional monetary policy. *Journal of Economic Literature* 60 (2): 527–597.
9. Chairman Ben Bernanke's announcement on 19 June 2013 that the Fed intended to reduce its pace of bond purchases led to an upward jump in bond prices and an increase in the foreign exchange value of the US dollar which marked the first episode of the "taper tantrum." See Neely, C.J. (2014). Lessons

from the taper tantrum. *Federal Reserve Bank of St. Louis Economic Synopses*, Number 2.

10. The illustration is a modified and expanded version of Figure 1 in Ihrig, J.E., Meade, E.E., and Weinbach, G.C. (2015). Rewriting monetary policy 101: What's the Fed's preferred post-crisis approach to raising interest rates? *Journal of Economic Perspectives* 29 (4): 177–198.
11. Payment of interest on reserves was authorized by the Financial Services Regulatory Relief Act of 2006 with an effective date of 1 January 2011 (109th Congress, PL 351). The effective date was moved up to 1 October 2008 by the Emergency Economic Stabilization Act of 2008 (110th Congress, PL 343).
12. The European Central Bank and the Bank of Japan expanded their balance sheets by purchasing debt from the banking system, which only served to create larger reserve balances. As a result, recessions in Europe and Japan were deeper than those experienced in the United States. See Hanke, S.H. and Sekerke, M. (2017). Bank regulation as monetary policy: Lessons from the great recession. *Cato Journal* 37: 385–405 for an analysis.
13. FOMC, "Policy Normalization Principles and Plans," 17 September 2014.
14. Afonso, G., Kim, K., Martin, A. et al. (2020b). Monetary policy implementation with an ample supply of reserves. *Federal Reserve Bank of Chicago Working Paper 2020-02*.
15. FOMC, "Policy Normalization Principles and Plans," 17 September 2014.
16. Federal Reserve, "Timelines of Policy Actions and Communications: Forward Guidance about the Federal Funds Rate," 22 February 2019. https://www.federalreserve.gov/monetarypolicy/timeline-forward-guidance-about-the-federal-funds-rate.htm.
17. Gertler, M. and Karadi, P. (2013). QE 1 vs. 2 vs. 3…: A framework for analyzing large-scale asset purchases as a monetary policy tool. *International Journal of Central Banking* 9 (S1): 5–53.
18. Minutes of 12 June 2011 FOMC meeting ("Exit Strategy Principles").
19. Ibid.
20. FOMC, "Policy Normalization Principles and Plans," 17 September 2014.
21. FOMC, "Addendum to the Policy Normalization Principles and Plans," 14 June 2017.
22. See the timeline in Clarida, R.H., Duygan-Bump, B., and Scotti, C. (2021). The COVID-19 crisis and the Federal Reserve's policy response. *Federal Reserve Board Finance and Economics Discussion Series 2021-035*.
23. FOMC, "Statement Regarding Monetary Policy Implementation and Balance Sheet Normalization," 30 January 2019.

24. Nelson, B. (2024). How the Federal Reserve got so huge, and why and how it can shrink. *Bank Policy Institute*, February 7: 9–10.
25. See https://www.federalreserve.gov/aboutthefed/files/combinedfinstmt2023.pdf.
26. Michael S. Derby, "Fed's paper losses top the $200 bln mark," Reuters, 3 October 2024.
27. Cavallo, M., Negro, M.D., Frame, W.S. et al. (2019). Fiscal implications of the Federal Reserve's balance sheet normalization. *International Journal of Central Banking* 15 (5): 255–306.
28. Quoted in Labonte, M. (2024). The Fed's balance sheet and quantitative tightening. *Congressional Research Service*, June 24.
29. Available at www.chicagofed.org/webpages/banking/financial_institution_reports/bhc_data.cfm, cdr.ffiec.gov/public, and www.fhlb-of.com/ofweb_user/pageBuilder/fhlbank-financial-data-36.
30. Afonso, G., Entz, A., and La Sueur, E. (2013). Who's lending in the Fed Funds market? *Liberty Street Economics*, December 2.
31. Afonso, G., Cipriani, M., La Spada, G. et al. (2020a). A new reserves regime? COVID-19 and the Federal Reserve balance sheet. *Liberty Street Economics*, July 7.
32. Ibid.
33. While all institutions with access to the Fed Funds market can lend, only commercial banks can borrow reserves.
34. Quarterly data from 2006Q4 to 2012Q4 is available at www.newyorkfed.org/fed-funds-lending.
35. Afonso, G., Entz, A., and La Sueur, E. (2013). Who's lending in the Fed Funds market? *Liberty Street Economics*, December 2.
36. Du, W. (2023). Foreign banking organizations in the United States and the price of dollar liquidity. *Liberty Street Economics*, January 11. Lean on wholesale funding because their deposits are not FDIC insured.
37. Afonso, G., Cisternas, G., Gowen, B. et al. (2023). Who's borrowing and lending in the Fed Funds market today? *Liberty Street Economics*, October 10, using data from nonpublic forms FR 2420 ("Report of Selected Money Market Rates").
38. Federal Register 85(82), 23445–23448, 28 April 2020.
39. Kroeger, A., McGowan, J., and Sarkar, A. (2018). The pre-crisis monetary policy implementation framework. *Federal Reserve Bank of New York Economic Policy Review* 24 (2): 38–70 discuss autonomous factors prior to the GFC.
40. Nelson, B. (2024). How the Federal Reserve got so huge, and why and how it can shrink. *Bank Policy Institute*, February 7, "Note that there is no record that the decisions to let the TGA increase or to expand the foreign reverse repo pool were discussed with the FOMC, even though they became

important reasons why the FOMC could not return to a necessary-reserves framework." (p. 16)

41. Choi, M., Goldberg, L., Lerman, R. et al. (2022). The Fed's central bank swap lines and FIMA repo facility. *Federal Reserve Bank of New York Economic Policy Review* 28 (1): 93–113.
42. Committee on the Global Financial System. (2020). US dollar funding: An international perspective. *CGFS Papers No. 65*.
43. Committee on the Global Financial System. (2021). Changing patterns of capital flows. *CGFS Papers No. 66*. See also the discussion of foreign exchange dealing in Chapter 2.
44. Choi, M., Goldberg, L., Lerman, R. et al. (2022). The Fed's central bank swap lines and FIMA repo facility. *Federal Reserve Bank of New York Economic Policy Review* 28 (1): 93–113.
45. Ibid.
46. Ibid.
47. Ibid.
48. The classification depends on the elasticity of demand for reserves, or how many basis points the Fed Funds—IOER spread moves for a change in aggregate reserves equal to 1% of banking system assets. When reserves are abundant, the elasticity of demand is zero; ample and scarce reserve supply regimes are identifiable when the elasticity is modestly negative or negative and large, respectively. See Afonso, G., Kim, K., Martin, A. et al. (2020b). Monetary policy implementation with an ample supply of reserves. *Federal Reserve Bank of Chicago Working Paper 2020-02*, Afonso, G., Giannone, D., La Spada, G. et al. (2024). Scarce, abundant, or ample? A time-varying model of the reserve demand curve. *Federal Reserve Bank of New York Staff Report No. 1019 (revised)*, April.
49. FBOs are better able to earn the arbitrage spread because the size of their balance sheets is less constrained by the supplementary leverage ratio (SLR), which is administered more strictly in the United States than abroad. The SLR was introduced by the BCBS in 2010 and finalized in January 2014. The ratio is defined as Tier 1 capital divided by Total Exposure, with the denominator capturing on- and off-balance sheet positions. The SLR was adopted as a final rule in the United States on 3 September 2014 and became effective 1 January 2015. The extended SLR (eSLR) became effective 1 January 2018. The United States averages daily levels while other jurisdictions look at period-end values. The Basel SLR must exceed 3%, while the eSLR must exceed 5%. Section 171 of the Dodd-Frank Act required an SLR of at least 4% prior to the Basel rules. See Tufts, R. and Moloney, P. (2022b). The history

of supervisory expectations for capital adequacy: Part II (1984–2021). *Moments in History: Economic Insights from the History of the Federal Banking System (OCC)* and Haubrich, J. (2020). A brief history of bank capital requirements in the United States. *Federal Reserve Bank of Cleveland Economic Commentary 2020-05* for more details.

50. Du, W. (2023). Foreign banking organizations in the United States and the price of dollar liquidity. *Liberty Street Economics*, January 11.
51. Afonso, G., Giannone, D., La Spada, G. et al. (2024). Scarce, abundant, or ample? A time-varying model of the reserve demand curve. *Federal Reserve Bank of New York Staff Report No. 1019 (revised)*, April. An interactive chart showing the Federal Reserve's estimates of reserve demand elasticity is available at https://www.newyorkfed.org/research/reserve-demand-elasticity/#interactive.
52. See Greenwood, J. (2021). Monetary policy is not about interest rates: The liquidity effect and the Fisher effect. *Working Paper, Johns Hopkins Institute for Applied Economics, Global Health, and the Study of Business Enterprise, Studies in Applied Economics 190*, September for an analysis.
53. Bauer, M. and Swanson, E.T. (2023). A reassessment of monetary policy surprises and high-frequency identification. *NBER Macroeconomics Annual* 37: 87–156. The authors call their preferred metric the "orthogonalized monetary policy surprise." It consists of the residuals of a regression of the monetary policy surprise on six potential confounding factors. The monetary policy surprise is defined as the first principal component of post-announcement movements in the first four Eurodollar futures contracts.
54. Bauer, M. and Swanson, E.T. (2023). A reassessment of monetary policy surprises and high-frequency identification. *NBER Macroeconomics Annual* 37: 87–156.
55. Fabo, B., Jancoková, M., Kempf, E. et al. (2021). Fifty shades of QE: Comparing findings of central banks and academics. *Journal of Monetary Economics* 120: 1–20; Fabo, B., Jancoková, M., Kempf, E. et al. (2024). Fifty shades of QE: Robust evidence. *Journal of Banking and Finance* 159: 107065.
56. Caldara, D., Gagnon, E., Martínez-García, E. et al. (2021). Monetary policy and economic performance since the financial crisis. *Federal Reserve Bank of St. Louis Review*, 2021Q4: 425–460: Table 1; Gagnon, J., Raskin, M., Remache, J. et al. (2011). The financial market effects of the Federal Reserve's large-scale asset purchases. *International Journal of Central Banking* 7 (1): 3–43.
57. Hesse, H., Hofmann, B., and Weber, J.M. (2018). The macroeconomic effects of asset purchases revisited. *Journal of Macroeconomics* 58: 115–138.

58. Walentin, K. (2014). Business cycle implications of mortgage spreads. *Journal of Monetary Economics* 67: 62–77.
59. Hesse, H., Hofmann, B., and Weber, J.M. (2018). The macroeconomic effects of asset purchases revisited. *Journal of Macroeconomics* 58: 115–138.
60. Gorea, D., Kryvstov, O., and Kudlyak, M. (2022). House price responses to monetary policy surprises: Evidence from the U.S. listings data. *Federal Reserve Bank of San Francisco Working Paper 2022-16*.
61. Bianchi, F., Lettau, M., and Ludvigson, S.C. (2022). Monetary policy and asset valuation. *Journal of Finance* 77 (2): 967–1017.
62. Hanson, S.G. and Stein, J.C. (2015). Monetary policy and long-term real rates. *Journal of Financial Economics* 115: 429–448; Di Maggio, M. and Kacperczyk, M.T. (2015). The unintended consequences of the zero lower bound policy. *Working Paper*, Columbia Business School; Choi, J. and Kronlund, M. (2018). Reaching for yield in corporate bond mutual funds. *Review of Financial Studies* 31: 1930–1965; Bianchi, F., Lettau, M., and Ludvigson, S.C. (2022). Monetary policy and asset valuation. *Journal of Finance* 77 (2): 967–1017.
63. See our discussion in Chapter 7.
64. We analyze the differences between QE in the United States, the Eurozone, and Japan in Hanke, S.H. and Sekerke, M. (2017). Bank regulation as monetary policy: Lessons from the great recession. *Cato Journal* 37: 385–405. See also Greenwood, J. (2016). Why negative rates are not a solution for Japan or the Eurozone. *Working Paper, Johns Hopkins Institute for Applied Economics, Global Health, and the Study of Business Enterprise, Studies in Applied Economics 56*, June.
65. Data are from Flow of Funds Table L.110.
66. Quarles, R.K. (2020a). The adaptability of stress testing. *Remarks delivered June 19, 2020*, Quarles, R.K. (2020b). Stress testing: A decade of continuity and change. *Remarks delivered July 9, 2020*.
67. Board of Governors of the Federal Reserve System, *Comprehensive Capital Analysis and Review: Objectives and Overview*, 18 March 2011 at 3–4.
68. Hirtle, B. (2017). What explains shareholder payouts by large banks. *Liberty Street Economics*, October 18. The CCAR program indicated that dividend rates above 30% of net income would "receive particularly close scrutiny."
69. Quarles, R.K. (2020b). Stress testing: A decade of continuity and change. *Remarks delivered July 9, 2020*: 6.
70. Board of Governors of the Federal Reserve System Press Release, "Federal Reserve announces temporary and additional restrictions on bank holding company dividends and share repurchases currently in place will end for most

firms after June 30, based on results from upcoming stress test," 25 March 2021. The final rule establishing the stress capital buffer is available at https://www.federalreserve.gov/newsevents/pressreleases/files/bcreg20200304a2.pdf.
71. https://www.centerforfinancialstability.org/amfm/Divisia_Aug24.pdf.
72. See Belongia, M.T. and Ireland, P.N. (2022). A reconsideration of money growth rules. *Journal of Economic Dynamics & Control* 135: 104312 and references therein.

Part Three

REWRITING THE RULES OF OUR FINANCIAL SYSTEM

Chapter 11

Defining Neutral Monetary Policy

We are now ready to begin thinking about reforms to the financial system. Part One and Part Two established the structure and function of the monetary system and construed monetary policy as all the mechanisms of public policy that can affect the rules of monetary policy. Now, it is time to imagine the structure and function of a system that is, in some sense, optimal.

This chapter defines optimality in terms of a criterion we call *neutrality*. For monetary policy to seek neutrality is not new. Current thinking on monetary policy considers the policy stance to be neutral when the targeted interest rate is equal to the "natural rate" of interest. We define neutrality differently. Our overarching concern is with the distributional effects of monetary policy. Rather than focusing on the short-term interest rate—a single price prevailing in financial markets—we are concerned with monetary policy's impact on the money supply, broadly measured, and its effect on prices, incomes, output, and expenditures across relevant sectors of the economy. These may be defined as individual industries, a stratification of households by income or wealth, or the Flow of Funds sectors, among other segmentations of the economy.

The first aspect of neutral monetary policy we present is based on the desire to achieve balanced growth and inflation outcomes throughout the economy. While differences in growth and inflation are to be expected due to sectoral differences in technology and productivity, we can make the objective of policy to *minimize monetary contributions to the variance of growth and inflation*. When this objective is met, the impact of monetary conditions on relative prices across sectors will be minimized. Our goal is for money to work with minimal disruption to the price system, avoiding the misallocation of resources and related losses of efficiency.

The second aspect has a more structural flavor. We consider features of the capital and credit markets that influence the formation of investable and bankable projects. These microeconomic conditions shape the channels into which savings and credit can flow. If structural obstacles to credit creation lie in the way of sectoral money demand, monetary policy may be fairly helpless to achieve better outcomes. Optimal policy considered from this perspective seeks the *efficient use of global savings*. The division of finance between the banking system and the capital markets is implicated in the analysis, as well as the investment of effort by banks and capital markets firms to reduce informational asymmetries, develop innovative products, and design new financial contracts.[1]

This chapter is just for objectives. After considering structural conditions in banking and capital markets in Chapters 12 and 13, respectively, we will turn to the implementation of neutral monetary policy in Chapter 14.

Neutral Monetary Policy

Given our overarching concern with the effect of monetary policy on relative prices, income, and output, we begin with a framework for disaggregating the impact of monetary conditions.

In Chapters 7 and 9, we presented two variations on a system to trace the mutual influence of money, prices, and output on each other. Movements in money, prices, and output are modeled as reactions to deviations between money supply and demand, as well as their lagged movements. In a world where the quantity of money matters, we would expect all variables to respond to deviations between money supply and demand, and for prices and output to respond to lagged movements in the quantity of money. Because the system is centered on deviations of money supply from money demand, we refer to it as a money demand system.

Now we imagine a money demand system disaggregated over multiple sectors indexed $i = 1, \ldots, N$. These could be Flow of Funds sectors, industries, or households stratified by wealth. We distinguish the fiscal contribution to sectoral money balances M_{it}^G from money supplied through private channels M_{it}^P, so that total money supply $M_{it}^S = M_{it}^G + M_{it}^P$. The fiscal contribution represents the excess of within-sector expenditure over sectoral taxes, net of the sector's increase in government bond holdings. We assume that Divisia quantity indices can be constructed for the fiscal and private contributions to the money supply.

A stable money demand equation $M^D_{it} = f_i(M^P_{it}, M^G_{it}, P_{it}, Y_{it})$ is assumed to exist, with $\varepsilon_{it} = M^S_{it} - M^D_{it}$ measuring the deviations of money supply from money demand. Money demand and the larger money demand system may further depend on other variables, but we suppress them here.

The price and quantity indices P_{it} and Y_{it} in the money demand equation may correspond to sectoral income or expenditure, depending on which disaggregation is pursued and one's priors about the nature of money demand. In an aggregated system where Y is GDP and the trade balance accounts for a small share of GDP, the distinction between income and output may not be very important. However, in a disaggregated system, the difference can be material, particularly if one distinguishes between gross output and value added. It may be sensible to model sector inputs, sector outputs, or both. We will write everything as P_{it} and Y_{it} below, but the reader should bear in mind the potential for the interpretation of the price and quantity indices to shift depending on the stratification employed, the availability of data, and the empirical evidence in favor of different specifications. We will refer to income/output and consumer/producer prices to capture this ambiguity.

With these definitions, our disaggregated money demand system now has the form

$$\Delta \ln M^P_{it} = \alpha^{MP}_i \varepsilon_{it} + \beta^{MP}_{iMPi} \cdot \Delta \ln M^P_{itl} + \beta^{MP}_{MGi} \cdot \Delta \ln M^G_{itl}$$
$$+ \gamma^{MP}_i \cdot \Delta \ln P_{itl} + \delta^{MP}_i \cdot \Delta \ln Y_{itl} + \cdots$$

$$\Delta \ln M^G_{it} = \alpha^{MG}_i \varepsilon_{it} + \beta^{MG}_{MPi} \cdot \Delta \ln M^P_{itl} + \beta^{MG}_{MGi} \cdot \Delta \ln M^G_{itl}$$
$$+ \gamma^{MG}_i \cdot \Delta \ln P_{itl} + \delta^{MG}_i \cdot \Delta \ln Y_{itl} + \cdots$$

$$\Delta \ln P_{it} = \alpha^{P}_i \varepsilon_{it} + \beta^{P}_{MPi} \cdot \Delta \ln M^P_{itl} + \beta^{P}_{MGi} \cdot \Delta \ln M^G_{itl}$$
$$+ \gamma^{P}_i \cdot \Delta \ln P_{itl} + \delta^{P}_i \cdot \Delta \ln Y_{itl} + \cdots$$

$$\Delta \ln Y_{it} = \alpha^{Y}_i \varepsilon_{it} + \beta^{Y}_{MPi} \cdot \Delta \ln M^P_{itl} + \beta^{Y}_{MGi} \cdot \Delta \ln M^G_{itl}$$
$$+ \gamma^{Y}_i \cdot \Delta \ln P_{itl} + \delta^{Y}_i \cdot \Delta \ln Y_{itl} + \cdots$$

The sums of lagged variables we had on the right-hand side of the system in Chapter 7 have been replaced with vectors of coefficients and lagged variables (subscripted *itl*). We would have a copy of this system for each sector $i = 1, \ldots, N$. We assume that the coefficients are known, or that they can be estimated using appropriate data. The superscripts on the coefficients indicate the response variable of the equation in which the coefficients appear.

Some coefficients of particular interest in the money demand system are the income/output multipliers of private and government money creation

β^Y_{MPi} and β^Y_{MGi}, the contribution to consumer/producer price inflation from private and government money creation β^P_{MPi} and β^P_{MGi}, the coefficients α^{MP}_i and α^{MG}_i, which describe how private credit supply and government budget deficits react to imbalances in money supply, and the coefficients α^P_i and α^Y_i, which show how consumer/producer prices and income/output react to money supply errors.

The individual evolutions and effects of government and private monetary sources point to the importance of coordination between fiscal policy and monetary policy. We will assume that fiscal policy is given and does not attempt to influence monetary conditions *per se*, so that $\alpha^{MG}_i = 0$.[2] Stability in the money supply then requires $\alpha^{MP}_i < 0$.

The mere construction and parameterization of such a system would provide crucial insight into how much money matters across sectors. Differences in coefficients at the sector level will show where credit and fiscal policy are most stimulative to income and output growth. In addition, the analysis will lay bare where prices are most distorted by changes in money supply and fiscal policy. The usefulness of such a system for the evaluation of fiscal policy is a particularly interesting feature. Not only can the multipliers to government spending be isolated, but the interaction of government spending with monetary conditions can also be captured to evaluate whether government stimulus indeed compensates a shortfall in private finance.

Defining Neutrality

The point of monetary policy is not to achieve identical rates of inflation and income/output growth in all sectors. Differences in output growth across sectors reflect technological and productivity developments and other conditions. Some dispersion in inflation across sectors is also to be expected given differences in the composition of expenditures.

The first objective of neutral monetary policy is to choose a path for $\{M^P_{it}\}$ that contributes to income/output growth without excessively increasing the rate of inflation. Taking the expectation of the equation for inflation, we have

$$E[\Delta \ln P_{it}] = \beta^P_{MPi} \cdot E[\Delta \ln M^P_{itl}] + \beta^P_{MGi} \cdot E[\Delta \ln M^G_{itl}] + \gamma^P_i \cdot E[\Delta \ln P_{itl}]$$
$$+ \delta^P_i \cdot E[\Delta \ln Y_{i,t-1}] + \cdots$$

under the assumption that $E[e_{it}] = 0$. A similar expression holds in the equation for real output. We further assume that a rational fiscal policy will not subsidize any sector in perpetuity so we can set $\mathrm{E}\left[\Delta \ln M_{itl}^{G}\right] = 0$. Then part of the problem of neutral monetary policy is to choose an average growth rate for the private supply of money $\mu_i^{MP} = \mathrm{E}\left[\Delta \ln M_{itl}^{P}\right]$ which is compatible with a low rate of inflation after accounting for feedback from past price changes $\mathrm{E}\left[\Delta \ln P_{itl}\right]$ and income/output growth $\mathrm{E}\left[\Delta \ln Y_{itl}\right]$.

As a second aspect of our objectives, we would like to choose $\{M_{it}^{P}\}$ so that the contribution of monetary factors to the *variability* of output and inflation is minimized. We cannot minimize variability overall—and we would not want to—because some variability is attributable to changes in technology and other non-monetary factors which should affect relative prices. A straightforward calculation shows that the monetary influence on the variance of inflation is equal to (abusing notation[3]):

$$\frac{\left(\alpha_i^P\right)^2 \sigma^2(\varepsilon_{it}) + \left(\beta_{MPi}^P\right)^2 \sigma^2(\Delta \ln M_{itl}^P) + \left(\beta_{MGi}^P\right)^2 \sigma^2(\Delta \ln M_{itl}^G)}{\sigma^2(\Delta \ln P_{it})}$$
$$+ \frac{\beta_{MPi}^P \beta_{MGi}^P \sigma^2(\Delta \ln M_{itl}^P, \Delta \ln M_{itl}^G)}{\sigma^2(\Delta \ln P_{it})}$$

The variance in real output attributable to monetary factors has a similar expression. We are dealing with a fraction that has a value between zero and one. Monetary factors explain less of the variance in inflation to the extent that inflation depends on its own lagged values, on lagged growth rates, or on any other variables in the demand system.

Under our assumption that fiscal policy is given, the path of private money $\{M_{it}^P\}$ contributes to the variability of inflation through three terms. The variance of private money growth $\sigma^2(\Delta \ln M_{itl}^P)$ and its covariance with the monetary impact of fiscal policy $\sigma^2(\Delta \ln M_{itl}^P, \Delta \ln M_{itl}^G)$ are both minimized when the volatility of private money growth $\sigma_i^{MP} = \sigma(\Delta \ln M_{itl}^P)$ is minimized. Somewhat less obviously, the contribution of inflation's response to money supply errors $(\alpha_i^P)^2 \sigma^2(\varepsilon_{it})$ is minimized when money supply reliably meets money demand, thereby reducing the variance of money supply errors $\sigma^2(\varepsilon_{it})$.

Under neutral monetary policy, the supply of money grows in line with money demand, and as near as possible to a constant growth rate μ_i^{MP}. The balance between the two objectives depends on the relative size of the coefficients α_i^P and β_{MPi}^P. These conditions bound the monetary contribution to growth and output within the sector and minimize σ_i^{MP}, the monetary contribution to variability in growth and output.

Neutrality is achieved when these objectives are met *across sectors*. Monetary policy must meet $2N$ conditions, rather than a single inflation target and/or output growth target, in order to avoid creating distortions to the economy. It is not enough that an overall price index or rate of income/output be achieved for the entire economy, because such requirements can paper over gross differences at the sectoral level.

Why Neutrality?

In Part Two, we presented evidence which suggests that certain sectors of the economy have been systematically favored by banking regulation, such as the markets for housing and consumer credit. We brought out the differences in monetary conditions across sectors of the economy and across households stratified by income. We further showed that fiscal policy is not evenly distributed and that its monetary effects are not dissipated by financial intermediation. We have good reason to believe that monetary conditions are not homogeneously distributed in society, unlike a reference interest rate or a general price level.

When the monetary contribution to variability in income, growth, and inflation is minimized across sectors, the power of monetary policy to distort relative prices is tamed. A distortion in relative prices means that the price of a sector's inputs or outputs becomes relatively cheaper or more expensive than those of other sectors due to monetary factors, rather than because of differences in technology or productivity. In response to the price change, the demand for the sector's output may be affected, or the sector's ability to purchase inputs on favorable terms may change. As Friedrich Hayek wrote in *Prices and Production* (1935: 220–221):

> *What we are interested in is only how the relative values of goods as sources of income or as means of satisfaction of wants are affected by money.*
>
> The problem is never to explain any "general value" of money but only how and when money influences the relative values of goods and under what conditions it leaves these relative values undisturbed, or, to use a happy phrase of Wicksell, when money remains *neutral* relative to goods. Not a money that is *stable* in value but a *neutral* money must therefore form the starting point for the theoretical analysis of monetary influences on production, and the first object of monetary theory should be to clear up the conditions under which money might be considered to be neutral in this sense.[4]

Neutrality is the starting point for Hayek's analysis of monetary influences on production because non-neutrality leads to inefficient patterns of production and investment. Decisions about the allocation of production and consumption, as well as the distribution of intermediate goods production across industries can all be influenced by monetary conditions, pushing them away from the output levels that would prevail if monetary conditions were homogeneously distributed. When left to fester unchecked, the efficiency losses from distorted relative prices can be instrumental in creating business cycles.

Our definition of neutrality is explicitly conditioned on fiscal policy to ensure that fiscal policy has its intended effect, and that monetary conditions are balanced by fiscal policy. It is rare to see fiscal policy evaluated on a disaggregated basis, with its impact on prices, incomes, and output explicitly measured. But these are—in our view, at least—minimal requirements for verifying that the policies implemented by government are effective and reaching their intended targets. In particular, it is desirable to avoid adding monetary stimulus in areas where the supply of money and credit is already abundant, or to enforce austerity in sectors where the monetary system has already done so.

We are not interested in equalizing inflation rates across sectors because, as we have said, these also vary for reasons that are unrelated to monetary conditions. However, in a system where the monetary standard is defined in terms of a price index, dispersion across price indices means that somewhat different monetary standards prevail in various domains of the economy. For individual sectors to absorb a decline in the monetary standard disproportionately would be unfair. The evolution of sector-specific price indices should at least be monitored to ensure that the burden of inflation is borne equitably.

Efficient Use of Global Savings

Thus far our definition of neutrality depends on defining a path for private money creation that meets money demand and introduces minimal variability in income, output, and prices. Such a definition tacitly assumes that no material obstacles lie in the way of private money creation on a sectoral level. In other words, we have assumed that any target growth rate can be achieved.

In Part One, we argued that a sufficient supply of bankable projects was a global constraint faced by the monetary system. Certain microeconomic conditions influence the formation of investable and bankable projects, configuring the channels into which savings and credit may flow. In the event that features of the institutional environment or the financial system severely limit the formation of investable and bankable projects in some domains of the economy, money demand may be persistently rationed, regardless of monetary policy actions.

Hence, the pursuit of neutral monetary policy requires certain structural conditions. Those conditions can loosely be summarized as the efficient use of global savings in the capital markets and productive credit creation in the banking system. In both cases, efficiency and productivity depend on investments in information that are made within the financial sector.

Formation of Investable Projects

In Chapter 4, we described the formation of investable projects as an equilibrium position of the system of financial intermediation. Entrepreneurs bid for savings based on the expected returns of their projects, but the set of projects that becomes investable depends on the risk of the project and the prevailing information environment between entrepreneurs and savers. Where financial intermediaries are able to produce, monitor, and disseminate relevant information, risky projects can obtain capital and savings flow from savers to entrepreneurs. If the production of information by intermediaries cannot make enough risky projects ready for investment, savings are idled in safe assets.

We are interested in the case where the allocation to risky assets is below the efficient allocation. In this case, allocations to safe assets expand while equity rationing becomes more severe. The resulting set of funded investment projects thus has too little risk to achieve the efficient rate of return on investment, and global growth suffers.

To achieve a larger allocation to safe assets, it may be tempting for capital markets to cannibalize bankable projects. In previous chapters, we have suggested that bonds are winning at the expense of banks, and that the production of monetary services has suffered as a result. Why are investors keen to trade the return on equity in a bank for the return on a portfolio of bonds? A possibility is that bank equity, though it buys more exposure to safe assets per dollar, nevertheless involves an unacceptable level of risk for the population of savers. In Chapter 13, we will identify the major sources of savings that have prevailed during the Basel era, which provides some clues about investors' choice of asset allocation.

An excessive allocation to safe assets in capital markets may reflect decisions on the supply side of financial markets as well. Decisions are made within universal banks about allocations between bank equity and capital markets business. Since the return on equity from fee-based capital markets business is so much greater than that from banking, a universal bank may choose to underinvest in the banking business and invest heavily in debt capital markets business. Savers get more bonds because universal banks make more money from issuing and trading bonds than they do from making loans. In Chapter 12, we will discuss how

Formation of Bankable Projects

In Chapter 5, we argued that an efficient allocation of equity capital is a prerequisite for creating a broad base of bankable projects. We care about the supply of bankable projects because they are, in effect, the substrate on which the money supply can grow in a fiat money system. We also care about the quality of the supply of bankable projects because the productivity of bank credit creation is not indifferent to the character of the project.

The connection between finance and growth has been investigated for decades.[5] However, it is only recently that substantial evidence has begun to connect bank finance to growth and productivity. Studies using large panel data sets exploit country- and industry-level variation in credit flows to isolate the causal effect of bank credit on productivity.

Beck et al. (2023) estimates that a 10% expansion of per-capita bank balance sheet size raises the trend of GDP growth by more than a percentage point.[6] They find that bank lending is closely connected with the formation of tangible assets, especially in industries where debt financing is not abundantly available from capital markets. Similarly, Müller and Verner (2024) find that credit expansion in tradable goods sectors lifts growth and productivity and reduces crisis risk, while expansion to non-tradable sectors increases the risk of crisis.[7] The latter is weighed down by real estate-based lending. Credit growth in non-tradable sectors is associated with a shift in economic activity toward non-tradable sectors and reduced productivity, whereas expansion in tradable goods sectors lifts productivity in the short and medium run.

Accordingly, we consider the formation of bankable projects as the foundation of the money supply, as well as the quality of bankable projects as a source of economic fluctuations. In the next chapter, we will connect bankable project formation to competition in the banking sector and incentives within universal banks. Chapter 13 examines the pathological character of real estate as the paradigmatic bankable project.

Notes

1. Our definition of neutrality has some affinity with the way that economists define optimal tax policy: first ensuring that the tax system does not change the character of economic activity, and second to properly define the tax base

and protect its integrity. See, for example, Adam, S., Besley, T., Blundell, R. et al. (2011). *Tax by Design*. Oxford University Press: Chapter 2.
2. Other mixes of fiscal and monetary policy are possible, but we do not pursue them here.
3. The variance and covariance terms in the numerator should be written in terms of matrices since the coefficients are vectors. We abuse notation by treating the vectors like constants. The intention of the expression should be clear.
4. Hayek, F. (2008 [1935]). *Prices and Production*, 2e, Reprint. Ludwig von Mises Institute: 220–221 (emphasis in original).
5. The modern literature begins with Gerschenkron, A. (1962). *Economic Backwardness in Historical Perspective*. Harvard University Press and is surveyed in Levine, R. (2004). Finance and growth: Theory and evidence. *NBER Working Paper 10766* and Popov, A. (2018). Evidence on finance and economic growth. In: *Handbook of Finance and Development* (eds. T. Beck and R. Levine), 63–104. Edward Elgar. Berger, A.N., Molyneux, P., and Wilson, J.O.S. (2020). Banks and the real economy: An assessment of the research. *Journal of Corporate Finance* 62: 101513 offers a review focused specifically on the relationship between banking and growth.
6. Beck, T., Döttling, R., Lambert, T., et al. (2023). Liquidity creation, investment, and growth. *Journal of Economic Growth* 28: 297–336.
7. Müller, K. and Verner, E. (2024). Credit allocation and macroeconomic fluctuations. *Review of Economic Studies* 91 (6): 3645–3676.

Chapter 12

Universal Banks in the Monetary System

We have repeatedly emphasized the importance of the commercial banking system in the system of fiat money. Most monetary services are produced by the deposit money created by commercial banks against their extensions of credit or, less frequently, against reserve flows received from the government's account. The condition of the monetary system is thus intimately connected to the condition of the commercial banking system. Similarly, we have noted the importance of capital markets in the formation of investable projects and the allocation of capital. Capital markets are closely intertwined with commercial banking, providing equity that subordinates bank lending, but also cannibalizing bankable projects in several domains.

This chapter examines the fitness for purpose of the universal banking firm in accomplishing its dual objectives of efficiently allocating existing savings through capital markets transactions and efficiently creating money to finance bankable projects without using existing savings. The ability of any firm to achieve outcomes in line with economic efficiency is achieved through a combination of competition, corporate governance, and regulation.[1] In this chapter, we consider how each of these mechanisms has influenced the behavior of universal banks and weigh the prospects of achieving better outcomes through reforms to each.

In a market economy, we generally rely on competition to achieve outcomes that maximize productivity and deliver goods and services to customers at the lowest cost. Consumer sensitivity to price favors those firms that produce output with minimal resource input. When we become dissatisfied with outcomes in a market, an inquiry into the state of competition naturally follows. The degree of competition in a market and the competitive strategies employed by firms active in the market determine the structure of an industry along with the nature of industry technology. The actions of incumbent firms and potential entrants alike shape competitive dynamics.

Traditional attempts to apply the tools of competitive analysis (industrial organization) to the commercial banking industry largely misunderstand the business of banking and fail to provide useful explanations of competition in the sector.[2] We begin by clarifying how banks compete. We contrast competition in banking with competition in capital markets. Finally, we examine how banking and capital markets businesses compete across the banking-capital markets boundary. Throughout the analysis, we are concerned with the way the universal banking firm conditions competition internally and among bank subsidiaries in the credit market.

The results of competition are often realized through the entry of new firms and the exit of failing firms. Exit occurs through the bankruptcy process. In banking and capital markets, the loss of a failing firm can threaten the solvency of other firms linked to the bankrupt firm through contracts and clearing systems and potentially devalue the claims on the bankrupt firm if adequate resources do not exist to redeem them. Accordingly, one frequently encounters discussions of the "trade-off" between competition and financial stability in banking.[3] While the tradeoff undoubtedly exists, its importance is limited so long as the conditions for "exit" can be decoupled from the complete insolvency of the financial firm. Prudential regulation and (in the case of banking) deposit insurance exist to achieve this decoupling.[4] Thus our analysis of competition must be sensitive to the presence of prudential regulation and deposit insurance, and the design of competition policy is best undertaken jointly with the design of the prudential regime.

Our discussion then turns to the corporate governance of the universal banking firm. We examine profit-maximizing strategies for the universal banking firm that is simultaneously active in banking and capital markets business, the incentives used by the owners of such firms to align management's interests with their own, and the compatibility of the resulting ownership and control structures with welfare-maximizing outcomes in banking and capital markets. The question at hand is whether owners of a universal banking firm can design an incentive scheme that simultaneously implements desired outcomes for the banking book and the trading book. In the absence of such a scheme, separating the ownership and control of the banking book from that of the trading book becomes a more compelling proposition.

Finally, we analyze the potential for regulation to create better outcomes where competition and corporate governance reach their limits. Concentration within the industry may already be prohibitive for regulator-led solutions. The interaction of prudential regulation with a concentrated universal banking industry leads to a peculiar sort of hold-up problem in which responsible banking practices are ransomed for accommodation in the capital markets business. It is high time such hostage-taking is preempted by sane policy.

Competition in Commercial Banking

For much of the period from the Great Depression through the 1970s, competition in banking was not a priority for public policy.[5] Steps toward liberalization of the sector in the 1970s and 1980s put competition back on the agenda but did so at the nadir of academic understanding of the banking business.[6] As a result, thinking about bank competition has long focused on assessing the effectiveness of banks in "intermediating" savings between depositors and borrowers, with the "intermediation spread" between loan and deposit rates providing a rough-and-ready index of competition among banks. One imagines banks participating in separate deposit and loan markets and resolving any imbalance between sources and uses of funds in the interbank market.

The model of banks as competing intermediaries is capable of multiple refinements. Deposit contracts and loans can be supplied on perfectly competitive terms, in an oligopoly framework, or through some variety of monopolistic competition. In the latter case, banks are thought to enjoy market power due to geographic concentration or some degree of product differentiation which makes demand for their product less than perfectly elastic. When inelastic demand is combined with network effects, bank "intermediation" becomes a problem of platform competition in which banks appeal to depositors and borrowers by offering a rich set of potential interconnections between the groups which would not otherwise exist.[7]

Such models completely miss the mark in banking. Banks' ability to lend is in no way constrained by their ability to first attract deposits because they create whatever funding they need in the process of lending. Instead, banks compete to originate loans and to offer deposit terms that stabilize their liquidity balances. Though the bank must compete successfully and simultaneously in both domains, they need not synchronize their loan and deposit strategies to establish matches between networks of borrowers and lenders.

On the lending side, banks compete in their ability to underwrite and originate profitable loans. Some information for loan origination is public, such as prevailing market interest rates, collateral values, and borrower credit ratings. However, much of the other relevant information is private and must be discovered by the bank by developing a relationship with the potential borrower, investigating the economics of various investment projects, transacting in collateral markets, and modeling the residual risks of potential loan transactions. The question for the bank is whether the information asymmetry between itself and the borrower can be sufficiently reduced to make new projects bankable. To make a previously rationed project bankable is to make it suitable for profitable lending at a risk-adjusted interest rate. That is, the unobservable "character" of the borrower can be ascertained sufficiently well to mitigate the bank's risk of adverse selection. Alternatively, the bank can offer innovative contracts which allow for corrective action to be taken when information unknown at the time of underwriting becomes available.

On the deposit side, banks offer a set of bundles that screen depositors according to their desired mix of monetary and investment services. Recall from our construction of the Divisia broad money aggregates that the user cost of monetary liabilities is equal to the amount of risk-free investment income foregone in favor of liquidity. In choosing which deposit liabilities to hold, from demand and savings deposits to time deposits and MMFs, bank customers select from a menu of contracts offering various degrees of liquidity and investment income. Banks offer a menu of different options not only to stabilize their reserve flows, but also to observe signals about individual deposit customers. Those who commit to less liquid money balances are more likely to be assured of their incomes, for example. Such private information can be valuable when offering credit.

The banking business is thus one of technologies for discovering, producing, and processing information from a nexus of relationships with potential borrowers and depositors. As a result, we would expect the dynamics of competition between banks to be governed by the technological frontier in generating such information—how readily it can be discovered by a new entrant, transferred by a customer from one bank to another, and/or deployed at scale. Likewise, we are concerned with the consequences of a new entrant's information endowment relative to those of incumbents. Are new banks likely to succumb to extreme adverse selection in their quest to build up their balance sheets because higher-quality customers have already been acquired by incumbents?

One's sense of the prevailing degree of competition in banking is thus highly indexed to perceptions of saturation in lending markets. If nearly all bankable projects are funded and the potential to make new projects bankable at reasonable cost is slim, further expansion of the banking sector is unlikely to be profitable, and new entrants are unlikely to succeed. Loan portfolio growth will slow and banks will tend to hold more resources in securities, eking out a minimal spread over whatever deposit liabilities they manage to attract. Underwriting capacity deteriorates, becoming formulaic and undifferentiated.

In an environment of healthy competition, by contrast, banks find responsible ways to make credit available to new borrowers and to finance new kinds of projects. They develop new *credit products*. As new kinds of capital projects become pervasive in the economy, banks become experts in their costs and returns, outrunning the capacity of individual entrepreneurs to assess prospects and potential payoffs. They develop a sense of what sort of ventures and borrowers are likely to succeed. They connect with potential users of the new capital and monitor secondary markets for information about depreciation and liquidity. They create credit that supports new projects rather than transferring the same assets among a fixed set of owners, or refinancing the same assets for the same borrower. New deposit balances created by lending are not immediately destroyed by paying off the principal of existing loans. New monetary services persist as liquid balances rather than being invested nearer to short-term bond rates. The notion of what is bankable expands judiciously, through the disciplined discovery of private information and the thoughtful design of loan contracts.

We presented several views of the Flow of Funds data in Chapter 7 that suggest the degree of competition in the banking sector has declined significantly since the GFC. The pace of loan growth has slowed in the aggregate, with growth concentrated (for a time) in real estate and consumer lending. Banks are devoting less of their balance sheets to loans, favoring securities and liquid assets. Corporate lending has struggled, while new mortgage credit has been difficult to come by for borrowers without accumulated home equity or sterling credit profiles. More anecdotally, new entry by fintech companies has focused on payments and short-term consumer lending rather than the development of new lending markets. New contracts and new borrower populations have not appeared for a long time. Very few new national bank charters have been sought or approved since the GFC. Whereas roughly 100 new banks were chartered annually in the years preceding the GFC, the rate is now roughly 10 per year.[8]

We have also seen some high-profile exits. Silicon Valley Bank's ability to attract deposits from startups and VC funds far outstripped its ability to originate profitable loans. It loaded up on long-term government bonds and agency MBS, stretching for yield by investing in long-duration obligations. When interest rates rose, SVB's securities investments lost so much value that management had to seek new equity to remain solvent. Announcing that the bank was raising new equity triggered a run on the bank. First Republic Bank sought the business of high-net worth clients by offering cut-rate mortgage refinancing in exchange for deposit balances. They, too, were undone by rising interest rates. Other banks failed because they were making advances against cryptocurrency, an asset with no potential to generate a surplus beyond the willingness of a greater fool to purchase them at a higher price. Though much of the commentary around these failures has focused on interest rate risk management, which is not entirely wrong, the fact is that no bank would have faced so much interest rate risk if their growth had been driven by lending rather than overpaying for existing deposit balances.

Competition in Capital Markets

Competition in capital markets business is a different animal. Primary capital markets business consists of underwriting new offerings of debt and equity securities on behalf of corporate issuers. These new offerings then trade in secondary markets, where capital markets firms make markets in securities, repackage offerings into legal forms and risk profiles better suited to investor needs, and offer and hedge derivative securities. Each of these businesses generates significant flows of information which can be sold separately as capital markets advisory services and sell-side investment research, among other information products and services.

Capital markets business is inherently an intermediation business in which the existence of networks creates externalities for demand on each side of the market. Corporate security issuers want to offer their debt and equity through underwriters who are connected to enough investors that the offering will raise the targeted amount of capital at a reasonable valuation. Similarly, investors want to develop relationships with underwriters who will allocate material amounts of new issues to them so their due diligence and research efforts are not wasted. Each primary capital markets business is indeed a platform, but the ability of issuers and investors to do business with multiple platforms ("multihoming") and price sensitivity on both sides of the market ensures that the market can sustain multiple competing underwriting platforms and prices for underwriting services are constrained by competition. The same is true for secondary trading and derivative businesses, where the extent of a firm's client network determines the availability of liquidity, a network externality produced by the platform that no one customer can internalize themselves.[9]

Analyzing capital markets business in terms of platform competition is a far cry from how such businesses were understood in the 1990s, when a groundswell of support emerged for allowing American banks to merge with capital markets firms, undermining the last vestiges of the Glass-Steagall Act. At that time, capital markets firms were viewed essentially as large mutual funds, holding a variety of financial risks and offering claims on such risks to investors. Given a large number of investments, the effect of extreme outcomes would be attenuated and diversification would reduce the overall risk of the claims held by the firm's customers. If, furthermore, the investments were less than perfectly correlated with the risk of bank loans, diversification benefits could be realized by combining banking and capital markets business.[10] The economic theory that sold the Gramm-Leach-Bliley Act was indeed this thin, and taken to its logical conclusion, it would imply we would all be best off with a single financial services firm for everything. In line with other thinking about competition from that era, whatever lack of discipline from U.S. competition might arise from deregulation would be contained by competition on a global scale. Never mind that five large firms dominate U.S. capital markets; we need to worry about banks already operating on this scale in other jurisdictions.[11]

Under the platform competition paradigm, the potential for vigorous competition in capital markets business appears to be a more plausible prospect. At the very least, one would have to inquire seriously into the ability of customers to switch between platforms and respond to changes in pricing, as well as the efforts made by firms to differentiate their offerings and network coverage.

Competition Within Universal Banks

What happens to competition in banking and capital markets when the largest incumbent firms have significant footprints in both domains and considerable discretion over how projects are funded? And what happens when nonbank firms try to compete with banks for bankable projects?

Our answer to the first question focuses on the mirroring of banking book lending business in a universal bank's debt capital markets business. For every loan product line, it seems, there is a security-based competitor. Residential and commercial mortgage lending compete with RMBS and CMBS. Consumer lending and asset-based commercial lending compete with ABS. Corporate lending competes with CLOs and corporate bonds. A universal bank can choose how it wants to participate across the base of bankable projects. It can lend and hold risk on its balance sheet. Alternatively, it can originate loans and sell them on the capital markets side, earning origination and servicing fees, and then earn revenue structuring securities and making markets in the bonds created.

Prior to the GFC, many of the resulting bonds created on the debt capital markets side ended up back in the trading book, earning further income and enjoying benign regulatory capital treatment. Today, the regulatory capital treatment is less benign, and the ability of U.S. banks to hold trading book positions for their own account has been curtailed by the Volcker Rule of the Dodd-Frank Act. Enforcement of the Volcker Rule has been weak, however, so there is still room for proprietary trading in securities to masquerade as market-making inventory.

But even without the ability to eventually hold investments in bankable projects in security form, the debt capital markets business looks pretty attractive relative to the banking book. It is hard to beat immediate fee income with little required equity for an institution interested in maximizing returns on equity. While the private-label securitization business has contracted post-GFC, agency MBS volumes have remained robust, and both corporate debt and CLO volumes have accelerated, as we pointed out in Chapter 7. In the United States at least, abundant flows of savings have continued to favor capital markets funding for bankable projects.

Banks also face challenges from unregulated capital markets loan originators outside of universal banks. These challengers aim to stake out market share in banking business without the burden of a large balance sheet or regulatory capital requirements. Countrywide Financial was a leading example pre-GFC; after the GFC "financial technology" or "fintech" firms entered the fray.

Competition from nonbank financial firms tends to harm banking book business by depressing prices. Countrywide priced mortgages aggressively, and fintech firms grew by the venture capital playbook of losing money on every transaction to capture market share. Banks are forced to match prices if they wish to maintain share, regardless of the bank's own view of risk-based pricing. They are compelled toward recklessness by institutions with no obligations to be prudent.

The trading book business tends to encourage these incursions by nonbanks. Nonbank originators rely on the securitization infrastructure of the universal banks, which are happy to earn fees from any source. Private equity firms are cultivated as sponsors of CLOs, both for the securitization business and to get a leg up on future initial public offering (IPO) underwriting opportunities. They are also convenient counterparties for synthetic transfers of risk from the trading book.

The capital markets business of a universal bank contributes to the cannibalization of bankable projects from the banking book, while putting pressure on the banking book to take more risk without commensurate reward. Though it is challenging to quantify exactly, it seems that commercial banks face more competitive pressure from within the bank holding company than from other commercial banks.

Competition Versus Financial Stability

Since the GFC, there has been a tendency to tolerate concentration in universal banking in exchange for the perceived benefits to financial stability. Most of the bank assets in the United States are now held by "global, systemically important banks" (GSIBs) which are subject to more stringent legal and regulatory requirements under the Dodd-Frank Act and Basel III. Policymakers have encouraged the absorption of failing institutions by GSIBs—beginning with Bear Stearns, Countrywide Financial, Lehman Brothers, and Merrill Lynch—both to bring them within this heightened regulatory perimeter and to benefit from the perceived financial strength of GSIBs.

Such a tendency runs contrary to the existing corpus of bank legislation in the United States, which is oriented toward maintaining competition in the banking system and the wider economy.[12] The country that once feared "money trusts" above all else now actively facilitates their formation, in the name of preserving access to safe and sound banking.

Does encouraging concentration among universal banks lead to safer banking? Not when those institutions are dominated by fee-based capital markets business. Though some exceptions exist, an abundance of research shows that increases in capital markets business (measured by non-interest income in bank holding companies) are associated with increased risk at the individual bank level.[13] These increases in risk do not disappear as universal banks become larger.

To make matters worse, capital markets business contributes to increases in systemic risk. The risk of one universal bank tends to increase the risk of all universal banks, because interconnections are especially strong on the capital markets side of the business. Higher ratios of non-interest income to assets are associated with increased systemic risk, tail risk, and interconnectedness. Increased non-interest income is also associated with reduced interest income, consistent with our cannibalization thesis.[14]

Therefore, we doubt whether the tradeoff between competition and stability actually exists in the United States when the institutions involved are universal banks. More competition is still likely to produce more benefits than its absence. However, it is evident that some additional control from corporate governance or regulation is needed to ensure balance between the businesses united in universal banks.

Governance

The foundational problem of corporate governance is the separation of ownership and control in the modern corporation.[15] Shareholders own the company, while senior managers make day-to-day decisions about what the corporation will do, how its resources will be deployed, and how the gains from the enterprise will be distributed. How can senior managers be made to act in the best interest of the owners, rather than dissipating the resources of the corporation and arrogating its gains for their own purposes? How do the owners define their best interests, and what mechanisms are available to owners (principals) to implement their best interests in the presence of self-interested managers (agents)?[16]

Current thinking on corporate governance boils down to a few basic principles. The board of directors, which represents shareholders' interests, should be independent of senior management. A simple way to maintain independence is to require the board chairman and the CEO to be different people. Senior managers should be incentivized to maximize the value of the company through a well-designed executive compensation plan. And if management maximizes the value of the firm, it will simultaneously achieve the best outcomes for the firm and for society.

Based on this scorecard, the corporate governance of universal banks was quite good prior to the GFC.[17] Needless to say, however, the GFC was not a welfare-maximizing outcome. While universal banks were not the only important actors in creating the GFC, following the canons of accepted practice in corporate governance clearly did not achieve desired outcomes. Accordingly, we must go back to the basics to ponder the governance framework that will best align the behavior of universal banks with the expectations attached to them by shareholders, depositors, regulators, and other stakeholders.

It is probably not right to presume that the universal banking firm is like any other corporation. From chartering to everyday operations to restructuring and resolution in bankruptcy—indeed, from cradle to grave—the legal and institutional treatment of banks is different from the treatment of other corporations. Much of a universal bank's funding is created by the bank itself, rather than raised from outside investors. That funding must trade at par with the unit of account. In a bankruptcy, depositors do not take control of the firm like a creditor's committee. Holders of deposit money have interests that are different than those of a garden variety unsecured creditor.

Within the universal banking firm, control is delegated through multiple layers of hierarchy and distributed across dozens, if not hundreds of subsidiaries.[18] It is challenging to properly incentivize so much management. Nor is it obvious that managers individually maximizing within their domains will result in an optimal outcome for the universal bank, as we have emphasized with respect to the banking/trading book divide. It may not be anyone's responsibility to adjudicate these conflicts and ensure coordination. Incentives are based on achieving short-term results from long-term contracts. Origination targets are easy to reward, while slowly developing problems can be blamed on external factors.

There is ample scope for management to influence the presentation of the firm's performance and risk profile to shareholders, the board, and outside auditors.

Even when accounts are presented faithfully and risk is modeled responsibly the sheer scale of the assumptions and calculations involved in presenting a large universal bank's financial condition can easily overwhelm a nonspecialist. Accountability is especially difficult to achieve.

Better governance could address some of universal banks' peculiarities. Managers could be made to write out-of-the-money put options back to the bank when receiving bonuses, which would return compensation in the event of a subsequent share price decline. Or, as Goodhart and Lastra (2020)[19] suggest, bank insiders could be issued a distinct class of equity with multiple liability to concentrate their minds on potential downside scenarios.[20] However, other reforms seem more difficult to achieve. Shareholders are unlikely to create duties for themselves vis-à-vis holders of deposit money. And it may be necessary to dismantle a business before restructuring it.[21]

Regulation

That leaves regulation to deal with the blind spots of corporate governance and competition among universal banks. Competition authorities could certainly encourage more entry and the unbundling of larger firms for the sake of generating some dynamism in the sector. Failing firms need not be swallowed by the largest incumbents.

U.S. regulators lean on corporate governance in vague but not ineffective ways. An understanding prevails among the FDIC, OCC, Federal Reserve, and bank directors that directors owe some duties to depositors, particularly after the passage of the Dodd-Frank Act.[22] Section 956 of the Dodd-Frank Act also directed bank regulators to promulgate a rule on incentive compensation for bank managers. A rule proposed in 2016 has been reproposed in 2024, perhaps to become a binding regulation this time.

But even if all of these reforms were forthcoming and equipped with teeth they would not speak directly to the problem of balancing banking and capital markets business to achieve the social purpose of each. Instead of delivering banks that respond elastically to money demand and intermediaries that connect savings to risky projects, our system gives us banks that struggle to create money and capital markets that plunder the safe projects banks need to grow. What can regulation do about that?

Basel III attempts to rebalance the banking book and the trading book by ensuring that significant risk weights are attached to trading book activity. However, as we argued in Chapter 8, this does not liberate the banking book so much as bleed its capital and liquidity for the sake of the trading book. The impossibility of issuing equity solely for the purpose of recapitalizing trading book business leaves the banking book's capital at the mercy of the trading book's capital needs.[23]

The Basel III approach is a complete about-face from Basel II's solution, which sought to align the regulatory capital of the universal bank with rational economic capital management. Weaknesses in governance doomed this solution after the GFC. Post-GFC governance reforms probably have not progressed far enough to have confidence in the Basel II approach. This is unfortunate, as it closes off many paths to rational balance between the businesses. Embedding economic capital management in well-governed firms remains a worthy goal.

Therefore, we are skeptical that a mix of competition, governance, and regulation can simultaneously achieve efficient outcomes for capital markets and the monetary system, when the largest firms in each market stand astride both markets.[24] In Chapter 14, we make the case for divorce between the banking book and the trading book.

Notes

1. The three pillars of Basel II lean indirectly on competition and corporate governance through the "market discipline" pillar, which requires disclosure of the bank's risk and capital management procedures. The minimum capital and supervisory review pillars sit squarely in the domain of regulation. In general, Basel leaves the management of competition and corporate governance to national authorities.
2. The touchstone in this genre is the Monti-Klein model. See Freixas, X. and Rochet, J-C. (2008). *Microeconomics of banking*. MIT Press.
3. See, for example, Gali, J. (2015). *Monetary Policy, Inflation, and the Business Cycle: An Introduction to the New Keynesian Framework and its Applications*, 2e. Princeton University Press.
4. The insolvency regime created by the Dodd-Frank Act in the United States is a major advance in this regard.
5. Grossman, R.S. (2010). *Unsettled Account: The Evolution of Banking in the Industrialized World Since 1800*. Princeton University Press.
6. Santos, J.C. dos. (1996). Commercial banks in the securities business: A review. *Federal Reserve Bank of Cleveland Working Paper 96-10* surveys the state of the literature at the time.

7. For example, Rajan, R.G. (1996). Why banks have a future: Toward a new theory of commercial banking. *Journal of Applied Corporate Finance* 9 (2): 114–129 argues that banks enjoy scale economies in the provision of liquidity and reduce their risks by pooling assets and deposit liabilities. Commercial banking "institutions bring market power, scale, and the ability to pool liquidity demands and enhance contractual possibilities when they undertake the traditional activities of offering demand deposits and originating illiquid loans." (p. 118)
8. Data from the FDIC's BankFind Suite: Commercial Banks—Structure, Changes in Number of Institutions.
9. For an introduction to the economics of platform competition, see Belleflamme, P. and Peitz, M. (2021). *The Economics of Platforms: Concepts and Strategy*. Cambridge University Press.
10. Kwan, S.H. (1997). Securities activities by commercial banking firms' section 20 subsidiaries: Risk, return, and diversification benefits. *Federal Reserve Bank of San Francisco Working Paper*, October: 4 found that "banking organizations" securities subsidiaries tend to be riskier but not necessarily more profitable than their bank affiliates. Within the class of securities activities, I found that securities trading tends to be more profitable and riskier than banking activities, while securities underwriting is found to be riskier, and in some cases also less profitable, than banking activities. Nevertheless, banking firms seem to be able to attain diversification benefits from engaging in securities activities.'
11. Santos, J.C. dos. (1996). Commercial banks in the securities business: A review. *Federal Reserve Bank of Cleveland Working Paper 96-10* surveys the securities activities of banks in OECD countries and the corporate forms for combining banking and securities activities, concluding "a majority of the OECD countries allow banks to engage directly in securities underwriting, dealing, and brokering. Concerning banks" choice of where to undertake these activities within their organizational structure, the countries with the most restrictive regulations are Greece, Japan, and Norway, followed closely by the United States and Canada.
12. Omarova, S.T. and Steele, G.S. (2024). Banking and antitrust. *Cornell Law School Research Paper No. 24-03*.
13. Stiroh, K.J. (2004). Diversification in banking: Is noninterest income the answer? *Journal of Money, Credit and Banking* 36 (5): 853–882; Stiroh, K.J. (2006). A portfolio view of banking with interest and noninterest activities. *Journal of Money, Credit and Banking* 38 (5): 1351–1361; Stiroh, K.J. and Rumble, A. (2006). The dark side of diversification: The case of U.S. financial holding

companies. *Journal of Banking & Finance* 30: 2131–2161; Demirgüç-Kunt, A. and Huizinga, H. (2010). Bank activity and funding strategies: The impact on risk and returns. *Journal of Financial Economics* 98: 626–650; DeYoung, R. and Torna, G. (2013). Nontraditional banking activities and bank failures during the financial crisis. *Journal of Financial Intermediation* 22: 397–421.
14. Brunnermeier, M.K., Dong, G.N., and Palia, D. (2020). Banks' noninterest income and systemic risk. *Review of Corporate Finance Studies* 9: 229–255.
15. Berle, A.A. and Means, G.C. (1932). *The Modern Corporation and Private Property*. Macmillan.
16. Jensen, M.C. and Meckling, W.H. (1976). Theory of the firm: Managerial behavior, agency costs and ownership structure. *Journal of Financial Economics* 3 (4): 305–360; Shleifer, A. and Vishny, R.W. (1997). A survey of corporate governance. *Journal of Finance* 52 (2): 737–783.
17. Armour, J. (2018). Bank governance. In: *The Oxford Handbook of Corporate Law and Governance* (ed. J.N. Gordon and W.-G. Ringe), 1108–1127. Oxford University Press.
18. See Cetorelli, N. and Prazad, S. (2024). The nonbank footprint of banks. *Federal Reserve Bank of New York Staff Report No. 1118*, September on the evolution of BHC complexity.
19. Goodhart, C. and Lastra, R. (2020). Equity finance: Matching liability to power. *Journal of Financial Regulation* 6 (1): 1–40.
20. Both of these proposals are, admittedly, subject to non-trivial counterparty credit risk.
21. An interesting example is UBS's rebuilding of its investment bank following the GFC.
22. Peck, R.R. and Halloran, M.J. (2016). Fiduciary duties of financial institution directors and officers in the post Dodd-Frank era. *International Journal of Disclosure and Governance* 13 (3): 221–235.
23. Recall that the banking book and the trading book both depend on one endowment of capital. Any equity issue may be perceived as a signal about the solvency of the banking book, which could trigger a run on the bank.
24. Rather than first-best efficiency, it may be more correct to speak of constrained efficiency, but our point should be clear.

Chapter 13

The Base of Investable and Bankable Projects

Our goal for the economic reform of the rules governing our financial system is to achieve a more efficient use of global savings for financing global investment. Vibrant capital markets influence the formation of investable projects and shape the channels into which savings can flow. Ventures that are well-capitalized with equity can also become bankable projects and support credit creation.

The goal of the present chapter is to infer some lessons about the base of investable and bankable projects from secular trends in the flows of global savings. The sources and uses of global savings tell us something about how well financial intermediaries have matched the supply of savings to demand.

Since the 1990s, the major sources of savings in the United States have been foreign capital flows (the "rest of the world"), nonfinancial business, and the wealthiest households. Foreign capital flows come from central banks seeking to ensure adequate dollar liquidity for international trade and to stabilize their exchange rates against the U.S. dollar as well as private investors. Nonfinancial business, once a destination for household savings, has now become a net supplier of funds to households. And within the household sector, the wealthiest households have become suppliers of funds to less wealthy households. We explain how these shifts in savings patterns follow the distribution of income from trade, the capital share, and skilled work, and investigate the destinations of those funding flows to determine how efficiently such massive resources are being used.

One of the leading sinks for savings from all sources is real estate. We take an excursion into the economics of real estate prices to understand why real estate projects are so favored as destinations for savings and as bankable projects. Real estate projects allow their owners to appropriate land-based rents that are taxed as capital income (if they are taxed at all) despite their infinite lifetime and non-depreciation. The credible claim to surplus that is underwritten in a real estate project is thus underpinned by the value of the land and the tax shields it affords, perhaps even more so than the future surplus of the borrower. Fluctuations in land values lead to collapses in real estate prices and precipitate banking crises through mortgage exposure. We recommend a land value tax to divorce banks' real estate exposure from cycles of land speculation and decouple credit from real estate cycles. If real estate projects will continue to dominate the bankable project base it is best to align their underwriting with borrower income and improvements to the land, rather than volatile, cyclical land values.

Might the dominance of real estate and consumer credit in bank balance sheets be evidence of change in the character of commercial business? We critically examine the thesis that corporate lending has receded because the assets of nonfinancial business are increasingly intangible. Given the flexibility afforded by intangible assets for shifting profits into different tax jurisdictions, nonfinancial business is well-incentivized to represent their operations as less physical affairs. Yet, physical production remains integral to the economy, even as it has become more "cloud-based" in the popular imagination. Reports of the demise of tangible capital appear to be premature.

Ultimately, we believe the fate of the base of investable and bankable projects is bound up with the state of competition in banking and financial intermediation, as well as the nonfinancial economy itself. As discussed in the previous chapter, there is ample scope for innovation in making new projects investable and bankable given sufficient investments in information. If banking and financial services can be made more competitive, the supply of projects will take care of itself.

Of Savings Gluts and Safe Assets

Beginning in the mid-1990s, the United States began running a series of current account deficits, meaning the United States was importing significantly more goods and services than it was exporting. At the time, economists pondered what failure in U.S. economic policy might be responsible for the persistent deficits. A decline in manufacturing or competitiveness? Monetary policy fostering an excessively strong U.S. dollar?

In 2005, Fed Governor Ben Bernanke suggested that to look inward was to miss the point.[1] The deficits, according to Bernanke, had their origin not in U.S. policies, but in conditions in the world outside the United States. The necessary counterpart of the United States importing more than the value of exports was borrowing in international capital markets, with the rest of the world loaning funds to close the gap.[2] What if the rest of the world's desire to invest savings in the United States was actually the *cause* of the U.S. current account deficit, rather than the *effect* of the trade balance?

Bernanke pointed to two sources of global savings that potentially benefited the United States. First, in Europe and the remainder of the developed world outside the United States, demographic developments were well underway in which larger proportions of the population were aging. A shift in the age structure of society toward larger shares of older citizens meant that more of the developed world's population was in a high-saving phase of their lifecycle. When these savings exhausted the ability of their local capital markets to absorb them, the next stop would naturally be the deep markets of the United States.

Second, developing economies had been stung by a series of currency crises, sovereign debt defaults, and banking system collapses. Beginning in Latin America and reverberating through Southeast Asia, central banks depleted their foreign currency reserves in a brutal series of crises while defending exchange rate pegs against the U.S. dollar. Eager to avoid more such episodes, developing country central banks began accumulating U.S. dollar reserves and paying down dollar-denominated debt. Central banks mobilized domestic savings for the effort by issuing local currency bonds and investing the proceeds in foreign currency.

Together, these phenomena mobilized hundreds of billions of dollars of international capital flows into the United States each year for nearly a decade. Awash in a "global saving glut," U.S. households reduced their saving rates and began to buy more imported products, generating the current account deficit. Our concern is to explain what happened in U.S. capital markets to find a destination for these massive flows of savings. But before we answer that question, we consider two further secular shifts in the sources and uses of savings in U.S. capital markets.

Shifts in the Balance of Domestic Saving

The "global saving glut" posited by Bernanke explains an increase in funds available to the entire U.S. economy but does not dwell at length on the sectoral disposition of those funds. Bernanke observes that the household sector was a prime beneficiary of the glut, using funds to increase investment in housing.[3] The government absorbed a material share of the inflows with new debt, though far from enough to be a major contributor to explaining the current account deficit. Investment by nonfinancial business was not obviously boosted, either.

There were at least two other major changes in the distribution of saving and borrowing with the United States happening concurrently with the global saving glut. Developments in the sources of saving followed developments in the distribution of income. Since the 1980s, labor's share of income has declined relative to the profit share; hence, business savings increased and demand for household funds declined. And since the 1980s, more of labor's share has been captured by top earners, creating a divergence between the savings rates of the wealthy and all other households.[4]

Two major changes in fund flows followed these domestic saving gluts. The first of these was a change in the relationship between the household and business sectors.[5] From the end of World War II until the 1990s, the household sector was a reliable source of savings that were consumed by the business sector. Funds were channeled from households to fund business investment, as in workhorse models of the macroeconomy. However, beginning in the 1990s, the situation reversed: the business sector began to accumulate savings within itself, while the household sector began to reduce its savings. Firms contributed to dissaving by households directly through dividends and share repurchases, and indirectly through financial intermediaries as lenders of funds. A second major shift occurred within the household sector.[6] As real income gains accelerated at the top of the income distribution and were more elusive for those with lower incomes, savings accumulated among the wealthiest households. It became a major task to intermediate these savings to a destination outside the nonfinancial business sector, which no longer needed them.

Safe Assets as a Sink for the Saving Glut

What is surprising about the international and domestic saving gluts and changes in the distribution of savings is not so much their sources or their magnitudes, but the tendency for these new funds to be absorbed by safe assets rather than riskier capital projects. Bernanke noted the dominance of residential real estate in absorbing global capital flows. The new savings of business were predominantly held as cash and cash equivalents rather than deployed in new structures and capital equipment.[7] And the increased savings of the rich more often found their way to mortgages financing housing for those lower in the income distribution, Treasury bonds, and municipal debt than to venture capital funds and "angel investment" projects.[8] Indeed, it is remarkable that capital markets opened a channel through which savings could be intermediated within the household sector (via securitized mortgages), which had previously depended on bank finance and funds mobilized by the mortgage GSEs.

That these savings gluts found their way to safe assets suggests that the wealthiest actors in society are shockingly risk averse. Economists tend to assume that wealth has diminishing marginal utility, so that a billionaire suffers less upon losing $100 million than someone with a net worth of $110 million. The voracious demand for safe assets among the wealthiest suggests that people dislike losses equally at any level of wealth. The willingness of foreign investors and central banks to save in safe assets is understandable, however, and is a plausible explanation for the long-term decline in risk-free interest rates.

The other side of these inflows to safe assets is the supply of risky equity investment opportunities that were not created. Cumulative flows of equity to the nonfinancial business sector were negative throughout the 1990s and early 2000s. From 2003 to 2007, the sector bought back $5 trillion in stock.[9] Not all business is corporate business, but the lack of equity flowing to the sector is stunning.

Though we can provide no definitive answer here, in sketching and tracing these trends we can begin to answer some questions that have obsessed us throughout the book. How did savings become so plentiful that they could be used to fund projects which could otherwise be funded by bank credit creation without using savings? Having built a financial system on the assumption of plentiful savings, can we be assured that savings will remain abundant for generations to come? If trends in saving were to change, what would be the consequences for banking and capital markets? And is the time ripe for the pendulum to saving back in favor of bank funding?

Après le deluge

The phenomena driving the global and domestic saving gluts appear to be receding. Aging populations in the rich world are now simply retiring, entering a dissaving phase of their lifecycle that will not reverse. Demographic trends do not suggest that a wave of new births will rebalance the population age distribution, and stagnating economic growth rates will generate few new savings.[10]

Among central banks, the last great accumulator of foreign reserves—the People's Bank of China—has reduced its holdings of Treasury debt significantly in recent years, and many other developing world central banks are now so well-equipped with reserve war chests that further additions seem superfluous.

Within the United States, long-term swings in labor's share of income and the distribution of income need not reverse, though they seem to be reaching a political limit. It would seem odd in a democratic society to assume that gross levels of inequality will only expand, business will become ever more concentrated and profitable, and the economy will split into a bacchanale for the few and subsistence for the many. To make plans on this basis would probably be a failure.

There is, at any rate, good reason to believe that the flows that have been supporting growth in safe assets cannot be assured of continuing. Unless the use of savings can be economized, we should expect a world with higher real interest rates and a growing reserve of unfunded investment initiatives, with potentially disastrous consequences for economic growth, government debt dynamics, and the stability of the monetary system. Safe investments will not produce the growth dividend we need to stabilize the debt and defend the monetary standard.

The Pathological Character of Land and Real Estate

In our construct developed in Chapter 4, a bankable project is an investable project with additional characteristics that make it an essentially riskless proposition for a bank lending to finance it. As an investable project, a bankable project will have a positive net present value (NPV) (or satisfy another appropriate criterion). The bankable project will also grant the lending bank assurance in the form of collateral assets, borrower equity, and/or limitations on the use of the funds, all of which limit the risk of the loan and provide resources that can be mobilized to retire the loan if the positive NPV fails to materialize. Together, the positive NPV and assurances of a bankable project give rise to what we have called a "credible claim to a future surplus."

In Chapter 7, we saw that the majority of bank lending is against real estate. The share of real estate loans in bank lending would be even greater were it not for the additional $10 trillion in real estate loans funded in the capital markets through agency and non-agency MBS. In this section, we argue that the disproportionate representation of land-based projects in the set of bankable projects is the result of modern tax systems' blindness to income derived from land, inherited from neoclassical economists' blindness to land as a factor of production. The resulting implicit tax subsidy to land enhances bankability, at the cost of degrading bank underwriting and tying the banking system to cycles in land speculation.

Investable Projects Involving Land

Land is a very special basis for bankable projects. Following the classical economists, we take land to mean the category of resources which are not produced by labor or capital. Land includes physical space, of course, in urban, suburban, and rural forms; but it also includes mineral resources, fossil fuel energy resources, the productivity of the soil and cultivated crops, the growth and fecundity of livestock and fisheries, sunshine, wind, forests, and other natural resources. While labor and capital can increase the productivity of land when used in conjunction with land, the productivity of land is not itself the product of labor or capital. Whether anyone intends it or not, a seed that roots in the soil of the forest grows, and if it is later harvested as timber, its value is only partially related to the saw and the hand that operates it.

Just as economics forgot the power of banks to create money out of nothing, the field has also forgotten land as a factor of production. Whereas the classical economists like the physiocrats, Adam Smith, David Ricardo, and John Stuart Mill, were closely concerned with the produce of land, neoclassical economists have eliminated land entirely from the process of production, or have lumped land in with capital as an especially long-lived capital asset.

The economic character of land is its ability to produce a yield without additional input. Forested land produces trees without human labor or capital investment. Mineral and energy deposits precede human intervention. To be sure, the value of land can be augmented by integrating it into production processes: agriculture employs labor and specialized equipment to increase crop yields far beyond their uncultivated state, and both forestry and mineral-based businesses require labor and capital for extraction and transport, at a minimum. But that does not mean the output was produced solely with labor and capital. The residual value of the land-based product, net of the wages that compensate labor productivity and the interest and depreciation allowance that compensate capital, is the *rent* of land. Land rent is a yield realized in land-based production over and above the value of complementary inputs to production. Capitalizing this yield—summing its discounted value over an infinite horizon—gives the economic value of land.

Similar considerations apply to urban (and suburban) land. The service flow of urban land consists not in a flow of natural products but in its proximity to opportunities. Its value can be enhanced by improving it in a manner well-suited to its location: creating office space in a commercial district, or cultural centers in a residential area, for example. But just as productive agricultural land yields value that cannot be attributed to labor or capital, urban land yields value unrelated to how it is improved. The rent of urban land arises from its location, which is a function of improvements to all the land around it, rather than improvements to one's own parcel.

Land is a productive factor distinct from capital. Space, of course, does not depreciate like capital—an acre is still an acre 10 years from now, regardless of how it is used. And while natural resources may be depleted or exploited beyond their capacity to renew themselves, the lost productive capacity cannot be offset by investment in the way depreciating capital is renewed by investment. The evolution of the economic value of the stock of land is thus determined by the intensity of its use and physical or "bioeconomic" considerations. Accordingly, the remuneration of land as a productive resource is not determined by the forces that determine the remuneration of capital, which are generally understood as interest, depreciation, and premiums for bearing risk. Rent is not earned as a result of labor or deferring consumption in order to invest. The value of land is the sum of the stream of rents it will produce, discounted at an appropriate rate.

It is easy to see that workers earn wages and the owners of capital appropriate interest—but who appropriates land rent? In the time of the classical economists, a separate class of rentiers owned the land and explicitly collected rent from its (mostly agricultural) users. Indeed, in feudal society the lords who possessed the land would collect the rent in kind, taking a share of the crop from the serfs who farmed it. Now, however, ownership of land tends to coincide with ownership of capital. Before one builds a farm, a factory, or a high-rise building, one purchases the land on which it is built. Rent is appropriated by those who own land or otherwise have the right to dispose of its product. This coincidence of ownership is one factor that leads economists to treat land as a species of capital.[11]

The Bankability of Investable Projects Involving Land

It is easy to lose sight of what is actually underwritten in a real estate loan. The credible claim to future surpluses offered by a potential real estate borrower comes not from potential appreciation of the property but from the borrower's ability to grow their income during their tenure at the property. A residential mortgage borrower repays their mortgage with growth in their labor income that arises from their local opportunity set, the accrual of their experience, and their tenure with particular employers. Similarly, a commercial mortgage borrower repays their mortgage by supplying apartments, hotel rooms, office space, retail space, etc. in areas where people wish to live, travel, work, and shop. In both cases, the surpluses being realized come from increased productivity: producing more value on the job, reducing search costs, and making joint production possible.

The unique characteristics of land in production make lending against real estate (and natural resources) a special kind of bankable project, however. Real estate is generally a zoned bundle of land and improvements (capital), while natural resource projects are bundles of physical or bioeconomic resource streams, investments in capital, and the labor employed in their exploitation. As a result, the revenue earned by real estate and natural resource projects reflects the productivity of land, labor, and capital, but only labor and capital are explicitly remunerated. Land rent accrues as a residual to the owner of the project. As a result, land-based projects are almost assured a positive NPV, and the credible claims to future surpluses from real estate and natural resource projects arise predominantly from the ability of the entrepreneurs in land-based projects to pledge those rents as a source of value to retire the loan.[12] Similarly, the embodied value of those rents in land enhances the value of land as collateral, reinforcing the bankability of the project. It is extremely tempting for banks to underwrite these future surpluses rather than the borrower's non-rent income.

Rents earned by land make an additional contribution to the bankability of real estate projects because land is generally taxed as if it were capital. Like capital, gains on land are not recognized and taxed until the land is sold, so the owner's after-tax return increases with his holding period.[13] While land does not actually depreciate, owners of real estate are generally able to depreciate some (or all) of the cost of the land according to the same schedule as the improvements on the land, either because tax rules do not distinguish between land and improvements, or because they afford owners wide latitude in allocating purchase prices between land and improvements.[14]

Thus, whenever someone buys a (zoned) bundle of land and improvements, one acquires a non-depreciating asset that yields a flow of rents and a depreciating asset that yields a flow of capital services.[15] The tax system treats the bundle as if the whole thing were a depreciating asset yielding a flow of capital services. Depreciation is a tax shield. Slippage between the tax system and economic reality allows the owner of the land to appropriate some of the flow of land rent on a tax-free basis. This untaxed land rent is, of course, capitalized into the land value. The tax code thus amplifies the after-tax value of real estate projects relative to other potentially bankable projects and encourages owners to hold their projects indefinitely, continuously renewing their financing.

The desirability of lending against real estate independently of the borrower's creditworthiness has been well-appreciated as a factor in the housing and mortgage finance bubbles that preceded the GFC. These conditions were not a passing phenomenon but are inherent in real estate investment. Should a hapless borrower fail to generate a surplus from their real estate rents—because the rest of their income collapses, or because the tax shields given to real estate are not as valuable to a borrower in a low tax bracket—then the underwriter of the loan obtains a relatively liquid collateral asset which is likely to have appreciated in value. As the supply of capital seeking exposure to real estate projects exploded, underwriting efforts shifted away from evaluating a borrower's projected future income to forecasting the price at which zoned bundles of land and improvements could be liquidated in future economic scenarios. The asset became the focal point rather than the surplus income being pledged.

The bank's problem of renewing its loan portfolio is also simplified when it is heavily exposed to real estate. Rather than finding and underwriting new projects, the same set of real estate projects can be refinanced again and again at higher valuations—especially in an environment of falling interest rates. It is little wonder that banks prefer to cruise on their informational investments in real estate rather than shoulder the fixed costs of learning to lend against projects collateralized by smaller and riskier groups of assets.

Exposure of the Banking System to Land Values

Downturns in real estate occur because land values fall. Defaults on real estate loans follow a particular geographic pattern. When real estate investment expands, new development occurs on marginal land on the periphery of established residential and commercial centers. The development lifts the value of the land, which becomes a new potential locus for agglomeration.[16] However, when the appetite for further development in peripheral areas is lost—usually because new buyers or tenants cannot be found—the new area fails to reach "critical mass," the potential for future agglomeration is falsified, and the upward trend in land value reverses.[17]

Fluctuations in land values are sufficient to explain real estate downturns because land values comprise a substantial portion of real estate prices. The share of land value in the aggregate value of real estate was just over 40% in 2019, and skews much higher in more desirable areas.[18] More importantly, most of the risk in residential and commercial property values reflects risk to the price of the land, consistent with our baby model of real estate cycles and the "land leverage" hypothesis.[19] From 2006 to 2009 the Case-Shiller housing index fell by roughly 20%, while the value of urban land fell by 40%.[20]

Every credit crisis in recent memory has also been a real estate crisis, which is to say, a reversal in the trend of land prices. In the post-World War II era, collapses of credit-fueled speculative housing bubbles have been responsible for the deepest and longest recessions in the developed world.[21] The currency crises that ripped through East and Southeast Asia in 1997 were also real estate crises, catalyzed by waves of speculation and inflated appraisals.[22]

It is easy to see how real estate crisis propagates through the banking system to create a credit crisis. When real estate loans default, banks amortize loans out of their own equity resources, and their diminished capital base provides thin support for new lending. The loss of money and financing drags on the economy, threatening all the income streams that have been pledged in support of bank credit.[23] Unsurprisingly, bank failures follow real estate crises with depressing regularity.

Our analysis implies that the coincidence of real estate crises, credit crises, and bank failures is not accidental. The temptation to expand real estate lending in periods of increased land speculation is nearly irresistible, and when the speculative wave loses momentum, the reversal is swift and painful. Yet real estate remains the basis on which the banking system creates most of the money supply. A primary challenge for reform of the financial system is to reduce the sensitivity of banking system capital to fluctuations in land prices, without collapsing the money supplied by underwriting real estate projects.

Land rents can be rendered unimportant sources of value in real estate projects by taxation. An efficient tax on land does not distort an owner's decision about how long to own the land relative to a world without taxation. The current system of taxation allows land owners to reduce the present value of their tax burden by holding land indefinitely: all taxes are paid at the time of sale.[24] The only tax that does not affect decisions about the duration of land tenure is an annual tax levied on the value of the land.[25] That is, a Georgist tax on the value of the land, excluding improvements to the land, is both economically efficient (neutral) and effective in preventing the rent of land from being privately appropriated and capitalized in land values.[26]

A Georgist land value tax would make bank capital less sensitive to land prices without intervening in real estate loan underwriting. Banks would remain free to evaluate a potential borrower's income and risks to income, and to demand borrower equity on that basis. Underwriting will become harder work as the rapid appreciation of real estate collateral will no longer be assured. However, a major source of correlation in borrower defaults will be dampened so that risk can be managed through loan-level pricing and reserves rather than general-purpose bank capital buffers. Real estate projects would remain a substantial basis for the creation of deposit money for a wider base of borrowers. Reducing the importance of land in real estate underwriting would also help level the playing field across the wealth distribution for borrowers seeking credit.

Finally, from a fiscal perspective, a land value tax would offer a substantial non-distortionary source of revenue at a time when deficits and debt threaten to crowd out private saving and investment. The value of all urban land in 2006 has been estimated at $30 trillion.[27] At the time of writing, the Case-Shiller U.S. National Home Price Index has increased 77% since December 2006. Since land values tend to appreciate more quickly than the value of structures, it is reasonable to assume that the aggregate value of urban land now exceeds $50 trillion. A 1% annual tax on land values would therefore raise over $500 billion in revenue, more than the tax revenue generated from corporate income tax. Shifting the tax base toward land would mitigate longstanding and well-documented distortions of incentives to work and save created by the taxation of earned income. We should take advantage of shifting the burden to reduce these distortions. It would also significantly reduce the cost of purchasing a home.[28] Whether additional revenue is sought beyond current aggregate tax revenue is a separate question.

Is Technology Making Fewer Projects Bankable?

There is some reason to fear that fewer investment projects in the business sector are bankable. Whereas extensive plant, equipment, and working capital investments were once necessary for production, the assets of modern corporations are increasingly intangible: patents, know-how, data, software, etc. While the returns to producing intangible assets can be impressive, they do not generally result in collateral that can be seized in the event of a default and resold in a deep and liquid secondary market.[29]

It is true that the share of manufacturing in U.S. GDP has declined from roughly 25% in 1947 to about 10%–12% in recent years. Nevertheless, we should stress test the underlying assumption that the U.S. economy has become somehow more virtualized than it was in the immediate postwar era. Industries with physical products like mining, utilities, construction, manufacturing, trade and transportation consistently account for more than 40% of private gross output, which has grown at a compound annual rate of about 4% since the late 1990s. Though the output of such industries is predominantly sold to other industries, its production still depends on significant investments in land, plant, and equipment, and results in a stream of marketable intermediate products which require working capital to support.

Perhaps what has changed most noticeably in the way that goods are produced is the shift toward just-in-time production planning, which seeks to economize on working capital. Reducing inventories shrinks a producing firm's balance sheet, increasing the return on the firm's capital without the use of bank credit. Another important trend is the increasing vertical integration of production, which connects stages of production within a single self-financing firm and further reduces the stock of work in process.

We should also stress test the idea that the intangible assets created by modern firms are indeed so intangible and so idiosyncratic. Intangible assets are easily moved offshore and can be used to reduce corporate tax bills through internal transfer payments—off-market transactions at dubious prices—which creates an incentive for business to overstate their value and importance and to recharacterize tangible investments as intangible investments whenever possible. Much internal knowledge is captured in data and software that would be readily usable by other firms—hence the brutality with which former employees are pursued should they take any bit of it with them. And then there are items like mailing and contact lists, contracts, and other items that are easily transferred or assigned, saving the recipient or assignee the considerable effort of developing the same asset themselves.

The problem may not be so much that valuable, resalable collateral does not exist in technology-driven industries, but that it is difficult to define a lien on it within the commercial code, to restrict the use of loan proceeds to a particular project, or to take possession of the asset through the bankruptcy process. Which is to say that additional legal and monitoring effort is needed to render investments in intangible assets bankable. In our view, this is not a dead end or a call for policy intervention but the nature of innovation and investment in banking itself. Banking cannot grow unless banks can configure new bankable projects.

How to Expand the Base

We have seen fairly little innovation in banking for more than a generation. The expansion in banking has largely been a story of pushing the same products to existing customers in greater volumes, and to new customers along the margins of credit rationing. As a result, lending has remained tied to a few classes of collateral—real estate, consumer durables, industrial plant and equipment, inventories—where it is supported with adequate equity, and in rare cases, the expected savings of individuals and firms. Does the economy now lack general-purpose technologies against which banks can lend with confidence? Have savings become so plentiful that bank borrowing has become superfluous?

We believe the answer to the first question is negative. There is no shortage of general-purpose technology in the new economy, from data centers and cell phone towers to photovoltaic arrays and wind turbines. However, we see investments in these technologies being funded through private credit markets and securitizations rather than the banking system. Private equity firms and capital markets businesses are making the necessary investments in information, contracting, and secondary marketability to support lending at large scale. That banks are unable to do the same is somewhat shocking.

In Chapter 12, we described how banks and financial intermediaries expand the bases of bankable and investable projects in the normal course of healthy competition. Technology and entrepreneurship deliver projects with positive NPVs, but it takes informational investments by banks and financial intermediaries to make them bankable and investable. Chapter 12 also touched on the state of competition in banking and capital markets. The debt capital markets business of the major universal banks has enjoyed favorable conditions for more than a generation, benefiting from a torrent of concentrated inflows. Bank lending has been diminished in several of its best-established domains. Even so, the largest banks remain dominant and would be highly profitable if they could avoid being penalized for their failures of governance. They remain too big to fail and coast on their bigness. In this environment, there has been little innovation opening up new domains to lending or changing the form of lending in existing markets. Banks remain the cash cow subsidiaries of the universal bank, supporting and hedging the risks of more profitable and more volatile capital markets business.

The banking system's ability to monetize the rent of land has kept the sector buoyant and profitable for a long time. Leaving land rent untaxed is a massive subsidy to real estate ownership that elevates prices and fuels speculative frenzies. It also subsidizes the banking system while undermining its stability. It is time for a land value tax to eliminate the subsidy, contribute to stabilizing the government budget, and remove an artificial source of value from the base of bankable projects.

Taking away the crutch of land rents will help to reinvigorate competition in underwriting and grow the base of bankable projects. Competition would be greatly facilitated by removing regulations that attempt to steer credit to preferred sectors. Perhaps more importantly, the banking system would benefit from the opportunity to manage itself independently of capital markets business. Banking needs to be more than the junior partner in a universal bank. If you take care of competition in financial services, the base of projects will largely take care of itself.

Notes

1. Bernanke, B.S. (2005). The global saving glut and the U.S. current account deficit. *Remarks delivered March 10.*
2. Bernanke identifies the ultimate cause of the current account deficit as occurring outside the United States. For an alternative view, see Hanke, S.H. and Li, E. (2019). The strange and futile world of trade wars. *Journal of Applied Corporate Finance* 31 (4): 59–67, who argue that the current account deficit has been homegrown for many years.
3. We emphasize that investment in residential housing is distinct from homeownership. Imagine half the housing stock is owner-occupied, while the other half is owned by landlords who rent it to tenants. If half of the tenants purchase their homes from the landlords, no new investment in housing takes

place, even though the rate of homeownership has increased from one-half to three-quarters. Ownership has simply passed from the landlords to the tenants. Thus, an individual household's investment in housing does not entail investment in the aggregate. As a result, the origination of new mortgages is only loosely connected to housing investment. Only new builds and renovations are investment in housing stock.

4. Piketty, T. (2014). *Capital in the 21st century* (trans. A. Goldhammer). Harvard University Press.
5. Chen, P., Karabarbounis, L., and Neiman, B. (2017). The global risk of corporate saving. *Journal of Monetary Economics* 89: 1–19 and references therein.
6. Mian, A.R., Straub, L., and Sufi, A. (2021). The saving glut of the rich. *NBER Working Paper 26941*.
7. Chen, P., Karabarbounis, L., and Neiman, B. (2017). The global risk of corporate saving. *Journal of Monetary Economics* 89: 1–19.
8. Mian, A.R., Straub, L., and Sufi, A. (2021). The saving glut of the rich. *NBER Working Paper 26941*.
9. Flow of Funds Table F.224.
10. For a deeper analysis, see Goodhart, C. and Pradhan, M. (2020). *The Great Demographic Reversal: Ageing Societies, Waning Inequality, and an Inflation Revival.* Palgrave-Macmillan.
11. The coincidence of ownership is not universal. In Singapore, for example, land remains owned by the state and is leased to private households. See Phang, S-Y. (2018). *Policy Innovations for Affordable Housing in Singapore: From Colony to Global City.* Palgrave for an insightful analysis.
12. In the context of natural resource projects, there is more of a presumption of payment for the land rent. When access to the land is leased by a government or special taxation measures are attached, the possibility exists that rents will not be appropriated by the entrepreneur. Casual empiricism suggests, however, that governments rarely realize the full value of land rents, and the design of better auction structures for resource leases remains an area for improvement.
13. Accumulated depreciation can be "recaptured" at the time of sale because it reduces the tax basis of the property. Undoubtedly, there are ways for a clever accountant to mitigate this.
14. The bundled purchase of land and improvements gives the purchaser some leeway in allocating the purchase price to each component. Attributing most of the price to the improvements smuggles land into capital for commercial real estate purchases. In residential real estate the tax shield for mortgage

interest implies a path of accelerated depreciation which is common to the land and the residence alike.

15. Franke, M.K. and van de Minne, A.M. (2017). Land, structure and depreciation. *Real Estate Economics* 45 (2): 415–451 show that the depreciation of improvements is non-negligible. A minimally maintained property will lose 43% of its value over 50 years.

16. Agglomeration refers to the benefit of locating an activity in an area where similar or complementary activities are undertaken. Two simple examples are locating a retail business in a district with other retail shopping opportunities or finding housing in an area with good schools.

17. In this section, we work out the 1982 notes of Mason Gaffney, "Causes of Downturns: An Austro-Georgist Synthesis," available at www.masongaffney.org.

18. Davis, M.A., Larson, W.D., Oliner, S.D. et al. (2021). The price of residential land for counties, ZIP codes, and census tracts in the United States. *Journal of Monetary Economics* 118: 413–431 describe the most recent housing boom and bust as "a land boom and bust." See Davis, M.A. and Heathcote, J. (2007). The price and quantity of residential land in the United States. *Journal of Monetary Economics* 54: 2595–2620; Davis, M.A. and Palumbo, M.G. (2008). The price of residential land in large US cities. *Journal of Urban Economics* 63: 352–384; Haughwout, A., Orr, J., and Bedoll, D. (2008). The price of land in the New York Metropolitan area. *Federal Reserve Bank of New York Current Issues in Economics and Finance*; Kok, N., Monkkonen, P., and Quigley, J.M. (2014). Land use regulations and the value of land and housing: An intra-metropolitan analysis. *Journal of Urban Economics* 81: 136–148; Nichols, J.B., Oliner, S.D., and Mulhall, M.R. (2013). Swings in commercial and residential land prices in the United States. *Journal of Urban Economics* 73: 57–76; and Davis, M.A., Oliner, S.D., Pinto, E.J. et al. (2017). Residential land values in the Washington, DC metro area: New insights from big data. *Regional Science and Urban Economics* 66: 234–246.

19. Bostic, R.W., Longhofer, S.D., and Redfearn, C. (2007). Land leverage: Decomposition home price dynamics. *Real Estate Economics* 35: 183–208. Nichols, J.B., Oliner, S.D., and Mulhall, M.R. (2013). Swings in commercial and residential land prices in the United States. *Journal of Urban Economics* 73: 57–76 attribute the difference in volatility between land and structures to differences in the elasticity of supply for each.

20. Albouy, D., Ehrlich, G., and Shin, M. (2018). Metropolitan land values. *Review of Economics and Statistics* 100 (3): 454–466. Nichols, J.B., Oliner, S.D., and Mulhall, M.R. (2013). Swings in commercial and residential land prices in

the United States. *Journal of Urban Economics* 73: 57–76 estimate a peak-to-trough decline of 50% using different methods.

21. Jorda, Ò., Schularick, M., and Taylor, A.M. (2015). Leveraged Bubbles. *Journal of Monetary Economics* 76: S1–S20.
22. Quigley, J.M. (2001). Real estate and the Asian crisis. *Journal of Housing Economics* 10: 129–161.
23. Gan, J. (2007). The real effects of asset market bubbles: Loan- and firm-level evidence of a lending channel. *Review of Financial Studies* 20 (5): 1941–1973.
24. Unsurprisingly, some choose to never sell, passing properties in trust to family members, or utilizing so-called 1031 exchanges, which allow gains on property sales to be rolled over into new purchases. Parents tap their home equity to finance home purchases for their children as well; see Benetton, M., Kudlyak, M., and Mondragon, J. (2024). Dynastic Home Equity. *Federal Reserve Bank of San Francisco Working Paper 2022-13*.
25. Gaffney, M. (1970a). Tax-induced slow turnover of capital, I. *American Journal of Economics and Sociology* 29 (1): 25–32; Gaffney, M. (1970b). Tax-induced slow turnover of capital, II. *American Journal of Economics and Sociology* 29 (2): 179–197; Gaffney; M. (1970c). Tax-induced slow turnover of capital, III. *American Journal of Economics and Sociology* 29 (3): 277–287; Gaffney, M. (1970d). Tax-induced slow turnover of capital, IV. *American Journal of Economics and Sociology* 29 (4): 409–424; Gaffney; M. (1971). Tax-induced slow turnover of capital, V. *American Journal of Economics and Sociology* 30 (1): 105–111. Improvements to land would be taxed as capital, and Gaffney's analysis of distortions in the taxation of capital would apply *mutatis mutandis*, but distortions in the taxation of capital are not peculiar to real estate markets.
26. Such a tax is called Georgist in honor of its original proponent Henry George. The late Mason Gaffney was perhaps the most distinguished of the modern Georgist economists. George's influence has not disappeared entirely from modern economics. See, for example, Arnott, R.J. and Stiglitz, J.E. (1979). Aggregate land rents, expenditure on public goods, and optimal city size. *Quarterly Journal of Economics* 93 (4): 471–500, which defends the generality of the "Henry George Theorem": Yeager, L. (2011). *Is the Market a Test of Truth and Beauty? Essays in Political Economy*. Ludwig von Mises Institute: 51–71, 209–224; and Goodhart, C. (2024). Reeves has the best chance since Lloyd George of reforming property tax. *Financial Times*, August 15, which argues for a land tax to play a central role in the UK's fiscal system.
27. Albouy, D., Ehrlich, G., and Shin, M. (2018). Metropolitan land values. *Review of Economics and Statistics* 100 (3): 454–466.

28. Goodhart, C. (2024). Reeves has the best chance since Lloyd George of reforming property tax. *Financial Times*, August 15 calculates that a 0.6 percent land value tax in the UK—an annual levy of GBP 3,000 on a GBP 1m property in which half of the value is accounted for by land—would raise GBP 22 billion in revenue while reducing home prices by 7%. Crowe, C., Dell'Ariccia, G., Igan, D. et al. (2013). How to deal with real estate booms: Lessons from country experiences. *Journal of Financial Stability* 9: 300–319 model the impact of increasing property taxes in the United States from the lowest rate (0.26%) to the highest (2.6%). While this tax would fall on the value of improvements as well as land, the authors estimate it would lower home price appreciation by 4.3 percentage points a year, putting it in the range of 1–2% per year.
29. Haskel, J. and Westlake, S. (2018). *Capitalism without Capital: The Rise of the Intangible Economy.* Princeton University Press.

Chapter 14

Rewriting the Rules

We conclude with a provisional sketch of a quantity-based monetary policy. Rather than target a short-term interest rate, the central bank targets a growth rate for a Divisia broad money index. Its primary instrument of control is the rate at which the banking system's capital expands. The central bank controls its own balance sheet to align the overnight lending rate for reserve money with other short-term interest rates. The target growth rate for broad money is chosen to meet aggregate demand for broad money, consistent with the potential growth rate of the economy and a low rate of general inflation. The success of policy is monitored at a finer level of granularity for neutrality, as articulated in Chapter 11.

Our vision for monetary policy is more structural than tactical, oriented toward keeping results within long-term bounds rather than reacting to daily market developments. Hence, we suggest structural reforms in the service of neutral money creation. We argue for commercial and investment banking to be split, for credit risk weights to be set in a more neutral manner, for an expansion and consolidation of standing liquidity facilities at the central bank, and for increased regulatory attention to loan pricing and underwriting. We also advocate for a reduction of the government's footprint in capital markets and greater urgency for innovation in public and private capital markets.

We outline a model in which the central bank targets the growth rate of broad money. Previous attempts to regulate broad money supply relied on proposed linkages between the central bank's supply of reserve money and the supply of deposit money by the banking system. We propose an alternative framework in which the supply of Divisia broad money is linked to the supply of bank capital through three straightforward relationships. The supply of broad money may then be controlled by managing the accumulation and release of bank equity. We also propose a passive role for central bank rate-setting in the market for reserve money and suggest a larger role for standing facilities that can co-opt lending currently managed through the Federal Home Loan Bank (FHLB) system.

Next, we advocate the divorce of commercial banking from investment banking and consider revisions to the regulation of commercial banks. We are primarily concerned with distortions to the distribution of lending encouraged by regulators' credit risk weights. Neutral risk weights can be designed by focusing on the relative profitability of bank business lines, rather than their relative loss exposures in a stress scenario. This insight focuses attention on bank underwriting and pricing operations, powerful levers through which banks set the terms of accepting risk. Current liquidity regulation reinforces the distortions created by regulatory credit risk weights, makes banking less efficient, and stifles the interbank lending market. We recommend shifting the management of bank liquidity risk from the current self-help regime to a greater reliance on standing facilities at the central bank.

We conclude with some suggestions to encourage more efficient capital markets. The need to free up global savings for other projects is signaled elegantly by the global rise in real interest rates. Interest rates are rising now because a globally large generation has now entered the dissaving phase of their lifecycle, and reliable sources of new savings like central bank reserve policy and Chinese credit creation have left the scene. Mobilizing new savings will require either a global reduction in consumption—what we usually call a recession—or the recycling of savings currently tied up in unproductive projects. We believe it will be far less painful to pursue the latter course. It is difficult to defend the $10 trillion footprint of United States government agencies related to housing policy in the global capital markets. Similarly, the Federal Reserve's balance sheet weighs heavily on the state of the capital markets and impedes the conduct of central bank policy needed today.

Toward a New Central Bank Operating Model

The unconventional monetary policy that followed the GFC has become fiscally costly and increasingly challenging to implement. We need a new operating model for central banking that does not depend on an enormous balance sheet, an interbank market oversaturated with liquidity, and payment of administered rates on bank reserves. The new operating model should be guided by the overarching goal of neutrality, rather than efforts to lean against the interest rate determined by an elusive capital markets equilibrium.

In a quantity-based operating framework for monetary policy, the Cambridge equation links the supply of broad money to output and inflation, the final target variables of monetary policy. It is the starting point for elaborating a transmission mechanism connecting quantities of money to primary policy objectives. We formalized a disaggregated quantity-based money demand framework in Chapter 11 that connected broad money and the monetary impact of fiscal policy to prices and transactions at the sectoral level. Monetary demand systems of this kind can be used to ensure that monetary policy is aligned with the goals of neutrality and a stable monetary standard. It remains to describe how quantity-based policy can be animated. What instruments are controlled by the central bank, and how?

Errors of the Old Monetarism

The first attempts at monetarism in the United States relied on controlling a narrow monetary aggregate by adjusting the monetary base on the balance sheet of the central bank.[1] Following a classic analysis by Phillips, changes in the targeted aggregate were thought to be predictable based on the assumption of a stable "multiplier" connecting it to base money.[2]

The monetary base consists of cash and reserves, $M_0 = C + R$. The monetary aggregate consists of cash and demandable deposit money, $M_1 = C + D$. The nonbank public holds a proportion w of its monetary balances in cash, so $C = wM_1$ and $D = (1 - w)M_1$. Reserves are connected to deposits by the reserve requirement fraction, $R = \rho D$, assuming no excess reserves are held, so we have $R = \rho(1 - w)M_1$. We can now express the relationship between the monetary base and the monetary aggregate as

$$M_0 = C + R = wM_1 + \rho(1 - w)M_1 = M_1[w + \rho(1 - w)]$$

so that $M_1 = \mu_1 M_0$, where $\mu_1 = [w + \rho(1 - w)]^{-1}$ is the reserve *multiplier*. If you know the fraction of money balances held as cash w and the reserve requirement fraction ρ, you can compute the multiplier.

The same logic works for broader aggregates, so long as each component of the aggregate is subject to its own reserve requirement. Labeling different kinds of deposits $D_1, \ldots, D_n$, reserve fractions $\rho_1, \ldots, \rho_n$, and assigning weights $w_0, w_1, \ldots, w_n$ to cash and deposits which sum to one, the multiplier becomes $\mu_n = [w_0 + \rho_1 w_1 + \cdots + \rho_n w_n]^{-1}$. Ostensibly, the central bank can set the reserve fractions, but it must now rely on the stability of the distribution of money holdings to a much greater extent if a broad aggregate is to be controlled by adjusting the monetary base.

Control over the monetary base is difficult to achieve. Cash demand is difficult to forecast. Reserve demand forecasts are complicated by autonomous factors such as movements in the government's current account at the central bank, demand for excess reserves, and bank use of central bank standing facilities. Errors in control over the base propagate through errors in computing the multiplier, which would depend on stability in the composition of money demand, even if the central bank were to enact more reserve requirements than the banking system has seen or tolerated in recent history.

Targeting Divisia Money

Let us take another look at the problem. Suppose the monetary aggregate being targeted is a Divisia aggregate. The evolution of the Divisia aggregate is given by

$$\ln g_t = \sum_{i \in A} \bar{s}_{it} \ln f_{it}$$

where the f_{it} are the log growth rates of the monetary components and the $\bar{s}_{it}$ are the growth factor weights. The growth factor weights are two-period averages of

$$s_{it} = p_{it} q_{it} / \sum_{j \in A} p_{jt} q_{jt}$$

which weight the outstanding quantities q_{it} by their user cost $p_{it} = R_t - r_{it}$. We are now well beyond a tractable formula linking the target aggregate to the monetary base. Yet we can continue to imagine a policy regime in which control over a monetary aggregate is maintained.

The potential control variables for a Divisia aggregate include the component quantities q_{it} and the interest rates R_t and r_{it}. It seems best to take R as given and assume that interest rates on monetary liabilities r_{it} are left to the market. Bank competition for deposits and the demand for monetary services will determine the user costs p_{it}.

That leaves control of the quantities. In a large aggregate, the list of quantities q_{it} can be dauntingly long, but relatively few are consequential at any time. Demand and savings deposits invariably dominate, followed by cash and money market funds. Each of these has a clear origin in the banking system, at the central bank, and in the capital markets, respectively. Thus, it may be possible to control the evolution of a Divisia aggregate reasonably well with three controls operating through each institutional locus. Of these three, control of bank money is undoubtedly the most important.

We propose a simple framework for the control of broad money growth using bank capital as the policy instrument. The linkage between bank capital and bank money comprises the following elements:

1. A *lending reaction function*. The lending reaction function recognizes that new loan origination takes time and does not depend solely on the availability of capital. The availability of bankable projects is further constrained by interest rates, collateral, equity, and other observable and unobservable factors. Accordingly, it will take time for new loan principal to emerge in response to accumulated capital, with the rate depending on a potentially long list of variables. In addition, there is lending that has already been underwritten but whose timing is uncertain. Contingent credit lines may be drawn at the option of the borrower at any time within the term of the credit facility. This behavior must also be anticipated. An estimate of the lending reaction function lets us forecast how loan principal will emerge over various horizons in response to new capital, given the level of interest rates and other information concerning the state of the economy.

2. An *amortization forecast*. Loan amortization destroys deposit money. Some amortization is easily forecastable: loans generally have an amortization schedule, which performing borrowers respect. Performing borrowers may voluntarily prepay principal as well, reducing the principal balance below its scheduled level or eliminating it all together. Non-performing borrowers, conversely, will not amortize principal on schedule. If no further payments are made, principal will be repaid in a lump sum when any collateral supporting the loan is liquidated. Principal not repaid from liquidation will be repaid from bank reserves and/or capital, completing the unscheduled amortization. Loan performance, prepayment, default, and liquidation may each be modeled as a function of interest rates, credit-related variables, and the state of the economy.

3. A *monetary liability transition matrix* that models how balances migrate between different forms of money, and especially how newly created deposit money migrates to other forms of money. Combining the lending reaction function with an amortization forecast results in an estimate of the net change in deposit money. The new deposit money provides maximal monetary services. Not all of these monetary services will be needed. Downstream recipients of deposit money will decide how much monetary services to retain and how much to give up in exchange for interest, based on interest rates and the state of the economy. The monetary liability transition matrix forecasts the distribution of net money creation by the banking system across components of the money supply. The most challenging component to forecast will be

balances held in cash and store-of-value money like MMFs and repos, which depend on supply and demand factors outside of the banking system.

The framework leads from changes in bank capital to net deposit money creation and the disposition of money balances across all forms of monetary liabilities. Each element may be estimated from abundantly available data, and supplemented by expert judgment and ongoing learning. Estimates would ideally be developed at the bank level, perhaps with banks participating in the forecasting process themselves.

The three elements of this framework connect changes in bank capital to changes in each component of the broad money supply (f_{it}, q_{it}) over a chosen horizon. Hence, given market interest rates and the state of the economy, one can anticipate the growth rate of a Divisia aggregate corresponding to a given increase in bank capital. The basic framework is easy to grasp and not harder to implement (in principle) than the historical central bank framework targeting equilibrium in the reserve market.

To control the growth rate of broad money, then, one must forecast and control the growth rate of bank capital. The capital constraint is at once our most powerful lever in controlling the growth rate of broad money and the greatest risk to the neutrality of broad money growth.

We argued in Chapter 10 that Federal Reserve policy following the GFC regulated the growth rate of broad money by controlling capital distributions in this way. The Dodd-Frank stress testing regime and the Federal Reserve's CCAR process created a gating process for capital distributions run by the Federal Reserve as the primary regulator of the banking system. Though the process was not without controversy, the banking system rebuilt its capital over the 2010s, and broad money grew at a reliably steady rate.

Bank capital increases by a bank's net interest margin (NIM) and is reduced by non-interest expense, loss provisioning, and distributions to shareholders. Drechsler et al. (2018)[3] document that NIM is surprisingly stable, fluctuating within a range of 2.2%–3.8% since 1955, despite short-term interest rates ranging from 0% to 16%. Accordingly, the rate at which bank capital grows can be predicted with confidence.[4]

Restrictions on bank capital distributions are a potential policy tool for controlling the expansion of banking system capital and broad money growth. Reducing distributions (dividends and share repurchases) keeps more capital in the system, permitting more rapid loan growth rates, while increasing the amount of permitted dividends can slow loan growth by bleeding capital from the system. We imagine the bank regulators would set a ceiling and floor for capital distributions. Banks would advise on their distribution plans and seek the regulator's approval. Changes to the distribution limits can be made cyclically, increasing ceilings when NIMs are elevated above long-term averages and lowering the limits when NIMs are depressed.

Reserve Management

If the central bank no longer uses the interbank rate as a policy instrument nor uses the monetary base to regulate broad money, what does it do as monopoly issuer of reserves? In the new operating regime, the central bank will keep the overnight rate on loans of reserve money within a narrow target band around short-term market interest rates. It will conduct open-market operations to change the supply of reserves accordingly. The operations needed to achieve these outcomes are well-known from the pre-GFC era. What is different is their passivity. The central bank will passively follow market rates, rather than attempt to align market rates with an exogenous policy rate.[5]

Passively following market interest rates is still an interest rate policy of sorts. It is an interest rate policy in which there is very little divergence between the equilibrium rate and the interbank rate. The stance of monetary policy will no longer be communicated by the difference between the policy rate and the unobservable equilibrium rate. Whether monetary policy is loose or tight will depend on the controls in effect for bank capital distributions.

Work must be done to return the interbank market for borrowing and lending reserves to a functioning state. Our proposal in the following section for a QE sinking fund would leave behind a central bank with a reasonably sized balance sheet supplying reserves to the banking system, where reserves are actively borrowed and lent between banks.

Standing Facilities

Short-term interbank rates can be volatile, particularly when there are short-term spikes in demand for interbank liquidity. While such spikes cannot be eliminated, their peaks may be shaved with the aid of well-designed standing liquidity facilities at the central bank. Such facilities allow banks to swap a menu of assets for reserve money subject to haircuts on asset values and at a penalty interest rate. Rather than define the penalty rate as a spread over a policy rate, it will be a spread over the reference market rate followed to accommodate the interbank market. The spread puts a provisional upper bound on rate spikes.

The liquidity regulations added in Basel III foisted a self-help liquidity regime on the banking system, requiring banks to stand prepared to liquidate large shares of their on- and off-balance sheet liabilities without recourse to central bank facilities. The balance sheet space given over to liquidity portfolios to comply with the new requirements amounted to some 10% of bank assets, coming almost entirely at the expense of loan volumes. Surely, the banking system can insure itself in 99% of adverse liquidity scenarios with far fewer resources than those required for 100% insurance, relying on standing facilities at the central bank for the worst 1% of outcomes. When weighing the potential cost of such facilities against the productivity of new bank lending, some willingness to incur costs on standing facilities is justified.[6]

Standing liquidity facilities should be rule-based, broad-based, and stigma-free apart from the penalty rates and haircuts at which they are accessed. The Fed's discount window is a broad-based facility, but its use has always carried a stigma because it is taken as a signal of mismanagement, and the names of its users are published. Its use invites bank runs rather than arresting them. Instead, we want standing facilities that allow banks to continue making prudent loans without the fear that they will be unable to settle short-term obligations in periods of distress.

Haircuts for standing facilities should be comprehensive and announced well in advance so banks can access their ability to raise funds as their portfolios evolve, allowing the central bank to become a "pawnbroker for all seasons," in Mervyn King's phrase.[7] The desire for easily administered facilities favors the use of pledged securities to raise funds. Central banks should similarly investigate and deploy standardized terms for advancing funds against performing loan portfolios, secured by net interest income. For example, insured mortgages underwritten to GSE guidelines could be pledged without requiring them to be securitized in agency MBS. While few banks would prefer raising funds by this avenue, it would allow highly distressed banks to remain going concerns in exchange for granting something like preferred equity to the government via the central bank. It would also bring the Federal Reserve regime into line with the FHLB advancing system, which should be integrated with Federal Reserve facilities.

Overall, we imagine an operational framework for central bank policy that is more structural than strategic. Policy will establish conditions according to which the money supply can grow evenly and at a predictable rate over longer horizons. Such a regime will not lurch from monetary policy meeting to monetary policy meeting or hang on every word of a silver-tongued central banker. It will leave most of the work to banks and capital markets to establish the quantity and price of money that is compatible with the state of technology and the potential output of the economy. We may even find that we no longer miss the monetary policy shocks generated by the central bank, which are as likely to cause a recession as to cure one.

Monitoring the Distributional Impact of Broad Money Growth

In Chapter 11, we argued that monetary policy should strive to avoid creating imbalances in economic activity and inflation across segments of the economy. While we are not inclined to recommend setting money growth targets at a segment level, we believe it is essential to monitor outcomes at that level to enforce the neutrality of monetary policy.

Accordingly, we imagine that the authorities will set a target for aggregate broad money growth that is consistent with a low rate of inflation and the potential growth rate of the economy. At the sectoral level, private money growth and the monetary impact of fiscal policy should be monitored using sector-specific Divisia indices. The demand system framework of Chapter 11 can be used to evaluate the contribution of money to income, expenditure, and inflation relative to monetary policy targets, technical developments in the sector, and factors influencing credit rationing.

If a sectoral imbalance is spotted, how should the authorities intervene? The proper course of action should be evaluated on a case-by-case basis. The most effective intervention may take the form of fiscal policy changes, structural interventions in credit markets, a temporary adjustment to credit risk weights, or a decision to tolerate the outcome because of an idiosyncratic growth dynamic. Developing the requisite instrumentation to be able to measure distortions of this kind is a worthy goal in itself. We would particularly like to see monetary policy monitored at the industry level and across households stratified by wealth.

Fixing Bank Regulation

Fixing bank regulation begins with fixing the universal banking firm. We see the divorce of commercial and investment banking as a more elegant solution than a more complicated regime of regulation, corporate governance, and competition enforcement. After splitting the businesses and their regulatory structures, we are still confronted with the task of reforming commercial bank regulation. We propose three main reforms.

First, the credit risk weights that are applied to calculating bank capital adequacy favor certain categories of assets. Categories which carry lower risk weights are "cheaper" for a capital-constrained bank to pursue in the absence of significant return differentials. The artificial prices created for different types of lending by bank capital regulation distort the allocation of credit and economic activity. Following, we describe a solution to the design of credit risk weights that removes their influence on credit allocation, aligning with our overarching goal of neutrality.

Second, we see obvious inefficiency in the self-help liquidity regime decreed by Basel III. Pre-positioning immense resources at every bank to manage a GFC-level liquidity crisis without central bank support is an unnecessary tax on the entire system. It would be better to design institutions through which banks could access standing facilities at the central bank to meet extraordinary and temporary liquidity needs. We also discuss evidence suggesting that bank failures are most commonly traceable to insolvency rather than illiquidity, undermining a key argument for regulators' fixation on liquidity regulation.

Third, bank regulation relies too much on risk management and not enough on the integrity of banks' underwriting and pricing policies. If banks are better at originating good loans and pricing risks appropriately *ex ante*, there should be fewer risks to react to *ex post*.

If we can revise credit risk weight-setting and transition from a self-help regime of liquidity management to standing central bank facilities, the existing Basel system of bank regulation can be moved away from its current, prescriptive bent toward the vision of economic capital management glimpsed in Basel II. Some degree of international harmonization can persist without Basel's tendencies to favor certain kinds of lending. The existing regime will also serve as useful scaffolding for building up a regime of capital regulation for investment banks.

Splitting the Banking Book and the Trading Book

Banking and capital market business cannot both be managed optimally when both are capitalized by a single pool of equity. Getting both institutions to discharge their economic roles effectively cannot be achieved by market discipline, by any unified corporate governance scheme, or by an ever-more complicated system of universal bank regulation. The activity supported by a marginal dollar of capital in a capital markets business will almost always be more profitable and realize cash returns more quickly than it will within a large commercial bank. Universal banks will therefore remain well-incentivized to continue cannibalizing projects from their commercial banking business. As we have repeatedly emphasized, global savings are much better used funding actual risk-taking in equity markets or capitalizing actual banks rather than by creating miniature securitized banks for narrow clienteles. Investment banking must be split off from commercial banking. Doing so would pave the way for better capitalized trading book operations, allowing investment banks to raise more capital without raising doubts about the solvency of a commercial banking subsidiary.

That the largest institutions have not already split themselves can be attributed to several factors. Owners may doubt that the trading book business would be so generously capitalized on a standalone basis. They may enjoy the comfort of blending volatile financial results of trading with the steady profits of lending business, an attachment to the liquidity offered by a captive internal bank, or the ability to use the banking book as a hostage when excessive trading risk threatens the business. None of these are good reasons to keep investment banks attached to commercial banks. The notion that a holding company containing an investment bank will be a source of strength for a commercial bank in a time of distress is also highly questionable. In most other industries, conglomeration has been considered a squandering of senior management's focus and a disservice to investors. After splitting the businesses, investors who wish to obtain the return profile of a universal bank can simply hold both commercial bank and investment bank shares in their portfolios, with weights that reflect their desired risk exposures.

It would be wise for some kind of capital regulation to remain in place for the trading business once it is split from commercial banking.[8] There is a public interest in sound derivatives, rates trading, and securitization markets, among other activities that currently live on the capital markets side of universal banks.[9] The sudden collapse of a major dealer bank would still reverberate throughout the world financial system to the detriment of everyone. However, the regulation of such trading book activities can be far less burdensome because investment bank losses will no longer directly threaten the redemption of deposits in a commercial banking business. It may even be possible to pull significant business back into a regulated investment banking environment from private equity, hedge funds, and the wider shadow banking system once the potential for banking crises is removed from the equation.

The new FRTB regulations would provide an exemplary model for trading book capital were they not calibrated to the conditions prevailing immediately after the collapse of Lehman Brothers. Thanks to the reforms of the Dodd-Frank Act, the risk of a second Lehman Brothers-level event must be assigned a very slim chance.

Among the positive aspects of the FRTB regulations is that they condition a bank's ability to use internal models on the observability of risk factors, and that observability must be proven continuously. In other words, a bank can model the dynamics of risk in its trading book using any predictor it likes, so long as changes in that predictor can be observed with the aid of market prices.[10] Requiring observability prevents risk measurements from being tethered to arbitrary parameters and ensures that risk measurements do not become opaque if trading slows. FRTB further requires that internal models explain a large share of variation in the bank's accounting profit and loss, which puts pressure on banks to update their valuations promptly. Both requirements are excellent correctives to internal risk modeling which should allow capital regulation to rely more heavily on internal models.

The unanswered questions about competition and governance we raised in Chapter 12 can be evaluated and answered more effectively following a divorce of the trading book from the banking book. We expect that product innovation and differentiation will become a bigger feature of the competitive landscape in banking, and that platform competition between financial intermediaries will be less of a muddle. Corporate governance can be more precisely calibrated to the economic roles of each institution.

Neutral Credit Risk Weights

Standardized credit risk weights for bank capital favor consumer exposures over commercial exposures, property-based lending over lending based on other assets, and larger entities over smaller ones.[11] When credit risk weights are set with the aid of VaR or expected shortfall models, the ranking of risk weights follows the relative performance of asset categories in adverse economic scenarios, which again reinforces the ordering of risks prescribed by the standardized risk weights. It is not obvious that a profit-maximizing bank would make portfolio decisions based on these criteria. The divergence between the economic allocation that would be chosen by the bank and the allocation that is optimal under the regulator's risk weighting scheme changes the distribution of monetary growth, with consequences for the distribution of inflation and growth rates across economic domains.

It turns out that minimum levels of capital can be enforced by a regulator without deviating from the bank's efficient choice of loan allocation or being blind to differences in performance across classes of loans. The key, as shown by Paul Glasserman and Wanmo Kang, is to align risk weights to the risk-adjusted excess returns of various loan types.[12] The allocation-neutral risk weights can be found using straightforward mathematical tools. Most of the math is in the appendix at the end of this chapter. We explain here for those who will take us at our word.

The management of a bank's balance sheet may be framed as a portfolio optimization problem in the spirit pioneered by Harry Markowitz. Investors like excess returns above the risk-free rate, but dislike risk. If returns are jointly distributed according to a multivariate normal distribution, their properties are completely described by the excess return μ and the variance-covariance matrix Σ.[13] The investor's problem is thus to choose an allocation x that maximizes

$$\mu'x - \frac{\gamma}{2}x'\Sigma x$$

where γ is a parameter that expresses how much the investor dislikes risk. Both μ and x are vectors and Σ is a matrix, but the objective being maximized is just a scalar (a number).

Banks are not investors simply buying and selling securities, so it is worth dwelling a bit on what x is and the circumstances under which the bank's opportunity set can be represented by μ and Σ. Organizing the data in vector and matrix form assumes that the bank's business can be grouped into a not-too-long list of product types, which is a commonly maintained assumption in management, reporting, and capital regulation. Within each of these product lines, the number of loans, securities, off-balance sheet commitments, etc. is large enough that their (marginal) financial outcomes converge toward a continuous probability distribution reasonably well-approximated by the normal distribution, while their joint outcomes are reasonably well-modeled by their volatilities and pairwise correlations. Again, these are commonly maintained assumptions, and there are relatively few joint probability models that can compete with the multivariate normal for tractability and interpretability. Hence, we are fairly comfortable discussing the outcomes of a small number of business lines in terms of their mean expected returns and their associated covariance matrix.

Expected returns for each bank business line include interest earnings and/or fees net of loss reserves, operational costs, and funding costs. Each of these is easily attributed on a business line level, though some amount of overhead expense will have to be allocated according to management judgment. Loans will have lower funding costs, as deposit funding created by the bank will supply funds at low cost. Securities are financed out of the bank's own funds using debt and equity, with additional leverage potentially coming from repo markets. The relatively higher funding cost of securities is compensated by lower operational costs and loss reserving, which can be substantial for loans. Thus, with some accounting effort, returns on bank business lines can be evaluated on equal footing and decent assumptions made about their variances and covariances. Some residual balance sheet items like cash, reserves, and high-quality government bonds may be treated as risk-free assets, with their share controlled by the parameter γ.[14]

For new lending products, one can begin by assuming that excess returns will be close to (and correlated with) those of adjacent products.[15] The variance of excess returns should begin from an inflated value to reflect uncertainty about the new product's performance. As results become available, risk and return parameters can be re-estimated. It would be wise to continue inflating variances for an initial period to avoid erroneous conclusions about risk.[16]

With the problem set up in this way, x may be interpreted as the amount of assets in the bank's home currency allocated to each business line. The source of funds for x includes the relevant mix of deposits, wholesale funding and regulatory capital. We can form the bank's risk-weighted assets by collecting each business line's risk weight into a vector w, and require that $w'x$ exceed some minimal prudential level. Regulators are assumed to set an upper bound η on the bank portfolio's standard deviation, and to require the bank's equity to be at least as large as some percentage β of its risk-weighted assets. Thus, if we require *equity* > $\beta w'x$, then $\kappa = \beta^{-1} \cdot$ *equity* is the upper bound on risk-weighted assets. We assume equity is given and constant for purposes of determining κ.[17]

We know the solution to the bank's unconstrained maximization problem is

$$x^o = \frac{1}{\gamma}\Sigma^{-1}\mu$$

where one can see that larger values of γ will scale down allocations to risky assets encompassed in the opportunity set $\{\mu, \Sigma\}$. We can also work out (see Appendix 14.A) the allocation that is optimal under the regulator's risk preferences

$$x_r = \frac{\eta}{\sqrt{\mu'\Sigma^{-1}\mu}}\Sigma^{-1}\mu$$

and the allocation that will be optimal for the bank when constrained by credit risk weights

$$x_c = \frac{1}{\gamma}\Sigma^{-1}\mu - \frac{1}{\gamma}\frac{(w'\Sigma^{-1}\mu - \gamma\kappa)^+}{w'\Sigma^{-1}w}\Sigma^{-1}w$$

We can see that the regulator's preferred allocation x_r replaces the bank's risk preferences γ^{-1} with the regulator's risk preferences $\left(\frac{\sqrt{\mu'\Sigma^{-1}\mu}}{\eta}\right)^{-1}$. Under the regulator's chosen risk weights, the bank's preferred allocation x_c is the same as its unconstrained optimal allocation if $\gamma\kappa \geq w'\Sigma^{-1}\mu$ (the risk capital weights are not a binding constraint) but is otherwise scaled down by the second term in the expression, which depends on the vector of risk weights.

The question at hand is whether there is any vector of risk weights w^o that implements the regulator's risk preferences such that the bank's portfolio allocation under the regulator's risk weights is proportional to the allocation it would choose under its own preferences, x_c. If such weights exist, the requirement for the bank to hold a minimum of regulatory capital can be enforced without creating an uneconomic allocation of credit or inefficiently influencing the split between loans and securities on the bank's balance sheet.

Glasserman and Kang show that a neutral set of risk weights does exist. Instead of being proportional to the *risk* of different business lines, which is the common point of reference when "calibrating" risk weights, the neutral risk weights are proportional to μ, the *expected returns* for each business line. Thus, $w^o = \alpha\mu$ for some scaling factor α are optimal and neutral credit risk weights. Glasserman and Kang show the result holds when asset allocations are constrained to be long-only (non-negative), for more general risk measures than Σ, and when banks have access to heterogeneous opportunity sets $\{\mu_i, \Sigma_i\}$.

We can work out the value of α that implements the regulator's risk constraint by substituting $w = \alpha\mu$ into x_c and setting the result equal to x_r (see Appendix 14.A):

$$\alpha = \frac{\kappa}{\eta\sqrt{\mu'\Sigma^{-1}\mu}} = \frac{equity}{\beta\eta^2} \cdot \frac{\eta}{\sqrt{\mu'\Sigma^{-1}\mu}}$$

The final expression represents α as the product of two terms. The second is the scaling factor implied by the regulator's risk preferences. The first represents the upper bound of risk-weighted assets in units of variance, evaluated at the regulator's preferred variance bound η^2. Thus, α gives the bank a risk-weighted asset "budget" scaled according to the regulator's risk preferences.

The question naturally arises whether regulators can observe μ at the bank or system level sufficiently well to set w^o. Glasserman and Kang show that μ and Σ can be approached through an iterative scheme.

Glasserman and Kang's analysis rests on the assumption that bank equity and the regulatory capital budget established by the risk weights are the only binding constraints faced by the bank. In our discussion of the bank's optimization problem in Chapter 5, we conceived of the bank's portfolio decision being subject to many additional constraints. The availability of suitable lending opportunities, collateral, and borrower equity also constrain loan origination and bank balance sheets. Hence, we explore a bit beyond Glasserman and Kang to ask whether w^o continues to be neutral when the baseline portfolio allocation problem also includes binding constraints on x from above which are unobservable to the regulator.

The solution is easy to work out intuitively. If any constraint binds from above there is at least one element of x (say, x_i) that is equal to the bound at the optimum, so we have $x_i = \tau$ for some constant τ. In the absence of the constraint, the bank would choose $\bar{x}_i > \tau$. When the regulator prescribes risk weights, all elements of x will be scaled down by a common factor, including $\bar{x}_i$. As a result, x_i will be scaled down by less than the other elements of x, and may potentially remain at $x_i = \tau$. Thus, the bank's allocation to business line i will increase on a relative basis in the presence of risk weights versus its allocation in the absence of risk weights.

Is this a problem? Under the regulator's risk weights, the bank increases its relative allocation to x_i not because it is gaming the system, but because its reduced risk budget introduces some slack relative to the constraint binding from above. Glasserman and Kang's result remains neutral in this case because the non-regulatory constraint would also bind in an unregulated scenario.

Liquidity Risk Management

In the above framework, the high-quality liquid assets (HQLA) required by Basel III's liquidity regulations will be those with small excess returns, low variances, and minimal correlation with risky assets. Allocations to HQLA will increase if the regulator reduces the variance bound η^2, just as they would for larger γ in the unconstrained portfolio problem. Credit risk weights already imply a certain proportion of HQLA holdings. Adding requirements on top of that would imply the regulator wants the bank to choose risky assets as if it had a larger risk budget than when it chooses safe assets, which seems counterproductive.

The opportunity cost of additional HQLA requirements is a proportional loss of lending and securities holdings. These restrictions weigh adversely on bank profitability and sacrifice growth and productivity gains that can be obtained with efficient lending. When these potential benefits are weighed against the administrative costs of maintaining standing liquidity facilities at the central bank, it is difficult to justify the self-help liquidity regime of Basel III.

The adverse treatment of corporate deposits under Basel III is also needlessly punitive and biased against credit creation for the corporate sector. Whether they are initiated by corporate or retail deposit holders, bank runs are caused by fears of insolvency rather than a lack of liquidity.[18] Incremental holdings of HQLA will do relatively little to arrest the risk of bank runs, apart from artificially lowering the volatility of bank earnings.

We would prefer to jettison the liquidity regulations of Basel III. When excess reserve balances can be drained from the interbank market, returning to a simple and binding reserve requirement would be useful in stabilizing interbank lending rates.

Underwriting, Pricing, and Innovation

Transitioning to a system of risk weights based on profitability shifts regulatory emphasis from worst case outcomes to *pricing*. In competitive markets for bank lending, additional profits earned by banks must be compensation for additional risk. The optimization models underneath the Glasserman-Kang analysis incorporate risk via the variance-covariance matrix for expected returns. If a bank chooses to overweight some form of lending or investment in its portfolio, it must be earning some excess return not accounted for in the risk measure. In a multivariate normal model, the extra compensation might be for a tail risk not captured in the covariance matrix. However, even in more general models of risk, an excess allocation suggests some premium is being earned in excess of the risk that has been measured. Is this a free lunch, evidence of market power, or a chimera that arises when risk models are incomplete?

In a world that relies on "big data" and a regulatory regime populated by accountants, it is important to remember that some component of lending and investment risk remains, by its nature, unobservable. The incomplete observability of risk is what creates the phenomenon of credit rationing, as we explained back in Chapter 3. Rationing results in a subset of borrowers obtaining credit from an observationally equivalent population. So, how does the bank decide who is rationed and who is not? One way would be to have a lottery among all qualified borrowers. However, a more likely way is for the bank to decide based on some criterion outside the set of information that makes those borrowers observationally equivalent. These criteria, which loan officers refer to vaguely as "character," serve to further differentiate the population of potential borrowers. They are observable to the banker, but not the risk management team. The bank must price the unobservable character of the borrower as well as the observable characteristics of the loan if the bank is to be compensated properly for risk. As a further precaution, the risk-return ratios of all business lines should be shrunken toward a grand mean, limiting the amount by which any business line can diverge from overall performance.

We cannot simply assume the efficiency of loan pricing. To convince ourselves one way or the other, prudential focus must shift to *underwriting*, which receives far less regulatory attention than risk management. Increased expectations for underwriting capture risks at origination, rather than at the point of deterioration or default. Expecting risk management to compensate bad underwriting is like expecting the healthcare profession to extend average lifespans when society otherwise provides increasingly unsafe levels of nutrition, pollution, hazards, and violence.

How does one price the unobservable? Underwriters must have a sense of how well their underwriting criteria explain the variation in *ex post* borrower performance. Every underwriting process will have some error rate associated with it. The question is whether underwriting can reduce the error rate sufficiently to make loans available with an acceptable risk premium. Such questions must be answered with a combination of data and judgment. While bank directors can be liable for reckless underwriting, management judgment could be exposed to more scrutiny to further promote responsible behavior.

Whereas regulators have generally focused on banks' risk management capabilities and have been willing to offer more generous risk budgets to banks with strong abilities in this area, we would like to suggest rebalancing attention toward pricing and underwriting capabilities. A bank which can demonstrate discipline and competence in managing risk-based pricing and controlling error rates *ex ante* in a rational framework aligned with management's risk appetite and theses about the economy will have fewer *ex post* risk management problems to solve. As regulators will struggle to evaluate banks' lending programs independently and banks will be reluctant to share pricing details, the challenge of supervising underwriting is to create incentives that encourage banks to do the work, along with simple performance indicators that regulators can trust but verify.

Using Savings More Efficiently

Much of Part Three has been devoted to pondering how savings become so abundant that debt capital markets could eat the business of banks and generate falling interest rates. To the global saving glut famously identified by Ben Bernanke we have appended the saving glut of the wealthiest households and the saving glut of a more concentrated corporate sector. We were surprised to see that these actors were so risk-averse despite their enormous wealth, contrary to economic intuition about the diminishing marginal utility of wealth. We also pointed a finger at universal banks, which were content to see banking business migrate into the "trading book," where it would earn a superior return on capital. The result of this confluence was enormous growth in debt capital markets, as well as a lost opportunity to redistribute equity capital to investable projects with greater return potential.

To use savings more efficiently, we propose reducing the government's borrowing footprint, shrinking the Federal Reserve's balance sheet, and building more vigorous equity capital markets.

Reducing Government's Footprint in the Capital Markets

The U.S. government and its agencies occupy a disproportionate footprint in the global debt capital markets. At the end of 2023, there was $140.7 trillion outstanding in global fixed income markets. Debt issued by U.S. entities accounted for $55.3 trillion (39.3%) of the total, of which $37.7 trillion was public sector debt.[19] Subtracting $26.4 trillion in outstanding Treasury debt leaves $11.3 trillion in agency debt, which includes MBS issued by Fannie Mae and Freddie Mac, debt issued by Fannie Mae and Freddie Mac, and obligations issued by the FHLB system. These government-sponsored enterprises thus channel more than $10 trillion in global savings to projects which could be funded more efficiently by the banking system and the central bank.

In Chapter 9, we lamented that so many prototypically bankable projects were lost to the banking system due to U.S. housing policy. Since the 1970s, the commercial banking system has consistently lost share in aggregate mortgage lending because of the mortgage GSEs' stunning expansion. Bank regulations favoring liquid agency MBS over mortgage loans made the retain-or-sell decision a no-brainer for banks originating mortgages. The trend toward preferring MBS over mortgages accelerated in the 1990s and 2000s as universal banks built up their capital markets divisions and designed their own securitization structures for mortgages that could not be sold to the mortgage GSEs.

In Chapter 9, we also began to sketch a gradualist solution for the mortgage GSEs. Rather than fully funding the purchase of mortgage loans from bank originators, the mortgage GSEs could provide risk transfer services. Mortgage loans would remain on the balance sheets of originating banks. Credit risk could be transferred to the mortgage GSEs through a standard-form insurance contract. To the extent that the banks are unable to transfer unwanted interest rate risk through existing markets, the mortgage GSEs could assume interest rate risk on mortgages through derivatives. The lost liquidity of a mortgage-backed security could be compensated by central bank facilities for advances against GSE-guaranteed mortgages. Such reforms would isolate the risk transfers involved in government housing support from volume of turnover, as well as the funding channeled into mortgages. The mortgage GSEs could concentrate on pricing risks properly—developing actuarially fair mortgage insurance rates and prices for interest rate derivatives—rather than enabling gigantic securitization operations.

The maximalist solution for the mortgage GSEs is of course to wind them down all together. In this case, our gradualist solution would be a useful intermediate step. Once the extent of risk transfer from residential housing markets to the government is made visible, decisions can be made about how much risk to accept. It would not be advisable to privatize them without first severing them completely from housing policy and government support. Were the mortgage GSEs to disappear, it should be regarded as a success story: the measures that were needed to develop mortgage markets in the 1960s and 1970s are no longer needed because we have now accumulated the needed expertise to extend mortgage credit to a substantial share of the population.

On a smaller scale—which nevertheless approaches a trillion dollars—the FHLB system channels capital market funds into the banking system. They pursue a barbell strategy. On one hand, the FHLBs make overnight loans to the U.S. branches of non-U.S. banks through the interbank market, earning slightly less than the interest rate on reserves paid by the Federal Reserve. On the other hand, the FHLBs extend lifelines to smaller U.S. banks in the form of term loans secured by swathes of assets. The problem with these activities is not that they are inherently bad, but that they can be done more efficiently and transparently by the central bank. The Federal Reserve has expanded facilities to make dollar liquidity available to foreign official institutions; surely some effort can be made to connect them to U.S. branches of non-U.S. banks as well. And there would be merit in ceding the FHLB's unofficial lender of last resort activity to the official lender of last resort. FHLB lending offers a model for standing facilities based on loan collateral, whereas the Federal Reserve has invariably preferred securities collateral.

Unwinding the Federal Reserve Balance Sheet

The other domain where the government has disproportionate influence in the debt capital markets is on the post-QE balance sheet of the Federal Reserve. The Fed is not alone in this regard. Most developed country central banks have seen their balance sheets swell since the GFC, none more than Japan. Central banks the world over must plot a course toward more normal balance sheets without tanking markets for their government's debt.

The large balance sheet was monetary policy itself in the post-GFC era. Now that the case for keeping long-term interest rates depressed is no longer in evidence, large central bank balance sheets are a heavy vestige impeding everyday policy implementation. The problem of balance sheet reduction is even more urgent because the world's largest central banks are producing enormous fiscal losses (in the hundreds of billions of dollars). Persistently inverted yield curves and enormous balance sheets suggest interest paid on reserves will exceed earnings on bond portfolios and losses will continue for a long time. And if yield curves normalize because long-term rates rise—contrary to the dominant assumption that short-term rates will eventually fall—central bank losses will crystallize rapidly as the values of their long-term bond holdings collapse. Whether it happens fast or slow, this era of central banking will end with enormous fiscal losses. We are concerned with how these losses can be minimized, as well as the transition to an operating model with fewer unintended consequences and a stronger claim on neutrality. Though releasing most of the Fed's securities portfolio into the markets will consume aggregate savings, it will remove the pricing distortions created by past unconventional monetary policy.

Central bank losses can be stemmed by shrinking balance sheets and paying less interest on fewer liabilities. There is little prospect of the central bank achieving either goal on its own in a reasonable amount of time. Selling trillions in assets would take trillions of dollars out of circulation, tightening the money supply and prompting deflation, recession, or both.[20] Eliminating interest on trillions in bank reserves would send banks piling into other assets that qualify as HQLA, potentially at rates below the floor of the central bank corridor.[21]

The best course of action is to explicitly realize and fiscalize central bank losses rather than allow central banks to speculate on their ability to trade out of their bond portfolios. The fiscal authority should set up a separate "bad central bank"—we might call it a "QE sinking fund"—which acquires excess assets from the central bank. The QE sinking fund will be financed by issuing a new series of short-term bills which are general obligations of the government. These new bills will be auctioned in periodic tranches to commercial banks and other participants in the reserve market. As banks trade their reserves for bills, the QE sinking fund will obtain funds to purchase bonds from the central bank at market prices. Sinking fund bond purchases will redeem and destroy reserves by returning them to their issuer. Auctions of bills will continue until the banking system reaches its desired quantity of reserves and bills, simultaneously solving for the optimal size of the QE sinking fund and the legacy central bank balance sheet.

The QE sinking fund removes the size of the central bank's balance sheet as a constraint on future policy actions and allows the banking system to swap reserves for another interest-earning security at market rates. These actions will bring the market for reserves into line with reserve demand, which is an important step toward restoring a functional interbank lending market. Indeed, the reserve market will be "tight" once again when reserves may be borrowed and lent at rates close to the sinking fund bill rate. And because the government, central bank, and banking system are transacting among themselves, there will be no immediate impact on the money supply or the net government debt in the hands of the public.

The primary risk in the transaction is that the banking system trades collusively or holds up the QE sinking fund when short-term debt issues are to be rolled over. Such risk can be mitigated through good market design, and (if necessary) by putting a floor beneath bank holdings of the newly issued securities, similar to a reserve requirement. MMFs may also become important bidders for the new bills, allowing the nonbank public to absorb some of the debt as store-of-value money.

The mission of the QE sinking fund will be to shrink its balance sheet prudently and quickly. Sinking fund purchases of bonds from the central bank will allow the embedded losses in the central bank portfolio to be valued at market rates. In between subsequent auctions of bonds, the sinking fund may put its portfolio out for bids, selling its holdings whenever a minimum density of bids is obtained and the value of the transaction is acceptable.[22] Realized sales will reduce the volume of bills to be rolled over in the next auction. The process would allow an essentially passive and market-driven wind-down of the QE sinking fund. Once it reaches some minimal size, the sinking fund can simply be wound up, with its obligations retired and the remainder of its portfolio sold at prevailing market prices. The sinking fund's charter should automatically terminate once the fund is wound up. In this way, the problem of balance sheet reduction can be separated from the central bank's problem of transitioning to a sustainable operating model.

Unfinished Business

Our analysis of the savings gluts of the wealthiest households and the largest businesses shows that inattention to distribution of income comes back to bite in the form of capital market anomalies. The deep development of securitization markets and new forms of store-of-value money may be traced to the desire of these clienteles to keep their surpluses safe, rather than invest them in risky projects with better growth potential.

The concentration of income in the corporate sector is closely linked to the emergence of a few large, dominant technology companies. It has become standard to hold enormous cash piles with which to swallow other companies when opportunities arise, and to fund internal projects that preempt new entrants as often as they lead the way to new products and services. There is widespread feeling that competition policy has been asleep throughout these developments, though that feeling will have to prove its mettle in court against decades of precedent set during competition policy's slumber.

Throughout the book we have emphasized the special role of equity capital in making projects investable, as well as the impasse generated for entrepreneurs by equity rationing. We are concerned with equity capital formation because it enables investable projects to go forward that cannot be funded any other way and because it separates the possibility of entrepreneurship from the boundaries of friends' and family savings. Those investable projects that succeed and grow can later become bankable, supporting the renewal of the money supply.

A well-developed system now exists for channeling equity capital to entrepreneurs in technology startups. This venture capital system centered around Silicon Valley has been criticized for a fair amount of hubris in recent years. The system of venture capital disproportionately favors a certain kind of founder and a certain kind of business model. The result has been an inordinate number of startups in which founders—in their first or second job—set out to disrupt one or another industry by turning it into a computer science problem. The targets for disruption faithfully represent the preoccupations of their young founders: dating, food delivery, online advertising, and so on.

To accept that the Silicon Valley startup ecosystem is a complete solution to the formation of equity in early-stage ventures is to accept a considerable foreshortening of our intelligence as a species. An inordinate number of Silicon Valley startups fail because very few important economic problems are easily and profitably beaten into a cybernetic mold. Most of them involve engaging with the human "wetware" that Silicon Valley's leading lights would rather consign to permanent unemployment, exchanging an endowment of cryptocurrency for Soylent and internet access. Entrepreneurial talent exists to reach these opportunities, but it is older, more widely dispersed, and less than infinitely scalable. To Silicon Valley, there is more risk in backing an experienced person with concrete business plans and reasonable compensation expectations than new graduates living off their parents and raising a pre-seed round with no ideas at all.

We submit there is untapped opportunity for early-stage equity capital that has been rationed from the capital markets not by economic considerations but by the ideology of Silicon Valley. This white space in the market is the result of a lack of competition in venture capital, which might be construed as professional investment but prefers a more messianic image. Efforts to replicate venture capital ecosystems outside of the United States stumble by slavishly imitating the most superficial aspects of the Silicon Valley model.

Beyond early-stage investments, it is becoming clear that exchange-listed equity is in short supply. Non-U.S. stock exchanges consistently lose listings to U.S. exchanges, which in turn lose listings to private equity funds. The price discovery and liquidity afforded by an exchange listing are familiar to all finance professionals. A loss of exchange listings thwarts the disclosure of information won through the grinding work of accounting and auditing which could make other projects investable. It also shunts the valuation of business ventures out of public view and into the opaque accounting policies of fund managers. We should be more curious about whether the migration of equity from public to private markets is driven more by the costs of being a public company or by the incentives of fund managers and their investors to launder the volatility of a public listing to create the appearance of steady performance. We should be concerned with the loss of public companies not because IPOs are the only way to connect equity to risky ventures, but because the informational externality created by a deep roster of listed companies with publicly reported financials reduces informational asymmetry for competitive ventures.

The projected capital formation needs of the next decades run into the hundreds of trillions of dollars to maintain the capital stock, decarbonize emissions-intensive production, reconfigure the geography of supply chains, and bring cutting-edge technologies to market. These funds cannot be conjured through a modern monetary theory fantasy. If we are to meet the challenge of creating the future we want, we will have to make more efficient use of our savings, the institutions that make credit creation and financial intermediation possible, and a neutral monetary policy framework.

Appendix 14.A Neutral Credit Risk Weights

In this appendix, we derive the optimal allocations x^o, x_r, and x_c, which allow us to solve for neutral risk weights following Glasserman and Kang (2014).

The solution to the unconstrained portfolio problem is found by differentiating the objective and setting it to zero. The objective is

$$\max \mu'x - \frac{\gamma}{2}x'\Sigma x$$

Taking the derivative with respect to x gives

$$\mu - \gamma \Sigma x$$

Setting the derivative to zero and solving yields $x^o = \frac{1}{\gamma}\Sigma^{-1}\mu$.

When the regulator imposes an upper bound η^2 on the variance of the portfolio $x'\Sigma x$, we substitute the constraint $x'\Sigma x = \eta^2$ for the bank's risk aversion in the objective and solve the Lagrangian

$$\max \mu'x - \lambda_0(x'\Sigma x - \eta^2)$$

Taking the derivative with respect to x gives

$$\mu - 2\lambda_0 \Sigma x$$

Setting the derivative to zero and solving yields

$$x_r = \frac{1}{2\lambda_0}\Sigma^{-1}\mu$$

The optimum is given by the complementary slackness conditions on λ_0 and the associated constraint. There are two cases to consider: $\lambda_0 = 0$ with $x'\Sigma x < \eta^2$ and $\lambda_0 > 0$ with $x'\Sigma x = \eta^2$. The first case is never optimal because more profit can always be obtained by increasing the variance of the bank portfolio. Hence, we consider the second case:

$$\eta^2 = x'\Sigma x = \left(\frac{1}{2\lambda_0}\Sigma^{-1}\mu\right)'\Sigma\left(\frac{1}{2\lambda_0}\Sigma^{-1}\mu\right) = \frac{1}{4\lambda_0^2}\mu'\Sigma^{-1}\Sigma\Sigma^{-1}\mu = \frac{1}{4\lambda_0^2}\mu'\Sigma^{-1}\mu$$

where we have used the symmetry of the covariance matrix in the third equality. Solving for λ_0 we obtain

$$\lambda_0 = \frac{\sqrt{\mu'\Sigma\mu}}{2\eta}$$

which yields the optimal allocation under the regulator's risk preferences:

$$x_r = \frac{\eta}{\sqrt{\mu'\Sigma\mu}}\Sigma^{-1}\mu$$

Finally, in the presence of risk weights w, the bank faces an upper bound on risk-weighted assets $\kappa \geq w'x$, where κ is proportional to the bank's equity. The bound on risk-weighted assets becomes an additional constraint on the bank's original maximization problem, which we append to the objective:

$$\max \mu'x - \frac{\gamma}{2}x'\Sigma x - \lambda_1(w'x - \kappa) = (\mu - \lambda_1 w)'x - \frac{\gamma}{2}x'\Sigma x + \lambda_1\kappa$$

Differentiating with respect to x, setting the derivative equal to zero and solving yields

$$x = \frac{1}{\gamma}\Sigma^{-1}\mu - \frac{\lambda_1}{\gamma}\Sigma^{-1}w$$

Again, we consider the two cases $\lambda_1 = 0$ with $w'x - \kappa < 0$ and $\lambda_1 > 0$ with $w'x - \kappa = 0$. In the first case, the risk weights are not binding, and the optimum is the same as in the unconstrained problem. In the second case,

$$w'x = \kappa$$
$$w'\left(\frac{1}{\gamma}\Sigma^{-1}\mu - \frac{\lambda_1}{\gamma}\Sigma^{-1}w\right) = \kappa$$
$$w'\Sigma^{-1}\mu - \lambda_1 w'\Sigma^{-1}w = \gamma\kappa$$

Solving for λ_1 and combining with the first case yields

$$\lambda_1 = \frac{(w'\Sigma^{-1}\mu - \gamma\kappa)^+}{w'\Sigma^{-1}w}$$

which gives the optimal constrained allocation

$$x_c = \frac{1}{\gamma}\Sigma^{-1}\mu - \frac{1}{\gamma}\frac{(w'\Sigma^{-1}\mu - \gamma\kappa)^+}{w'\Sigma^{-1}w}\Sigma^{-1}w$$

Now we want to solve for the risk weights that implement the regulator's restriction on the variance of bank earnings without changing the bank's optimal allocation. Put $w = \alpha\mu$ and let $w'x = \kappa = \alpha\mu'x$:

$$\begin{aligned}
x_c &= \frac{1}{\gamma}\Sigma^{-1}\mu - \frac{1}{\gamma}\frac{\alpha\mu'\Sigma^{-1}\mu - \gamma\kappa}{\alpha^2\mu'\Sigma^{-1}\mu}\alpha\Sigma^{-1}\mu \\
&= \frac{1}{\gamma}\left(1 - \frac{\alpha^2\mu'\Sigma^{-1}\mu - \alpha\gamma\kappa}{\alpha^2\mu'\Sigma^{-1}\mu}\right)\Sigma^{-1}\mu \\
&= \frac{1}{\gamma}\left(\frac{\gamma\kappa}{\alpha\mu'\Sigma^{-1}\mu}\right)\Sigma^{-1}\mu \\
&= \frac{\kappa}{\alpha\mu'\Sigma^{-1}\mu}\Sigma^{-1}\mu
\end{aligned}$$

Setting this allocation equal to x_r implies

$$\frac{\eta}{\sqrt{\mu'\Sigma\mu}} = \frac{\kappa}{\alpha\mu'\Sigma^{-1}\mu}$$

Solving for α gives the neutral credit risk weights

$$w = \frac{\kappa}{\eta\sqrt{\mu'\Sigma\mu}}\mu$$

Notes

1. Following Bindseil, U. (2004). *Monetary Policy Implementation: Theory – Past – Present*. Oxford University Press: 20–29. See also Goodhart, C. (2011). *The Basel Committee on Banking Supervision: A History of the Early Years, 1974–1997*. Cambridge University Press: 29–30.

2. Phillips, C.A. (1920). *Bank Credit*. Macmillan.
3. Drechsler, I., Savov, A., and Schabl, P. (2018). Banking on deposits: Maturity transformation without interest-rate risk. *NBER Working Paper 24582*, May.
4. Non-interest expense is a slow-moving variable, as is the percentage of capital distributed to shareholders. Changes in loss reserves are more volatile but foreseeable.
5. This will, of course, require some care to ensure that open market operations do not amplify market interest rate dynamics.
6. See Beck, T., Döttling, R., Lambert, T., et al. (2023). Liquidity creation, investment, and growth. *Journal of Economic Growth* 28: 297–336 and Müller, K. and Verner, E. (2024). Credit allocation and macroeconomic fluctuations. *Review of Economic Studies* 91 (6): 3645–3676.
7. King, M. (2017). *The End of Alchemy: Money, Banking and the Future of the Global Economy*. Abacus: 269–81.
8. Reforms are also needed in equity markets, where IPO volumes have long been out of step with the issuance of other savings vehicles.
9. Rates trading encompasses foreign exchange and interest rates (government bonds and money market instruments).
10. An observable option price makes implied volatility observable as well, for example.
11. Unless they are small enough to enjoy the special treatment afforded to SMEs.
12. Glasserman, P. and Kang, W. (2014). Design of risk weights. *Operations Research* 62 (6): 1204–1220. See also the comments by Duffie, D. (2014). Comment on: "Design of Risk Weights" by Paul Glasserman and Wanmo Kang. *Operations Research* 62 (6): supplement and Rochet, J-C. (2014). Comments on the article by Paul Glasserman and Wanmo Kang: "Design of risk weights". *Operations Research* 62 (6): supplement.
13. The variance-covariance matrix is notoriously difficult to estimate. See Sekerke, M. (2015). *Bayesian risk management: A guide to model risk and sequential learning in financial markets*. Wiley Finance.
14. The unconstrained portfolio problem does not require that the portfolio be fully invested. Larger values of γ will result in less risk-taking, leaving unallocated balances available for risk-free assets.
15. That is, the excess returns of a new mortgage product will closely approximate those of existing mortgage products.
16. See the discussion of variance discounting in Sekerke, M. (2015). *Bayesian risk management: A guide to model risk and sequential learning in financial markets*. Wiley Finance.

17. The units in Glasserman and Kang's analysis are a bit difficult for those used to seeing a portfolio problem as a scale-free allocation decision. For the allocation to be represented in dollar terms, γ^{-1} must be expressed in dollars risked per risk-adjusted unit of return. Similar interpretations attach to other risk parameters that appear in the analysis that follows.
18. See Correia, S.A., Luck, S., and Verner, E. (2024). Failing Banks. *NBER Working Paper 32907*, September.
19. SIFMA. (2024). *2024 Capital Markets Fact Book* (SIFMA), July, World Bank Quarterly Public Sector Debt statistics.
20. The results would depend on who buys the assets sold by the Federal Reserve.
21. The Fed would have to reintroduce reserve requirements to create a distinction between required and excess reserves to end interest on excess reserves; otherwise, it could stop paying interest on all reserves.
22. The sinking fund could be endowed with a level of equity that allows it to realize additional losses after acquiring the bonds or required to resell at a price greater than or equal to its purchase price.

About the Authors

Matt Sekerke is an economist and advisor to the world's leading financial institutions. He is currently a Managing Director at SEDA Experts, an elite expert witness firm specializing in financial services, and Senior Macro Advisor at Hiddenite Capital Partners, a fundamental equity long-short firm focused on investments in industrials, technology, and adjacent sectors, globally. He pursues research in monetary economics and finance as a Fellow at the Institute for Applied Economics, Global Health, and the Study of Business Enterprise at the Johns Hopkins University and Visiting Fellow in the Department of Finance at Durham University Business School. Matt earned his Ph.D. in economics from Durham University after graduating from Columbia University, the University of Chicago, and the Johns Hopkins University. He is the author of *Bayesian Risk Management* (Wiley Finance, 2015).

Steve H. Hanke is a professor of applied economics and founder and codirector of the Institute for Applied Economics, Global Health, and the Study of Business Enterprise at the Johns Hopkins University in Baltimore. Hanke holds nine honorary doctorates and four honorary professorships in recognition of his scholarship on exchange-rate regimes. He served on President Reagan's Council of Economic Advisers where he was Reagan's privatization guru. Hanke has acted as an adviser to governments and heads of state in Europe, South America, and Asia. Hanke is a well-known currency and commodity trader. Currently, he serves as chairman of the Supervisory Board of AMG Critical Materials in Amsterdam and chairman emeritus of the Friedberg Mercantile Group in Toronto. During the 1990s, he served as president of Toronto Trust Argentina in Buenos Aires, the world's best-performing emerging market mutual fund in 1995. He is the co-author of *Capital, Interest and Waiting* (2024) with Leland B. Yeager. Hanke and his wife, Liliane, reside in Baltimore and Paris.

Index

Note: Page numbers followed by *f* and *t* refer to figures and tables, respectively.

A

ABS, *see* Asset-backed securities
Admati, A., 31n23, 187
Adverse selection, 85, 90, 217, 274
Amortization, 82–83, 85, 87, 119n5, 307
Analyzing Bank Capital framework, 179
Assets:
    and capital adequacy before Basel era, 179
    as collateral, 86, 89–90
    high-quality liquid assets, 190–193, 195, 242, 243, 318, 323
    household, 56–57
    intangible, 55–56, 178, 276, 286, 296–297
    and interest rate policy, 245–247, 251
    large-scale asset purchases, 127, 221, 235–236, 238, 239, 246–248
    and lending to nonbank financial institutions, 114–115
    level of, in banking system, 151–153
    liquid, 50, 125–126, 174, 189, 194, 215, 248–249, 275. *See also* High-Quality Liquid Assets
    of money market funds, 50–51
    and neutral credit risk weights, 314–317
    in nonfinancial business sector, 55
    and propogation of financial impulses, 224–225
    and risk transformation, 109–114, 117
    risk-weighted, 125, 126, 180, 181
    safe, 9–10, 175, 268, 288–290, 318
    seignorage, 40–41
    and system of claims, 60–61
Asset-backed securities (ABS):
    as collateral, 186, 216
    in consolidated financial intermediation sector, 49, 51–53, 52*t*, 77
    credit card, 172n55
    and risk transformation, 109, 183
    solar, 112
    student loan, 161, 214
Asset managers, 48–50, 49*t*, 53, 76

B

Balance of payments accounting, 57
Balance sheet(s):
    broad trends in bank, 150–154
    capital adequacy evaluated through, 179
    of central banks, 36–41, 38*t*–40*t*, 322–324
    of commercial banks, 41–43, 42*t*, 130, 149–151

334 INDEX

Balance sheet(s) (*Cont.*)
  details of bank, 154–156
  evolution of bank, 149–163, 150*t*, 151*t*–152*t*
  Federal Reserve, 232–244, 236*t*, 239*t*, 241*t*, 322–324
  of financial intermediaries, 46, 48–54, 49*t*, 51*t*–53*t*
  fiscal authority, 37–38, 37*t*–39*t*
  of governments, 40–41, 40*t*
  of households, 56–57, 56*t*
  and liquidity coverage ratio, 190–193
  loans on, 49–50, 49*t*, 152, 184
  of monetary system, 58–59, 58*t*
  of nonfinancial businesses, 54–55, 55*t*
  with risk-weighted assets, 181
  and supplementary leverage ratio, 189, 256n50
  of universal banks, 104, 105*t*, 189
Balance sheet schema, 35–61
Banks (banking system). *See also* Central banks (central bank policy); Commercial banks (commercial banking system); Risk management by banks; Universal banks
  credit creation by, *see* Credit creation
  deposit creation by individual, 43–44
  in fiat money systems, 13–29
  and foreign exchange, 25–27
  and government sector, 36–41, 234, 236, 240, 244, 250, 264
  and metallic standards, 21–23
  money creation by, 18–19, 41–48, 81–98, 130, 142, 164–166. *See also* Credit creation
  and neutral monetary policy, 9, 262, 268–269, 303–305, 311, 322
  role and functions of, 5–7
Bankable projects, 285–298
  about, 8, 10, 81–88
  cannibalization of, 165, 268, 271, 278
  and competition within universal banks, 107–108, 277
  and credit creation, 96–97, 213
  defined, 8, 42, 81–82
  expanding the supply of, 297–298
  formation of, 85–88, 269
  funding of, 85–88, 156, 174–175
  and government budget, 203, 204
  and information asymmetry, 85, 274
  investable projects qualified as, 81–82, 84–85, 107–108, 203

  in land, 290–296
  and nonbank public, 54, 56
  in real estate sector, 286, 290, 292–295
  and savings glut, 286–290
  supply of, 10, 27, 68, 85–88, 96, 126, 130, 134, 267, 307
  and technology, 296–297
Bank capital:
  after first Basel Accord, 180–181, 183–184
  before Basel era, 179–180
  defining, 177–179
  1996 market risk amendment, 182–183
  regulation of, 176–184
Bank equity, 43, 89, 90, 99n14, 156, 177–179, 268, 304, 317
Bank for International Settlements (BIS), 27, 43, 180, 182, 185, 189
Bank Holdings Companies Act (1956), 174
Banking books, 118, 182–189, 195, 196, 251, 272, 277, 278, 281–282, 312–314
Bank lending. *See also* Loan(s)
  capital market finance vs., 156–163
  competition in, 273–279
Bank liquidity:
  liquidity coverage ratio, 95, 190–194
  net stable funding ratio, 45–46, 194–195. *See also* High-Quality Liquid Assets
  regulation of, 189–195
Bank liquidity risk management, 88
Bank of America, 41, 105
Bank of Japan, 253n12
Bank regulation:
  approaches to fixing, 311–320
  Basel I Accord, *see* Basel I Accord
  Basel II Accord, *see* Basel II Accord
  Basel III Accord, *see* Basel III Accord
  BIS and, 27, 43, 180, 182, 185, 189
  capital regulation, 187–189
  features of, 125–126
  and internal risk modeling, 186–188, 195, 199n34, 313–314
  liquidity regulation, 189–195
  supervision, 22, 27, 180, 187–188, 192, 242, 320
Barnett, William A., 135
Basel I Accord, 150*t*, 155, 157, 165, 180–185, 187, 194, 318
Basel II Accord, 183, 185, 187, 188, 282, 282n1, 312

Basel III Accord, 150, 150t, 153, 183–185, 187–196, 237, 243, 279, 281, 282, 309–310, 312, 318
Basel Committee on Banking Supervision (BCBS), 27, 180, 182, 185, 189
Bear Stearns, 105, 279
Bernanke, B., 253n9, 287, 288
BIS, *see* Bank for International Settlements
Bitcoin, 28, 33n48. *See also* Cryptocurrency(-ies)
BlackRock, 50
Borrower equity, 81, 82, 86, 87, 295, 317. *See also* Credit rationing
Bretton Woods system, 24–26, 143, 150, 150t, 179, 244
Broad money:
  and banking system, 5–7
  components of, 59, 59t, 135–148
  controlling supply of, 303–304, 306–309
  Divisia aggregation of, 135–148. *See also* Divisia broad money
  growth of, 127, 232–233, 240, 247–251, 303–304, 307, 311
  indices for, 136–137
  and interest rate policy, 125, 136, 140, 144, 234, 303, 307–309
  measures of, 60, 129–134
  money supply as, 35, 129–130, 133–144
  and nonbank public, 59–60
  by sectors and strata, 144–148, 145f–148f, 262–267, 305, 311
  simple sum aggregates, 138–141, 138t, 139t, 140f–141f
  sources of, 59t, 141–144, 142t
  targets for, 122–125
Brunner, K., 3
Budget, government, *see* Government budget

C

Cambridge equation, 132, 305
Capital markets:
  bankable projects in, 85, 116–117, 165, 278
  and banking, 103–106, 118, 196n3, 262, 272
  bank lending vs., 156–163
  and borrower equity, 86
  competition in, 107–108, 276–279, 306, 314, 324–326
  crowding-out in, 216–217
  debt capital markets, 216, 268, 277–278, 298, 320
  derivatives in, 114
  economic growth with, 96–98
  efficiency in, 68, 266–269, 285, 304, 312, 320–322
  equity capital markets, 77, 216–217, 320
  equity rationing in, 8, 74–75, 85–86, 217
  financial intermediaries in, 67–78
  government-sponsored entities in, 37, 112, 157–163, 211, 213–214, 304, 320–322
  and interest rate risk, 91–92
  international and U.S., 57–58, 287
  investable projects in, 68, 74–75, 81, 268–269
  linked to credit creation, 82, 96–98
  private equity, 77, 115, 278, 297, 325
  and regulation, 281–282
  and securitization, 109
  underwriting in, 76, 276
  and universal banks, 41, 103–104, 113, 184–185, 278–279
  venture capital, 48, 77, 116, 175, 238, 324–325
Capital stock, 69, 286, 296–297
CBDCs, *see* Central bank digital currencies
CCAR, *see* Comprehensive Capital Analysis and Review
CDS, *see* Credit default swaps
Central banks (central bank policy). *See also* Federal Reserve (Fed); Monetary policy(-ies)
  about, 36–41, 231–233
  balance sheets of, 36–41, 38t–40t, 322–324
  and bank liquidity risk management, 88, 93–96, 113, 114, 117–118, 189–195, 214, 238, 245, 247, 304, 318
  Bank of Japan, 253n12
  cash issued by, 38
  consumer price standard implemented by, 24, 246
  and COVID interventions, 238–244
  in developing countries, 27, 57–58, 287, 289
  European Central Bank, 123, 253n12
  in fiat systems, 36–37
  as foreign exchange dealers, 25
  and Global Financial Crisis (2007–2009), 233–245, 247
  government abuse of, 63n6
  and government budgets, 203, 204

Central banks (central bank policy). *See also* Federal Reserve (Fed); Monetary policy(-ies) (*Cont.*)
   and growth of broad money, 303–304
   and interbank market, 43, 153, 166, 215, 234, 237, 242–243, 304, 309
   interest rate policy, 7–8, 125, 245–247, 251, 303, 307–309
   and interest rates, 4–5, 123–124, 127, 237–238, 251–252, 309
   limitations of, 121
   liquidity facilities at, 153, 186, 309–310, 312, 318
   monetary policy of, *see* Monetary policy(-ies)
   proposed operational framework for, 304–311
   quantitative easing by, 143, 234–236, 246
   quantity policy, 125, 127, 247, 305
   reserve money issued by, 38
   successes of, 21, 23, 247–251
   transactions of, in government obligations, 210–211
   U.S. dollar reserves held by, 26–27, 287, 289–290
Central bank digital currencies (CBDCs), 62n4
Chase, 41, 105
Combined government, 40, 40*f*
Commercial banks (commercial banking system), 41–48
   about, 41–43
   balance sheets of, 130, 149–151
   and bankable projects, 42, 54, 68, 85–88. *See also* Bankable projects
   as "banking book" of universal banks, 118
   and central bank policy, 106, 122, 124, 231, 233–234, 237, 242, 244, 312–314
   competition in, 107–108, 171n45, 273–279
   in consolidated financial intermediation sector, 53–54, 53*t*
   and credit card networks, 172n55
   credit creation by, 43–48, 81–98. *See also* Credit creation
   and fiat money, 28, 31n21, 36–37, 271
   governance, 279–282, 282n1, 312, 314
   investment banks vs., 171n45, 304, 312–314
   loans from, 49, 49*t*, 161
   and mortgage GSEs, 111–112, 155–161, 165, 212–214, 321
   and mortgage lending, 104, 105, 154, 156–161, 164–165, 211, 277, 321
   notes issued by, 31n21
   and reserve market, 242
   reserves held by, 39, 39*t*, 40*t*, 41–42
   risk management by, 88–96, 186–188, 195, 199n34, 313–314
   savings and loan associations, 181
   securities activities of, 283nn10–11, 312–313
   securities holdings of, 152–153, 155
   as source of broad money, 59–60, 60*t*, 138*t*, 141–143, 142*t*, 164
   and universal banks, 103–108, 118, 165
Competition:
   in banking and capital markets, 107–108, 276–279, 306, 314, 324–326
   in deposits, 274
   stability vs., 278–279
   with universal banks, 273–279
Comprehensive Capital Analysis and Review (CCAR), 249–250
Consolidated banking system, 42*t*, 125, 151, 248
Consolidated financial intermediation sector, 53–54, 53*t*
Consolidated government, 39–41
Consumer price standards, 21–27, 246
Countrywide Financial, 279
COVID-19 pandemic, 5, 151, 232, 238–244, 239*t*
Credit creation, 81–98
   about, 81–82
   bankable projects, 85–88
   and Basel III framework, 189, 318
   and capital markets, 96–98
   credit rationing, 8, 85–88
   financial intermediation vs., 54, 67–68. *See also* Financial intermediation
   and foreign exchange, 25
   fractional reserve theory vs., 45
   by individual commercial banks, 43–45
   in macroeconomic thinking, 4, 25, 67–70, 121
   and monetary policy, 21, 106
   and monetary theory, 61, 64n17
   productivity of, 269
   removing obstacles to, 166, 262
   reserve multiplier theory vs., 45
   risk management in, 88–96
   savings and investments, 82–85
   Schumpeter on, 5–6
   and underwriting, 8, 16, 17, 81, 84–85, 90, 164

Credit default swaps (CDS), 114
Credit rationing, 8, 9, 11n11, 81, 85–88, 97, 99n9, 108, 134, 297, 311, 319
Credit risk management, 89–91, 176, 181, 182, 184, 188–189, 191–195
Cryptocurrency(-ies), 27, 275, 325

D

Deadweight losses, 174
Debt:
  deposit insurance, 208–209
  and fiscal authority, 36–38
  government, 39–41, 40t, 205–209
  government's ability to redeem, 6
  regulation of, 178–179
  securities, banks holding, 43
  stability conditions, 205–208
Debt capital markets, 216, 268, 277–278, 298, 320
Deposits:
  competition in, 274
  creation of, 43–48
  term, 44
Deposit insurance, 208–209. See also Federal Deposit Insurance Corporation
Derivatives:
  and Basel I, 181, 182
  and Basel III, 185
  in capital markets, 276
  and credit creation, 26
  in financial intermediation, 104
  and interest rates, 92–93
  liquidity rules for, 190
  risk transfer with, 49, 113–114
Divisia broad money, 129, 135–148
  about, 135–136
  indices for, 136–137
  by sectors and strata, 144–148, 145f–148f
  simple sum aggregates vs., 138–141, 138t, 139t, 140f–141f
  sources of, 141–144, 142t
  as target for quantity-based policy, 306–309
  user cost of money, 135–137, 141, 141t, 144, 146, 146t, 148, 148t
Dodd-Frank Act, 115, 119n8, 249, 277, 279, 281, 308, 313
Domestic savings, 287–288
Dynamic stochastic general equilibrium (DSGE), 4, 123

E

ECB, see European Central Bank
Economic growth, 84, 96–98, 127, 139, 146, 232–233, 240, 247–251, 303–304, 307, 311
Endogeneity, 60
Equation of exchange, 124–125, 129–134, 136, 164
Equilibrium, 7–8, 28, 29n1, 61, 68–72, 74, 79n15, 82, 83, 97, 98n1, 124, 132, 268, 304, 309
Equity capital markets, 77, 216–217, 320
Equity rationing, 8–10, 74–75, 85, 217, 238, 268, 324
European Central Bank (ECB), 123, 253n12

F

Fannie Mae, see Federal National Mortgage Association
FBOs, see Foreign banking organizations
Federal Deposit Insurance Corporation (FDIC), 174. See also Deposit insurance
Federal Home Loan Banks (FHLBs), 214–216, 304, 321–322
Federal Home Loan Mortgage Corporation (FHLMC, Freddie Mac), 111–112, 159, 211, 321
Federal Housing Finance Authority (FHFA), 111
Federal National Mortgage Association (FNMA, Fannie Mae), 111–112, 159, 211, 321
Federal Reserve (Fed):
  Analyzing Bank Capital framework of, 179
  balance sheets of, 232–244, 236t, 239t, 241t, 322–324
  changing targets of, 123, 235, 237, 239, 242, 247
  Distributional Financial Accounts compiled by, 147
  and FHLBs, 214–216, 304, 321–322
  government debt held by, 62n5
  interest rate policy of, 232, 235, 238, 245–247, 251–252
  and LSAPs, 235, 237–239
  monetary policy of, 3, 247–251, 308, 310, 322
  real bills doctrine of, 23–24
  as regulatory agency, 173–174

Federal Reserve (Fed) (*Cont.*)
  reserve requirements of, 45, 192–193
  Supervisory Capital Assessment Program of, 249
Federal Reserve Act (1913), 24, 173–174
FHFA, *see* Federal Housing Finance Authority
FHLBs, *see* Federal Home Loan Banks
FHLMC, *see* Federal Home Loan Mortgage Corporation
Fiat money, 21–27. *See also* Money
  after metallic standards, 23–24
  and banking, 13–29
  and commercial banks, 28, 31n21, 36–37, 271
  credit- and claim-based nature of, 6, 35–36, 59t, 60–61
  in foreign exchange, 25–27
  and metallic standards, 21–23
  underwriting of, 6, 17, 28, 35, 203–204
Final target variables, 122, 123
Financial intermediation, 48–54
  asset-backed securities, 51–52
  asset managers, 49–50
  balance sheets, 46, 48–54, 49t, 51t–53t, 114–116
  in capital markets, 67–78
  competition in, 107–108
  consolidated financial intermediation sector, 53–54
  credit creation vs., 54, 67–68. *See also* Credit creation
  institutions, 48–49
  money market funds, 50–51
  productivity of, 85, 96–97, 98n4
  and project stratification, 75–78
  risk management, 116–118
  subsectors of, 48–49
  by universal banks, 103–104
First Republic Bank, 215, 275
Fiscal authority, 36–38, 37t, 39t. *See also* Government (government sector)
Fiscal impulse, 220–225
Fisher, I., 3, 5, 131–132
Flow of Funds data, 61n1, 149–151, 150t–152t, 154, 154t–156t, 164, 275
FNMA, *see* Federal National Mortgage Association
Foreign banking organizations (FBOs), 242–243, 256n50

Foreign exchange:
  and international money standard, 25–27
  and nature of money, 14
Fractional reserve theory, 45
Freddie Mac, *see* Federal Home Loan Mortgage Corporation
"Free banking," 31n21
Friedman, M., 3, 136
Fundamental Review of the Trading Book (FRTB), 186–187, 313

G

GFC, *see* Global Financial Crisis of 2007-2009
Ginnie Mae, *see* Government National Mortgage Association
Glasserman, P., 314, 317–319, 326
GLBA, *see* Gramm-Leach-Bliley Act
Global Financial Crisis of 2007-2009 (GFC):
  and bank holdings, 152–157
  and bank reserves, 39, 104–106, 247
  and Basel Accords, 183, 184
  causes of, 104–106
  and central bank policy implementation, 233–245
  competition in banking following, 275, 277–278
  Divisia broad money during, 143
  effects of, xvii
  and governance, 280, 282
  government debt following, 205
  growth following, 146, 247–249
  and home equity loans, 160, 161, 164
  and monetary economics, 5
  monetary growth during, 139
  monetary policy following, 232, 235, 238, 239, 245–247, 251, 304, 308
  mortgages following, 159, 235–236, 243, 246
  and quantitative easing, 234–236
  responses to, 232
  structural changes following, 242–245
Global savings, 267–269
Global systemically-important banks (GSIBs), 278–279
Goldman Sachs, 41, 105
Gold standard, 22–23, 36. *See also* Metallic standards
Governance, of universal banks, 279–281, 312, 314. *See also* Bank regulation

Government (government sector), 36–41
   central banks of, *see* Central banks (central bank policy)
   consolidated, 39–41, 40f
   fiscal authority, 36–38
   monetary authority, 38–39
   necessity for existence of monetary system, 17–19
   role of, in monetary policy, 203–225
Government budget, 203–225
   about, 203–204
   agencies, 203, 204, 211–213, 216, 220
   aggregate conditions in, 209–217
   disaggregated, 217–223
   distributional impact of, 203–205, 217–221
   fiscal balances, 203, 206–207, 209–211, 217–218
   and government debt, 36–41, 40t, 62n2, 63n6, 205–209
   monetary impact of, 203–209, 213–214, 217, 223
Government National Mortgage Association (GNMA, Ginnie Mae), 37, 105, 111–112, 155, 157, 211, 213, 227n21
Government-sponsored enterprises (GSEs):
   credit enhancements by, 111
   Federal Home Loan Banks, 214–216, 304, 321–322
   Federal Home Loan Mortgage Corporation, 111–112, 159, 211, 321
   Federal Housing Finance Authority, 111
   Federal National Mortgage Association, 111–112, 159, 211, 321
   footprint in capital markets, 37, 112, 211, 213–214
   in mortgage market, 157–161, 211–213, 321
   privatization, 214, 321
   and quantitative easing, 236
   reserve market activity, 243
   risk weights for GSE securities, 181–182, 314–318, 326–328
   in securities portfolios, 155
Gramm-Leach-Bliley Act (GLBA), 118, 184
Great Depression, 159, 247, 273
GSEs, *see* Government-sponsored enterprises
GSIBs, *see* Global, systemically-important banks

H

Hayek, F., 266–267
Hellwig, M., 31n23, 187
High-Quality Liquid Assets (HQLA), 190–193, 195, 242, 243, 318, 323
Holding companies, 6, 41, 43, 103–104, 118, 151, 178, 278, 313
Homogeneity, 31n26
Household sector, 56–57, 56t, 146, 221, 222t, 223, 285, 287–288

I

Inflation, 5
   causes of, 136
   and central bank policy, 233
   changes caused by, 134
   consumer price standard for, 24
   and cost price index, 141
   and interest rate, 124
   and monetary policy, 204, 206
   and neutrality, 218–220, 264–266
   as target of central bank policy, 123
   and user cost of money, 135–137, 141, 141t, 144, 146, 146t, 148, 148t
Information asymmetry:
   in bankable projects, 85–88
   between banks and borrowers, 274
   between investors and entrepreneurs, 72–75
   mitigation or reduction of, 81, 262, 326
Ingham, G., 14
Institutional structure of economy, 35–61
Intangible assets, 55–56, 178, 286, 296–297
Interbank liquidity, 309–310
Interbank rate, 123
Interest rates:
   and central bank policy, 123
   risk management, 91–93
   r-star, 5
   short-term, 123, 232, 235, 237–238, 245–246, 309
Interest rate policy, 7–8
   and asset prices, 245–247, 251
   and broad money, 125, 136, 140, 144, 234, 303, 307–309
   of central banks, 7–8, 125, 245–247, 251, 303, 307–309
   of Federal Reserve, 232, 235, 238, 245–247, 251–252

Intermediaries, financial, *see* Financial intermediation
International Monetary Fund, 27
International monetary standard, 25–27
Investable projects, 68, 72–75, 77, 285–298
    and asymmetric information, 72–73
    bankable vs., 81
    in capital markets, 107–108, 324
    defined, 8, 68
    and economic growth, 97
    and entrepreneurship, 72–77
    and financial intermediation, 96
    formation of, 268–269
    and government budgets, 203, 216
    involving land, 290–294
    and NPVs, 72, 74–75
    and safe assets, 268
    supply of, 68
Investment(s). *See also* Bankable projects; Investable projects
    and adverse selection, 85, 90, 217, 274
    and claims to future savings/surplus, 17, 42, 44, 81–85
    and equity rationing, 8–10, 74–75, 85, 217, 238, 268, 324
    and information asymmetry, 72–75, 85–88
    NPV criterion for, 71–72
    in residential housing, 299–300n3
    and safe assets, 9–10, 175, 268, 288–290, 318
    and savings glut, 286–290

J
JPMorgan, 41, 105

K
Kang, W., 314, 317–319, 326
Keynes, J. M., 5

L
Land, 286, 290–296. *See also* Real estate
    investable projects involving, 290–294
    land value tax on, 286, 295, 298, 302n28
    mortgages secured by, 156
    rents on, 298
    and taxation, 220, 293, 295
    value of, 294–296
Large-Scale Asset Purchases (LSAPs), 127, 221, 235–236, 238, 239, 246–248

LCR, *see* Liquidity Coverage Ratio
Lehman Brothers, 105, 185, 186, 279, 313
Lending, *see* Bank lending
Lending reaction function, 307
Limited liability, 73, 177
Liquid assets, 50, 125–126, 174, 189, 215, 248–249, 275. *See also* High-Quality Liquid Assets
Liquidity:
    bank, 88, 93–96, 152–153, 152t, 174–176, 185–186, 189–195, 208
    household, 146
    interbank, 309–310
    of money market funds, 50
    and mortgage GSE guarantees, 214
    offshore-dollar, 243, 244
    self-help regime, 189, 195, 304, 309, 312, 318
Liquidity Coverage Ratio (LCR), 189–195, 243
Liquidity risk, 88, 93–96, 113, 114, 117–118, 189–195, 214, 238, 245, 247, 304, 318
Liquidity rules (liquidity requirements), 126, 174–176, 184, 189–195, 304
Loan(s):
    about, 5
    amortization of, 82–83, 85, 87, 119n5, 307
    and asset-based securities, 52
    on balance sheet, 49–50, 49t, 152, 184
    and broad money growth, 43–47, 307
    commercial, 116, 165
    consumer, 56
    and credit rationing, 85–88
    and credit risk/default, 43, 89–91
    and interest rate risk, 91–93
    and liquidity risk, 93–96
    and money supply, 16–17
    to nonbank financial institutions, 114–116
    risk-based, pricing, 89
    and securitization markets, 109–111
    security for, 55
    servicing of, 82–83, 85
    student, 161
    underwriting of, 44, 50, 105, 273–274
Loanable funds, 20, 53, 54, 56, 67–68, 70–76, 82
Loan loss reserves, 43, 178, 181
LSAPs, *see* Large-Scale Asset Purchases

M

Macroeconomics, 4–5, 25, 61, 67–70, 84, 246. *See also* Monetary economics
Marshall, A., 5, 132
Maturity Extension Program, 235
Meltzer, A., 3
Merrill Lynch, 105, 279
Metallic standards, 21–25
Microeconomics, 70–75
MMFs, *see* Money market funds
Modigliani-Miller theorem, 79n15
Monetarism, 3, 5, 134–136, 305–306
Monetary authority(-ies), 36, 38–43, 39t, 40t, 210, 244
Monetary economics:
   banking systems, 5–7
   and fiat monetary standards, 21–27
   foundations of, 27–29
Monetary liability transition matrix, 307–308
Monetary policy(-ies):
   conventional view of, 54, 232, 235, 304, 323
   distributional impact of, 9, 41, 84, 131, 200, 204, 261
   expanded view of, 121–127
   frameworks for, 122, 127, 129, 302–309
   instruments of, 5, 122–126, 232, 236, 245
   interest-rate vs. quantity-based, 7–8, 305
   and monetary standards, 13–15
   neutral, 9, 13, 21, 164, 261–269, 304–305, 311
Monetary standards:
   consumer price standards, 21–27
   and deposit insurance, 47–48, 173–174, 191, 196n2, 197n8, 208–209, 272
   gold standards, 22–23, 36
   metallic standards, 21–25
Money, 38
   broad, *see* Broad money; Divisia broad money
   as claim or credit, 16–18
   and economic growth problem, 84
   in economic process, 19–21
   in economic theory, 3–5
   fiat, *see* Fiat money
   reserve, 38
   state as basis for, 18–19. *See also* Government (government sector)
   store-of-value, 18, 19, 49, 51, 53, 59, 60, 130, 139, 143, 146, 164, 184, 324
   systems of, 13–14

Money market funds (MMFs), 47, 49–51, 51t
Money supply, 129–166
   about, 58–60
   and bank balance sheets, 149–163
   Divisia broad money, 135–148
   equation of exchange for, 130–134
   frameworks for measuring, 129–130
Morgan Stanley, 105
Mortgage markets, 157, 157f–159f, 159–163, 292–293

N

National Bank Act (1863), 173
Neo-Keynesianism, 4, 123, 134
Net present value (NPV), 8, 20, 71–72, 113, 290
Net Stable Funding Ratio (NSFR), 189–190, 194–195
Neutrality (neutral monetary policy), 261–269
   defined, 261, 264–266, 269–270n1
   as goal of monetary policy, 9, 13, 21, 164, 304–305
   Hayek on, 266–267
   monitoring, 311
Nonbank financial institutions, 114–116. *See also* Shadow banks (shadow banking)
Nonbank public, 54–57
   households, 56–57
   and money supply, 58–60
   nonfinancial businesses, 54–55
Non-depreciating assets, 293
Nonfinancial business sector, 54–55, 55t
NPV, *see* Net present value
NSFR, *see* Net Stable Funding Ratio

O

Office of the Comptroller of the Currency (OCC), 173
Operational frameworks, 122

P

People's Bank of China, 289
Pigou, A. C., 132
Policy rate, 123
Prices, in sticky-price models, 4
Project stratification, 75–78
Purchasing power, 20

Q

Quantitative easing (QE), xvii, 169n25, 234–236, 236t, 322–324
Quantity-based policies, 7–8, 306–309
Quarles, R., 250

R

Real bills doctrine, 23–24
Real business cycle (RBC) model, 4–5
Real estate, 290–296
    as collateral, 56
    and credit cycles, 181, 286, 290–296
    exposure in securities portfolios, 154–156
    home ownership vs. residential housing investments, 299–300n3
    investable projects involving, 290–294
    land rent, 220, 291–293, 295, 298, 299n12
    land value tax on, 286, 295, 298, 302n28
    and monetary policy, 232–233
    mortgages secured by, 156
    overexposure to, 105–106
    and taxation, 220, 293, 295
    tax incentives for, 220, 228n38, 299–300n14
    and uneven credit creation, 20
    value of, 294–296
Regulation, see Bank regulation
Reserve balances:
    bank deposits as, 47–48
    commercial bank, 42–43
    management of, 309
    requirements for, 45–46
Reserve market, structural changes in, 242–245
Reserve money, 38
Reserve multiplier theory, 45, 305
Residential mortgage-backed securities (RMBS), 111–112, 127, 155, 155t, 156t, 157, 159, 277
Resolution Trust Corporation, 181
Risk-based loan pricing, 89
Risk management by banks, 88–96, 182–189
    credit risk, 89–91
    government-sponsored enterprises in, 203
    interest rate risk, 91–93
    liquidity risk, 93–96, 318
    market risk, 182–189
    risk transfer contracts, 111–114, 119n5
    in securitization markets, 109–111
    underwriting vs., 318–320
    in universal banks, 116–119

Risk-weighted assets (RWAs), 125, 126, 180, 181
RMBS, see Residential mortgage-backed securities
r-star, 5

S

Safe assets, 9–10, 175, 268, 288–290, 318
Savings, 286–290, 320–326
    domestic, 287–288
    global, 267–269
Savings and loan associations, 143, 181
Savings glut, 286–290, 324
Schumpeter, J., 5–6
Secondary Mortgage Market Enhancement Act (1984), 153
Securitization, 109–111, 113–117, 120nn11–12
Seigniorage, 40–41, 40t, 58
Self-help liquidity regime, 189, 195, 304, 309, 312, 318
Shadow banks (shadow banking), xvii, 7, 29
    money creation by, 174, 184
    and securitization, 104, 105
    universal banks, 103–105
    unregulated institutions and, 193, 214, 216
Short-term interest rates, 123, 232, 235, 237–238, 245–246, 309
Silicon Valley, 324–325
Silicon Valley Bank, 215, 275
SLR, see Supplementary leverage ratio
SOEs, see State-owned enterprises
Special purpose vehicles (SPVs), 49, 51–52, 107, 109, 113
Stability:
    competition vs., 278–279
    debt, 205–208
State-owned enterprises (SOEs), 37
Sticky-price models, 4
Store-of-value money, 18, 19, 49, 51, 53, 59, 60, 130, 139, 143, 146, 164, 184, 324
Stratification, 75–78, 147, 261, 263
Student loans, 112, 154, 161, 214
Supplementary leverage ratio (SLR), 189, 256n50
SWIFT system, 25

T

Taxation:
    capital gains, 50
    and creation/destruction of money, 16–17
    and deadweight losses, 174
    and fiscal authority, 36–38

and government debt, 205
and land, 220, 293, 295
and loan loss reserves, 178
and sector-level fiscal influence, 219–220
and the state, 18
Taylor rule, 124
Technology, 4, 68, 71, 72, 77, 78n5, 88, 97, 115, 134, 223–224, 261, 265, 266, 272, 278, 296–297, 310, 324
Term premium, 91
Trading books, 106, 118, 182–187, 189, 191–192, 195, 196, 272, 277, 278, 281–282, 312–314, 320
Treasury General Account (TGA), 240

U

Underwriting:
  in capital markets, 76, 276
  of credible claims to savings/surplus, 6, 28, 203–204, 286
  and credit creation, 8, 16, 17, 81, 84–85, 90, 164
  and creditworthiness, 17
  defining, 17, 30n14, 60, 76
  due diligence in, 76
  and expected surplus, 20, 28, 44, 81, 82, 84–85, 286
  of fiat money, 28, 35, 203–204
  of loans, 44, 50, 105, 273–274
  of real estate loans, 292–295
  and risk-based pricing, 90
  risk management vs., 318–320
Universal banks, 6–7, 103–118, 271–282. *See also* Commercial banks (commercial banking system)
  about, 103–106, 273
  balance sheet of, 104, 105t, 189
  bank capital, regulation of, 176–184
  banking book of, 118, 182–189, 195, 196, 251, 272, 277–278, 281–282, 312–314
  and Basel I Accord, 180–184
  and Basel III initiatives, 187–189
  in capital markets, 276–277
  competition within, 107–108, 277–279
  decisions about equity allocation within, 268–269
  dual functions of, 41, 54
  and financial stability, 278–279
  governance of, 279–281
  legal form of, 144
  liquidity regulation with, 189–195
  in monetary system, 271–282
  and 1996 market risk amendment, 182–183
  regulation of, 173–196, 281–282, 311–313
  risk management in, 116–119
  and risk transfer contracts, 111–114
  and risk transformation in securitization markets, 109–111
  and shadow banks and nonbank financial institutions, 103–105, 114–116
  trading book of, 106, 118, 182–187, 189, 191–192, 195, 196, 272, 277, 278, 281–282, 312–314, 320
Unlimited liability, 73, 177
Urban land, 291, 294, 295
U.S. dollar, 24, 26–27, 175, 179, 243, 244, 246, 285–287
Utility, 14–15, 31n26, 69, 83

V

Value at Risk (VaR), 182–183, 198n26, 199n27
Venture capital (VC), 48, 77, 116, 175, 238, 324–325
Volcker, P., 3, 140, 144, 146, 247
Volcker Rule, 199n36, 277

W

Walras, L., 5
Wicksell, K., 5, 98n4, 266
World Bank, 192